D1202662

Anatomy
of the
Bear

Lessons From Wall Street's
Four Great Bottoms

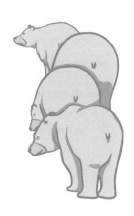

by

Russell Napier

BOOKS

Hong Kong Tokyo Singapore New York London

CLSA BOOKS
CLSA Asia-Pacific Markets
18/F, One Pacific Place
88 Queensway, Hong Kong

Printed November 2005

The text of this book is set in Goudy, with display set in Optima.

Cover design by Aligo Mok and team.

Printed in Hong Kong
ISBN: 962-86067-9-4

For Karen

CLSA
BOOKS

Contents

Acknowledgements

This book was written through a frustration with modern capital market theory and also most available financial history books. The first approach downplays the study of history and the second downplays the practical elements of history. The aim of this book is to provide a practical history of financial markets. In doing this I have been inspired by other practitioners who have already made a contribution in this field - Barrie Wigmore (*The Crash and Its Aftermath, Securities Markets in the 1980s*), Sandy Nairn (*Engines That Move Markets: Technology Investing from Railroads to the Internet and Beyond*), John Littlewood (*The Stock Market: Fifty Years of Capitalism At Work*), Mark Faber (*The Great Money Illusion* and *Tomorrow's Gold*) and of course George Goodman aka 'Adam Smith' (*The Money Game, Super Money, Paper Money*). If this book turns out to be half as useful as those authors' contributions, it will not have been a waste of two years' effort. If this book also convinces other practitioners that they too can add to the literature of the practical history of financial markets then it will have achieved it goals.

This book would not exist if it were not for Gary Coull, Executive Chairman of CLSA Asia-Pacific Markets. It was Gary's idea that CLSA get into the business of publishing books and also his idea that I should write one. Although I agreed readily, I delivered very, very slowly. As an employee of CLSA I am an admirer of many of the company's qualities but the discovery that they also include patience came as a surprise and a relief. I would like to thank Gary and other employees, past and present, of CLSA from whom I have learnt so much over the years: Dr. Jim Walker, Edmund Bradley, Jonathan Slone, Jonathan Compton, Mike McCoy and Richard

Pyvis.

It would not have been possible to write this book without access to a great deal of data. In finding that data I was set off in the right direction by Murray Scott, who knows his way around the data mines better than anyone I know. When one data vein appeared to be extinguished, Richard Sylla was a sure guide to a new source and a new field of enquiry. When all else failed and a flight to the US seemed essential, the staff of the New York Public Library came to the rescue and I thank them for their help for someone they have never met many thousands of miles away. This book relies particularly upon primary research in the back issues of *The Wall Street Journal*. Reading through sixteen months of this venerable daily was a mammoth task and one I probably would not have even contemplated had it not been for the services of ProQuest (www.proquest.co.uk). The ProQuest service offers remote access to every article and advertisement published in the *Journal* since 1889. While already recognised as a wonderful resource for historians, I think its usefulness to investment practitioners is not yet fully recognised. For those who seek guidance to the investment future a fully searchable database of over one hundred years of *WSJ* articles is a wonderful resource.

For the past four years, I have been involved in creating and running a course called A Practical History of Financial Markets (www.sifeco.org). I owe this opportunity to learn and contribute to financial market understanding to the trustees of the Stewart Ivory Foundation, a charity which funds the development and running of this course and many other projects. In this task I have been very fortunate in that some of the best minds in finance have agreed to contribute to the project. It has been a wonderful opportunity to learn from a team of authors and teachers who have combined practical experience of more than two hundred years. In relation to this book I would like to acknowledge the assistance of four of the course author/teachers in particular: Michael Oliver, Gordon Pepper, Andrew Smithers and Stephen Wright. Michael and Gordon have done their best to steer me through the minefield of monetary data interpretation necessary in this book. Andrew and Stephen have been kind enough to allow me to quote from their book, *Valuing Wall Street*. Any errors which may appear in these pages on the subject of q ratios or money are those of the student rather than the teacher. For those who also wish to learn from the teachers please come and join us on the Practical History of Financial Markets course, buy a copy of *Valuing Wall Street* or Gordon Pepper's forthcoming publication, *The Liquidity Theory of Asset Prices*.

I hope this book is now digestible to the average reader. It was not always so. Even hardened investment professionals, such as my friend PJ King, found it very hard going. PJ, in the blunt but kind way perhaps unique to men of County Cork, made very clear what should be changed. Of course, coming from the other end of Ireland, I did not agree easily to all of this. This is where the Antipodeans come in. Editors Tim Cribb and Simon Harris beat down my rambling prose into something which hopefully is now digestible for all. Without the considerable efforts of Tim and Simon I would probably still be writing and finding more subjects which simply had to be covered. I am neither qualified by aptitude or spirit to be an editor and I admire their skill and fortitude when confronted with such a stubborn author.

In just about every book I have ever read, the author acknowledges the support of their immediate family. Only if you have written a book can you really understand why this is so necessary. I would like to thank my partner Sheila and my sons Rory and Dylan for putting up with my long absences and frequent boring discursions on times long past. In particular I would like to thank my parents for their guidance and support over many decades. Thanks to my father who, as it was to turn out, had already taught me most of what I needed to know about business in his butcher's shop in Belfast. Thanks to my mother, who taught me that there are many things in life much more important than business.

Russell Napier,
Newbattle, Scotland
November 2005

Foreword: Marc Faber

Russell Napier's *Anatomy of the Bear: Lessons From Wall Street's Four Great Bottoms* is an outstanding "must read" for any student of financial markets.

Conventional wisdom has it that great market bottoms, which offer lifetime buying opportunities, occur quite soon after devastating market crashes. But, as Russell shows in this book, great bear markets have long life-spans. The key element to identifying extreme undervaluation is to find a period of time "when the advance in stock prices has failed to keep pace with economic and earnings growth" within the system. He shows, for instance, that at its 1921 low, the Dow Jones Industrial Average was no higher than it had been in 1899 - 22 years earlier - while during that period nominal GDP had increased by 383% and real GDP by 88%! Similarly, by August 1982, the Dow was no higher than it had been in April 1964, and was down by 70% in real, inflation-adjusted terms. According to Russell, August 1982 represented the fourth best buying opportunity for US equities in the last century, aside from 1921, 1932 and 1949.

The important message of Russell's book is that it usually takes a long time - about 14 years - for stocks to travel from peaks of overvaluation to depths of undervaluation, and that the nominal low in stock prices is not always the best time to buy equities. What is more important is the *real* level of equity prices and the various valuation parameters that indicate deep undervaluation. Thus, while the Dow Jones bottomed out on 9 December 1974 at 570, and stood at the 9 August 1982 low at 769, in real terms it had lost another 15% since the 1974 low.

Investors tend to associate major market lows with total despair among market participants, panic, depression in the asset class, bankruptcies in the affected sector and overwhelming negative sentiment. But Russell exposes as another myth the idea that stock market lows lead economic recovery by six-to-nine months and that the news is universally bearish at major market lows - by showing that economic improvement and better news in the media led the four major 20th Century stock market recoveries by several months.

Russell has filled a void with *Anatomy of the Bear*. It is the first book to my knowledge that traces, with many pertinent insights, the swings of US stock prices from undervaluation to overvaluation *and back* over the last 100 years. The book provides much food for thought. If equity prices swing between over and undervaluation, other asset markets such as real estate, commodities and bonds will do the same. Thus, I suppose that, in the same way US bonds were grossly overvalued in the 1940s, Japanese bonds were grossly overvalued in June 2003, when the yield on JGBs had declined to less than 0.50%. At the same time, the April 2003 low for the Nikkei Index at less than 8,000 may have been this generation's best ever buying opportunity in Japan.

In fact, the 2003 low in Japanese equity prices and interest rates shared similarities with the 1940s lows in US equities and interest rates. After the 1940s, US stocks rallied into 1973 but bond prices collapsed into 1981. Similarly, the stock market rally in Japan, which began in 2003, could last for many years and be accompanied by a significant bear market in Japanese bonds, which would drive local institutions and Japanese households out of their overweight bond and cash positions, which benefited during the 1990s deflation, into equities and real estate.

Moreover, if, as Russell explains, 1921, 1932, 1949 and 1982 provided outstanding buying opportunities for achieving subsequent high returns - which tended to last for a minimum of eight years (1921-29) but usually much longer - then I suppose that, taking the late April 2003 low of Japanese equities as a generational low, the bull market in Japanese equities could easily last until at least 2010 or even longer and significantly outperform US equities.

Another lesson from Russell's book could very well be that other Asian equity markets remain grossly undervalued relative to other assets, despite their post-1998 recovery. After all, many Asian stock markets are, in US dollar terms or in real terms, still down by more than 50% from the highs reached between 1990 and 1994. Also if, as Russell outlines, it takes about 14 years for equities to make the journey from overvaluation to undervaluation, the severity of the 20-year commodities bear market from 1980 to the turn of the millennium is evident. Put in proper perspective, commodity prices were, in the 1998 to 2001 period, in real (inflation adjusted) terms, at the lowest level in the history of capitalism. And, although some industrial commodity prices may suffer from a significant phase of profit-taking in 2006, given that commodity bull markets tend to last between 20 to 30 years, we may just be at the beginning of an extended rise in the price of natural resources.

There is another point I should like to add to Russell's excellent study. In a world of rapid monetary and credit expansion, extreme undervaluation of the Dow Jones might occur with the Index at 36,000, 40,000 or 100,000 or even more - at stock price levels that were predicted by several analysts in 1999. How so? At present the Dow is at around 10,500 and the price of gold is at $460. Let us assume that, as a result of the Bernanke paper money printing machine - which incidentally has been in existence since the formation of the Federal Reserve Board in 1913 and accounted for the dollar's 92% loss in purchasing power since then - the Dow Jones rises to 36,000 in the next few years (it will not take another 100 years for the US dollar to lose another 92% of purchasing power, but more likely only 10-20 years). If this was the case, the price of gold could rise from $460 to $3,600. This would bring down the Dow/gold ratio from currently about 25:1 to only 1 - as was the case in 1932 and in 1980! Thus in nominal terms the Dow would have trebled from the present level, but lost significantly in real terms - a scenario I regard as highly probable. This would naturally be devastating for US bond prices.

Finally, I am constantly asked about the best investment opportunities. I think the acquisition of knowledge and a broad understanding of historical price trends may be one of the best personal investments a fund manager, broker or trader can make at this time. I have no doubt that *Anatomy of the Bear* will become an investment book classic, read by students of financial trends for generations. To read this book is the best Christmas 2005 gift you can give yourself and your friends!

Marc Faber
Hong Kong
November 2005

Introduction

Before beginning a Hunt, it is wise to ask someone what
you are looking for before you begin looking for it.

Pooh's Little Instruction Book by Joan Powers, inspired by A. A. Milne,

As a fly fisherman, I have occasionally found myself deep in the woods of
North America. This is where the bears live. As an Ulsterman, my
experience has not been in dodging bears and I have sought the advice of
the experts on what to do should one appear on the river bank. The US
National Parks Service has been particularly helpful.

Make as much noise as possible to scare it away. Yell. Bang pots
together. If there's someone with you, stand together to present a more
intimidating figure. All of this might prevent your name joining the list of
56 people so far killed in bear attacks in North America over the past two
decades.

This book is about what to do should you spot a bear of a different kind,
but one no less dangerous. It is a field guide for the financial bear, which
can shred a portfolio and seriously damage your wealth. And this type of
bear is a much greater threat to most individuals than anything found in the
wild.

There are some 84 million shareholders of US equities alone,[1] and
millions upon millions more around the globe, whose financial futures could
be destroyed or seriously damaged by one of these bears, which are not

---

[1] New York Stock Exchange *Factbook*.

1

nearly as easy to recognise as a member of the *urisidae* family in the woods of North America. Even if you can recognise this bear, making a lot of noise or standing tough with friends won't scare it away, though you may feel a lot better.

This is a good time to look at the financial bear. The large decline in the price of US equities that erupted in March 2000 petered out in late 2002. Was this the end of the bear market? Informed commentators are divided on the issue, even by the autumn of 2005 when equity prices remain well above their lows. Did a new bull market begin in 2002, or is it just a bounce in a longer bear market? There are few more important questions to be answered in modern finance and this book, by looking at all the previous major bear markets that have followed on from periods of extreme overvaluation, offers an answer to that question. We remain in a bear market. When will it end? How much lower will the market have to go? What events will help you determine when the market has bottomed? The answers are in this book.

As with everything in life - except, perhaps, water in your waders in the middle of a particularly cold stream - there is an upside to a bear market. According to Professor Jeremy Siegel's analysis of total real returns since 1802, all an investor needs do is hold for 17 years, and they will never lose money in the stock market. If you sit it out and ignore market prices, history suggests that in sometime less than 17 years the bear will simply go away, leaving your real purchasing power undamaged. When it comes to investment in equities, it is indeed true that everything comes to he who waits. If you have that time horizon, you don't need a financial field guide.

Few investors are sanguine enough to ignore market movements for 17 years. Indeed, New York Stock Exchange (NYSE) statistics for the first half of 2005 show the average holding period of the 84 million stockowners in the US was just 12 months (the average holding period from 1900-2002 was just 18 months). In the 20th Century, the real annual return on US equities was negative for 35 of those 100 years. In eight of those years, the negative return exceeded 20%. So, the average investor will likely encounter a bear market every three years or so, and every 13 years the bear will be particularly mean.

Granted that much of the volume on the NYSE is created by hedge fund managers and operators with near 20/20 short-term foresight, let's assume the average investor is more patient than the statistics suggest and works on a time horizon of ten years. This, of course, is wishful thinking as NYSE average turnover rates show only one year in the past hundred where the average investor had a time horizon of this duration. However if we assume a ten-year holding period, that still makes a bear encounter somewhat likely. For nine of the years of the past century, subsequent ten-year total real returns from US equities were negative. This is frequent enough, even for an investor with a ten-year time horizon, to face the risk of committing capital in the one dud year in 11. And big bears tend to linger. Periods of rising prices, before a further fall, are not uncommon in long bear markets. A financial field guide helps to avoid mistaking a rise in prices for the onset of a new bull market.

As you will discover, it seems highly likely that the rise in US equity prices since October 2002 has been just such a false dawn. That's important information, even if you have a ten-year time horizon.

Bears, however, can be beautiful in their way, and an alternative title for this book might have been *How I Learned to Stop Worrying and Love the Bear*. Bear markets mean lower prices. Consumers don't object to lower prices and neither should investors if they are buying rather than selling. Avoiding bears preserves wealth, but buying cheap in a bear market, given the positive real long-term returns from equities, is even more profitable. This field guide to the financial bear focuses on the very lucrative periods in history when equity prices had been pushed well below fair value and rebound was imminent.

As US baseball legend Yogi Berra once said, 'You can observe a lot just by watching'. By watching the financial bears, we can observe the point at which a number of potential factors come together to signal the market can only get better. Those factors include low valuations, improved earnings, improving liquidity, falling bond yields, and changes in how the market is perceived by those who play it. The aim of this guide is to help recognise factors that have, in the past, proven to be good markers to the future, and those that have been misleading. Albert Einstein once said the secret of his success was to ask the right questions, and keep going until he got the answer. In financial markets just asking the right questions can be incredibly difficult. This book, by studying financial history, offers the questions to ask when confronted by the bear. You have an advantage over Einstein. The beauty of finance over physics is that you don't need to provide the right answers, just better answers than most everyone else. Hopefully, this guide will help you on the way to finding those better answers.

3

Using financial history as a tool to understand the anatomy of the bear market is contentious, and Henry Ford was right in a way to say that 'history is more or less bunk'. Ford was talking about "tradition", a form of extrapolation that is inherently dangerous for any investor. A man of capital trapped in a mindset of behaving the same way as his forebears would probably still be clutching an equity portfolio rigid with the scrip of the Anglo-American Brush Light Company (the patent holder of the arc-light made redundant by the work of Edison) and The Locomobile Company (its steam car lost its one-third share of the US automobile market). Unfortunately, Ford's aphorism became imbedded in the academic approach to financial markets in 1952 when Harry M. Markowitz published his paper 'Portfolio Selection'.[2] This paper began an assault by academia on the value of history to investors. Markowitz assumed markets were efficient, and he came to some clear conclusions about the benefits of building a diversified portfolio of stocks. This dalliance of science with the concept of efficiency in relation to financial markets soon became a courtship and marriage in the form of the "efficient market hypothesis".

The birth of this theory was, for many, proof that history was indeed "bunk". What value, they asked, can there be in studying the history of financial markets if the stock market efficiently and immediately reflected all available information? Wasn't history simply an accumulation of all available past information? By the 1970s, the belief that market prices already reflect all available information had gained Wall Street's endorsement. As Peter Bernstein puts it:

> Had it not been for the crash of 1974, few financial practitioners would have paid attention to the ideas that had been stirring in ivory towers for some twenty years. But when it turned out that improvised strategies to beat the market served only to jeopardize their clients' interests, practitioners realized that they had to change their ways. Reluctantly they began to show interest in converting the abstract ideas of the academics into methods to control risk and to staunch the losses their clients were suffering. This was the motivating force of the revolution that shaped the new Wall Street.[3]

The new Wall Street came to replace the old. The acolytes of efficiency created a shrine to mathematical modelling of risk and return, all based on the assumption of efficiency. As is the wont of all new sects, iconoclasts damned the methodology of their predecessors as barbaric. However, even

---

[2] *Journal of Finance* Vol. III, No. 1 (March)
[3] Peter Bernstein, *Capital Ideas: The Improbable Origins of Modern Wall Street*

as this new sect became the orthodoxy, there were incidents that struck at its core beliefs. In 1987, the new Wall Street created a derivative product that offered investors a type of portfolio insurance. It failed to deliver, exacerbating the stock market crash of that year.

The new Wall Street may have created products for the management of risk, but it could not eradicate the risk of human greed and stupidity, as the citizens of California's Orange County and the shareholders of Gibson Greetings discovered.[4] In 1998, the acolytes closest to the shrine felt the tremors as Long Term Capital Management, perhaps the ultimate creation of the new Wall Street, imploded. Picking through the wreckage, there was evidence in the boom and bust of 1995 to 2002 that the new Wall Street was no more successful in protecting clients' interests than the failed "improvised strategies" of 1974.

Whatever the truths inherent in the ascendant orthodoxy, was it really so wise to discard the lessons of those who had gone before? The events of 1995 to 2002 indicate that some synthesis of old Wall Street thinking and new Wall Street ideas could create a more relevant and useful approach for financial practitioners. And that brings us back to the value of financial history.

The recent expansion and busting of yet another stock market bubble may be a good enough reason to suggest there is more in heaven and earth than is dreamed of in the philosophy of efficiency. There is also another reason. In 2002, the behavioural psychologist Daniel Kahneman, along with Vernon I. Smith, was awarded the Nobel Prize in economics for 'having integrated insights from psychological research into economic science, especially concerning human judgement and decision-making under uncertainty'.[5]

The Nobel Committee believed Kahneman had elucidated some of the errors in human judgement that eradicate the surety of efficiency. Ironically, Kahneman's first published article on the concept appeared in 1974, just as Wall Street was coming to embrace market efficiency. The Nobel Committee had previously honoured the acolytes of efficiency - Harry Markowitz, Merton Miller and William Sharpe in 1990, and Myron Scholes and Robert Merton in 1997. It now recognises a psychologist who

---

[4] Both sets of investors wound up nursing huge financial loses, having misunderstood the financial risks inherent in derivative products.
[5] Press release from Royal Swedish Academy of Sciences, 9 October 2002

questions whether human judgement, even in aggregate, lends itself to efficiency.

If there is a legitimate role for the study of human judgement and decision-making under uncertainty, then financial history is redeemed. What is financial history if not such a study? The behaviouralist school of psychology, around for nearly a century, is based on observing reactions to selected stimuli. Financial history looks at market prices, which are a reflection of the behaviour of thousands of participants to certain stimuli. In behavioural economics, history is a useful tool for observing how financial markets work, rather than theorising about how they should work.

Such historical studies have not yet lent themselves to the comforts of empiricism. This, in itself, may be enough of a reason for many to reject the approach. However, the inability to translate all understanding into binary code does not necessarily denude it of value and insight. If psychology is a soft science, then using financial history to assess human decision-making in times of uncertainty is softer still. For those who accept that human judgement and decision-making cannot be divined by equations, financial market history is a guide to understanding the future.

The particular value in financial market history comes from its insight into the operation of human judgement under uncertainty, in particular its examination of contemporaneous opinion. While any historian is liable to hindsight bias, a focus on contemporary comments and reactions at least reduces the risks of projecting one's own order on things. As a historical source, newspapers offer an efficient daily collation of events and, in the financial press, with a focus on the markets, this has been the best practical repository of contemporary opinion for the past century or more. The boom in press coverage of the stock market dates from around the birth of the railway, when the emerging middle classes found investing in the new technology almost irresistible. If we focus on this particularly rich vein of information, we find a largely reliable source that dates back to around 1850.

To discover what the bottom of past bear markets looked like, and how the investor was reacting, I analysed some 70,000 articles from *The Wall Street Journal* written in the two months either side of the four great bear market bottoms. I report my findings in these pages. My aim is to provide as accurate a picture as possible of a bear-market bottom based on contemporary comment. This is where any understanding of human decision-making in times of past investment uncertainty must begin. The pages of the *WSJ* take us close to the primary sources on what was happening at the time and, at various points in the book, the reader will be immersed in this contemporary coverage of events and the approaches that have worked in assessing when the bear is about to become the bull. What also emerges is an understanding of how similar the great four bear-market bottoms were, in turn leading us to a set of signals to guide investment strategy.

In this book, I focus on the history of bear markets. Such periods have important practical implications for today's investor, but seem to be the chapter missing from most books on financial history. Booms and bust make for attractive analyses, but what of the moment the bust ends and the boom begins. Picking that point must surely minimise losses and optimise profit. But which of the many bear markets in the many financial jurisdictions occurring since 1850 will lead us to the right conclusions? Looking for the best available financial market coverage and the largest financial market, we are drawn to the United States, rather than the United Kingdom. So, which of the US bear markets will tell the most complete story? Those bear market bottoms that were followed by the best subsequent returns have the advantage of at least suggesting practical ramifications from the exercise. Whatever subjectivity there may be in discussing whether markets are below fair value, the subsequent superior returns from these lows are the best objective indicator that value did exist.

Andrew Smithers and Stephen Wright published a book in 2000 called *Valuing Wall Street*, in which the authors calculate the best years in the 20th Century to have invested in equities. They defined a measure of "hindsight value", calculated by taking the average of 40 discrete periods of subsequent returns over one-to-40 years. By taking the average of returns over 40 different holding periods, "hindsight value" would represent the range of holding periods of the very differing investors who have bought equities in any given year. This study showed the best three years to buy US equities were 1920, 1932 and 1948. These years do not necessarily coincide with the period when the Dow Jones Industrial Index (DJIA) reached its low. This difference is mainly because the return calculations are done using year-end levels, and the equity market has a habit of not necessarily being at its low on 31 December. When adjustment is made for intra-year movement, the three best times to invest in US equities emerge as August 1921, July 1932 and June 1949.

"Hindsight value" can only be calculated for those years where there is at least a subsequent 40 years of returns. Subjectivity does play a part in leading us to the fourth period for analysis in this book, but there are good reasons to believe 1982 will prove to be one of the four best years to have invested in US equities. It is certainly in the top four, 23 years down the track.

As equities produced the best returns after these four periods, we can state with the benefit of hindsight that equities were at their cheapest in 1921, 1932, 1949 and 1982. This is a measure of value only observable some 40 years after the event and, thus, of limited immediate use. For the purposes of this book, we need a reliable measure of value available to investors facing the market on a day-to-day basis. There are many competing valuation metrics, but fortunately Andrew Smithers and Stephen Wright narrowed the field to just two. In *Valuing Wall Street*, they subject the most common valuation measures to various tests, importantly the reliability of those measures relative to subsequent returns as indicated by "hindsight value". What we find is there were measures of value available to investors at the time that showed equities to be very cheap in 1921, 1932, 1949 and 1982. While accepting the usefulness of the cyclically adjusted PE - the chosen measure of value of Yale's Robert Shiller - Smithers and Wright found that the q ratio has been a particularly accurate indicator of superior future returns. Given its usefulness, at least over the long term, we will use the q ratio to assess how equity valuations have altered over different periods.

The q ratio is effectively a measure of the stock-market valuation of a company relative to the replacement value of its assets. In this book, a statement such as 'equities were trading below fair value' simply means the prevailing q ratio was below the geometric mean of the ratio. The four periods we study in this book are the only occasions when equities were at more than a 70% discount to replacement value. The role of this book is to explain the forces that reduced prices to such levels, and identify the factors pushing them back to replacement value and beyond.

To tell the story of the four-month period around the four great bear market bottoms, we cannot ignore the bigger picture. To understand the forces pushing equity prices back towards fair value, one must understand the fears that drove them to such discounts to fair value. That excursion, often through decades of investment history, is a book in itself and much has had to be omitted in the interest of brevity. In Part I, the backstory can be found under the heading 'The road to August 1921' - a similar heading is used to set up the subsequent three periods under discussion. It is also necessary to provide a brief description of the structure of the financial markets in each of the periods studied. There are important structural differences in each period that need to be borne in mind by investors seeking to apply the lessons of history to today's markets. For example, major financial institutions were not listed on the NYSE in the first of the periods we examine. A brief overview can be found under the heading 'Structure of the markets'. Having sketched the cause of the market decline and its contemporary structure, we then focus on the factors signalling the end of the bear market, under the heading 'At the bottom with the bear'. Examination of the behaviour of the fixed-interest markets - a book in itself - focuses on the salient events directly affecting equity prices.

Readers will also notice that extended attention is paid to the events of 1929-32. This is because there are important differences between this great bear market and the other three analysed in this book. It is also because 1929-32 is often held up as being typical of a bear market; and events of that period often colour opinions about what a bear market looks like. It is therefore useful to spend some time with this bear, if only to understand more about how unique it was in financial history.

This book is aimed at both the professional investor and those wanting to exercise their own judgement in making the best financial provisions for their future. Throughout the book are boxes to help the lay investor seeking to understand the complexities that professionals sometimes neglect to explain. Still, there is likely to be jargon that has gone unexplained. A useful aid in understanding this jargon is the excellent online encyclopaedia at the Economic History Services website at www.eh.net.

Sections of text have been bolded to guide the reader with conclusions that may be drawn from events as they are discussed, building towards a set of universal conclusions about bear-market bottoms, their identification and strategies to optimise profit.

Throughout this book are epigraphs from some of the 20th Century's greatest writers. They were living amid enormous economic turbulence and financial uncertainty and their work around the time of our analysis allows us to hold the mirror of literature to the events we examine. The central characters in these novels made propitious financial decisions just as the stock market was reaching its bottom. F. Scott Fitzgerald had Nick Carraway give up his job on Wall Street in 1922, following Gatsby's death, and return to Wisconsin. Whether he was happy there we shall never know but he headed east just as the greatest equity bull market in US history began. For James T. Farrell, poor Studs Lonigan had an even worse fate. He flung his nest egg into the market in 1931, just as the worst portion of the financial collapse began. Before the equity market bottomed in July 1932, Studs was dead. In the late 1940s, Robert Holton had to decide whether to take a risk and head off to Italy with a married woman, or to play it safe and stay on Wall Street. Gore Vidal decided Holton should stay behind - and outside the pages he would no doubt have benefited handsomely from one of the longest bull markets in the history of America. This is not to say he wouldn't rather have been in Italy. Holton appears to have been the only one of these characters to have made a financially astute decision. For John Updike's Harry 'Rabbit' Angstrom, gold, in the form of krugerrands, was the best investment for his future. His fateful purchase almost coincided with gold's all-time high.

Can it be coincidence that the four years covered in this book - 1921, 1932, 1949, 1982 - also mark momentous change in American society. There was the birth of the consumer society (1921), the birth of big government (1932), the birth of the military-industrial complex (1949) and the rebirth of free markets (1982). Each of the fictional characters in this book struggles with a particular societal transition, all the while wrestling with the impact of that change on their financial future.

I had lunch with a man who has come across quite a few bears in his time, polar explorer and mountaineer David Hempleman-Adams. I asked him what to do when confronted with a bear and his advice was brief: 'Shoot the bastard.' Guns offer no protection from the financial bear. This book, I hope, makes it a fairer fight.

Part I
August 1921

'I wouldn't ask too much of her,' I ventured. 'You can't repeat the past.'
'Can't repeat the past?' he cried incredulously. 'Why of course you can!'

F Scott Fitzgerald, *The Great Gatsby*

Despite the boom in US stock markets during the early years of WWI, by August 1921 the Dow Jones & Co. Index of Industrial shares was back to its level of 22 years ago. Investors who had shunned this dangerous new sector of the market had fared even worse with their blue chip railroad shares back at 1881 prices. But now was a wonderful time to buy, with equities trading at a 70% discount to the replacement value of their assets. By September 1929, equities were close to a 100% premium to their replacement value and the DJIA had risen almost fivefold. This was the greatest bull market in the almost 140-year history of the New York Stock Exchange. What changed in 1921, and how could investors have anticipated the bottom of the market to profit from the Roaring Twenties?

The road to August 1921

The course of the Dow - 1896-1921

It was the end of summer in lower Manhattan when the air was ripped asunder by a thunderous explosion outside the offices of JP Morgan & Co on Wall Street. The area went dark and a huge cloud of smoke swathed the financial centre of America. Brokers at the New York Stock Exchange ran to avoid the flying glass. Windows shattered up to half a mile away. The death toll would reach 40 and the date was 16 September 1920. It has never been determined who planted the bomb. The press and public used one of Wall Street's favourite analytical tools in assessing the situation: extrapolation. In April 1920, bombs had been mailed to 18 prominent people known in their politics to be anti-labour. It was assumed the Wall Street bomb was also a "red" attack, this time on the centre of US, and increasingly world, capitalism. The bomb was not the only disturbance on Wall Street - a vicious bear market was also wreaking havoc.

Bear markets are the field of study of this book. This is not due to any predilection of the author to chronicle the more depressing periods of our investment history, quite the reverse. Buying at the bottom is the goal, perhaps only a dream, of every investor. This book is thus an identification guide to those seeking to establish that period when the bear turns into the bull. This is the most profitable time to invest in equities, and the summer of 1921 was probably the most profitable time in the history of Wall Street. To create such an identification guide it is important to, paraphrasing the estimable Mrs Beeton, 'first catch your bear', but defining a bear market is not easy, even today, with the S&P 500 and the Dow Jones Industrial Average (DJIA) sometimes telling quite different stories. In 1921, it was far more complicated as there was no index representative of the whole market. To gauge market movements, one had to watch two distinct sectors: the Dow, Jones & Co 20 Industrial Stock Average, and the Dow, Jones & Co 20 Railroad Stock Average.

The development of the two separate stock indices by Charles Dow tells the story of the development of the stock market itself as it headed down the road to the bear market of 1919-21. In 1896, industrial share sales accounted for 48% of volume on the NYSE, compared with 52% of volume for the railroad stocks. There was an extremely low level of market activity in general - reflected in a 41% decline in the price of NYSE memberships over the previous decade - and in railroad shares in particular, as the market recovered from the panic of 1893-95.

JP Morgan's amalgamation of bankrupt and distressed railroads in the wake of the crisis of 1893-95 panic breathed new life into that moribund sector. Merger mania followed soon after the launch of the industrials index, and the number of business mergers in the United States rose from 69 in 1897 to more than 1,200 in 1899. The positive impact from such mergers was greatest for the railroad sector, where profitability had been crushed by excess capacity. A merger-driven bull market in railroad shares drove up the railroad index from 1896 to 1902, far surpassing the rise in the industrials index, where excess capacity had not previously been as damaging to profitability. Dow's creation of an industrial average in 1896 marked the high-point of interest in the industrial stocks and their share of total market turnover did not rise above the 1896 level again until 1911.

The **Dow Jones Industrial Average (DJIA)** was first published in May 1896 and was calculated by averaging the share prices of 12 component companies. Charles Dow created his original index in 1884, at which time it was dominated by railroad shares. The need for a second index for industrials was evident by 1896, indicating the growing importance to investors of the "smokestack" companies. In October 1916, the number of stocks in the index was expanded to 20, and in October 1928 to the current 30. The index continues to be weighted by price rather than market capitalisation. References throughout this book to "the market" refer to the DJIA. Throughout the four periods covered, investors looked to the DJIA as their guide to what the market was doing. In analysing the investor's perception of the market, we also focus on the DJIA. Sometimes it is necessary to refer to another index, the S&P Composite Index, but such divergence is confined to valuation and earnings, where the data is of superior quality to that available for the DJIA.

The highpoint for activity in railroad stocks ended with the assassination of William McKinley in 1901 and the ascendancy of Theodore Roosevelt. The new president was less sympathetic to the numerous combines of businesses formed as legal trusts and acted to control pricing in many industries. The trust-busting activities of the new administration hit the mature railroad business with greater ferocity than the growing industrial sector. By 1911, the industrial sector's share of total turnover breached the 1896 level and, for the first time, exceeded activity in railroad stocks. Activity and interest in both asset classes were then roughly equal until the start of World War I, when a dramatic divergence in activity and prices developed.

Figure 1

RAILROAD/INDUSTRIALS MARKET SHARE (%) 1895-1921

Source: New York Stock Exchange

Investors seeking to survive and profit in the 1919-21 bear market were dealing with a market which had been structurally transformed by WWI. By the end of the war, industrials accounted for more than 80% of NYSE volume and most of the railroads had been nationalised. The war also produced a disturbance to the general price level, which was to lead directly to the bear market of 1919-21. Market reaction to the assassination of Archduke Franz Ferdinand on 28 June 1914 had been relatively calm. However, on 25 July, Austria and Germany refused to attend a conference of the six Great Powers (Russia, Great Britain, France, Austria-Hungary, Italy and Germany). The apparent inevitability of an outright war heightened the prospects for a mass selling of stocks. Investors feared a heavy outflow of gold from the US, a debtor nation, to finance a European war and an ensuing tightening of domestic liquidity. On 28 July, Austria declared war on Serbia, and the stock exchanges of Montreal, Toronto, and Madrid closed, followed the next day by Vienna, Budapest, Brussels, Antwerp, Rome and Berlin. On 31 July, the London exchange closed and the NYSE was left with little choice but to follow suit rather than be faced with the prospect of having to absorb huge forces of liquidation from global investors. The DJIA stood at 71.42 and the railroad average at 89.41.

With certain restrictions on trading, the market reopened on 12 December 1914, a Saturday. On the Monday, the *Wall Street Journal* published the first Dow Jones averages for more than four months. The railroad average had risen to 90.21. The industrials average, however, ended 12 December at 54, down 32% from the 30 July level. The industrials average bottomed just below that level within days before a major bull market that lasted through 1915. Instead of the feared capital outflow, funds poured into the US as the warring nations bought necessary materials from the neutral industrial powerhouse.

Figure 2

DOW JONES INDUSTRIAL AVERAGE - INCEPTION TO 1921 BEAR MARKET BOTTOM

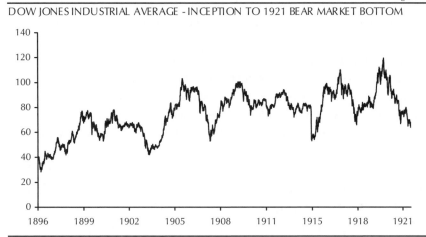

Source: Dow Jones & Co.

As well as improving liquidity, industrial stock prices benefited from booming profits. It is important to stress the incredible magnitude of the profit boom in that period. In nominal terms profits did not exceed the 1916 level until 1949. In real terms, it was not until December 1955 that 1916 earnings were exceeded, and thereafter there were numerous subsequent declines to pre-1916 levels. As late as January 1992, S&P Composite real earnings were below the 1916 level. Indeed, when real earnings bottomed in March 2002, they were just 4.7% above the 1916 level. Not surprisingly in this environment investors quickly came to favour industrial stocks referred to as "war brides" - those accruing huge war orders from Europe. Following this major bull market, railroad and industrial stocks traded largely sideways through 1916, before a major downturn in prices in 1917 on the growing likelihood of the US entering the war and an early peace. Further contributing to the 1917 bear market was government intervention to control commodity prices, the failure of the railroads to secure rate increases from the Interstate Commerce Commission (ICC), rising costs, the introduction of an excess profits tax and increased government debt issues.

As the stalemated war in Europe turned to attrition, the industrial and railroad indexes traded sideways through 1918. It was not until after the war, in 1919, that the industrials enjoyed another bull market, reaching an all-time high in November 1919. The vast discrepancy in performance of the two sectors during and immediately after WWI resulted from many factors, but the nationalisation of the railroads at noon on 28 December 1917 was clearly a key factor. This effectively converted railroad equity into bonds, with the government paying the stock owners a fixed dividend based on the average earnings of their companies prior to nationalisation.

With returns to railroad stockholders thus constrained, investor focus shifted to industrial stocks, where companies were benefiting from the wartime boom. When the industrials' bull market peaked in 1919, turnover in railroad shares accounted for just 13.8% of the total trading volume. But investors in stocks continued to focus on both indexes through 1919-21. Many investors believed the decline in railroad stocks was a temporary phenomenon that would disappear with the end of nationalisation in March 1920. By 1921, investors were still looking to the railroad and industrial indices in assessing the scale of the bear market, even though volume in the industrials sector now far surpassed activity in the railroads.

Living with the Fed – A whole new ball game (I)

It would be easy, and dangerous, to assume that markets worked in 1921 as they do today. Before looking at the stock market in detail for the period of June to October - two months either side of the August bottom - it is worth pausing to consider key institutional differences in the workings of the financial markets then against now. In particular, in setting the scene for the events of late summer 1921, it is important to consider the emergence of an unknown new factor in markets - the Federal Reserve System, established in 1914.

This system consisted of the Federal Reserve Board and 12 Federal Reserve Banks. The Reserve Banks were free to determine discount rates but, according to the legislation, such decisions were 'subject to review and determination of the Federal Reserve Board'. However, no such review and determination was given to the Federal Reserve Board when it came to the open market operations of the Federal Reserve Banks. There was, thus, the possibility of a high degree of autonomy for the Federal Reserve Banks within the system. This autonomy led, in the early years of the system, to the Federal Reserve Bank of New York, operating as it did in the financial capital of America, becoming a key driver of the system's monetary policy.

The decentralised structure of the system complicated the business of forecasting future policy and also led to conflicts within the system itself, which were to have important consequences in the not too distant future. The dramatic impact of the creation of this institution at the time might be understood by the modern investor if one imagined the impact on investment decisions if the system was abolished tomorrow.

The creation of a central bank altered the operation of a monetary mechanism that had been familiar to US investors since the post-Civil War resumption of the gold standard in 1879. The Federal Reserve System created an element of uncertainty for investors. It was difficult to know how this extra, human element would work. Indeed, there had been a long-held belief, summed up by the report of the Bullion Committee to the British House of Commons in 1810, that the introduction of any human element in the monetary process could be dangerous.

> The most detailed knowledge of the actual trade of the country, combined with the profound Science in all the principles of Money and circulation, would not enable any man or set of men to adjust, and keep always adjusted, the right proportion of circulating medium in a country to the wants of trade.[6]

The US did not have an official central bank - President Andrew Jackson vetoed the renewal of the charter of the Second Bank of the United States in 1832.

Just how the new system would interact with the gold standard to influence liquidity, interest rates and financial markets was difficult to predict, given its mandate:

> To provide for the establishment of Federal reserve banks, to furnish an elastic currency, to afford means of rediscounting commercial paper, to establish a more effective supervision of banking in the United States, and for other purposes.[7]

---

[6] Report from the select committee of the House of Commons on the high price of gold bullion (1810).

[7] Preamble to the *Federal Reserve Act 1913*

Such a step was believed necessary because, twice in the recent past, the inability to 'furnish an elastic currency' had brought the United States close to bankruptcy. In February 1895, only a loan from JP Morgan and the Rothschilds had prevented the exhaustion of the US government gold reserve and the end of the gold standard. In 1907, JP Morgan again brokered a deal to prevent the bankruptcy of key financial institutions and saved the financial system. Despite significant political opposition, Wilson's Democrats enacted the legislation that created the Federal Reserve System and the "elastic currency" that was supposed to remove from private hands the role of de facto lender of last resort.

The **gold standard** was a monetary system, under which gold coin was legal tender and bank notes could be redeemed for gold at a fixed price. Many countries adopted this monetary system, each declaring a fixed price in gold for their domestic currency. As each national currency was redeemable for a fixed amount of gold, the value of each currency was effectively fixed relative to each other. This had important implications for the supply of money in the economy, and economic activity and prices. If the US, for instance, ran a balance of payments surplus, there would be more buyers than sellers of US dollars. In that situation, more dollars would have to be created to retain the fixed rate of exchange. A sufficiently large increase in the amount of dollars would likely produce higher economic activity, but also higher prices. Higher prices would eventually erode US competitiveness and the balance of payments would eventually move into deficit. In a situation where there were more sellers than buyers of the currency, the process would be reversed. After WWI a variation of the gold standard was introduced in which some authorities would hold other currencies, which themselves were redeemable for gold, as part of their reserves. This system was known as the gold exchange standard.

In practice, the Federal Reserve System furnished elasticity by creating Federal Reserve banknotes and accepting commercial bank deposits with the Fed as satisfying legal reserve requirements. The Fed created these two types of money by receipt of gold, rediscounting of eligible paper, discounting of foreign trade acceptances, and open market purchases of government securities, banker's acceptances and bills of exchange. This ability to create money based on rediscounting bank assets was known as the real bills criterion. The difficult question for investors to answer was how such an elastic currency would operate while the country also adhered to the gold standard? The apparent conflict is that the gold standard dictates the stock of money necessary to balance international payments while the real bills doctrine does not limit the quantity of money. Milton Friedman and Anna Jacobson Schwarz argued that this contradiction was 'more apparent than real'.

> While the gold standard determines the longer-term movements in the total stock of money, it leaves much leeway in shorter-run movements. Gold reserves and the international capital market provide cushions for temporary imbalances. More important, the gold standard does not determine the division of the total stock of money between currency and deposits, whereas the real bills criterion was linked to this division.[8]

The crises of 1895 and 1907 were exacerbated by the public's shift from bank deposits to cash. Thus, the new legislation was aimed at creating a system that would allow such a shift to occur without producing bank failures or the restriction of cash payments by banks. The elastic currency could be rapidly expanded in such situations and banks could rapidly access currency by discounting their assets with the new reserve bank.

In theory, an investor should expect that the Fed would operate only to alleviate any rush to currency that would imperil the banking system. The problem for those allocating capital was that, in practice, something very different occurred. From the creation of the Federal Reserve System in November 1914 to June 1920 the "elastic" money was stretched and the stock of money more than doubled. To complicate matters further for investors, the Fed's role in money-creation was inconsistent and unpredictable.

Figure 3

SOURCES OF CHANGE IN HIGH-POWERED MONEY (Total change = 1.00)	US neutrality Jun 1914 -Mar 1917	War Mar 1917 -Nov 1918	Peace Nov 1918 -May 1920
Monetary gold stock	0.87	0.04	(0.41)
Federal Reserve claims on public and banks	0.15	1.24	1.44
Other physical assets and fiat of monetary authorities	(0.02)	(0.28)	0.03

Source: Friedman and Schwartz

---

[8] Milton Friedman and Anna Jacobson Schwartz, A *Monetary History of the United States, 1867-1960*.

High-powered money (also known as the monetary base) is a term for a combination of all the forms of money, over which the Federal Reserve has almost complete control. It is known as high-powered money because small changes produce much larger impacts on the total amount of money in the economy. By impacting the total amount of money in the economy, changes in high-powered money can have major impacts on economic activity and inflation. Prior to the creation of the Federal Reserve System the key determinant of change to high-powered money had been gold inflows and outflows under the operation of the gold standard. This mechanism continued to impact the growth of high-powered money after the creation of the Fed, but the Fed could also act independently to influence high-powered money. Over the years, equity investors have watched the performance of high-powered money as a leading indicator of future trends in the economy, inflation and the stock market.

As we can see from Figure 3, the Federal Reserve System played only a minor role in money-creation prior to US entry into the war. The initial surge in the growth of high-powered money was due to a major gold inflow as belligerent governments purchased goods, liquidated investments and borrowed money. This process produced a turnaround in the US international investment position. A deficit of $3.7 billion in 1914 became a surplus of similar size by 1919. At this stage in its history, the Fed could only rediscount selected commercial bank assets to create Federal Reserve money. It had accumulated few assets, so had none to sell to "sterilise" an increase in high-powered money caused by the accumulation of gold. In more simple terms, the Fed could stretch the elastic currency in its early years but, until it had been first stretched, it could not be an instrument for monetary tightening. For the investor, the Fed System had little impact on liquidity adjustment and its consequent influence on stock market prices from the system's creation until the US entered the war in 1917.

US entry into the war created a clear monetary shift. The country now sold goods to its allies on US government credit rather than in return for gold. The flow of gold to the US ceased. In this period the increase in the monetary gold stock now played a negligible role in the increase in high-powered money. A second monetary change due to the US entry into the war was the government's need to finance the military. Although taxes rose, revenue was insufficient. Money reation through the central bank now played a role in enabling the government to raise finance domestically. Investors now had to understand the role of the elastic currency in propping up government finances rather than preventing the liquidity crises for which it had been designed. How "elastic" would be the new currency in this situation and, assuming the US won the war, what would be the magnitude of its subsequent contraction? Investors who answered these two questions correctly would make the optimal investment decisions of 1917-21.

Entry into the war produced a dramatic stretch in the elastic currency. Fed money accounted for 21% of high-powered money in April 1917, but by November 1918 this had risen to 59%. The member banks of the Federal Reserve System accomplished this by lending to their customers for the purchase of government bonds and then rediscounting these loans at one of the 12 Reserve Banks. After 1917, the Fed clearly utilised its new powers to 'furnish an elastic currency', not to alleviate or prevent a money panic, but to assist government war financing. WWI was the first major conflict to be fought by the United States since its Civil War. On that occasion, it was necessary to suspend the gold standard. On this occasion, the newly introduced currency elasticity permitted the country to remain on the gold standard. For US investors in 1917, the "elastic currency" kept money easy during a period of war and the gold standard in place. Investors who expected a suspension of the gold standard or its maintenance with associated tight money had failed to understand how the creation of the Federal Reserve System had changed the operation of the monetary system.

It was to be expected that the cessation of hostilities would depress the high levels of war demand, and bring about economic contraction. Just such an economic decline began in August 1918, even before the Armistice. But while many expected a prolonged decline, the contraction had run its course by March 1919. The public shifted to holding less cash than it had in the war period, and more deposits. This return of high-powered money into the commercial banking system helped to stabilise monetary growth. Just as important were the actions of the Fed Board, which kept interest rates low through 1919 and at a significant discount to market rates. This further encouraged member banks to borrow from the system and increase lending. The Fed justified its action as necessary to fund the government's floating debt and to prevent a slide in the price of government bonds, now a key asset and source of collateral to the banking system. In performing this support operation the Fed stretched the elastic currency as much in this postwar period as during the conflict (see Figure 3).

Although there was significant debate within the Fed and the Treasury, the belief was that somehow the system could distinguish "legitimate" borrowing from "speculative" during this period of artificially low rates. This was not the case, and a speculative bull market in industrial equities and commodities raged through 1919. It had long been a basic principle of investment that wartime inflation would be followed by postwar deflation due to the operation of the gold standard. However, now the reverse occurred as the Fed stretched the elasticity of the currency even further to assist the government with its funding requirements. Investors playing by the old rules missed the bull market in stocks and commodities in 1919.

It was in this postwar period that investors seriously misread how the monetary system would operate. The ability or willingness of the Fed to exercise the power of elasticity was subsequently misconstrued due to its activities in 1919. Many assumed the Fed's willingness to stretch the elastic currency had sufficiently circumvented the operation of the gold standard to prevent any future dramatic rise in interest rates. The Fed, which provided the system with no credit prior to November 1914, was providing around $3 billion by the end of 1919, a sum equivalent to almost 4% of GDP. With Fed credit rising from a base of zero, it was not surprising that some investors could believe that much higher levels of elasticity could be permitted. In this new environment, it was believed that borrowing funds for speculation in rising asset prices was a lot less risky than it had been before the birth of the Federal Reserve System. It was this misjudgement by investors that led, after the stock market party of 1919, to the more painful hangover of 1920-21.

What had apparently been forgotten was the statutory limit to the elasticity of the currency, which was rapidly being reached. The legislation required the Fed to hold gold reserves of 40% against notes, and 35% legal tender reserves against net deposits. Internally, the Federal Reserve had established its own minimum of 40% total reserves against net deposits and note liability. With gold leaving the country and the commercial banks encouraged to lend by sub-market rates provided by the Fed, a decline in the reserve ratio ensued. Having already declined significantly during the war, the ratio fell from 48.1% in December 1918 to 42.7% in January 1920. The Fed watched the decline without action, but in the first quarter of 1920, there was room for manoeuvre as the government began to retire federal debt.

The key reason for continuing to stretch the elastic currency was now gone. While the statutory power existed to suspend the reserve requirement and continue the stretching, the performance of the money market was suggesting early in 1919 that no suspension was expected. Tightness in the money market was already evident, with call money rates at 15% by June 1919, rising to 30% by November. The Fed made its first move to prevent the continuing decline of the reserve ratio in November/December 1919 by raising the discount rate - most banks increasing the discount rate to 4.75% in that period, with all banks increasing the rate to 6.0% by January/February 1920. The willingness of the Fed to stretch the elasticity of the currency to its limit played a role in the postwar bull market in industrial stocks. The reaction forced by the decline in the Fed's reserve ratio towards its statutory limit was to play a major role in the ensuing bear market.

As well as a heavy focus on the new monetary institution, investors in 1921 paid particular attention to alterations in the general price level. While inflation is regularly a topic of discussion in today's financial press, there was a far greater focus in 1921. This focus for investors on prices was dictated by the operation of the gold standard and its impact on the prices of securities. Under the operation of the gold standard, bear markets in stocks were normally associated with a loss of competitiveness, deterioration in the external accounts, tightening liquidity, economic contraction and a decline in the general price level.

Figure 4

FEDERAL RESERVE BANK OF NEW YORK DISCOUNT RATE - 1914-24

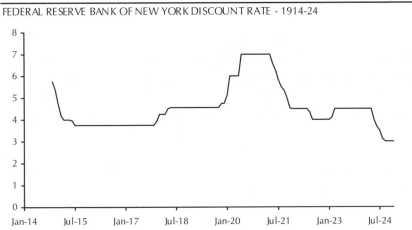

Source: Federal Reserve, *Banking and Monetary Statistics*

A question for any investor in assessing the end of this process was whether domestic prices had become competitive relative to prices of key trading partners. If this was the case, the process could reverse, with improving external accounts, easier liquidity, and economic expansion all acting to produce an improvement in equity prices. Judging when the deflation, begun in 1920, would be complete was particularly difficult due to the scale of prior price adjustments; from June 1914 to May 1920, wholesale prices in the US rose 147%. Judging how competitive the US was after such inflation was further complicated by the high wartime inflation of its key trading partners, which were operating with flexible exchange rates.

In the immediate postwar era, declines in the French franc, mark and sterling against the US dollar produced material capital flows into these jurisdictions as foreign investors bet on a return of these currencies to the gold standard at their pre-war levels. However, such confidence increasingly evaporated and a slide in exchange rates began in 1919. From the beginning of 1919 to the start of 1921, the franc and the mark had fallen by more than 60% and sterling almost 30% against the dollar. There had also been very high levels of inflation in other nations and it was thus not clear to what extent prices in the US would have to deflate to produce a balance in the external accounts under the gold standard.

Judging how large this adjustment would need to be was the key to understanding how tight liquidity would be and how much economic activity would be depressed. As the bull market in industrial shares lasted until November 1919, there were those who believed no such adjustment was necessary. They were wrong.

How did an investor in the postwar era assess the level of domestic prices dictated by the operation of the gold standard? It was not surprising that many were confused due to the scale of the dislocation to the global economy caused by WWI. The magnitude of price rises had been the largest witnessed in the US since the Civil War and nobody knew exactly how the relatively new Federal Reserve System would influence price determination. Prices had been rising before the US entered the war, and one might have expected that, with the Fed largely inactive until April 1917, the gold standard would have acted to restrain prices in that period. This was not the case as gold poured into the US (see Figure 5) and the stock of high-powered money increased.

Figure 5

YEAR-END GOLD STOCK HELD BY US TREASURY, ANNUAL NET IMPORT OF GOLD		
($m)	Gold stock	Net import
1914	1,526	-165
1915	2,025	+421
1916	2,556	+530
1917	2,868	+180
1918	2,873	+21
1919	2,707	-292
1920	2,639	+95

Source: US Bureau of the Census

In normal circumstances, the inevitable boost to liquidity would have resulted in rising prices, undermining US competitiveness and leading to a deflationary outflow of gold. However, in wartime such adjustments do not occur so smoothly. To some extent, the demand for munitions and materiel would always be less price-sensitive than the demand for foodstuffs and other material demands of peace. This would act to keep demand for US goods higher than it would otherwise be.

A deflationary monetary strain should have developed in those countries losing gold, resulting in their greater competitiveness, thus acting to bring gold back across the Atlantic. There were obvious new security issues which discouraged capitalists from bringing gold back to Europe. Also, during the war, the domestic scarcity of goods in Europe drove up prices despite the monetary drain illustrating how war production interrupted the normal operation of the gold standard. The price differential with the US was not big enough to produce a dramatic change in the current account situation and draw gold back to Europe in these extreme circumstances. Despite adhering to the gold standard, the US witnessed significant inflation before it entered the war (see Figure 6). In the postwar era, investors had to ponder how "sticky" this gold would be. How long would Europe take to rebuild and truly threaten US industry and national competitiveness? Would peace dictate the return of gold to Europe or would social chaos, evident in Russia and Germany, keep foreign gold in the US? Even analysing the future for general prices based purely on the gold standard was fraught with difficulty, further complicated by the Fed's actions from March 1917 to Nov 1919.

Figure 6

RISE IN WHOLESALE PRICES IN THREE PERIODS OF JUNE 1914-MAY 1920		
US neutrality Jun 1914-Mar 1917	War Mar 1917-Nov 1918	Peace Nov 1919-May 1920
65%	23%	22%

Source: Friedman and Schwarz, *A Monetary History of the United States 1857-1960*

In pondering what would happen to the flow of gold and how elastic the Fed would allow the currency to become, investors also had to assess the degree of permanence in the growth of the US economy and corporate earnings. Unless one could assess the normal peace time level of profitability of listed companies how could one value them? Even with the benefit of hindsight, it is not easy to accurately quantify how much growth in the US economy from 1914-19 was real and how much due to inflation. One can refer to monetary and price adjustments in the period with a high degree of certainty, but the alteration in the size of the economy is subject to greater uncertainty. The first published gross domestic product (GDP) statistics prepared by the US Department of Commerce relate to 1929. Prior to 1929, there are only estimates by economic historians of the growth in the US economy.

Figure 7

ANNUAL PERCENTAGE CHANGE IN GDP		
	Nominal GDP	Real GDP
1914	-6.3	-7.7
1915	+5.8	+3.4
1916	+26.4	+16.1
1917	+19.5	-0.2
1918	+26.4	+7.6
1919	+10.5	-3.2
End 1914 to end 1919	+123	+25

Source: Nathan Balke and Robert Gordon, *The Estimation of Pre-war GNP: Methodology and New Evidence.* NBER Working Papers 2674

While real economic growth had been strong from the end of 1914 to the end of 1919, much of that growth is accounted for by the boom year of 1916, when the war in Europe was demanding greater resources and neutral US helped provide them. Real growth of the economy in 1916 accounts for 70% of the total real growth in the five years 1915 to 1919. So apart from the difficult issue of assessing the necessary contraction in the elastic currency the wartime period also produced a significant problem in correctly valuing equities. In assessing the valuation of stocks in the postwar period, investors needed answers to some key questions. Was the boom of 1916 a permanent surge in the US share of world trade, and thus a permanent profit boost for US corporations? If the 1916 boom was unique, then didn't peace augur a major contraction in profitability? Could one value stocks in relation to their wartime profitability or was the pre-war level of profitability the correct basis for valuation?

Even if one came to the conclusion that the real growth in the economy was a permanent fixture, the wartime readjustment still held risks for investors. While the economy was clearly larger in real terms than it had been prior to the war, the wartime inflation still needed to be squeezed from the system. What scale of deflation would be necessary? What damage would such deflation inflict on the US financial system? How would the Federal Reserve's ability to provide an elastic currency influence the price adjustment and financial system stability? There were clearly fears that the whole 147% rise in wholesale prices might have to be squeezed out of the system, and such a level of deflation would produce severe economic hardship, particularly for those who had borrowed to purchase goods at such substantially higher prices. The Fed's actions November 1918 to late 1919 suggested it would stretch the currency to its extreme to prevent adjustment of such magnitude. Certainly, that was how it seemed to investors until the discount rate was raised in November 1919. It looked like some deflation would indeed be necessary, but how much and how long would it take?

While investors could expect postwar deflation, this would not necessarily be the case. There were other nations, admittedly free from the constraints of the gold standard, which sought a different way out of the postwar malaise. Investors were aware that there was another way, and in the summer of 1921 they debated whether Germany, Russia, Poland, Hungary and Austria were correct in pursuing this alternative approach. In these jurisdictions, where there was no longer any legal anchor to gold, the authorities printed money with a view to stimulating economic growth and employment and preventing deflation.

This policy worked, at least initially, but as Figure 8 shows, the gold backing of currencies fell dramatically in the process. Postwar deflation was avoided in Germany, where wholesale price inflation in 1921 was 29%, a contrast to the 24% deflation in France, 26% price decline in the UK and 11% drop in the US. In Germany, not only did prices rise, the economy did not enter a recession. There was even a stock-market boom:

> ... insofar as the inflation led to real exchange rate depreciation, on balance it stimulated exports, employment, and production... Investors had an incentive to protect their savings by drawing down their bank accounts. They should have purchased claims on firms in a position to pass along the rise in prices to their customers and hence to pay dividends that kept pace with inflation... Real share prices rose until the end of 1921.[9]

---

[9] Eichengreen, *Golden Fetters: The Gold Standard and the Great Depression 1919-1939*

Figure 8

GOLD-TO-NOTE COVERAGE RATIOS		
(%)	**1914**	**1921**
US	18	93
England	135	34
France	67	15
Italy	60	10
Belgium	35	5
Germany	54	1.5
Austria	54	.01
Switzerland	52	58
Holland	53	59
Spain	53	59
Sweden	42	35
Denmark	51	46
Japan	67	112

Source: *Wall Street Journal,* 2 July 1921

From March to August of 1921, the *Frankfurter Zeitung* stock average increased 40%. Indeed, the Berlin Stock Exchange suspended trading in early September 1921 as speculation was producing volumes its members could not handle. On 9 September 1921 the *WSJ* suggested the decline in the value of the mark was producing the bull market.

> Early in July paper marks began to show such a tendency toward depreciation that the investing classes in Germany took alarm and there was a mad rush to invest their paper in industrial and other securities before currency dropped further.

While the prospect of hyperinflationary disaster was becoming increasingly evident, there were still foreign investors who were optimistic. The German government estimated in mid-1921 that as much as $1 billion worth of German bank notes and bonds might have been held by investors outside the country. This accumulation had occurred during a period when the mark's value had fallen from US8¢ to US1¢. But the pages of the *WSJ* had only the most depressing outlook for Germany and its currency, and even Germans were aware of the likely consequences of this monetary policy. When the head of the British delegation to the Brussels Conference remarked that Germany was headed for the abyss, an anonymous German banker was quoted as replying:

> 'We do not care about the advice of the British. They are only thinking of themselves. Perhaps we are headed for the abyss, but then we will drag

France down with us, and that means the bankruptcy of all Europe.'[10]

The abyss was real. The four countries printing money to escape postwar deflation instead suffered hyperinflation.

Figure 9

GERMAN WHOLESALE PRICE INDEX 1918-1923	
1918	152
1919	291
1920	1,040
1921	1,338
1922	23,927
1923	11,634,000,000,000

Source: B.R. Mitchell, *European Historical Statistics 1750-1970*

The German experience, as shown in Figure 9, was the most extreme, with monthly price inflation peaking at just over three million percent. In the other jurisdictions, events were not quite as dramatic, but the peak monthly rate of inflation reached 213% in Russia, 275% in Poland, 134% in Austria and 98% in Hungary. What had appeared a positive policy for investors in 1921, compared with the deflationary policies pursued elsewhere, led to an almost complete loss of capital.

It is important to remember that US investors attempting to assess when the US price level would stabilise had to consider Germany's inflationary policies. For some time the policy worked. Its real exchange rate declined and it took market share in numerous products. If that continued, and Russia, Poland, Austria and Hungary could follow a similar path, the economic adjustment in the US might be much larger than anyone would normally expect. Without the gold standard, calculations as to when prices and the economy would bottom were considerably more complicated.

Structure of the market in 1921

> Up in the city, I tried for a while to list the quotations on an interminable amount of stock, then I fell asleep in my swivel-chair. Just before noon the phone woke me, and I started up with sweat breaking out on my forehead.
>
> F Scott Fitzgerald, *The Great Gatsby*

The stock market in 1921

The stock market in 1921 was not the usual domain of the institutional investor. Such investors did exist, but common stocks were still regarded as

---

[10] *Wall Street Journal*, 3 October 1921

of a speculative nature and the institutional investor was much more interested in the bond market. Figure 10 shows the stock market composition on 30 July 1921 for the New York Stock Exchange.

Figure 10

STOCK MARKET COMPOSITION 30 JULY 1921	
Total number of issues	586
Number of preferred stock issues	185
Number of companies with quoted stocks	382

Source: *Wall Street Journal*, 1 August 1921. Note: Many companies had more than one issue.

While the number of companies with NYSE-listed securities was just 382, compared to more than 2,500 today, there was still a broad range of industries available to investors. The key sectors were railroads, steels and oils. The issuance of stock in 1921 provides some indication of contemporary investor interest. Railroads accounted for less than 1% of the new stock issued in the first eight months of 1921, with the balance shared equally between public utilities and the industrial sector. One new growth business was rapidly gaining importance - the auto sector. Other key growth businesses were rubber, boosted by the boom in the auto industry, and cigarettes, as consumers were shifted towards manufactured sticks and away from more traditional forms of loose tobacco.

Railroads: US railway securities had been available to investors since Mohawk & Hudson Railroad joined the NYSE in 1830. From a very early stage, the business had been plagued by excessive competition, but despite numerous bankruptcies in the 19th Century, investors had a choice of numerous railway stocks, such as: Atchison Topeka & Santa Fe, Baltimore and Ohio, Canadian Pacific, Chesapeake and Ohio, New York Central Southern Pacific and Union Pacific.

Steel: The industry was still dominated by US Steel, put together by JP Morgan through the purchase of Carnegie Steel and other operations. The working capital of US Steel was almost double that of the other 12 listed companies combined. By 1921, capacity utilisation in US steel mills had fallen to 20%.

Automobiles: Ford was producing about half the autos in the US, but it did not list until 1956. Other dominant players, such as General Motors, were available on the market, as were stocks such as Studebaker, Pierce Arrow, Willys-Overland, Republic Motors and Maxwell Motors.

Oils: The sector was dominated by elements of the former Standard Oil trust which accounted for thirteen listed companies such as Standard Oil of

California, Standard Oil of New Jersey and Standard Oil of Ohio. The much smaller independent sector had seen a wartime boom and had a particular focus on Mexico. Companies such as Associated Oil, Cosden Oil, Houston Oil, Invincible Oil, Mexican Petroleum, Pacific Oil and Sinclair Oil were speculative favourites.

Rubber: Rubber companies had been doing good business since Goodyear's invention of vulcanisation made the material more practical for clothing and other uses. However, it was the arrival of the motorcar that produced a boom for the four listed rubber companies, among them Goodrich BF and US Rubber.

Mining: There had been a boom in mining during WWI and copper mining in particular had been a major beneficiary. The postwar collapse in price took a heavy toll, with the copper price falling back to the 1911 level. By 1921, copper was back to 12¢ a pound compared to 15.5¢ a pound it had averaged in the eight years prior to the war. Not until the mid-1950s did the copper price exceed the 1916 level. By 1921, only eight of the leading US copper mines were still producing. The mining stocks listed on the NYSE included the likes of Anaconda, Homestake and Dome.

Retail: The original listed retail stocks had been mail-order companies, but chain stores and department stores had also become large enough to gain listings. The key retails stocks to choose from included Sears-Roebuck, Woolworth's, Montgomery Ward, May Department Stores.

Sugar: There had been a bull market in sugar during and after the war. However, like other commodities, the 1920-21 recession badly hurt the price of sugar. Refined sugar had reached 26¢ a pound in 1920 but by summer 1921 it was just 5.5¢ a pound. This financial disaster resulted in National City Bank becoming, through the seizure of collateral on bad loans, one of the biggest sugar producers in Cuba. Production of sugar was concentrated in Cuba, where output had doubled over the previous six years and accounted for one-third of the national economy. The listed companies were involved in both production and refining of sugar - Guantanamo Sugar, Cuba Cane Sugar, American Sugar Refining Co.

Tobacco: The tobacco business was undergoing major change since the dismantling of the American Tobacco trust and the dramatic growth of the cigarette business. Among key tobacco investments of the day were Lorillard and Liggett & Myers.

Others: Outside the main sectors was a collection of companies involved in numerous emerging businesses, from the manufacture of submarines to makers of asphalt roofing. Many of the companies are still actively traded, in sectors that have gained considerable importance - American Express, AT&T, Coca Cola, Eastman Kodak, General Electric, National Biscuit Company (Nabisco), Otis Elevators and Westinghouse.

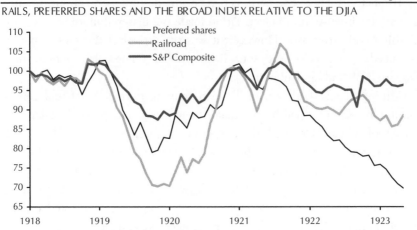

Figure 11

RAILS, PREFERRED SHARES AND THE BROAD INDEX RELATIVE TO THE DJIA

Source: NBER and www.econ.yale.edu/~shiller/data.htm

When the bear market came, investors fared best by accepting the guaranteed returns provided by the government. The nationalised railroads had completely failed to participate in the postwar boom in commodity prices and on the stock market. Investors could see little upside in investments with dividends pegged at historic levels by government fiat. Of course, when the economy took a dive in the 1920-21 recession, the stability of guaranteed dividends from the government had its benefits. As Figure 11 shows, the decline in the railroads index from the 1919 market peak to the bottom in August 1921 was only half that of the decline in the DJIA. It also shows how the broad S&P Composite Index and preferred shares performed far better than the then-20 component stocks of the DJIA.

Not all the major corporations were listed on the NYSE. The curb market, which until 28 June 1921 took place literally on the sidewalk at Broad Street, was the home of some companies that were to become global success stories in their respective industries. Literally on the street were the likes of British American Tobacco, Gillette, Philip Morris and Radio Corporation of America (RCA).

Many companies have faded somewhat from history, even if, in many cases, their operations continue. In 1921, investors keen to back the surviving Wright brother, Orville, had the opportunity to do so by buying the Wright Aeronautical Co, which the brothers had founded together. The company focused on aero-engines and despite a merger with Curtiss in 1929, was basically out of the aero business by the end of the 1950s. In 1921, the outlook for the Savage Arms Company was looking up as their lever-action rifle had been endorsed by Chief Lame Bear in 1919. Today's investors might have been interested in buying the stock of the National Acme Co; unfortunately the company produced what its chairman described as "labour-saving machinery" and not the ingenious products later in such great demand by Wile E Coyote. The name Guantanamo, linked with a sugar company in 1921, has very different associations today.

The bond market in 1921

'Young Parke's in trouble,' he said rapidly. 'They picked him up when he handed the bonds over the counter. They got a circular from New York giving 'em the numbers just five minutes before. What d'you know about that, hey? You never can tell in these hick towns.'

F Scott Fitzgerald, *The Great Gatsby*

A key factor producing the 1919-21 bear market in equities was the intensification of the long bear market in bonds. By 1921, investors in bonds had been subject to a prolonged bear market which had begun in 1899. The redemption yields on government securities during the 1899-1921 period do not provide an accurate reflection of returns to investors. Federal debt was in short supply in 1900-16, as the ratio of Federal debt outstanding to GDP averaged just 4.2%. As well as limited supply, demand was artificially raised by legislation permitting national banks to issue banknotes secured by government bonds - in 1913, 80% of the $965 million government debt was security for bank notes.

The artificial constraining of yields and restriction of liquidity on Federal debt forced investors to look at more liquid and higher-yielding debt securities. The prime investment medium for investors in 1899-1916 was thus the corporate bond. This market was almost 20-times larger than the entire US government bond market. The chart below shows the rise in average redemption yield of these instruments for 1900-21.

Figure 12

ANNUAL AVERAGE YIELD OF US PRIME CORPORATE BONDS

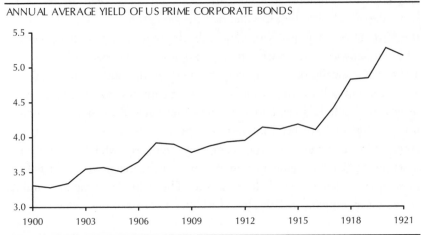

Source: Sidney Homer and Richard Sylla, *A History of Interest Rates*

Figure 12 reveals the slow-burning bear market in corporate bonds from 1899 to 1916 and the dramatic jump in yields from 1917-20. The Federal Reserve System kept interest rates low in 1914-18, but this did not prevent a significant decline in bond prices after the US entered WWI in 1917. The 23.6% price decline of prime corporate bonds from Jan 1917 to May 1920 made up more than half of the total decline for 1899-1920. This three-year period was the worst bear market in bonds since the start of the Civil War.

The US bond market changed dramatically with US entry into the war. In the aftermath, federal debt dominated the public debt markets. US Federal debt rose from 2.7% of GDP in 1916 to 32.9% in 1921. Relative to GDP, this was the largest level of debt in the country's history, edging out the 31.0% level reached in 1866, which was the financial legacy of the Civil War. The Federal debt had gone from being an illiquid, structurally over-priced instrument in 1916, to the most liquid and most widely-held instrument in 1918. By 1920 the federal debt had ballooned to $24.3 billion now surpassing in size the $18.0 billion corporate bond market. It is estimated there were 18 million subscribers to the four Liberty Bond issues of 1917-18 which is impressive when one considers that the population of the United States was just over 100 million at the time.

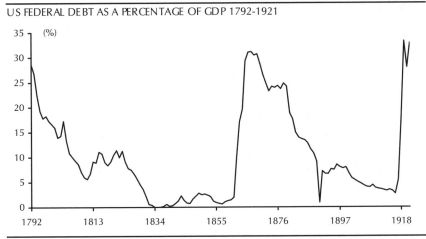

Source: US Bureau of the Census

Growth in the debt market through the issuance of Liberty Bonds and Victory Loans brought millions of new investors into the financial markets. Liberty Bond issues accounted for 71% of Federal debt outstanding in 1921 and the postwar Victory Loans took up a further 16% of the total. While the first Liberty Bond was issued to yield 3.5%, financing became more difficult and the fourth was issued to yield 4.25%. Peace did not bring any respite for bond investors as inflation accelerated in the short postwar economic boom. In the 1920-21 bear market in bonds, almost 80% of the original holders of Liberty Bonds sold out.

Average daily turnover for bonds on the NYSE in the summer of 1921 was about $10 million, compared with $36 million for stocks. Investor focus switched between Federal and other issues, but Federal debt always accounted for more than half, and sometimes as much as two-thirds of turnover. As the smallest Liberty Bond and Victory Loan issues were for $3.8 billion each, it was rare for trading in any corporate bond to exceed the volume of any one of these government issues. Other active bonds included Burlington, United Kingdom, Cuba Cane Sugar, Pennsylvania Rail Road, French Republic and Western Union.

Apart from Federal debt, the other bonds traded on the New York Stock Exchange were defined as "miscellaneous" and subdivided into three sectors - industrials, rails, and government and city (the only non-foreign issuer in the government and city sector was New York City).

Figure 14

MISCELLANEOUS BONDS 31 AUGUST 1921

	Number of issues
Government and city	41
Industrial	63
Rails	144

Source: *Wall Street Journal*

Of course, there were many bonds which were not listed on the NYSE and were traded off-market by various dealers. Already by 1920 much of the corporate bond business was shifting away from the NYSE. As Figure 15 shows, the bond market in total in 1920 had over 6,000 issues more than ten times the number of stocks traded on the NYSE.

Figure 15

US CORPORATE BONDS OUTSTANDING DECEMBER 1920

	Number of issues	$m
Railroads	1,700	9,631
Public Utilities	3,795	6,074
Industrials	868	2,380

Source: Braddock Hickman, *Statistical Measures of Corporate Bond Financing Since 1900*

The increasing number of foreign sovereign issues listed in New York was a clear sign of how the US had, particularly during the war, come to rival the UK as a global financial centre. In August 1921, the bonds of Argentina, Belgium, Brazil, Canada, Chile, Cuba, Denmark, Dominica, France, Japan, Mexico, Norway, Sweden, Switzerland, the UK and Uruguay traded on the NYSE. The transitional nature of global financial supremacy is evident in the fact that, although Japan, City of Tokyo, City of Zurich and Argentina had NYSE-listed bonds, they were denominated in sterling. However, the largest single issue and the largest combined issuer of foreign bonds was the UK itself. Liquidation of its US investments had not been in itself sufficient to finance the war, and, by 1921, the face value of its sovereign bonds listed on the NYSE had risen to $450 million. The junk sovereign issue of the day was Mexico. The price, in the low 30s, reflected that Mexico had been in default since 1914. In 1921 Imperial Russian Government bonds, unlikely to be redeemed unless there was a restoration of the monarchy in Russia, were trading at around 20 on the curb market.

At the bottom with the bear - Summer 1921

> But there was Jordan beside me, who, unlike Daisy, was too wise ever to carry well-forgotten dreams from age to age.
>
> F Scott Fitzgerald, *The Great Gatsby*

In major bear markets, equities are reduced to low valuations. However, as we shall see, this movement to extreme under-valuation is only partly due to this final down-draft in prices. A key element of the move to undervaluation is also a prolonged period of time, prior to the bear market itself, when the advance in stock prices has failed to keep pace with economic and earnings growth. As we shall see, the improvement in stock valuations, even prior to the bear market, has been a feature of all the bear market bottoms in the US with the exception of the 1929-32 episode. The DJIA's progress from its inception to its low on 24 August 1921 tells much of the story of how the discrepancy in stock prices and earnings had reduced valuations even prior to the eruption of the bear market (see Figure 16).

Figure 16

DOW, JONES AND CO INDUSTRIAL AVERAGE (1896-1921)

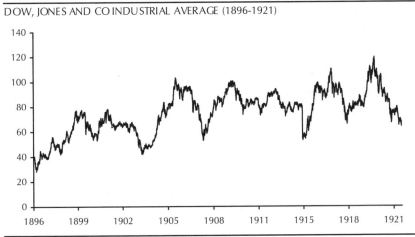

Source: Dow Jones & Co.

On 24 August 1921, the DJIA closed at 63.9, a level first reached on 27 January 1899. Essentially, the industrials index had gone nowhere in two decades. But this sideways movement in stocks contrasted sharply with the US economy. Figure 17 tells of amazing growth. Nominal GDP increased by 383%, real GDP by 88%. Much related to expanding population, yet real

37

GDP per capita increased 33% in the period. Listed companies, however, were in the best sectors to benefit. Figure 17 shows steel production rising more than four-fold and railroad track in operation increasing 148%. A number of listed companies participated in the exponential growth of the automobile business. Listed companies represented other growth industries, such as cigarettes, electricity and telephones.

			Figure 17
CHANGES IN THE US FROM 1899 TO END 1920			
	1899	**1920**	**+/- %**
Population (m)	75	106	+41
Economically active population (m)	29	42	+45
School enrolment (m)	16	23	+44
Average hourly earnings (manufacturing)	21¢	66¢	+214
Average earnings in all industries ($)	480	1,489	+210
Labour union membership	611,000	5,048,000	+726
Wholesale price index	52.2	154.4	+196
Cost of living index	66.1	203.7	+208
Retail price index	12.5	40.5	+224
Life expectancy in years	48	56	+17
Nominal GDP ($bn)	17.97	86.76	+383
Real GDP (billions of 2000 dollars)	322.1	606.6	+88
Number of farms	4,565	6,448	+41
Value of total mineral production (m)	798	6,084	+662
Physical volume of mineral production index	19.6	50.8	+159
Crude petroleum production (bbls m)	57	443	+677
Iron ore production (m long tons)	24	68	+183
Occupied dwelling units (m)	16	24	+50
Total residential mortgage debt ($bn)	3	9	+200
Book value capital in manufacturing (bn)	9	40	+344
Total steel ingots & castings (m long tons)	10	42	+320
Locomotives produced	2,475	3,672	+48
Value of output of autos ($m)	4	1,628	
Value of output of const. materials ($m)	1,006	4,777	+375
Railroad track operated (miles)	258,784	406,580	+57
Railroad employees (000s)	929	2,076	+123
Auto sales	4,192	1.9m	
Auto registrations	8,000	9.2m	
Number of telephones (000s)	1,005	13,329	
Exports ($m)	1,321	8,664	+563
Index of quantity of exports	70.8	141.8	+100
Net international investment ($m)	(2,797)	3,700	
Real gross private domestic product (index)	43.6	78.3	+80
Patents issued	23,278	37,060	+37
Total bank deposits ($m)	8,472	41,838	+394
Number of commercial banks	11,835	30,291	+161
Total currency in circulation ($m)	1,904	5,467	+187
Federal expenditure ($m)	605	6,403	+958
Public debt of Federal government ($m)	1,436	24,299	
Military personnel on active duty	100,166	343,302	+242

Source: US Bureau of the Census, and Balke and Gordon. Adjusted with addition of international factor income from Department of Commerce. Note: Blanks denote very large percentage increases.

The narrowness of the DJIA cannot be blamed for misrepresenting the actual returns from stocks over the period. This book focuses, as did investors at the time, on the DJIA as a measure of general stock market performance. But with hindsight we can compare the performance of this narrow index with a much broader index published by Alfred Cowles in 1938. Cowles was a private investor who was so disgruntled by the investment advice he received from so-called experts that he spent a significant portion of his life proving their incompetence. One element of this quest was the creation of a broader index to measure stock price performance. This broad index was based on:

> ... what would have happened to an investor's funds if he had bought at the beginning of 1871 all stocks quoted on the New York Stock Exchange, allocating his purchases among the individual issues in proportion to their total monetary value, and each month up to 1938 had by the same criterion redistributed his holdings among all quoted stocks.[11]

This broader index too shows little progress in the price of equities in the period 1899-1920, and even puts the broad market in August 1921 at a similar level to that of June 1881.

Cowles' index has been maintained and as the **Standard & Poor's Composite Index** (S&P 500) has become an increasingly important measure of US stock price performance. As this index has detailed earnings and dividend data back to 1871 it is often referred to in this book when issues relating to earnings and valuations are discussed. However in discussing market movements the focus is on the DJIA which obviously dominated investor perceptions and press headlines prior to the creation of the S&P Composite Index and continued to do so even up to the bear market of 1982.

In general, one might account for this discrepancy between the expansion of the economy and the stagnation of stock prices from 1881-1921 as an indication that corporate earnings growth had disappointed. Cowles' 1938 study shows earnings per share for the whole market declined 34% in the 40 years from 1881 until 1921, though earnings that year were very depressed. Figure 18 provides some of the low and high points for

---

[11] Alfred Cowles & Associates, *1938 Common Stock Indexes*

earnings per share.

Figure 18

S&P COMPOSITE INDEX (1871=100) - PEAKS AND TROUGHS FROM INCEPTION	
1880 - Peak 19th Century earnings	123
1894 - Trough 19th Century earnings	40
1916 - Peak pre-1929 20th Century earnings	383
1921 - Trough 20th Century earnings	73

Source: Robert Shiller, *Market Volatility*

So what constitutes the normal level of earnings to be utilised in computing earnings growth over the period? If we use 1916 earnings, then the markets' earnings growth over the 40 years was 250%. If we use 1921 earnings, then there was a contraction in earnings of 34%. Taking 1921 earnings as normal, the PE in January 1921 was 24.5x, but if 1916 earnings were considered normal, then the PE was 4.6x. Economic growth in 1916 was an exceptional 16.1% in real terms and investors were clearly sceptical that this was a representative year to judge profitability. With the benefit of hindsight investors had every reason to doubt as, apart from 1929, this level of earnings was not to be surpassed until 1947. If one utilises hindsight to declare that normalised earnings in 1921 were around the average of 1922-26, when the economy had recovered, then the January 1921 PE was 7x.

Listed sector earnings had still only increased 130% from 1881. In the same period, nominal GDP in the US grew 732% and real GDP 435%. So, while accepting the possibility of misrepresenting normalised earnings in this volatile period, it is still clear the earnings of listed companies had significantly lagged the general growth in the economy from 1881-1921.

A simple way of showing this lag is to compare an index of nominal GDP and the S&P Composite Index earnings from a similar start date in 1871. Figure 19 shows the growth differential between the economy and the reported earnings of listed companies. In this remarkable period of growth for the US economy shareholders clearly failed to benefit to the extent one would have expected. The failure of corporate earnings growth to keep pace with growth in the economy is one key reason why equities had disappointed investors even prior to the bear market of 1919-21.

Another reason for the apparent stagnation in share prices was the decline in valuations over the period. Using the 1922-26 average as normalised earnings, the market PE had declined to 7x by January 1921. The decline in the PE from very high levels is evident in Figure 20.

Figure 19

S&P COMPOSITE INDEX EARNINGS (1871=100) AS A RATIO OF US NOMINAL GDP

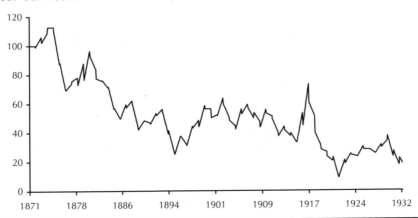

Source: www.econ.yale.edu/~shiller/data.htm. Balke and Gordon, *The Estimation of Pre-war GNP: Methodology and New Evidence*. NBER Working Papers 2674

Figure 20

PE OF S&P COMPOSITE INDEX (CYCLICALLY ADJUSTED EARNINGS) 1881-1921

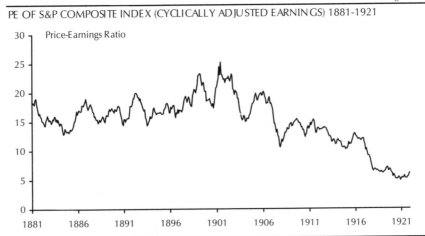

Source: www.econ.yale.edu/~shiller/data.htm

Even despite the depressed level of 1921 earnings, which suggested a PE of 25.2x in December 1921, there was ample evidence that stocks were cheap. The most dramatic demonstration of the discrepancy between corporate performance and share price performance is provided by the growth in cumulative retained earnings. From 1915 to 1920 the average retained earnings per share of the listed industrial sector was $48, which was the same as the average price of an industrial share in 1921. The situation was described in the *WSJ* on 19 September by an anonymous banker:

> ... the capitalisation of scores of concerns today is selling below working capital. In the case of many companies the shares are selling for less than the value of the plants. There are shares of copper mines that are selling below what it would cost to equip these respective mines... The shares of a large number of industrial corporations are selling at one-third their respective intrinsic values.

Investors chose to ignore such earnings power. The rise in the government debt from $1.1 billion in 1915 to $24 billion probably played a role in squeezing out the funds available for the purchase of stocks and distracting investors.

Figure 21

S&P COMPOSITE STOCK PRICE INDEX FROM INCEPTION TO AUGUST 1921

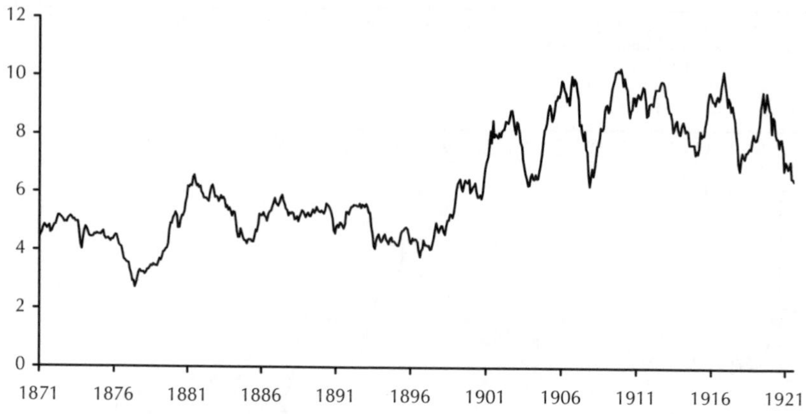

Source: www.econ.yale.edu/~shiller/data.htm

With the S&P Composite unchanged from 1881 to 1921 (Figure 22), investors secured no capital return over the period. Of course investors did receive dividends.

While reinvested dividends did exceed returns from investing in prime commercial paper, the difference over the 40-year period was small; a stock investor obtained only a marginally higher return than an investor in the highest quality fixed-interest securities. This stagnation in share prices occurred as the reported earnings growth of the listed sector significantly lagged the growth of the economy, and as the valuation placed on earnings almost halved. Payments of dividends failed to adequately compensate investors for these poor capital returns.

42

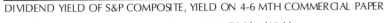

Figure 22

DIVIDEND YIELD OF S&P COMPOSITE, YIELD ON 4-6 MTH COMMERCIAL PAPER

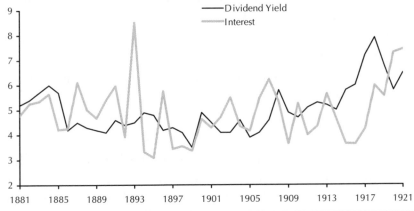

Source: Robert Shiller, *Market Volatility*

By 1921, the q ratio suggested equities were very cheap. As the replacement value of assets is only available from year-end, all annual q ratios are measured as of December in any given year. The peak reading for the q ratio in the first quarter of the 20th Century was 1.12x in December 1905, which was also when the market peaked. At year-end 1921, the q ratio was just 0.35x. There had been a significant market rally from August to December 1921, which suggests the q ratio in August was less that 0.3x and may have been as low as 0.28x. Equities were trading at more than a 70% discount to the replacement value of their assets.

Figure 23

DOW JONES INDUSTRIAL AVERAGE – 1919-21

Source: Dow Jones & Co.

Equities had become cheap by August 1921, but it was a situation that had been developing for a long time - arguably for 40 years, and at least since the bear market of 1907.

Good news and the bear

It was the hour of a profound human change, and excitement was generating in the air.

F Scott Fitzgerald, *The Great Gatsby*

There are many assertions trotted out by investors during bear markets - never catch a falling knife, nobody rings a bell at the bottom of the market, etc. However, perhaps the most common advice is that one should buy stocks when all the news is bad; and that the best indicator of this deluge is the press of the day. But an investor acting on this advice and not buying equities at the bottom on 24 August 1921, or anytime in 1921, would have missed the bull market of the "Roaring Twenties".

The *Wall Street Journal* in the summer of 1921 was teeming with news and well-informed opinion that the economic contraction and with it the bear market in stocks was ending. Not just the editorials expressed such opinions, but businessmen and even politicians were accurately predicting the end of the postwar adjustment. This general optimism, reflected in the following notes from the *WSJ* two months either side of the DJIA bottom on 24 August 1921, refutes the old market adage that investors should keep their powder dry until there is no good news at all.

25 June: Steel makers are taking a more cheerful view of the situation. They realise that consumers will eventually have to buy steel products and that an improvement in operation is not far off.

27 June: Federal Reserve Bulletin, final edition, declares that without waiting for improvement in the export and general foreign trade situation, domestic business has begun to show a turn for the better in several lines.

27 June: 'The wonderful improvement being made in condition of Federal Reserve banks undoubtedly forecasts cheaper money, and I believe we shall soon have 5% rates on commercial paper.' [Comments by Controller of the Currency, DR Crissinger.]

27 June: 'We have hit the bottom and when prices begin to rise slightly people will jump at opportunities to buy. When industries through the Federal Reserve banks can obtain sufficient funds at reasonable interest rates to expand, foreign trade and foreign loans will automatically be taken care of by business men themselves' [Harry F Sinclair (founder of Sinclair Consolidated Oil Corp.).]

30 June: 'Belated liquidation in such commodities as mineral oil, sugar, paper, and the like is allowed to outweigh in importance the accumulated evidences of stabilisation at lower levels of such things as copper, cotton, wool, silk, hides and grain.'

1 July: 'With productive prospects favourable and prices in some lines apparently reaching a condition of greater stability the outlook for the Autumn trade appears reasonably encouraging.' [Federal Reserve Board Business Review.]

1 July: Many bankers believe average commodity prices are now at or near bottom.

11 July: 'We are already entering the accumulation period between a bear and a bull market, during which time special recognition is bestowed on those companies already definitely on the upward path.' [JS Bache of JS Bache & Co.]

12 July: 'Meanwhile wise investors will continue to make profits by buying at the bottom of the long swings and selling at the top. We are now at, or very close to, the bottom of one of those long swings and investors who buy long-term bonds or investment stocks now should have a handsome profit in the next few years.'

14 July: Business has turned the corner of depression. This is the view expressed by Secretary Hoover in his Boston speech. Other men, prominent in business or political life, have recently expressed the same opinion. Among the fundamental conditions of recovery, the wage readjustments now going on are of great importance... Decreased purchasing power of the farmers had

much to do with the stagnation in industry. Prices cannot run all at once to a relative level but the gaps are being closed up and a bushel of wheat has a greater exchange value than at the first of the year.

15 July: Many leading commission houses are telling their customers that the dullness will probably continue into September. But the stock market discounts a change for the better or worse at least six months ahead and if, as many believe, business can be expected to pick up by November or December it is more than likely that Wall Street will begin to discount it very soon.

18 July: There is some improvement throughout the country in motor sales. Ford, Studebaker and Dodge are running nearly full while a number of other manufacturers who have been operating on moderate schedules report noticeable improvement in sales during the past ten days which is making increased operations necessary.

27 July: When the crops are on their way to the market and when certain important financing is completed, then perhaps the public will begin to recognize that improvement has begun, and that depression is ending and with that recognition will come a better feeling which of itself will stimulate industry and business.

1 August: Altogether trade sentiment was more optimistic and it is now generally believed that the bottom of the depression has been reached although really good business is not expected for some time to come. Two encouraging factors in the past week were the United States Steel Corporation's quarterly earnings statement which was about $10,000,000 better than had been expected generally, and the statement from the Bethlehem Steel Corporation that the six months' dividends on the common stocks had been fully earned.

1 August: Judge Gary does not qualify an opinion which he first voiced some time ago, for he says that some time in the future probably not distant there is to come 'the biggest business this country has ever witnessed.' [Judge Gary, chairman of US Steel]

1 August: 'Consumers demand as reflected in the volumes of retail trade (with due allowance for price declines), continues as good as or better than at this time last year. The improved condition noted during the past month or two as affecting textiles, boots and shoes, and other lines of business producing immediately consumable commodities, have been maintained. Probably the most hopeful feature in the outlook is, however, the continuing prospect of excellent food crop returns.' [Federal Reserve Board review of general conditions for July.]

1 August: The list of commodities that for so long a time resisted deflation is becoming less and less. With the gradual passing away of the period of price uncertainty a great obstacle to the making of forward commitments is being removed. Stocks are being run down and crucial to this is the increased purchasing power of the farming communities.'

1 August: 'Assurance is now doubly sure that we have reached the bottom of the business depression. One can feel it, so to speak under foot. The last month has brought a very marked change not only in security markets but in the whole outlook for American industry and business. Seemingly against the tide, bank clearings and railroad traffic have been increasing and there have been signs of firmer prices in many staple commodities.' [Blodget & Co letter to clients.]

2 August: National Bank of the Republic of Chicago states that it is possible to see evidence of the beginning of improvement. Price uncertainty has been the most potent cause of the drying up of forward business and now constitutes the principal deterrent to reduce industrial operations. Yet there's evidence that the downward swing of prices is nearing its end and commodities are reaching a level on which forward commitments may be undertaken safely... The long deadlock in the trade of farming communities is nearing an end. The early and heavy marketing of wheat has brought about a decided change in sentiment. A stimulation of rural trade must have a beneficial effect on industry in all parts of the country.

3 August: Throughout the country factory owners are putting in repairs which leads mechanical goods officials to believe that a resumption of industry is expected in the near future.

3 August: Steel prices are nearing bottom. The moderate improvement in orders over the last week or two may be the forerunner of a gradual improvement toward normal.

3 August: The revival in the leather business is nothing short of remarkable. Instead of operating 20% and 30% of capacity as they did only six months ago, some of the plants of the American Hide and Leather Co. are now running double shifts.

5 August: Many brokerage houses are advising the purchase of stocks on the theory that the tendency will be upward for the remainder of the year.

9 August: 'For the benefit of those who are inclined to indulge in gloom I want to say that we have entered the cycles of recovery. One of the best symptoms of recovery is the easier rates for money.' [Benjamin Strong Governor of the Federal Reserve Bank of New York.]

24 August: DJIA bottoms.

25 August: Business conditions reflect more clearly than a month ago the improvement then under way, though it was then, as now, somewhat obscured by the usual mid-Summer dullness. The increased availability of credit and the marked declines which have taken place in money rates in the last six months are among the surest evidences that the betterment is founded on improved fundamental conditions.

29 August: Resumption of operations by some of the high-grade paper mills on a broad scale, from various sections of the country.

1 September: Evidence is accumulating that a more optimistic feeling is developing in most sections. Many bankers in the rural districts express astonishment at the pessimism that prevails in Wall Street. It is likely that the situation will become still better when the effects of the harvest have been fully felt, over the territory under discussion. There is a better feeling. Most people have made their landing and realize where they are.

13 September: Better times are ahead based on these facts - Recent development in cotton which has released large sums of money. Increased railway tonnage. Government readiness and ability to help business. Aid to the cotton and livestock industries greatly accelerated their recovery, and helped the whole agricultural business. Depletion of stocks in almost all lines of business.

22 September: The greatest prosperity ever is just around the corner, Secretary of Labor Davis declared. `it will not be a return to normal, but a sweep beyond that to the highest pitch of good times,' Davis said. `I can see the greatest era of prosperity the United States has ever known near at hand. We are on the verge of it.'

23 September: 'All history shows that periods of prosperity and depression come in cycles, the rotation being about as follows; (1) Prosperity, (2) liquidation, (3) stagnation and (4) revival. At the present time the process of liquidation is well advanced... When the period of revival does definitely set in, to be followed by a new era of prosperity, let us remember that the greater the wave of prosperity and the more unrestrained the expansion and the speculation accompanying it, the sharper will be the depression that will follow. If, however, the lessons of the past two years are remembered, the next period of prosperity will be of longer duration, than any we have had before and the subsequent reaction will be far less severe.' [WPG Harding Governor of the Federal Reserve Board at the 'Made-in Carolinas' Exposition at Charlotte NC.]

2 October: The Federal Reserve board's review of business and financial conditions throughout the twelve Federal Reserve Districts, is the most hopeful in more than a year.

2 October: 'The trough of the business depression has, very clearly, been passed. The volume of manufacture halted its abrupt decline in February; prices of important commodities such as copper, tin, lead, rubber and cotton, have recovered after a long period of weakness, and of late unemployment in general has slightly decreased. These facts do not mean that business is not depressed, but rather that we are rising out of the trough and beginning an upward swing... If conditions in Europe were more nearly normal, and there were no possibility of a railroad strike in the United States, we could confidently count upon the continued improvement.' [Harvard University Committee on Economics Research.]

5 October: It is well to say that there is nothing in our domestic situation nor in the international situation that can sustain a pessimistic outlook, or a despondent view that the world has sunk into permanent depression. Gradual influences preventing the restoration of stable conditions are disappearing as prices move toward stability on an equitable basis... The full purchasing power that is necessary pre-requisite of normal prosperity is being recovered steadily as social and political conditions abroad improve. [John S Drum of the American Banker's Association address at the 47th Annual Convention.]

5 October: Idle cars are regarded as an infallible barometer of business, and the trend over the last few weeks has certainly reflected an improvement in commerce and industry. There are plenty of cars and locomotives at the moment to handle the business of the country which is on a 50% basis. A jump to 75% of normal would call for every car to handle freight consigned to the railroads. Normal business conditions would mean a car famine.

5 October: Captain Robert Dollar arrived Thursday aboard his own line the Robert Dollar from Shanghai after a six-month trip through the Orient. 'From observations I am firmly convinced that that bottom of business depression has been reached throughout the world and business conditions are gradually becoming better.'

21 October: Today there is a definite turning of the tide in the business and industrial activities of the country. This upward swing of the business pendulum is clearly defined to those who can read the economic signs of the times. [Personal message of Vice President Coolidge read to the Boston Chamber of Commerce.]

Waiting for an absence of good news before buying stocks would not have been wise. Of course, 1921 was not the bottom of any normal bear market. Stocks had reached a degree of undervaluation that would only be witnessed three times in the 20th Century. If 1921 was extreme, it still suggests that in periods of extreme undervaluation, which are the periods when every investor would like to enter the market, one should not be looking for the absence of good news to trigger investment.

Indeed, the 1921 example suggests the reverse is true; that, in periods

of undervaluation, investors may well ignore signs of an economic recovery with positive implications for corporate earnings and continue to sell. Indeed, in 1921, the improvement in the economy coincided with the improvement in the equity market. The National Bureau of Economic Research (NBER) reference date for the bottom of the economic contraction is July 1921 and the DJIA bottomed in August.

The bottom of this bear market was memorable for the failure of investors to react to good news. One can only admire the prescience of Judge Gary, chairman of US Steel, and James Davis, Secretary of Labor, who accurately forecast a rise to new levels of prosperity. Unfortunately, the prophetic words of William Harding of the Federal Reserve Board were subsequently forgotten.

> [If] the lessons of the past two years are remembered, the next period of prosperity will be of longer duration than any we have had before, and the subsequent reaction will be far less severe.[12]

Price stability & the bear

> A phrase began to beat in my ears with a sort of heady excitement: 'There are only the pursued, the pursuing, the busy, and the tired.'
>
> F Scott Fitzgerald, *The Great Gatsby*

In the summer of 1921 bullish forecasts by the *WSJ*, businessmen and government officials proved accurate. So what was the secret of success for those who proclaimed the bottom of the business cycle and the end of the bear market in stocks. One recurring piece of evidence cited by these commentators augured well for the end of the business contraction - the increasing stability of prices. Some of their more bullish declarations were:

> 'The accumulated evidences of stabilisation at lower levels of such things as copper, cotton, wool, silk, hides and grain.'

> 'Prices in some lines apparently reaching a condition of greater stability.'

> 'Prices cannot run all at once to a relative level but the gaps are being closed up.'

> 'There have been signs of firmer prices in many staple commodities.'

> 'The downward swing of prices is nearing its end and that one by one commodities are reaching a level on which forward commitments may be

---

[12] *Wall Street Journal*, 23 September 1921

undertaken with safety.'

'With the gradual passing away of the period of price uncertainty a great obstacle to the making of forward commitments is being removed.'

'Prices of important commodities such as copper, tin, lead, rubber and cotton, have recovered after a long period of weakness.'

'Gradual influences preventing the restoration of stable conditions are disappearing as prices move toward stability on an equitable basis.'

Adjustment in price levels is a prerequisite for any investor allocating capital in a jurisdiction operating a gold standard. During the contraction phase of the business cycle, the gold standard mechanism operated to reduce domestic prices until an improvement in competitiveness produced an improvement in the external accounts, a flow of gold back into the US and finally an easing of liquidity. Investors who could see evidence that prices were stabilising believed the mechanism had worked to reduce prices to such a level that easing liquidity and economic improvement would follow. As we have already seen assessing the correct price level was complicated in 1921 by numerous factors. While many could theorise on what level of deflation would be necessary, price stabilisation provided practical evidence that the adjustment process was over and economic recovery could begin. For these reasons, evidence of price stability was seized upon as signifying the end of the 1919-21 bear market in stocks.

When one considers the large range of opinions expressed by numerous commentators in the summer of 1921, the most accurate forecasts of the end of the bear market came from those who focused on the change in the trend in prices.

The modern investor will be surprised not just by the magnitude of the necessary deflation, but by the fact that the financial system coped so well when compared with the impact of post-1929 deflation. While popular memory associates deflation with the 1930s, the biggest annual postwar deflation occurred in 1921. This was not just a US phenomenon. In 1921, nine of the major economies of the world suffered their worst annual deflation recorded in the 20th Century: Australia, Canada, France, The Netherlands, South Africa, Sweden, Switzerland, the United Kingdom and the United States. This was largely due to a return to peace-time conditions and the prospect of a return to peace time prices. The US, Switzerland, Sweden, The Netherlands and Canada had recorded their highest level of inflation in the century during WWI. As prices continued to decline in

1921, investors wondered whether the deflation would have to take prices back to pre-war levels or whether some intermediate level would suffice. The pace of the adjustment and its magnitude were frightening.

This was very probably the sharpest decline in prices in US history. Labour was not immune - the price of unskilled labour fell from 60¢ an hour at its peak to as low as 25¢ by the summer of 1921. Figure 24 shows how difficult it must have been for the investor to guess in 1920 how large a deflation was necessitated by the operation of the gold standard. As it turned out, prices did not have to deflate to 1913 averages, although some, notably corn, cotton and hides, did just this. The increasing evidence of price stabilisation in the summer of 1921 was in itself a significant piece of evidence that the business downturn was ending. But how could stock investors be sure the stabilisation of prices around the summer of 1921 was not just a temporary hiatus before prices continued the correction to 1913 levels?

The one factor that seems to have convinced commentators that the stabilisation of prices represented the bottom was the response of demand to lower prices. In particular, the increasingly important automobile industry had seen demand improving from early summer in response to price cuts. Similar responses were evident in other industries.

Figure 24

DECLINE IN PRICES 1920-21 AND INFLATION FROM 1913 TO LOWEST LEVELS OF 1921

	% Decline from 1920 Peak	% above end 1913
Farm products	87.7	18
Food etc	72.2	52
Cloths and clothing	69.1	79
Fuel and lighting	55.4	82
Metals and metal products	78.9	20
Building materials	59.3	98
Chemicals and drugs	50.0	61
House furnishing goods	52.0	130
Miscellaneous	68.0	47
All commodities	69.8	52
Finished steel	78.4	37
Steel mill common labour	67.3	50

Source: US Bureau of Labor

The *WSJ* reported on 9 July 1921 that when phonograph companies, facing a "buyers strike", reduced prices by a third there was a considerable stimulation of sales in high-priced models.

The moral seems to be that the public has the power and the will to buy when it can get a bargain.

Evidence of increased demand was lifting confidence that future prices would be stable or rising. As the *WSJ* commented on 1 August, 'with the gradual passing away of the period of price uncertainty a great obstacle to making forward commitments is being removed'. In the same edition, there was evidence from the real world to confirm the theory. The *WSJ* reported that 'operators and middlemen' in the coal business were refusing to accept current spot prices for September delivery as they believed prices might rise. A further indicator was the improvement in supply dynamics.

> Advance in the price of iron, first noted last week in the Chicago district, then spreading to Buffalo and since to practically all parts of the country. It follows logically from the fact that producers have for some time been selling iron considerably below cost, a process which can not be continued indefinitely, and from the fact that stocks of iron have at last reduced to where it is impossible to make immediate shipment on many of the grades desired.[13]

As more and more commodity prices stabilised and firmed, investors grew more confident the list would grow.[14]

In such fashion, confidence in price stability spread and the bottom of the business cycle arrived. Even those investors who had seen the deflation coming had not necessarily been able to protect themselves. One broker expecting a postwar deflation bought $15,000 of diamonds in 1918. However, by 1921 even the pawnshops would only lend him 10% of the purchase price and he was forced to sell for $6,000. Even the girls' best friend had failed as a store of value in a deflationary period. With such shifts in value, it was not surprising a return to price stability was greeted with such excitement in the summer of 1921.

Liquidity and the bear

> I bought a dozen volumes on banking and credit and investment securities, and they stood on my shelf in red and gold like new money from the mint, promising to unfold the shining secrets that only Midas and Morgan and Maecenas knew.

> F Scott Fitzgerald, *The Great Gatsby*

The war had produced a major shift in wealth between the leading nations of the world. By 1921, the US held one third of the world's monetary gold

---

[13] *Wall Street Journal*, 18 August 1921
[14] *Wall Street Journal*, 11 October 1921

supply. This gold, along with Federal Reserve money, were the dominant components of high-powered money. With such a war chest flowing in, it seemed only a matter of time before a very significant increase in the money stock and credit would follow. Some pundits believed that forecasting this turn in the money/credit cycle would be the key to predicting better economic conditions and a better stock market. While the forecasts of an economic recovery in the *WSJ* in the summer of 1921 focused primarily on the importance of price stability, there was also frequent mention of the prospect of easier money:

> 'The wonderful improvement being made in condition of Federal Reserve banks undoubtedly forecasts cheaper money.' [DR Crissinger, Comptroller of the Currency.]

> 'When industries through the Federal Reserve banks can obtain sufficient funds at reasonable interest rates to expand, foreign trade and foreign loans will automatically be taken care of by business men themselves.' [Harry Sinclair, Controller of Sinclair Oil.]

> 'One of the best symptoms of recovery is the easier rates for money.' [Benjamin Strong, Governor the Federal Reserve Bank of New York.]

> The increased availability of credit and the marked declines which have taken place in money rates in the last six months are among the surest evidences that the betterment is founded on improved fundamental conditions.

Clearly contemporary commentators thought it was important to focus on the monetary situation but how easy was it to see the turning point that would result in a turnaround in the business cycle and the equity market? In theory, a monetary expansion results in price stabilisation, but in practice leads and lags created problems for investors. There was certainly a marked discrepancy between the behaviour of the price indices and outstanding bank credit in 1920-21. The NBER dates the peak of the economic expansion as January 1920. It appears selected price declines were the first warning signs for investors rather than any decline in credit associated with the rising discount rate in November/December 1919.

> The prices of certain articles, notably in the textile industry, began to decline as early as February and March of 1920, and the general price level as reflected in the Department of Labor index did not begin to fall until three months later. The volume of credit, however, remained high throughout the summer of 1920 and did not reach its maximum the country over until October, some five months later than the general maximum for

prices. Up to the present, when the Department of Labor price index is 46% below maximum and this bank's basic commodity index is 58% below maximum, the loans of national banks throughout the country are less than 14% below maximum.[15]

Commercial-bank loan books had increased 18% year-on-year in the second half of 1919, and the year-on-year increase was still 8% in the first half of 1920. The rapid rise in the discount rate - from 4% in November 1919 to 7% in June 1920, a level not surpassed until 1973 - took some time to affect the banks. The credit contraction was clearly not of the same magnitude as the general price deflation. Did this mean further credit contraction and deflation would follow, or that the link between credit and the general price level was not as direct as believed? Whatever the relationship between credit and the general price level, it was not a direct relationship that could be easily interpreted.

Monetary policy is formulated and implemented by the Board of Governors of the Federal Reserve System (prior to 1935 the Members of the Federal Reserve Board) and the Federal Open Markets Committee (prior to 1935 the Open Market Investment Committee for the Federal Reserve System). By controlling the cost and availability of bank reserves the Federal Reserve System impacts the supply of money, interest rates and credit availability. In impacting these monetary factors, the Fed hopes to steer the economy to produce a combination of high economic growth and low inflation. Having determined its monetary target, in 2005 a level for the Fed funds interest rate, changes in the bank reserves are the mechanism through which the target is met. Investors regularly assess changes in the Fed's balance sheet for the impact on bank reserves and, thus, monetary policy in general. Under the gold standard, the gold-exchange standard and the Bretton Woods agreements of July 1944, there were varying degrees of restraint placed on the Fed by the need to keep the dollar stable on the international exchanges. Since the 1970s, the Federal Reserve has been subject to no such fetters. Over the years investors have sought to assess whether monetary policy was loose, leading to potentially higher growth, but also higher inflation, or tight, leading to potentially lower growth and lower inflation.

A key determinant in assessing how much further such a contraction

---

[15] New York Federal Reserve Bank report, August 1921

would have to progress was the Fed's willingness to reverse the contraction in the elastic money begun in the middle of 1920. The *WSJ* explains how the study of the Federal Reserve System balance sheet in general, and the reserve ratio in particular, was the key in assessing the credit cycle:

> The Reserve ratio itself is the most important indicator.... The Federal Reserve law requires Federal Reserve banks to carry a gold reserve of 40% against Federal Reserve notes in actual circulation and 35% cash against net deposits. When the combined ratio declined to about 40% it was clear that expansion of credits could only be continued by huge imports of gold.... They [bankers] began to contract loans. This caused a lower level of prices. Lower prices influence the flow of gold to this country, which improved the reserve ratio. As prices declined and the volume of business contracted there was a smaller demand for Federal Reserve notes, which permitted a rapid retirement of those notes, and, resulted in a further improvement in the combined ratio. The ratio having improved slightly over 30 points from the record low, there is, of course, an enormous volume of unused cash in banks.[16]

The *WSJ* goes on to explain how this excess cash usually first seeks higher interest rates in bonds and how lower bond yields lead to an improvement in the stock market. It sounds straightforward, but just how easy was it for investors to predict each stage of this cycle, considering the *WSJ*'s view that the 'reserve ratio itself is the most important indicator'?

The first sign of preparedness to ease occurred with a reduction in the discount rate in May 1921, when the reserve ratio had risen to 56.4%, the highest level since August 1918. This cut in official interest rates occurred just three months before the equity market bottomed. The DJIA declined 20% in the intervening period.

It is unclear how any investor would have been able to foresee a contraction of such magnitude in the elastic currency before the Fed considered providing rediscount facilities at lower rates of interest. Federal Reserve Board meetings at the time were assessing the appropriate degree of deflation for the economy when determining policy. In particular, discussions make it clear that the Fed postponed any reduction in interest rates until there had been a reduction in wage rates, which the governors deemed necessary. This clearly suggests that the Federal Reserve Board was not steering monetary policy with regard to the degree of stretch in the elastic currency, but rather in relation to what adjustments it thought

---

[16] *Wall Street Journal*, 12 December 1921

necessary in the price level. In that environment, investors looking at the Fed's balance sheet for signs of easier monetary policy were misdirected. The Fed was not setting its course by the compass of its own balance sheet but was actively judging the appropriate monetary conditions necessary for the economy. The elastic currency invented to prevent financial collapse, had been used in 1917-19 to finance the government and now was being used to manage the economy. This element of subjectivity in Fed decisions made it very dangerous to assess future monetary conditions purely on the current condition of the Fed's balance sheet.

Those commentators who cited improvements in the condition of the Federal Reserve System as an indication that things would improve were, to some extent, right, but it would have been almost impossible to judge the level of improvement needed to trigger recovery in the economy and the stock market. There was a similar problem if the focus was on market rates of interest. There had been an improvement in market interest rates long before the stock market reached its low on 25 August 1921. In June 1920, the call-money rate ranged from 10% to 14%, and according to the Comptroller of the Currency at the time, some rates as high as 30% had been reported. Market rates of interest had declined significantly from 1920 to 1921 without halting the bear market in equities (see Figure 25).

Figure 25

KEY INTEREST RATES ON 31 AUGUST 1920 AND 31 AUGUST 1921			
	Call money (%)	Time money (%)	Commercial paper (%)	Bankers' acceptances (%)
1920	10	9	8.25	6 3/8
1921	5	6	6	5 1/8

Source: Federal Reserve, *Banking and Monetary Statistics*

There had been a steady decline in market rates since June 1921 and the *WSJ* was reporting 'a liberal supply' of call money at 5.0% in August 1921. By 28 July, call rates were at lows not seen since November 1919, and still the stock market declined. It is probably axiomatic to say that, at some level, these reductions would produce an economic recovery, but there is little in the economic record to indicate how investors would have estimated the stimulatory level. Based on this analysis it was those investors who focused on alterations in the general price level who were better able to gauge the turning point for the economy and the market. While the first signs of price stability did coincide with recovery the contraction of the Fed's balance sheet continued for years after the recovery had begun and market interest rates had been declining long before the stock market bottomed.

There is more to liquidity analysis than just analysing changes in the Fed's balance sheet. Though such changes have a direct impact on high-powered money, it is only a small part of the total money supply in any economy. The growth in broader measures of money can differ significantly from trends in high-powered money in the short term. If "liquidity analysis" focuses on this wider variable, do we find any better indications of the bottom of the bear market? There is a major discrepancy between the signals from M2 growth, depending upon whether one is looking at a nominal or inflation-adjusted series. The nominal series shows no improvement until the middle of 1922, well after the bottom of the bear market in equities. However, a marked improvement in the inflation adjusted series is evident in April-May of 1921 when a further 20+% decline in the DJIA was still to occur. Thus there may have been some useful indications from the growth of inflation-adjusted M2 in the period, but, as with following the first decline in the discount rate, it signalled a buy in May before the final down-leg in the DJIA.

If Fed balance-sheet changes have been difficult to read and broad measures of money misleading, what about credit growth as an indicator of better times for the economy and the stock market? Commercial-bank lending continued to expand long after the decline in economic activity had begun. It was also many months after the economy and stock market had bottomed before total loans began to expand. Monthly data is not available, but the annual data shows a decrease in total loans of 5.5% from June 1921 to June 1922. Over that period, the economy was expanding at almost 7% in real terms, and the DJIA rose almost 36%. Watching credit-growth numbers would not have been useful in trying to find the bottom of this particular bear market.

While an analysis of the monetary situation seems to throw little light on the ability of investors to predict the bottom of the equity market, it does raise an interesting structural issue. How did the US financial system weather this deflationary storm, when a similar storm from 1929-33 wiped out banks holding one-tenth of total US deposits? (We discuss this issue in detail in Part II.) The public accepted that the commercial banking system could take the strain in 1920-21 and increased their deposits; but such faith was lacking in 1929-33. Looking at the balance sheet of Chase National, the fourth-largest bank in the US, on 30 June 1920, it is not difficult to see why the public had such faith.

ANATOMY OF THE BEAR

Figure 26

CHASE NATIONAL BANK'S BALANCE SHEET ON 30 JUNE 1920	
	Percentage of total assets
Cash, exchanges and due from Federal Reserve	24
Demand loans	12
Bills discounted	24
Time loans	20
US Bonds and certificates of indebtedness	5
Bonds and stocks	7
Others	8
Total assets	100

Source: *Wall Street Journal*

The US commercial banking system was in a highly liquid position going into the 1919-21 deflation. Long accustomed to deflationary periods necessitated by the gold standard, it had built balance sheets to cope. This high degree of liquidity, and perhaps the creation of the Federal Reserve System itself, convinced the public the banking system was safe. In 1921, they were right.

The bulls and the bear

> There is no confusion like the confusion of a simple mind, and as we drove away Tom was feeling the hot whips of panic.

> F Scott Fitzgerald, *The Great Gatsby*

The analysis so far suggests savvy investors in 1921 were correctly forecasting a turnaround in the equity market by focusing on mounting evidence of price stability. Such a focus seems intellectually sound, given the operation of the gold standard, and it worked. Another approach with intellectual appeal was to monitor the balance sheet of the Federal Reserve System. Even with the benefit of hindsight, such an approach seems to have been highly subjective and less reliable than a focus on price stability.

Of course, not every market operator looks at things in the same way and such detached analysis is not always possible when one is in the grip of the bear on a daily basis. To get a better idea of life in the investment trenches we now focus on investor comment and reaction in the two months before and after the market bottom on 24 August 1921. In following the day-by-day progress of the bear market from 25 June 1921 to its nadir on 24 August and through the two months following, one sees how those wrestling the bear assessed the situation.

58

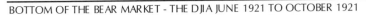

Figure 27

BOTTOM OF THE BEAR MARKET - THE DJIA JUNE 1921 TO OCTOBER 1921

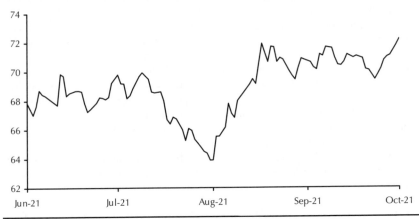

Source: Dow Jones & Co.

Notes from the pages of the *Wall Street Journal* indicate the factors contemporary opinion believed to be important in calling the bottom of the market in the summer of 1921:

25 June: The consensus is that the market is now acting as though it wanted to go up. Easy money has brought about considerable shifting from the bear to the bull-market side.

28 June: (Those) who acknowledge there has been no sign of business improvement as yet do not favour selling stocks short around current levels. They say it is unreasonable to compare stocks now purely on their earnings figures of 1921. It is the balance sheet that is even more important in times like these.

29 June: The bearish fraternity were bolder. These traders have made substantial profits during the long and painful period of liquidation and they have reached the stage where they refuse to regard any development as constructive... There is no disputing that confidence in the business future is growing stronger daily. Pessimism is slowly giving way to optimism, a development the stock market will reflect in due time. The market gives every indication that the urgent liquidation is over. It is a narrow market both ways, but on every drive by the bears support seems to be in evidence.

6 July: Dullest day of the year. The general list held up well despite the pressure on Mexican Petroleum. There is still a big short interest in the market.

7 July: Failure of the general list to go down on Tuesday during the violent break in Mexican Petroleum served as a warning to the bear crowd. It proved conclusively that the list was so oversold that the short interest was serving as a cushion to any general decline... a general covering movement set in and before the day was over the largest recovery of any single day this year was recorded.

13 July: The rank and file of the traders are still bearish and despite the run-up in prices last week there has been no appreciable diminishing of the short interest.

13 July: 'Stocks more recently do not appear to be in plentiful supply for lending purposes and, in other words, the technical situation would indicate that some constructive developments might easily be reflected in higher quotations for the better class of shares.' [Hornblower & Weeks letter to clients.]

13 July: It has been noticeable for some time that when the general list sells off, copper stocks hold firm.

13 July: Broker holdings of US Steel had been as high as 58% at December 1916 but investors took more stock and brokers held just 23% at end June 1921.

15 July: Traders on the floor are still finding it difficult to make any money. In fact it was said yesterday morning many of the floor men are not coming into town at all and will not until the market shows some signs of real activity.

18 July: Dullest market in three years... Very few of the usually active traders appeared in the financial district. We are in a typical summer market, with no incentive to do anything. It is acknowledged that the big money has already been made on the short side of the market, and as yet there is nothing in business conditions to make traders go long of stocks... There is absolutely no public participation in the market.

19 July: Most brokerage houses are advising their customers to keep out of the market until it becomes more active.

20 July: Industrial preferred stocks are being offered at prices some of which are bargains. Even the best, well-seasoned issues with a long dividend record are offered at prices to yield 7% to 10%, while money may be had around 6%... The omission of the last quarterly preferred dividends by five important companies may have been a contributory cause to the yielding of higher grade issues in sympathy.

21 July: The market became extremely dull on the decline, which the bulls considered a favourable sign.

22 July: Trading smallest in any five-hour session so far in 1921. Lowering of rediscount rate did not stimulate any interest. There is a big short interest in the steel stocks and some of the big operators are more inclined to cover short stocks on bad news than to put out new short lines. Premiums have been removed from the speculative stocks in the loan crowd and some stocks are loaning flat.

28 July: Lowest call rate since November 1919. 'It is a professional market of controlled fluctuation... The obvious seldom happens in a professional market at the time when expected.' [Hornblower & Weeks letter to clients.]

29 July: People in a position to know characterized the break in the equipment group as entirely due to a bear raid by the same interests that have staged other affairs of the sort during the last few months.

1 August: American Telephone $90 million stock offering was very successful. This follows a big loan for Burlington and the French government.

1 August: Brokerages bare of customers.

2 August: Motors failed to respond to the wonderful news from Studebaker. (Business for the second quarter was greater by 50% than the previous record quarter)

2 August: Bear Drives at Fruit (United Fruit Co.) uncover little real stock, for it is no secret that interests conversant with the company's outlook have been buying the shares on all dips.

3 August: Brokers loans lowest in about eight years. In the past two years these loans have contracted $1.25m to $500,000. The peak was reached on July 31st 1919. At the peak of the 1919 market the daily call market volume was around $45m but today it is around $15m to $10m.

5 August: Rise in railroad stocks has been going forward for nearly six weeks with slight intervening setbacks. Whereas in previous spurts in the rails the lower-priced shares were favourites, it has been notable that the features of the present advance were high-priced and investment railroad shares.

5 August: There are only 900,000 shares of Steel common held by Wall Street, compared with over 2,500,000 shares held a few years ago.

9 August: There is no body of small investors who provide market support in the darkest hour. If brokers depended on that kind of business the Exchange might properly close or convert itself into a moving picture theatre.

10 August: 'It is a fact however that my company has more potential buyers on hand today both in investment and speculative accounts than at anytime since 1914. I have clients who are straining at the leash to buy stocks, and I am holding them by main force.' [Quote from anonymous broker.]

11 August: There was no let-up in the selling for speculative account. They were helped by the passing of the American Sugar dividend which drove this stock to a new low for the year.

18 August: Premiums on a number of issues demonstrated that there had been little perceptible reduction in the extent of the short interest.

19 August: Over the past two days certain issues that have been under pressure have had a comeback, regarded by many as an attempt on the part of the shorts to cover their commitments. As an example, Pierce Arrow common is selling out of line with the preferred, but not withstanding this, the common has held around its present price for the last several weeks.

20 August: Absorption of stocks and bonds for investment is reaching larger proportions than one would imagine. There is very little buying for a quick turn. Majority of the buyers say they are picking up stocks for a pull of a year or two realizing they are cheap. These stocks are being paid for. This is a period of investment accumulation.

23 August: Liquidation in a number of stocks seems to be over. Proof of this is found in the fact that transactions are few and far between. This is particularly true of the copper issues.

24 August: DJIA bottoms.

25 August: 'So far as the averages are concerned they are far from encouraging to the bull, but they do not yet jointly indicate a definite resumption of the main bear movement.' [William Peter Hamilton's Dow Theory Analysis.]

25 August: International Paper common selling at $39.50 several months after the issuance of an annual report showing $53 a share available for common, is a stock market development without precedent... American International has sold down to 25 3/8 and the liquidating value of the securities it holds are $50.

27 August: Urgent short covering by bear operators frightened by the technically strong position of the market as well as some substantial buying orders, caused a vigorous rally in virtually all stocks which continued well into the afternoon.

28 August: Bears Trapped... The market had reached that stage where a technical rally was certain. The list of stocks commanding a premium in the loan crowd was the longest since the present bear market started two years ago... The rally that started before the end of the first hour was the best in the last three months... The bear rumors which have permeated Wall Street for the past month and which culminated Thursday in the false report about the deferring of dividend by the Mexican Petroleum Co. have aroused the constructive element in the Street; and it is reported that large financial interests have combined to force the prominent shorts to cover their lines and also to give warning that the campaign of untruth has been carried beyond unbearable limits.

29 August: Bear Attack Fails... Many companies have more cash than at any time in their history.

30 August: Houses bullish on GE tell their friends that the insiders intend giving the shorts a real lesson, and that the stock will be put much higher.

31 August: Shorts Driven In... The dropping of the rate of call money to 4.5%, the lowest rate in nearly a month, caused a considerable uneasiness in the ranks of the bear crowd.

1 September: There was a continuation of the upturn in stocks still containing a large short interest. The total of six stocks commanding a premium compares with fifteen stocks loaning at a premium last Thursday, just before the present upturn in prices got under way.

2 September: With the short interest eliminated there is now no one to buy stocks.

3 September: Demonstration Against Shorts... Additional encouragement is given by Wall Street's change of attitude toward the news of the day. Instead of stressing bearish factors - a state of mind which grew chronic during summer months - traders are tending to look on the brighter side.

7 September: 'It is time the American business man realised that the downward trend in business has been reached and the industries in the country, in general, have seen the end of the readjustment period. During the period of inflation, large numbers of businessmen found it necessary to expand their business in order to take care of the tremendous quantity of work coming their way, with the result that when the period of deflation had started, they found themselves with large quantities of high priced raw materials and finished products on hand which became practically unsaleable at anything like their cost. About that time great cry went out from the American public against the excessive prices of everything and the inevitable happened- a "buyer's" strike occurred. In order that this large accumulation of stock in hand might be disposed of, it was continually offered at low prices- from time to time, and gradually at the different levels, these goods have been liquidated. At the present time, instead of having large accumulated lines of goods on hand, there is actually a shortage in many channels...

... In order to partly bring about this state of liquidation, the producers of many materials voluntarily cut down their output mills were closed completely or running on very short time. But during this period the excessive amount of production was gradually being used up and once the American public realizes that prosperity is again ahead of them and that the Administration has been doing things along a constructive line and will continue to do so, there will be a scramble by every one to purchase what they need at the present prevailing low prices. Once that buying starts- with production at sub-normal levels, it is bound to turn the whole tide and prices will advance again- and, advancing prices always bring prosperity throughout the country.' [Jesse Livermore.]

7 **September:** The number of stocks reduced to loaning at a premium is two.

10 **September:** It might be said that a bear panic existed before the end of the day. The last of the Waldorf crowd, which had been persistently bearish on the market, was driven in.

12 **September:** During the current week thousands of shares of the better class of industrial and railroad stocks have been absorbed by large interests who are convinced that, with the inevitable reactions, the tendency of business as well as security markets, will be upward... The advance this week is undoubtedly due to an improvement in general business conditions...The bear crowd has been given one of the worst beatings in the history of Wall Street... Many brokerage houses who advised profit taking are now convinced by the action of the market that the rise is anything but a flurry engineered by professional operators.

14 **September:** 'As to the security market, the capitalizations of many concerns are today selling below net current assets over current liabilities. The shares of many corporations are selling at one-third of their respective book values. Security prices like these are too attractive to exist for any great length of time. Already we hear that the textile, shoe and many other industries are rapidly getting back to normal.' [William Boyce Thompson, mining entrepreneur and former director of the Federal Reserve Bank of New York.]

14 **September:** Outside of a handful of stocks, however there was little interest shown in the market and it was evident that the recent rise had not encouraged public participation.

16 **September:** Already the floating supply has been reduced and it may well be that in six months' time we shall be saying that there are not enough stocks to go around. Great price movements always overrun themselves and this is true of bull and bear markets alike. When tested

industrial properties show a book value far in excess of their common stock at the market price, ignoring their earning capacity altogether, we may at least say that the superior safety of tax-exempt municipal bonds has blinded the investor to equities which may well make the taxes seem small.

22 September: Most of them [rumours] concern a well known stock market operator and a prominent industrial leader. These two men are understood to have been largely responsible for the advance that started a month ago and lasted for nearly three weeks. Now it is said that there has been a falling out between the two and their friends are making all sorts of charges of double-crossing, selling out of the pool, and other charges of like character. From the action of the market it certainly appears that something has gone wrong on the inside because it is the pool stocks that are having the severest reactions. [This is a reference to Jessie Livermore]

23 September: A number of houses argue stocks are a sale because the public refuses to come into the market. It is traditional that an upward movement in stocks is not started by the public. The market for the last two years has reacted sharply after each rise, and selling stocks on bulges has become a habit. The recent rise did not have the same characteristics as previous advances. The strength of securities over the first half of the month followed the conviction of the largest bankers and financiers that the bottom of the depression had been reached. They have been the largest buyers of stocks. Professional operations have been in evidence in certain issues, but the real reason for the upward trend has been good buying for a long pull.... The

real source of stock market support is coming from the large banks and important financial interests. They turned bullish on the market more than two weeks ago and have been buyers of the good stocks. The sellers consist of houses that sold out and are now working a lower level.

26 September: 'We feel the principal thing to bear in mind is that the greatest necessity in the early stages of a bull market is patience because there is no question in anyone's mind, apparently, as to where prices will be selling a year from now but as usual the market of today keeps would-be purchasers in constant doubt and they will not buy stocks when they are dull and unattractive, but only when they are active and made to look very attractive for selling purposes.' [Hornblower & Weeks letter to clients.]

4 October: It cannot be too often said that the stock market reflects absolutely all everybody knows about the business of the country. When the market is taken by surprise there is panic and history records how seldom it is taken by surprise. [Editor of the *WSJ*, William Peter Hamilton.]

4 October: It is an easy matter to put a stock up on a short interest, but difficult to hold it after the short interest has been eliminated.

4 October: Many recriminations have been hurled at Jesse Livermore for the halting of the recent advance in the market due primarily to the inability of the general public to look upon a professional trader as anything but a pirate and a destroyer of values. Rather than halt the advance Livermore did all he could to keep it going. He and George J. Whelan, the tobacco magnate, were the prime movers in the manipulation. The pubic was totally absent and refused to come in. [During the upswing, the two men had fallen out regarding which stock should be used to lead the advance].

5 October: Market manipulators want the public when they are ready to distribute stock and do not want the public in upon their ground floor plans. Therefore when publication is made respecting financial plans, the whole matter is often held up indefinitely or set aside to be brought forward on an entirely new basis. The operators who had put the market up retired and the question is still unsettled as to whether as a market leader Mexican Petroleum, tobacco stocks, or railroad shares should have the right of way. But all the leaders agree the stock market has been liquidated out and that there is only one way for it to go and that is up. But how immediately, or in what time, nobody can agree.

5 October: Two bear factors which cannot be ignored are the bankruptcy of Germany and America's railroads.

7 October: The market has been permitted to take its own course for the past two weeks and speculative

authorities declare it has acted well. Developments have indicated that it will be no difficult matter to move it higher... Broker loans have increased very little.

10 October: According to the Pujo Committee only 14% of all trading is done by the so-called public. Will the other 86% wait upon the public's pleasure? The truth of the matter is that the 'public' whose presence seems so essential to the success of market ventures is very active in the bond market and its purchasing is putting Liberty bonds to new highs daily.

12 October: As copper, steel, petroleum and other prices tend upward and money rates downward ... the next move will be up. It is evident from the character of transactions that there is no actual liquidation... also that the big professionals are doing nothing on the short side.

24 October: Bearish operators, who had steadfastly refused to believe that the price movement was capable of a sustained rise, were badly punished in the upward drive and their hasty attempt to extricate themselves from a disastrous position gave further impetus to the advance.

For those in the trenches from June to August 1921, the watch phrase was clearly 'know your enemy'. One of the reasons cited for becoming more positive on the stock market is that the bears have 'reached that stage where they refuse to regard any development as constructive', even in a period when there was ample good news emerging. **The emergence of buying interest on every "drive" by the bears provided further evidence their day in the sun was ending.** In particular, on 19 August, just prior to the market bottom, it was noted that some common issues were selling out of line with preferred counterparts. This was taken as a sign that some shorts were being forced to cover their short positions in the common, creating the misalignment. The general emphasis on bad news was noted as a positive sign just two days before the market bottomed:

> Bear tips are now quite the thing, and any one who even intimates that a stock may go up is looked on with suspicion. Such a condition usually marks the end of a bear market.[17]

Just a few days later, an anonymous banker pointed out not just the proliferation of pessimism but the abundance of lies:

> 'I listen to a hundred confidences a day and recently the exaggerations I have heard from men in all walks of life are appalling. I have even kept still when men whispered reports on things of which they knew nothing, obviously wicked reports which were entirely incorrect. Bad news may travel fast but fake news has the wings of Mercury, that I know, and out of a possible 100 reports of disaster and tribulation I listen to weekly, perhaps one has an iota of truth in it and that one is never as black as it seems.'[18]

Not all companies accepted the proliferation of "fake news" lying down. Edward L Doheny of Mexican Petroleum succeeded in having newsletter writer WC Moore indicted on charges of criminal libel on the basis of a comment in one of his investment newsletters.

As we have already seen a flow of good news had been developing for some time and had previously been ignored. In due course, a turn in the market was apparent when investor focus switched from the bad news flow to the good news flow. Apart from these subjective criteria, it is clear from the extracts above that, investors also looked closely at lending activity. **When the supply of stocks for lending was decreasing and thus the cost of borrowing stocks rising, this was evidence the shorts were running out of ammunition.** It may have been coincidence, but the very bottom of the market occurred when the number of stocks being lent at a premium peaked. It was believed, rightly, that this was an indication the activity of the shorts was peaking and their activities to depress stocks were likely to wane from such high levels.

In 1921, long before institutional investors came to dominate the stock market, another part of knowing your enemy was to assess the general ownership of stocks. History had shown that, in significant bull markets, the concentration of ownership of stocks shifted to Wall Street. The bellwether stock at the time for assessing such shifts was US Steel, which had been the

---

[17] *Wall Street Journal*, 19 August 1921
[18] *Wall Street Journal*, 27 August 1921

largest listed company since its creation in 1901. Brokers' holdings of US Steel reached 58% by the peak of the stock market boom of 1916 and by the end of June 1921 had fallen to 23%. The general public had taken up the slack and investors watched the total number of shareholders of US Steel as another indication of when the bear market in stocks would end. The reasoning was that main-street investors would seek the haven of US Steel in times of difficulty. When the number holding US Steel reached historically high levels, it was taken to represent an expression of extreme conservatism among the public.

Peaks in the number of holders of US Steel had always previously coincided with nadirs of public participation in the market. This defensive position was only likely to reduce from such high levels, resulting in a greater commitment to the stock market in general. In the course of the 1919-21 bear market, AT&T came to be just as important as US Steel as a bellwether - and the number of holders of its stock actually exceeded US Steel.

The high number of shareholders in US Steel and AT&T in the summer of 1921 was once again a good indicator that the equity market was reaching its lows. Of course the public's conservative investment stance would only be slowly reversed. While some investors did watch odd-lot activity for a signal of a turnaround in the market, it was not widely expected the general public would lead the buying at the bottom of the market. The key buyers looked for at the bottom were the "big constructive interests". These were the men of wealth whom one would normally associate with significant ownership of stocks and who had been largely absent from the market for some years. Their public pronouncements suggest they were driven by considerations of value, but an easing of the wartime surtax - taxing stock market gains - was also a consideration. In 1921, it was these buyers who began to put a floor under certain stocks and squeeze the bears, sending the market sharply higher.

The bulls of 1921 focused on the value in shares and key technical factors which suggested that market prices would recover. There was little discussion on the immediate earnings outlook. While the market bottomed in August 1921 reported earnings had a further 37% to decline before they reached bottom in December 1921. An earnings recovery significantly lagged the recovery in the stock market.

As well as a focus on the activities of key players, investors in 1921 watched general behaviour in the market. Their bullishness was not just because volumes were low, but that a significant proportion of all the activity on the market was made up by shorting activity. When the shorts were dominant, and many brokers did not bother to come to their offices, this was a sign positive interest in the market was likely to increase. A decline in broker loans to historically low levels also indicated interest in the market had probably reached its low. **A market declining on particularly low volume was thought to be particularly bullish. This opinion is in conflict with a modern adage which states that bear markets will end with an act of capitulation involving a final slump in the market on heavy volume. As Figure 28 shows this is not the case and the final decline of the market in 1921 was attended by low rather than high volume. Presumably this low volume reflects a disinterest in stocks which augurs well for stock prices in the future where interest and accumulation increase. A rise in volumes after the first rebound in the DJIA suggests that the price rise may be sustainable.**

Figure 28

DJIA AND TWO-WEEK MOVING AVERAGE NYSE STOCK VOLUMES

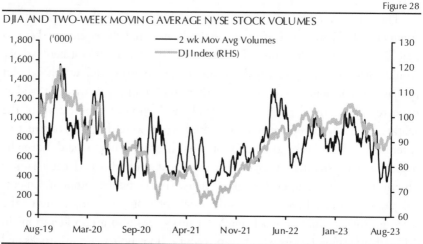

Source: NYSE and Dow Jones & Co.

It is worth dealing specifically with the comments of Jesse Livermore and William Peter Hamilton in the summer of 1921. Livermore had been recognised for many years as one of the most successful operators in the markets. By 1900 he was already banned from the "bucket shops" of New York and Boston for being too successful. In 1907, he made more than $3 million in one day shorting during the stock market crash. Livermore switched from the bears to the bulls almost exactly at the bottom of the 1921 bear market. His bullish comments to the *WSJ* reported on 7

September 1921 forecasting that 'the whole tide of prices will advance again and advancing prices always bring prosperity throughout the country' were part of an operation to talk-up the market. In justifying why the bear market in stocks was over, Livermore focused on the very low level of inventory in the system and the impact this was likely to have in producing price stability. In his opinion, this low level of inventory would prevent further price declines, spur buying activity and advance prices.

From Hamilton's editorials in the *Wall Street Journal* in the summer of 1921, it is clear his reading of the two averages (the DJIA and the Dow Jones & Co. Railroad index) that he accurately called the bottom of the 1921 bear market utilising the Dow Theory.

The **Dow Theory** has been elaborated at great length over the years after being first expounded in a piecemeal fashion by Charles H. Dow in his 'Review and Outlook' editorial, which began in the *WSJ* in April 1899.

Dow never formalised his theory. The first attempt to do so was by S.A. Nelson, who published 'Dow's Theory' in his 1903 publication *The ABC of Stock Speculation*. William Peter Hamilton had joined the *WSJ* in 1899 and had worked with Dow before Dow's death aged 51 in 1902. As editorial-page editor for the *WSJ* Hamilton often wrote about Dow's theory and its implications for the current stock market situation and he had plenty to say in the summer of 1921. In 1922 Hamilton gave his own explanation of Charles Dow's theory in the *Stock Market Barometer*.

Dow's theory is fundamentally simple. He showed that there are, simultaneously, three movements in progress in the stock market. The major is the primary movement... It will be shown that thus primary movement tends to run over a period of at least a year and is generally much longer. Coincident with it, or in the course of it, is Dow's secondary movement, represented by sharp rallies in a primary bear market and sharp reactions in a primary bull market... Concurrently with the primary and secondary movement of the market, and constant throughout, there obviously was, as Dow pointed out, the underlying fluctuation from day to day... Dow's theory in practice develops many implications. 'One of the best tested of them is that the two averages corroborate each other, and that there is never a primary movement, rarely a secondary movement, where they do not agree', Hamilton said.[19]

---

[19] William Peter Hamilton, *The Stock Market Barometer*

Bonds and the bear

A prolonged bear market in bonds had been underway since 1899 and escalated during the period of postwar inflation. Strictly speaking, the US corporate bond and Federal debt markets had bottomed in May 1920. The Dow Jones index of 40 corporation bonds posted its lowest reading of 57.29 in that month before commencing a rise. By the following June, the index had given up most of its gains to bottom at 57.75. Although still 0.8% above the May 1920 low, the June 1921 bottom was the beginning of a sharp rise in prices and a bull market that did not end until 1946.

Gains in the Liberty Bond market in 1920 proved more durable. As Figure 29 shows, Liberty Bond prices, unlike the prices of corporate bonds, did not retest the lows of May 1920. However, price gains in the thirteen months from May 1920 to June 1921 were roughly equal to the same gains made in the five months from June to October of 1921.

Figure 29

LIBERTY BOND PRICES

	First sales	May 1920 low	End June 1921	Price 6 Oct
3 1/2s, 1932-47	100.02	86.00	87.00	89.20
1st 4s cv 3 1/2s, 1932-47	97.30	83.00	87.20	92.20
2d 4s 2d Loan, 1927-42	100.00	81.40	86.60	91.50
1st 4 1/4s cv 3 1/2s, 1932-47	93.90	84.00	86.80	92.80
2d 4 1/4s cv 4s, 1927-42	93.94	81.10	86.72	91.94
3rd 4 1/4s 3d L'n, 1928	99.10	85.60	90.72	94.94
4th 4 1/4s 4th L'n, 1933-38	98.00	82.00	86.88	92.36

Source: *Wall Street Journal*, 7 October 1921

The bottom for the Liberty Bond market was clearly May 1920, but as with the corporate bond market, the real pickup for the 25-year bull market that followed began in the summer of 1921. While Liberty Bond prices did benefit from the deflation underway throughout 1920 and most of 1921, the corporate bond market traded sideways. In the summer of 1921, improvement in the bond market preceded that of stocks. Liberty Bond prices bottomed in the first week of June and the corporate bond index bottomed in the final week of June. The DJIA was not to bottom until 24 August.

The Dow Jones Composite Index of Corporation Bonds comprised four different sectors: highest-grade rails, second-grade rails, public utility bonds and industrial bonds. The industrial bonds were the last to bottom, which at the time was attributed to the fact that many industrial corporations omitted or cut dividends in the summer of 1921, while the dividend outlook for other sectors was more stable.

Figure 30

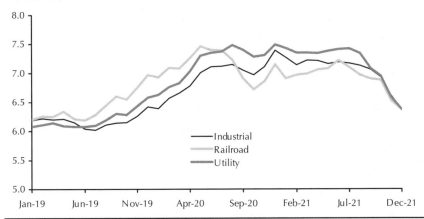

DOW, JONES & CO INDEX OF RAILWAY, UTILITY AND INDUSTRIAL BONDS

Source: Federal Reserve, *Banking and Monetary Statistics*

At this time, the outlook for bond and equity investors in the railroads was inextricably linked with politics. The key financial issue for both parties was whether the government would pay compensation for its underinvestment during the period of nationalisation, and if so, how much it would be? The early improvement in the railroad bond market was due to a combination of better-than-expected earnings results in the summer of 1921, but also progress on the political front. As Figure 31 shows, the rally in key bond issues was underway, as the decline of the stock market continued into August.

As Figure 31 shows, the bond market recovery was across-the-board, with particularly good gains to be had in high-yielding paper and among the second-grade rails and foreign-government issues. The maturity of the high-grade rail paper is significantly longer than other sectors and this reflects a willingness, which waned from 1900, for investors to accept long-dated paper in return for higher yields. (One non-callable railroad bond issued prior to this change in investment fashion had a maturity of 2862.) Liberty Bond yields for 8 August 1921 are shown in Figure 32.

The pattern for the bond market, at this stage, was for government bonds to lead the recovery, followed about three weeks later by the corporate bond market. Due to continued economic woes, the industrial sector was the last of the corporate bond sectors to see an improvement. Particularly important for the corporate bond market was evidence that deflation had run its course. Deflation had created havoc in the corporate

71

bond market as issuers were lumbered with numerous fixed costs, including bond interest payments, at a time when sales were contracting. Corporate bonds were thus particularly sensitive to any evidence deflation was ending. More so than for equities, the variable that bond investors watched when seeking to identify the bottom of the bond market was the trend in deflation.

Figure 31

KEY BONDS FROM LOWS (END JUNE 1921) TO 8 AUGUST 1921, YIELD ON 8 AUGUST

	Price rise (%)	Yield (%)
High grade rails		
Atchison gen 4s, 1995	6.1	5.45
Cent Pacific 1st 4s, 1942	5.2	6.25
C, B & Q gen 4s, 1958	6.0	5.28
NY Central 3 1/2s, 1997	8.0	5.27
Nor Pacific pr ln 34s, 1997	6.2	5.20
Penna 5s, 1968	8.3	5.77
Sou Pacific ref 4s, 1955	6.1	5.45
Union Pacific 1st 4s, 1947	5.8	5.23
Average	**6.5**	**5.49**
Lower grade rails		
Balt & Ohio conv 4 1/2s, 1933	9.6	8.60
Ches & Ohio conv 5s, 1946	6.0	6.30
Erie conv 4s D, 1953	17.6	9.80
Kansas City Sou 5s, 1950	7.8	6.75
Mo Pacific 4s, 1975	7.1	7.45
Pere Marquette 4s, 1956	6.4	6.32
St L & san Fran Inc 6s, 1960	32.2	10.30
Seaboard con 6s, 1945	12.2	13.40
Average	**12.4**	**8.62**
Foreign governments		
Belgium 7 1/2s, 1945	6.8	7.43
Chile 8s, 1941	7.6	8.10
French 8s, 1945	4.9	7.45
Italian treasury 6 1/2s, 1925	10.5	9.70
Norway 8s, 1940	7.4	7.65
Swiss 8s, 1940	4.2	7.40
Japanese 4s, 1931	25.9	8.40
Average	**9.6**	**8.02**
Public utilities		
Am Tel & Tel col Tr 5s, 1946	8.7	6.20
Bell Tel 7s, 1945	4.2	6.60
Detroit Edison 6s, 1940	2.3	7.15
Montana Power 5s, 1943	5.8	6.10
New York Tel 4 1/2s, 1939	9.8	6.12
Pacific Tel 5s, 1937	5.0	6.67
So Bell Tel 5s, 1941	2.9	6.55
Average	**5.5**	**6.48**
Industrials		
Armour 4 1/2s, 1939	6.7	6.35
Beth Steel rfg 5s, 1942	9.0	6.30
Cent Leather 5s, 1925	2.9	8.30
Gen Electric deb. 6s, 1952	3.1	7.05
US Rubber 5s, 1947	5.7	6.70
US Steel 5s, 1963	3.1	5.80
Wilson & Co 1st 6s, 1941	5.6	7.25
Average	**5.2**	**6.82**

Source: *Wall Street Journal*, 9 August 1921

Figure 32

YIELD TO MATURITY OF LIBERTY BONDS AND VICTORY NOTES (8 AUGUST 1921)		
	(%)	Date of maturity
Victory 3 3/4s	5.50	May 1923
Victory 4 3/4s	4.50	May 1923
Liberty Third 4 1/4s	5.63	September 1928
Liberty fourth 4 1/4s	5.25	October 1938
Liberty second 4s	4.94	November 1942
Liberty second converted 4 1/4s	5.21	November 1942
Liberty 3 1/2s	4.25	June 1947
Liberty second 4s	4.94	June 1947

Source: *Wall Street Journal*

As the *WSJ* regularly pointed out in the summer of 1921, many corporate bonds represented excellent investment opportunities when call money could be borrowed for as little as 4.5%. As with the equity market, there was no general despair at the bottom of this market, but a clamour of opinion backed by good news that it was the time to buy. In the summer of 1921 the lack of interest in such optimistic advice coincided with the bottom of the bear market rather than any general crescendo of pessimism.

The bullish dynamic for bonds was evident in the pages of the *Wall Street Journal*. In particular, the commercial banks were becoming increasingly large buyers of government bonds, as the demand for credit 'for expansion purposes has almost ceased' (*WSJ*, 27 June). The low cost of credit, with call money rates around 5%, made the purchase of corporate bonds particularly attractive as 'reasonably safe bonds are available at yields ranging from 8% to 17%' (*WSJ*, 30 June). There was ample advice around that investors should be taking advantage of the opportunity, and 'several banking houses which make a specialty in dealing on bonds are advising their clients to exchange holdings which mature in the next few years for long-term bonds' (*WSJ*, 23 July).

The key reason for investor nervousness on this obvious trade was the continuing negative impact of deflation on corporate balance sheets. So, as with the equity market, the stabilisation of prices reduced the risks to investors and thus encouraged more people to borrow short at around 5% and to buy bonds with considerably higher yields. Interestingly, the railroad bonds were already at six-month highs as the more speculative issues were still searching for a bottom. A key difference for railroads is that pricing in this industry was much more certain and, as late as 1920, the Interstate Commerce Commission had approved a 40% rise in freight rates and a 20% rise in passenger rates. It is noticeable that these bonds were able to see a turnaround much more quickly than those sectors reliant on market forces to produce price stabilisation. With prices stabilising and growing over-subscriptions for US and foreign government bond issues, all the indications were there that the corporate bond market was about to bottom.

US equities traded below fair value from 1917 to 1926. How was an investor to know that 1921 was the opportune moment to invest? As we have seen, there was a combination of signals in the summer of 1921 suggesting it was time to buy: improving demand at lower prices for selected goods, particularly autos; commodity price stabilisation; improving economic news being ignored by the market; rising volumes on a strong stock market; falling volumes on a weak stock market; a rising short interest; a final fall in equity prices on low volumes; reductions in Fed controlled interest rates; a rally in the government bond market; a rally in the corporate bond market; positive signals from the Dow Theory. This is the checklist of features one needs to focus on if one seeks the bottom of the bear market. The bad news was that the next bear market was very different, and more vicious in its nature. The good news was most of the signals were again flashing green at the bottom of the market.

Part II
July 1932

'Mort, the whole shooting match puzzles me,' Studs said, sipping coffee. 'I don't understand it. I guess there was a depression right after the war, but I didn't pay much attention to it.

'It wasn't anywheres near as frightful as this one.'

James T. Farrell, *Judgement Day*

The road to July 1932 leads through the most famous bull-and-bear markets in the history of American stocks. From 63.9 on 24 August 1921, the DJIA rose almost 500% to 381.2 on 3 September 1929. From there, it plunged 89% before bottoming out at 41.22 on 8 July 1932. These dramatic price adjustments alone would probably account for the fascination with this period of US history. However, as well as the sheer drama of wild price oscillation, the stock market mapped an irrevocable change in US society.

The road to July 1932

> And when his investments rose, he'd sell, bank his original capital, use the profits to play on other stocks. All these years he'd been so dumb he hadn't thought of making money this way. Other guys had cleaned up doing it, and he had been just too dumb to know it.

> James T. Farrell, *Judgement Day*

The commercial ballyhoo of the 1920s was the stage in American development when consumerism finally triumphed over almost everything that had gone before. And, as William Leach observes, Charles Cooley, pioneer founder of modern sociology, 'worried about this trend'.

> 'Pecuniary values,' he wrote in 1912, were not 'natural' or 'normal'; they were the historical outgrowth of a new economy and culture and 'by no means the work of the whole people acting homogenously'. In the past, values had taken their 'character from... the church', now they were deriving it from 'business and consumption'. Increasingly the worth of everything - even beauty, friendship, religion, the moral life - was being determined by what it could bring in the market. [20]

The words of F. Scott Fitzgerald from *The Great Gatsby* quoted in Part I of this book relate to the summer of 1922 and were so "of their time" because they perfectly illustrated the "new worth" of everything. The seal on the transformation of America was the publication of advertising man Bruce Barton's book *The Man Nobody Knows* in 1924. Barton wrote that:

> Some day ... someone will write a book about Jesus. Every businessman will read it and send it to his partners and his salesmen. For it will tell the story of the founder of modern business.

The previous values of America were transmuting with little subtlety into the consumer society. If there is one story from the newspapers of 1932 that illustrates the change in American's concept of worth over this period it is from the *Wall Street Journal* of 14 May.

> State Bank Commissioner Arthur Guy has advertised for sale at public auction June 6 a cemetery on Memorial Drive at the Maiden city line. It contains 44 graves and will be sold for the benefit of the depositors of the defunct Highland Trust Co., recently taken over by the bank commissioner. The trust company held a mortgage on the cemetery.

---

[20] William Leach, *Land of Desire: Merchants, Power and the Rise of a New American Culture*

In 1918, America honoured its war dead, in the 1920s they mortgaged them, and by the 1930s foreclosed on them. Given such a dramatic change, it is perhaps not surprising that this period of stock-market history has attracted so much attention, entwined as it is with the transformation of a country. However, undue focus on this one period has created a misleading impression of bear markets. **As we shall see through the course of this book there are key factors that make 1929-32 unlike the other three major bear markets of the 20th Century. While often cited as the classic example of a bear market, it may be more the exception than the rule and thus have misled generations of investors.**

The course of the Dow - 1921-29

Although the DJIA bottomed in August 1921 at 63.9, it was quite some time before the great bull market developed. As late as July 1924, the index was still below 100, and was below its November 1919 high as late as April 1925. By the end of 1924, earnings per share in the broad market were just above the 1919 level. One could categorise 1921-24 as a return to pre-recession profit and valuation. This return to "normalcy", a word favoured by Herbert Hoover in his run for the presidency in 1920, was very profitable for investors. By April 1925, the market had risen 87% from the August 1921 low, with an average dividend yield since 1921 of 6.4%. This was, however, just the beginning. Annual volume figures for the NYSE suggest rapidly growing interest in stocks from 1925.

Figure 33

DOW JONES INDUSTRIAL AVERAGE - 1 AUGUST 1921 TO 3 SEPTEMBER 1929

Source: Dow Jones & Co.

Even the insiders, those who bought and sold seats on the NYSE, did not begin to show anything but normal enthusiasm for the market outlook until 1925 (see Figure 35).

Figure 34

VOLUME ON THE NYSE - 1922-29

Year	Volume (Number of Shares)
1922	260,753,997
1923	237,276,927
1924	282,032,923
1925	452,211,399
1926	449,103,253
1927	576,990,875
1928	920,550,032
1929	1,124,990,980

Source: *New York Times*

Interest in the market was already growing, but the victory of Calvin Coolidge and the Republicans in the November 1924 presidential election is generally seen as the catalyst for an even greater belief in the positive outlook for US business. Although the decision of the voters was never in doubt, investors began to realise what another four years of Republican administration could mean for the stock market. Specifically, the Republicans had already proven themselves reluctant enforcers of anti-trust legislation, only the latest in a long history of inaction being the cessation of anti-trust action against the Aluminium Company of America. Andrew Mellon, Secretary of the Treasury and one of the richest men in America, had already delivered tax cuts and a significant reduction in government spending and more of the same was promised. For those in any doubt about Coolidge's intentions, he made himself crystal clear in his inaugural address on 4 March 1925:

> The collection of any taxes, which are not absolutely required, which do not beyond reasonable doubt contribute to the public welfare, is only a species of legalised larceny.

What happened after the 1924 election was singled out for special mention when the *WSJ* celebrated its 50th anniversary on 27 June 1932.

> Not for many years had Wall Street witnessed such a sensational advance in security prices as took place in the final two months of the year following the election of President Calvin Coolidge. Not only million-share days, but

two-million share days became common and the advances in prices day after day were spectacular and sensational, representing speculative as well as investment demand.

While the election provided a catalyst for the bull market in late 1924, it was not the underlying cause of the greatest upswing in the market's history. With the benefit of hindsight, one can trace many causes. However, the two key factors which are common in all major bull markets, a technological breakthrough and the increased availability of credit, were very evident in the great bull market of the 1920s.

Figure 35

PRICE OF A SEAT ON THE NYSE - 1920-27		
Year	High ($)	Low ($)
1920	115,000	85,000
1921	100,000	77,500
1922	100,000	86,000
1923	100,000	76,000
1924	101,000	76,000
1925	150,000	99,000
1926	175,000	133,000
1927	305,000	175,000
1928	595,000	290,000
1929	625,000	550,000

Source: New York Stock Exchange

The great technological breakthrough for the 1920s was rapidly increasing access to a technology first offered to the American consumer on 4 September 1882 - electricity. Growth in the use of electric power was slow, with only 8.0% of dwellings wired up by 1907. By 1921, 37.8% of US dwellings were connected. By 1929, 67.9% of homes had electricity. Against that backdrop, the percentage of factory machinery powered by electricity rose from 32% in 1919 to 49% in 1929. Sales of commercial electrical equipment in 1929 were 146% higher than in 1921. By 1929, the US produced more electric power than the rest of the world combined. The dramatic growth of this industry produced three key stimulants for a bull market in equities - a surge in productivity, a dampening effect on inflation, and a leap in demand for new electrical products.

The electrification of America boosted productivity and corporate earnings, providing one fundamental reason for the rise in stock prices during the 1920s. Real gross private domestic product per man hour increased 19% from 1921 to 1929. Each unit of capital added by business in 1929 was 23% more productive than it had been in 1921. Corporate America took an increasingly large share of the national wealth during the

79

decade. Data compiled by the Cowles Commission shows earnings per share for what was to become the S&P Composite Index rising 455% from 1921 to 1929. Granted that 1921 was a year of very depressed earnings, but even measured from the recovery year of 1923 earnings per share for the market increased 64% to 1929. The technology of electricity helped boost corporate profits. Perhaps even more importantly, the growth in productivity was a crucial element in reducing inflationary pressure. It is often thought that the exuberance of the 1920s must have been associated with rising inflation. If anything deflationary tendencies were more evident.

We have seen that 1919-21 was a period of gross deflation. More surprising, however, is that most prices in the US in 1929 were below 1921 levels.

Figure 36

PRICE INDICES - 1921 AND 1929

	1921	1929
All commodities	97.6	95.3
Food	88.4	104.9
Fuel and lighting	96.8	83.0
Metal and metal products	117.5	100.5
Building materials	97.4	95.4
Household furnishings	115.0	94.0
Textile products	94.5	90.4

Source: US Bureau of the Census.

Despite the surge in demand in the 1920s, supply was easily able to keep pace, thus dampening inflation. Much of the vast bulk of increased supply came from within the US and was driven by electrification and ensuing productivity gains. Food prices rose from the very low levels of 1921, but remained significantly below price levels of WWI. Most everything else fell in price. Another technological change, growth in the use of the motor car, played a key role in keeping food prices down. In 1900, one third of crop land of the US produced fodder for horses. This was increasingly turned over to producing food rather than feed as US horse numbers dwindled. On US farms alone there were five million fewer horses in 1929 than in 1921. To electrification, we can add the impact of mass production of the automobile on growing corporate profits, low inflation and low interest rates. That combination alone would have been sufficient for a bull market in equities, but the technological developments also produced a surge in demand.

The increasing number of households with electricity meant a bigger market for domestic electrical appliances. The dollar value of sales of electrical household appliances, even during this period of quiescent prices, increased 189% from 1921 to 1929. The most notable growth product was the radio, with sales rising almost 30-fold. Electrification increased demand for numerous items previously considered luxuries - phonographs, washing machines, sewing machines, vacuum cleaners and the 1919 invention once considered the ultimate in luxury - the electric refrigerator. New "growth" businesses sprang up, and investors only saw blue-sky potential. One thing was missing, however, and that was the hard cash needed by the American consumer to buy all these products produced by US "growth" companies.

A sudden expansion of consumer credit was a crucial feature of the 1920s bull market. Consumer credit in the US was, until then, based on instalment loans, which had been available in the US since at least 1807, though largely the province of furniture retailers. Instalment credit was popularised from the 1850s by the Singer Sewing Machine Company, and half the furniture retailers of Boston were offering instalment plans by 1899. Still, instalment credit was seen as rather working class, and this form of credit was anathema to other sectors of society. Anna Schwarz and Milton Friedman, in their *Monetary History of the United States 1867-1960*, observed that while instalment credit was available, it was "hardly known" in 1914. The key psychological change came in 1919, when General Motors Acceptance Corporation opened its doors. In order to buy a new and expensive consumer durable, the motor car, even the middle classes took instalment credit. Its social acceptability slowly increased and was extended to a range of consumer durables.

The percentage of households buying cars on instalment rose from 4.9% in 1919 to 15.2% in 1929. Writing in 1927, Wilbur Plummer showed how the instalment credit plan had been endorsed by most sections of society:

> It was found that forty per cent of the families canvassed in the poorer part of town bought on the instalment basis; twenty-five per cent of those canvassed in the middle class sections of town bought in this manner; and five per cent of the well-to-do families used the system.[21]

Instalment credit was most concentrated in the new goods made practical by increasing electrification.

Credit sales rose rapidly during the 1920s, especially in the field of consumer durables. By 1927, 15 per cent of all such goods - some $6 billion in value -

---

[21] Wilbur Plummer, *Social and Economic Consequences of Buying on the Instalment Plan* 1927

were bought through instalment contracts. Over 85 per cent of all furniture sales, 80 per cent of phonographs, 75 per cent of washing machines, and more than half the sales of radios, pianos, sewing machines, vacuum cleaners and refrigerators were made this way.[22]

When National City Bank, the largest bank in the US, entered the personal-credit business in 1928, buying consumer goods on credit received a further endorsement.

Clearly, such leverage could provide numerous benefits in any economic upturn, but it also increased the risks of greater-than-normal levels of default in the event of economic decline. The rapid development of instalment credit during the 1920s was extremely significant, as the overall monetary situation could not be described as particularly lax. The development of the instalment credit industry in the US at that time shows how, even in what seem to be periods of monetary moderation, new credit channels can appear offering credit where none previously had been available. Bull markets in consumption in key areas can be fuelled by such developments, even at a time when overall credit growth remains within normal boundaries.

Living with the Fed - A whole new ball game (II)

'All right, kid me. But I'm no sucker. I'm kicking out my twelve-fifty a share and when I collect on it, I'll be collecting fifty bucks a share. And then Pat, come round and ask me how about some real estate out on the lake,' Ike said.

James T. Farrell, *Judgement Day*

As this great technological displacement fed into the general prosperity of the US, what was the Federal Reserve doing? Could investors expect the Fed to now only utilise the elastic currency in the lender of last resort role as envisioned by the original legislation? Investors were to discover that the Fed, invigorated by its role in economic management from 1914-21, would continue to intervene to reduce the predictability of the operation of the gold standard. Fed activity had not been just an unavoidable consequence of the war and its aftermath but the birth of a new permanently active and unpredictable variable for investors. In the twenties an inflow of gold was dictating an easy monetary policy, but most members of the Federal Reserve Board believed something had to be done to curb the speculation associated with easier money. A tight monetary policy imposed by the Fed would

---

[22] Robert Sobel, *The Great Bull Market - Wall Street in the 1920s*

reduce the size of the current account deficit dictated by the gold standard alone and thus prevent gold and liquidity moving to America's trading partners. The longer this halt in the flow of gold, the more difficult it would be to accomplish reconstruction of the international gold standard. These dual objectives, to curb speculation and also to ensure adequate gold flows to trading partners, would complicate policy responses in 1927-29, when speculative activity reached ever-higher levels. Once again the Board believed there were exceptional circumstances that warranted management of the elastic currency and not the unfettered operation of the gold standard. Once again, as it had done from 1917-21, this was to significantly complicate things for investors.

There was good reason for the Fed to be concerned about permitting excessive economic growth in the postwar period. The Fed was concerned that gold would be naturally redistributed, as the gold standard was reconstructed, and it would be dangerous to permit the creation of credit structures in the US based on its permanency. This hesitancy to permit a large amount of credit to be built on the monetary gold stock is understandable when one looks at the scale of the flow of gold to the US. Since WWI, the US had been sitting on a monetary powder keg and the supply of "gunpowder" increased materially in the first half of the 1920s.

Figure 37

MONETARY GOLD HELD BY CENTRAL BANKS/TREASURIES (% OF WORLD TOTAL)

(metric tonne)	1920	1925	1930
United States	3,679.3 (32.6%)	5,998.2 (43.2%)	6,358.0 (38.7%)
France	1,622.2 (14.4%)	1,201.1 (8.7%)	3,160.0 (19.2%)
UK	863.8 (7.7%)	1,045.5 (7.5%)	1,080.0 (6.6%)
Japan	837.4 (7.4%)	866.4 (6.2%)	620.0 (3.8%)
Spain	708.6 (6.3%)	739.7 (5.3%)	709.0 (4.3%)
Argentina	699.7 (6.2%)	678.0 (4.9%)	620.0 (3.8%)
Germany	391.3 (3.4%)	432.1 (3.1%)	794.0 (4.8%)
Netherlands	385.2 (3.4%)	280.0 (2.0%)	257.0 (1.6%)
Italy	306.9 (2.7%)	498.0 (3.6%)	420.0 (2.6%)
Canada	278.3 (2.5%)	336.9 (2.4%)	165.0 (1.0%)
Balance	1,522.6 (13.5%)	1,815.6 (13.1%)	2,286.0 (13.9%)
Total	11,295.3	13,891.5	16,469.0

Source: Timothy Green, *Central Bank Gold Reserve*.

In 1921, only the United States and five other countries (Cuba, Nicaragua, Panama, Philippines and Salvador) remained on the gold standard. It was expected that, when the postwar economic adjustments had been completed, most countries would wish to return. Choosing an exchange rate for the return to the gold standard would be a political decision, and if politicians in other countries chose to deliberately undervalue their currencies, then major outflows of gold from the US could be expected. The Fed had contingency plans for a dramatic gold outflow. From 1923 to 1929, it intervened to sterilise gold inflows, acting to dampen the growth in high-powered money, the total monetary stock and therefore growth of credit and the economy. If the US had been operating without the Federal Reserve System, then money would have been considerably easier in the 1920s. However, as the decade wore on, the expected dramatic gold outflow failed to materialise, possibly due to war reparations and repayment of war debt. As Hugh Bancroft, President of the *Wall Street Journal* and husband of its owner, argued:

> The reparations and war-debt settlements set up a new and arbitrary force, not responsive to the normal operations of the law of demand and supply, which remorselessly drained $500 million a year from the rest of the world.... Finally, when more than 70% of the world's stock of monetary gold had been concentrated in the United States and France, there wasn't enough gold left in the rest of the world to sustain confidence....[23]

By the end of 1924, seven countries had returned to the gold standard and a further 11 did so in 1925, by which time the US authorities held 43.2% of world gold reserves. Fully 48 countries had returned to the gold standard by 1929. However, only after 1925 did the US share of gold reserves begin to slowly decline as some countries, notably France, chose to undervalue their currencies. While France undervalued its currency, a not surprising political decision, the British decided to return to the gold standard at a rate which clearly overvalued sterling. The net impact was that there was no dramatic drain in US reserves, and it can be argued that by sterilising the gold inflow and reducing monetary and economic growth, the Fed restrained the amount of gold that would otherwise have left the US because of balance of payments deterioration. If the Fed had not pursued a sterilisation policy, one can only surmise that the US would have undergone a boom-bust scenario much earlier in the decade - and it is unclear whether it would have been quite on the same scale as the boom-bust that did ensue. The Fed's monetary restraint was ratcheted up from 1928 onwards and the money stock at the peak of the economy in August

---

[23] *Wall Street Journal*, 1 August 1932

1929 was actually lower than it had been 16 months earlier. So the Fed's activities cannot be said to have added to the speculative frenzy of the 1920s. The figures for credit growth during the decade do not indicate too loose a monetary policy.

Figure 38

ALL BANKS' GROWTH IN TOTAL ASSETS, LOANS AND INVESTMENTS ($M)

	Total Loans		Investments		Total Assets	
1921	29,236		11,169		49,633	
1922	28,000	(-4.5%)	12,328	(+10.4%)	50,368	(+1.5%)
1923	30,734	(+9.8%)	13,474	(+9.3%)	54,144	(+7.5%)
1924	32,030	(+4.2%)	13,843	(+2.7%)	57,420	(+6.1%)
1925	34,378	(+7.3%)	15,056	(+8.8%)	62,232	(+8.4%)
1926	36,658	(+6.6%)	15,562	(+3.4%)	65,079	(+4.6%)
1927	37,949	(+3.5%)	16,649	(+6.9%)	67,893	(+4.3%)
1928	39,946	(+5.3%)	18,146	(+9.0%)	71,121	(+4.8%)
1929	41,944	(+5.0%)	17,305	(-4.6%)	72,315	(+1.7%)
Growth 1921-1929		+43.5%		+54.9%		+45.7%

Source: Federal Reserve, *Banking and Monetary Statistics*

The credit-growth figures in Figure 38 need to be viewed from the perspective of a 42% growth in nominal GDP from 1921 to 1929, against which bank credit growth does not necessarily suggest excess. It has been argued, by J.K. Galbraith among others, that the Fed should have adopted an even tighter monetary policy but this would have had dire consequences for the reconstruction of the international gold standard. Could the US economy really have remained unaffected by the economic chaos if the rest of the world has been forced again from the gold standard? Perhaps the failure to contract the elastic currency even further was driven by international considerations but they were international considerations which had very direct consequences for America. The Fed did act to constrain monetary growth and during the 1920s had considerable success. One could argue that such constraint, which restricted the flow of gold to those countries in desperate need of gold, was a key factor in creating the international crisis that was to hit America in September 1929. Clearly, this was a difficult balancing act for the Fed to get right.

There is little evidence of any general excessive easing in monetary policy during the period. As well as the sterilisation policy, the Fed, as in the commodity boom of 1919, attempted direct restraint in areas of speculative activity, and in the second half of the 20s the capital of speculative activity was Wall Street.

As early as 1925, just as the real bull market was getting underway, some members of the Fed were convinced that too much credit was being channelled towards "speculative" rather than "productive" purposes. It became clear that Wall Street in particular was increasingly attracting these so-called speculative loans. What could the Fed do about it? The method suggested by the majority of the Board to tackle this "abuse" of the system was to refuse rediscounting privileges to those member banks judged to be making excessive loans on securities. It was not entirely clear whether the Federal Reserve banks could legally do this. A split developed within the Federal Reserve Board amongst those who favoured such "direct" pressure to target speculative loans and those who believed a rise in the discount rate was the more appropriate response. Although debate continued, the need for action became more apparent by 1928 as the bull market in stocks showed no signs of abating.

Figure 39

BROKERS' LOANS BY SOURCE - 1924-29 ($M)			
	New York Banks	Outside Banks	Others	Total
Dec 31, 1924	1,150	530	550	2,230
June 30, 1925	1,150	770	740	2,660
Dec. 31,1925	1,450	1,050	1,050	3,550
June 30, 1926	1,060	780	1,090	2,930
Dec 31, 1926	1,160	830	1,300	3,290
June 30, 1927	1,130	970	1,470	3,570
Dec 31, 1927	1,550	1,050	1,830	4,430
June 30,1928	1,080	960	2,860	4,900
Dec 31, 1928	1,640	915	3,885	6,440
Oct. 4, 1929	1,095	760	6,640	8,525

Source: Federal Reserve, *Banking and Monetary Statistics*

Figure 39 shows how credit was being sucked in from across the country to finance the purchase of stocks. By the end of 1929, loans in the US banking system totalled $41.9 billion. Total loans to brokers in 1929, from all sources, were thus the equivalent of 20% of total bank loans outstanding. The Fed had drawn up a list of 100 member banks it considered to be financing speculation and should be subjected to "direct" pressure. This could perhaps have worked to reduce the amount of bank credit being directed towards Wall Street, but it was unlikely to prevent the rush of credit from other sources. The total value of all stocks and bonds listed on the NYSE rose from $27 billion at the end of 1924 to $89 billion by the end of October 1929. During that period, loans from New York banks to brokers barely increased, and loans from outside banks were lower in October 1929 than they had been in June 1925. As Figure 39 shows, the flow of credit for stock speculation was coming from non-banks. The source of the "speculative" loans rushing towards Wall Street was not the banking system, so it is not clear how "direct" pressure on member banks advocated by the Fed was going to work to reduce speculation. Indeed, there is ample anecdotal evidence that funds were flowing in from around the globe to finance the lending boom on Wall Street. Not until February 1928 did the Federal Reserve Bank of New York implement the first rise in interest rates, recognition in part that the attempt to target speculative lending had failed.

The New York Fed's discount rate rose from 3.5% in February 1928 to 6.0% by August 1929. However, as Figure 39 shows, the growth of loans to brokers accelerated during that period. The rise in the discount rate flowed into the call market and call-money rates rose from 4.24% in January 1928 to 9.23% in July 1929. There was a small panic in the stock market in March 1929 as call-money rates briefly exceeded 20%, though as rates came back down below 10% it was business as usual. Loans to brokers continued to grow and the stock market continued to rise. The apparent large rise in interest rates was too small to prevent more borrowing and speculation in an environment where excessive capital gains were assumed to be normal. By July 1929 came the first signs the rise in interest rates was affecting the economy, even if it was not interrupting the upward surge of the stock market. If the rise in interest rates worked to curb speculation, the evidence is that it did so by reducing economic activity, threatening corporate earnings growth and undermining the fundamental value of stocks. By September and October, the actions of the Fed were curbing speculation because they were curbing overall economic activity.

Investors might have originally expected the Fed would be a quiescent organisation ready to act as lender of last resort when necessary. It had been active since its inception primarily due to the national emergency of war. However, it became clear in the 1920s that it believed it had an active role in monetary policy. Fed-watching had been born, and in 1928-29 it was clear the policy of the Fed was to end the speculative frenzy in Wall Street. It took over a year, but the sledgehammer needed to crack the nut of speculative activity on Wall Street significantly damaged the economy in the process.

The course of the Dow - 1929-32

It's goddamn tough when a poor man saves a little money and thinks that he's got something put aside for his old age, and then the bank goes bust. It's goddamn rotten. And I suppose the crooked bankers who stole all the money will go free.

James T. Farrell, *Judgement Day*

So what brought the party to an end? Signs of slowing in the US economy were evident by the early summer of 1929. In June, the indices of industrial and factory production peaked, and year-on-year growth of motor vehicle production was slowing. The NBER reference date for the peak of the economic expansion is August 1929. A slowdown had been underway for sometime in other parts of the world. In Australia and the Netherlands, economic deterioration began as early as 1927, and by 1928 Germany and Brazil had slumped. Argentina, Canada and Poland followed in the first half of 1929.

Throughout the boom period of the 1920s, the US ran a current account surplus, and the failure of the country with 43% of the world's official gold reserves to run a current account deficit restricted growth opportunities in other countries returning to the gold standard. Higher US economic growth would have naturally led to an outflow of gold and easing monetary conditions overseas, but this did not occur. Further complicating the issue was that Wall Street acted as a magnet for capital, whether for direct investment in securities or lending at sometimes double-digit interest rates to investors for the purchase of securities. This capital, under more normal circumstances, may have found its way to other jurisdictions, easing liquidity conditions. The slowdown in capital outflow became particularly pronounced in 1929 when private capital outflows from the United States fell 42% from the average level of 1927-28.

Those countries seeking to maintain a commitment to the gold standard had no alternative but to pursue deflationary policies in the absence of any improvement of the current account when their access to foreign capital became restricted. The violent gyrations on Wall Street in September and October 1929 may have been partly a belated realisation that the rest of the world was being forced into deflation by trying to adhere to the gold standard. As 1929 progressed it became clearer that, if the gold standard was maintained, the US faced lower exports due to foreign deflationary policies, and if the gold standard broke then competitive devaluations threatened a similar disruption. Overseas economic deterioration may have been indicating the possibility of an economic deterioration in the US, which was becoming apparent to investors by September and October of 1929.[24]

The DJIA peaked on 3 September 1929 and had fallen 32% by 28 October, the eve of what would be known as 'the day the bubble burst'. Whatever factor was causing the liquidation of stocks was already in play well before that final mad week of October. As September wore on, evidence that the new global monetary system was under severe pressure became clearer. On 26 September, the Bank of England raised its discount rate from 5.5% to 6.5%. This was in response to a drain in gold and took interest rates to the highest level in eight years. Philip Snowden, the Chancellor of the Exchequer, said the action was necessary to prevent the drain of capital to that 'orgy of speculation 3,000 miles away'[25]. The interest-rate differential between the US and the UK changed dramatically, also driven by a decline in the call money rate from 10% to 5% in New York during the first two weeks of October. The demand for loans for the purchase of securities was drying up and the price of such loans was declining. With sterling strengthening, it was becoming increasingly likely a gold drain from the US would occur. The timing of the Bank of England's increase in interest rates thus helped unsettle investors in the US.

Other events in late September and early October further tested the nerve of investors. On 30 September, the UK business empire of Clarence Hatry collapsed. Hatry, who had been trying to consolidate the UK steel industry, was forging scrip to raise more finance. The stock market grew suspicious of the increased supply of shares in the market and the stock prices of Hatry's numerous interests went into free fall. The banks, seeing the value of their security shrink, restricted credit and the game was up for Hatry. The sudden collapse of a major business enterprise created concern about the foundations at other businesses. A further blow to confidence came on 11 October when the Massachusetts Department of Public Utilities refused permission to Boston Edison for a 4:1 stock split, and accompanied the decision with a statement that 'no one, in our judgement... on the basis of its earnings, would find it to his advantage to buy it'. The cover of *Time* magazine indicated the high levels of public interest in business and investment; on 28 October it featured Swedish financier Ivar Kreuger and on 4 November the Chicago utilities magnate

---

[24] Barry Eichengreen, *Golden Fetters: The Gold Standard And The Great Depression*, (1919-1939)
[25] Address to Labour Party Conference, Brighton, 3 October 1929

Samuel Insull. By 1932, Kreuger had committed suicide after his business empire collapsed and Insull was fighting extradition from Greece on charges of embezzlement and mail fraud.

Whatever triggered the decline in the market, there is general agreement as to why it was of such significant magnitude - the unwinding of many of the excesses of the bull market. In particular, any fall in the price of equities was likely to be exacerbated when leverage over these assets had reached such high levels.

Public participation in the market had risen dramatically. Best estimates suggest that half a million Americans owned securities prior to WWI. By 1929, the number had risen to as many as 20 million. It is unlikely all these small investors were conversant in the basic principles of equity valuation. When interest in the stock market began to wane, the downside for prices was likely to be larger than in periods of less public enthusiasm. The unwinding of public participation took its toll, as did the unwinding of the positions of some of the investment vehicles created to attract funds of small investors. While it is safe to assume the public was uneducated in the ways of the markets in the 1920s, the same could also be said for most "professional" investors. As Hugh Bullock opined in 1932:

> Investment management in Great Britain is a profession. There are approximately 200,000 seasoned, marketable securities in the world. It takes specialists to find the best. We in America are somewhat new to the business. But I believe you will see a class of men grow up who are as honest and able as those in Britain.[26]

Bullock's comments were made in light of the often negligent and sometimes fraudulent activities of the professional managers of investment trusts in the period. Although the investment-trust business had been playing an increasing role in the London Stock Exchange since 1868, by 1920 there were at most 40 investment trusts in the US, and they were of negligible importance. Then, between 1927 and 1930, 700 investment trusts and investment holding companies were created to take advantage of the public's demand for investment-management expertise. In 1929 alone, 265 new investment trusts were formed with $3 billion in capital subscribed. In September of that year, half of the $1.2 billion share capital raised through the NYSE was for investment-trust companies. At the peak

---

[26] Hugh Bullock, 'New Investment Trust Form Held Need of Financial Life' (*New York Evening Post* 4 January 1932)

of the market this sector accounted for at least $8 billion of market capitalisation. While many of these trusts were reputable investment vehicles, others indulged in dubious practices - the purchase of illiquid stock, buying shares from the company's own directors, manipulating the price of holdings, using funds to buy failed issues from connected parties, excessive gearing, stock-bonus allocations to managers, and extreme concentration of investments. Given the nature and extent of Wall Street's misallocation of capital in the economic upswing, it was not too surprising that significant capital destruction would follow. That the inevitable destruction of capital would be followed by a global depression was harder to foresee.

From its peak on 3 September 1929, the market fell 48% by 13 November. The initial decline to around mid-October was relatively mild, but from 10 October to 13 November the Dow Jones Industrial Average fell 44%. Although the pace of the October decline was unprecedented, the scale was not exceptional (Figure 40).

Figure 40

20TH CENTURY BEAR MARKETS IN THE US UP TO 1929 - DECLINES IN THE DJIA	
January 1907 to November 1907	(44%)
November 1916 to December 1917	(39%)
November 1919 to August 1921	(47%)
September 1929 to November 1929	(48%)

Source: Dow Jones & Co.

While the decline in prices had been unusually rapid, there was soon evidence the recovery might also occur more quickly than usual. By 17 April 1930, the market had recovered 52% of the decline and was back where it was at the beginning of 1929. The market was now just 23% below its high of 3 September 1929. The magnitude of the decline had not been abnormal and the rebound had been more rapid than normal. While the suddenness of the decline in prices in October 1929 plays some role in the historical legacy of "The Great Crash", it is events after April 1930 that are primarily responsible for this period of financial-market history looming so large in the psyche of investors today. Investors unfortunate enough to believe the market recovery was on a firm footing and who bought equities on 17 April 1930 saw the DJIA dive again, losing 86% of its value before it bottomed in July 1932. Thus the most dramatic landscape on the road to July 1932 came after April 1930.

If there is one key difference between other 20th Century bear markets and what happened in 1929-32, it is the collapse of the banking system. Bank collapse and fear of bank collapse had certainly played a role in previous bear markets and recessions. The panic of 1907 involved numerous bank and trust company failures, and that experience led directly to the creation of the Federal Reserve System. In 1916-17 and again in 1919-21, the new system seemed to work in containing the scourge of bank collapses, in even the most trying economic conditions. The ability of the Federal Reserve System to 'furnish an elastic currency' seemed to work, preventing money panic and mass bank closure. As Figure 41 indicates, what ultimately turned this "ordinary" bear market into the greatest stock market crash in US history were the banking crises.

Figure 41

BEAR MARKET 1929-32 - EACH PHASE AND ITS CONTRIBUTION TO DJIA DECLINE	Decline/rise in period (%)	Cumulative (%)
The Crash - 3 September 1929 to 13 November 1929	-48	-48
1st Rally – 13 November 1929 to 17 April 1930	+48	-23
Summer Decline – 17 April 1930 to 10 September 1930	-17	-36
First Banking Crisis – 10 September 1930 to 16 December 1930	-36	-59
2nd Rally- 16th December 1930 to February 24th 1931	+23	-49
Second Banking Crisis- February 24th 1931 to October 5th 1931	-56	-77
Potential Stability- October 5th 1931 to March 8th 1932	+3	-76
The gold drain- March 8th 1932 to July 8th 1932	-54	-89

Source: Dow Jones & Co.

Compare the stuttered decline of the stock market with events in the wider economy. Figure 42 uses available monthly and quarterly data to map the progress of the recession.

Figure 42

PROGRESS OF ECONOMIC DECLINE - END JUNE 1929 (INDEX = 100) TO JUNE 1934	GNP constant dollars	Index of real factory Payrolls	CPI	WPI	Department store sales price (Adjusted)
Jun 1929	100	100	100	100	100
Dec 1929	100.6	92.3	99.7	97.9	98.3
Jun 1930	98.2	83.8	99.1	91.2	90.6
Dec 1930	87.7	73.3	97.6	83.5	87.3
Jun 1931	89.5	70.0	94.8	75.8	92.4
Dec 1931	83.9	62.2	92.1	72.2	84.3
Jun 1932	77.8	48.6	88.2	67.2	74.9
Dec 1932	70.1	57.2	84.8	65.8	69.3
Jun 1933	77.5	58.6	81.3	68.1	76.2
Dec 1933	70.2	67.4	82.7	74.3	70.5
Jun 1934	80.6	76.7	82.4	78.3	72.4

Source: US Bureau of the Census.

Figure 42 maps the 1929-33 recession and shows that, by mid-1930, the US economy had not been greatly affected by the stock market crash eight months before. In the 12 months from June 1929, the economy contracted by 1.8% and the consumer price index fell 0.9%. The pace of decline was considerably more rapid in factory payrolls, the wholesale price index and department store sales. In the overall economy, the pace accelerated markedly in the second half of 1930, influenced by the first banking crisis, which erupted in October of that year. The first half of 1931 saw the only marginal recovery in the economy during the 1929-32 contraction as GNP and real department-store sales both increased. This recovery was thrown off track by the second banking crisis, apparent domestically in March 1931 and intensified by the banking crisis in Europe, which hit the headlines in early May.

In terms of the course of the recession, as measured by GNP in constant dollars, only 35% of what was to be the total contraction had occurred by the end of June 1931. The real break from the normal pattern of the business cycle was the impact of the second banking crisis and growing concern about exchange rate stability, which from June 1931 to December 1932 accounted for almost two-thirds of the total economic contraction. This tale of economic decline has a clear relationship with the decline in the stock market. By February 1931, the market's decline had been larger than that of 1907 and 1919-21, but not materially so. All the dreadful new experiences to be visited on investors came after the first half of 1931 - up until then, the economic contraction and the bear market had been "normal".

Bank failures had been running at high levels throughout the 1920s, with many years seeing a greater value of deposits affected by suspension than in the severe recessionary year of 1921.

The high level of bank failures during the 1920s was the result of hard times in the farming sector and increased competitive pressures due to bank amalgamations. However, even by those high standards of failure, something clearly different was underway in the final quarter of 1930. By the end of October 1930, the total value of deposits affected by bank suspensions for the year was $287 million. The Federal Reserve did not seem perturbed by the business contraction at that stage and, despite reducing the discount rate, had been reducing credit to member banks throughout the period. Based on the data available by June, one would have expected the total value of deposits affected by suspension to have been less than $350 million for the year - a high level by historical standards, but the US economy had not been unduly affected by the $260 million of deposits hit by bank suspension in 1926. However, November and December of 1930 produced $550 million worth of deposits tied up in 608 bank suspensions, putting the level of damage to the financial system on a whole new scale. Even in the fourth quarter of 1930 most failed banks were those in agricultural areas, already weakened by the hardships of the 1920s.

Figure 43

TOTAL COMMERCIAL BANK SUSPENSIONS BY TOTAL DEPOSITS ($M)

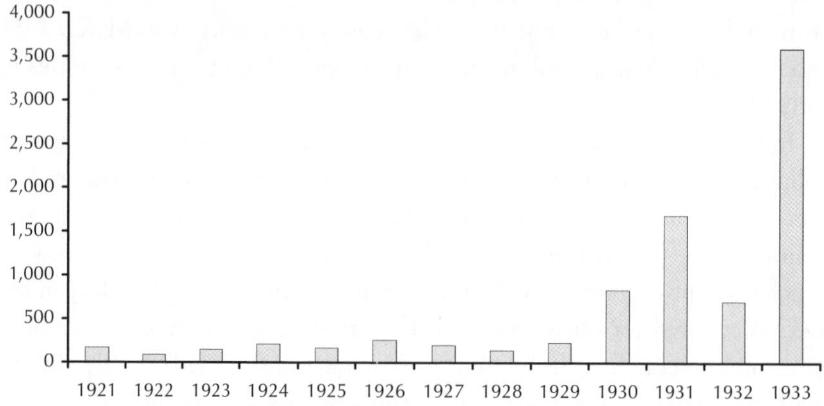

Source: Federal Reserve, *Banking and Monetary Statistics*

Crucially, one of the banks to fail in this period was the Bank of the United States, founded in 1791 and a member of the Federal Reserve System. It was the largest bank failure in US history. This was no country bank and its 400,000 depositors were heavily concentrated in New York City. When they lost their money, depositors elsewhere began to perceive material risk. From mid-September to mid-December 1930, the Dow Jones Industrial Average crashed through the November 1929 low, declining 36%.

Public behaviour changed, as did the behaviour of the banks. Up until October 1930, public willingness to hold bank deposits actually continued to increase. This increase in the ratio of deposits to currency held by the American public continued a trend which had been evident throughout the 1920s. By October 1930, the deposit-currency ratio was at a new high, indicating an unparalleled degree of faith in the banking system just as the first banking crisis arrived. There was now a major risk that even if the public decided to reduce its level of deposits to historically "normal" levels, a major monetary contraction would ensue. From October 1930, such a withdrawal of deposits began, but perhaps none could have anticipated the contraction in the deposit-currency ratio that ensued, from 11.5 in October 1930 to just 4.4 in March 1933. Before the public's withdrawal of its money was over, the deposit-currency ratio would be reduced to levels not seen since the end of the 19th Century. Given the operation of the fractional reserve banking system, where banks had to maintain cash balances much smaller than their deposit base, this drain of cash from the banks had a very negative impact. In this period the banks needed to reduce deposits by $14 in order to make $1 available for the public to hold as currency. The huge monetary impact of such deposit flight and the inability, or unwillingness, of the Federal Reserve to counteract it, is the key reason why the US recession of 1930 developed into the depression of 1931-32.

Total deposits in the US banking system declined from $59,828 million at the end of June 1930 to $58,092 million by the end of the year. This initial decline was modest but it kick-started a process which, combined with Fed inactivity, resulted in very negative impacts for bank balance sheets. The banks reacted normally to deposit flight by seeking more liquid assets for their balance sheets. This had a significant impact, as the banks tended to shift their holdings away from corporate bonds and into government securities. Prices of corporate bonds had been rising slowly since the stock market crash of October 1929. However, with the onset of the banking crisis of October 1930, prices began to decline. While slow at first, this was the beginning of a new price trend that would not run its course until the summer of 1932. It exacerbated problems for bankers going in to 1931 as they were forced to mark these liquid investments to market.

There were some signs of economic stability in early 1931, but this resulted in only a modest rally in the equity market. During the banking crisis, the DJIA reached a low of 157.5 on 16 December 1930. By 24 February 1931, it had risen 23% and was just 2.2% below the low of November 1929. Even at this stage, the magnitude of the decline in the index was only marginally in excess of the 1907 and 1919-21 bear markets. It was now that the second bank crisis hit. An investor committing funds to equities on 24 February 1931, almost 16 months after the October 1929 crash, would witness a 79% drop in the DJIA in the next 17 months. It was this period of decline that marked out the bear market as clearly different from anything before.

95

Prior to the first banking crisis, long- and short-term interest rates had been declining, as had yields on Baa-rated bonds. However, a yield spread then began to open, based on the quality of corporate credits. Banks searching for liquidity were dumping lower quality bonds for government securities. With the onset of another flood of bank suspensions in March 1931, the banks again strengthened their reserve positions. Bank failures increased rapidly in March and confidence was further undermined in May when Austria's largest private bank, Credit-Anstalt, failed. The Austrian authorities responded with numerous measures, one of which was exchange controls, freezing foreign bank balances in Austria. As Credit-Anstalt had a controlling interest in Hungary's biggest bank, a run on deposits began there in mid-May. The panic spread to Germany. The introduction of exchange controls in Austria had created concern among depositors in German banks that the balance sheet of their institutions may be undermined. As more than half of all German bank deposits were owned by non-Germans, a loss of confidence by these investors had very serious international consequences. There was a full-scale banking crisis in Germany by July and exchange controls followed. As US bank deposits in Austria, Hungary and Germany were frozen, the stability of US bank balance sheets were further undermined. This further question mark over US bank balance sheets prompted the American public to hold even greater cash balances at the expense of deposits. Total deposits of all banks declined from $58,092 million in December 1930 to $56,092 million in June 1931, then $49,509 million by December 1931. The US banking system held less in deposits in December 1931 than it had in December 1924. The banks were forced to again adjust their asset portfolios and corporate bonds were dumped with prices sinking further.

The US was now beset by its second banking crisis in less than a year. The country's leading experts had confidently predicted the Federal Reserve System would prevent such events. In the *Saturday Evening Post* of 14 April 1928, Secretary of the Treasury Andrew Mellon declared there to be:

> ... no longer any fear on the part of the banks or the business community that some sudden and temporary business crisis may develop and precipitate a financial panic such as visited the country in former years...We are no longer the victims of the vagaries of the business cycles. The Federal Reserve System is the antidote for money contraction and credit shortage.[27]

---

[27] Quoted in Harold B. Cleveland and Thomas F. Huertas, *Citibank 1812-1970*

The Federal Reserve System offered no such antidote. Those investors who remained committed to equities expecting the re-extension of the elastic currency must have watched in amazement as nothing was done. The Fed reduced the discount rate as recession and then depression developed, but there was no attempt to increase credit to member banks, even as the public withdrew deposits from the banking system and commercial banks dumped bonds in the scramble for liquidity. In 1921, one of the key questions for investors was how far Fed credit would shrink from its peak levels of around $3.5 billion in 1919. Few could have foreseen the contraction continuing until mid-1924, when it stood just below $1 billion. In summer 1931, Fed credit outstanding was again very close to that low of 1924. The economy expanded dramatically over that period and there was clearly ample scope to extend the "elastic currency" from these very low levels. However if, as Andrew Mellon had asserted, the Fed's ability to extend credit to the system was the antidote, then the doctors failed to administer it. Not until late in the summer of 1931 did the Fed begin any material purchase of bills and commence to extend credit to member banks. By that stage, however, the public's faith in the banking system had slumped, with the deposit-currency ratio below 9.0 from its peak of 11.5 in October 1930. As the banking system shook to its foundations, a new stage of the monetary crisis emerged as the US monetary gold stock, at an all time high of more than $4.7 billion as late as August 1931, began to drain away.

The damaging gold drain from the US began in September 1931 as investors were shocked by the devaluation of sterling. Eight other countries quickly followed suit, and a further four jumped ship in October. Foreign investors had, throughout the worsening economic problems, declining stock market and bank crises in the US, maintained their faith in the gold value of the US dollar. From September 1929 to August 1931, US gold stocks increased 15%, with 37% of the increase coming in May and June of 1931 as Europe's own banking crisis sent capital fleeing for the "safe haven" of the US. Britain's desertion of gold changed things dramatically and the US gold stocks declined 15% from August to October 1931, erasing the total inflow since 1929. Investors argued that if the UK could abandon the gold standard, there was a risk the US would follow.

The combination of a drain on gold reserves and currency withdrawals further exacerbated pressure on the commercial banking system, which was compounded by rising interest rates. The Federal Reserve acted as the gold

97

standard dictated, raising the discount rate from 1.5% to 3.5% in October with a view to halting the drain of gold from the country. Commercial banks once again rushed to dump assets in the scramble for liquidity. Now, for the first time in the recession, even the price of government securities declined. Investors who expected that government bonds would provide nominal returns in a deflationary period were now in for a major surprise. With banks forced to reduce the value of their government-bond holdings, balance sheet conditions further worsened. In the six-month period of August 1931 to January 1932, 1,860 banks with deposits of $1,449 million suspended operations - the same amount of deposits affected by bank suspensions in the entire 1921-29 period. The second banking crisis was of a much more serious nature than the first and, though operating from lower levels of the DJIA, accounted for 32% of the entire decline of the market from September 1929 to July 1932.

By 5 October 1931, the Dow had declined 77% from its peak in September 1929. Even the pessimistic investor may have considered that this scale of decline was sufficient to augur the end of any bear market. Some of the signs were indeed positive as the Hoover administration was finally spurred to try a new approach to the crisis. In October 1931, the National Credit Corporation was launched, aimed at extending loans to banks against assets deemed unacceptable as security for credit by the Federal Reserve System. In February 1932, the Republican administration created the Reconstruction Finance Corporation to provide loans to banks and railroads. By 26 February, the Federal Reserve Board was sufficiently relaxed about gold outflow to reduce the discount rate by 50 basis points to 3%. On 17 February, the *Glass-Steagall Act* was passed, permitting government bonds to serve as collateral against Federal Reserve bank notes, thus removing a technical bar to the creation of greater liquidity by the Federal Reserve System. The DJIA was marginally higher in March 1932 than it had been in October 1931. Investors who thought the worst was over and bought in at the March 1932 high were to lose 54% of their funds before the market bottomed in July.

The final blow to the market, which accounts for a quarter of the entire bear run, was primarily due to a renewed drain on gold from the US. From March 1932 to the end of July, US gold reserves declined a further 12%. At the time, the *Wall Street Journal* attributed the outflow to the growing number of bills before Congress seeking to increase government spending. The burgeoning fiscal deficit, it argued, convinced foreigners that US adherence to the gold standard was under threat. However, it is more likely the Federal Reserve's move to large-scale open-market purchases of government securities caused foreigners to take fright. Still, there was a heady cocktail of reasons for foreigners to be selling US dollars in early 1932. Barry Eichengreen argues that devaluations elsewhere threatened to erode America's current account surplus.

> The greater the pressure on the Federal Reserve Board to adopt reflationary initiatives, the greater the risk of dollar devaluation. The continued rise of American unemployment only intensified that pressure. With 1932 an election year, Congress was sure to exhort the Fed to respond more aggressively. Speculators consequently liquidated their dollar deposits, and central banks converted their dollar reserves into American gold.[28]

There is no doubt the Fed's launch of a significant open market operation at this late stage was prompted by the fear of direct political involvement in the monetary sphere. George Harrison, governor of the Federal Reserve Bank of New York, told the executive committee of his directors that 'the only way to forestall some sort of radical financial legislation by Congress, is to go further and faster with our own program'.[29] Investors had good reason to worry that politicians, by inclination prone to inflationary policies, were now in the driver's seat instead of the central bankers, doyens of sound money. These investors argued that Fed actions now showed that reflation, and not sound money, was the target. The change in policy was particularly alarming to foreign central banks holding US dollars in their reserves under the gold exchange standard. If this new policy alignment continued, then it was even more probable that the US would abandon the gold standard. Foreigners began to withdraw balances from the US and many on Wall Street believed devaluation of the dollar was likely by the summer. The Fed's belated conversion to reflationary policy, rather than encouraging investors, produced a final panic on Wall Street. Against this background of increasingly likely devaluation and continued economic deterioration, the bear market in equities continued. The DJIA, assailed by the crash of October 1929, the first banking crisis of October 1930, the second banking crisis of 1931 and the gold drain of 1932, was about to hit bottom.

---

[28] Barry Eichengreen, *op cit*
[29] Private notes of George L. Harrison (Governor of the Reserve Bank of New York), Quoted in Friedman and Schwartz.

Structure of the market in 1932

'It's this way, Joe. Now, what gave us good times? The automobile industry. Why? Because it was something new to develop. Now, what do we need now to bring back better times? Something else that's new, to develop. Well, that's the idea, see. This outfit I'm with has got something new. An electric shaver.'

James T. Farrell, *Judgement Day*

The stock market in 1932

Between each of the four periods covered in this book there were marked changes in the structure of the stock market. The intervening bull markets brought forth numerous new issues and new technologies, resulting in the emergence of new industries. While the 1921-32 period is the shortest gap between bear market bottoms it was still accompanied by significant structural change in the stock market. There were many more securities for investors to choose from in 1932 compared to 1921. Even following the darkest days of the crash and depression there were 1,278 NYSE-listed stocks at the end of 1932 compared with just 691 at the end of 1921. In contradiction of popular mythology the market remained active. For 1932 as a whole, 32% of the total shares listed were traded compared to 59% in 1921. Despite this decline in the turnover rate, 425 million shares were traded in 1932 compared to 173 million in 1921. The turnover rate declined, despite larger trading volumes because listed shares on the NYSE had increased 349% over the period.

As the stock market reached its lows in the last days of June 1932, the average weekly volume was just 3,047,183 shares. As the average stock price on 1 July was $11.89, the value of the weekly average turnover on the NYSE was $36.2 million. In understanding the structure of the market it is important to remember the preferred share was still an important asset class in 1932, accounting for 19% of the market value of common and preferred stock listed on the NYSE. On 1 July 1932, there were 808 common stocks listed on the market and 445 preferred stocks, and there was a significant business arbitraging the common and preferred stocks of the same issuer. On average through 1932, 50% of listed companies had both common and preferred issues outstanding. Although there were 1,253 listed shares in the summer of 1932, on a typical day's trading there would be activity in perhaps around 500 issues. In September 1929, the market value of common and preferred stocks reached $90 billion. The ensuing decline in value from 1929 to 1932 almost exactly mirrored the decline in average market capitalisation - between September 1929 and June 1932, as the number of total common and preferred stock issues only declined from 1,280 in September 1929 to 1,262 in July 1932.

In August 1929, the last period of normal trading prior to the slump, daily average volume was 3,677,053 shares. As the average peak monthly share price was $89.13, daily volume was around $328 million before the subsequent panic of September and October sent volumes to abnormally high levels. Thus the 89% decline in the DJIA in the 1929-32 bear market has to be seen against a 5% decline in the number of listed securities and a 98% decline in the value of daily trading volume.

These headline figures are often used to show that by 1932 the stock market was inactive and shunned by investors. However the fact is that 32% of all NYSE-listed shares were traded in 1932 and there were almost twice as many listed companies to choose from in 1932 compared to 1921. The DJIA may have fallen by 89% from its peak, but the total market capitalisation of NYSE-listed stocks was just 40% below the level reached by the end of 1924, when the first reliable market capitalisation data became available. While a 32% turnover of listed companies may have been low by historic standards, it was to prove to be higher than any level achieved from 1937 to 1979.

In understanding the structure of the market in 1932, it is important to realise the major changes which had occurred in American industry over the period. Figure 44 and Figure 45 show the market value of all the NYSE-listed sectors on 1 September 1929 and 1 July 1932. Perhaps the most surprising thing is that railroads still comprised the largest sector of the market in September 1929. This large weighting occurred despite the fact that the industrial sector had outperformed railroads by 86% from the lows of August 1921 to the peak of September 1929.

Although the bull market of the 1920s is often associated with the boom in autos and radios, the three largest sectors of the market - railroads, petroleum and chemicals - accounted for 31% of total market capitalisation at the market zenith in September 1929. The communications sector, which included the mighty AT&T, was notable for becoming an increasingly important sector of the market even though comprised of just a handful of companies. Even in September 1929, the financial sector, comprised largely of investment trusts, was less than 2.5% of total market capitalisation. As late as 1920, US Steel had been the largest listed company in America and part of a key sector of the stock market, but by 1929 the entire steel sector was just the 10th largest by market value.

Figure 44

MARKET VALUE SEPTEMBER 1929

	($m)	% of total	Number of issues
Railroad & Equipments	12,778	14.25	186
Petroleum	7,601	8.48	63
Chemicals	7,112	7.93	72
Autos & Accessories	6,162	6.87	66
Communications	5,315	5.93	13
Retail Merchandising	5,192	5.79	97
Electrical Equipment Manufacturing	5,096	5.68	19
Gas & Electiric Holdings Companies	5,045	5.63	34
Gas & Electric Operating Companies	4,796	5.35	38
Steel, Iron & Coke	4,403	4.91	47
Foods	4,178	4.66	86
Mining (excluding iron)	3,091	3.45	56
Machinery & Metals	3,010	3.36	85
US Companies Operating Abroad	2,861	3.19	41
Financial	2,221	2.48	31
Foreign Companies- Canada & Cuba	1,951	2.18	32
Tobacco	1,732	1.93	40
Farm Machinery	928	1.03	12
Amusements	926	1.03	27
Business & Office Equipment	868	0.97	12
Building	813	0.91	25
Paper & Publishing	805	0.90	26
Aviation	732	0.82	11
Rubber & Tires	507	0.57	18
Miscellaneous Utilities	376	0.42	37
Textiles	357	0.40	39
Miscellaneous Business	224	0.25	11
Land & Realty	186	0.21	8
Leather & Boots	147	0.16	20
Shipping Services	87	0.10	7
Garment Manufacturing	85	0.09	13
Shipping Operations & Buildings	85	0.09	8
Total	89,670	100.00	1,280

Source: *Wall Street Journal*, September 1929

It was during the 1929-32 bear market that the railroad sector finally lost its crown as the largest sector of the market. By July 1932, it accounted for just 8.7% of total market capitalisation. Just two decades earlier, it enjoyed more than 50% of NYSE turnover. The largest sector of the market in June 1932 was petroleum, although utility operating and holding companies, when grouped together, were the dominant sector accounting for 15% of total market capitalisation. Another sector to suffer a material decline in importance during the bear market was autos and accessories.

The auto industry suffered the Depression far more than the safe sectors of foods, tobacco, communications and utilities. There was also a degree of concentration during the period, with the 10 largest sectors accounting for 77% of market capitalisation in 1932, up from 71% in 1929. By 1932 the stock market was dominated by the utility, oil and communications sectors which together accounted for 37% of total market capitalisation.

Figure 45

MARKET VALUE JULY 1932 (TEN LARGEST SECTORS IN BOLD)			
	($m)	% of total	No. of issues
Railroad & Equipments	**1,364**	8.72	164
Petroleum	1,698	10.86	56
Chemicals	**1212**	7.75	76
Autos & Accessories	**668**	4.27	69
Communications	**1,686**	10.78	11
Retail Merchandising	**850**	5.44	103
Electrical Equipment Manufacturing	371	2.37	16
Gas & Electiric Holdings Companies	**929**	5.94	39
Gas & Electric Operating Companies	**1,492**	9.54	31
Steel, Iron & Coke	583	3.73	51
Foods	**1,243**	7.95	76
Mining (excluding iron)	360	2.30	55
Machinery & Metals	390	2.49	92
US Companies Operating Abroad	188	1.20	34
Financial	432	2.76	48
Foreign Companies- Canada & Cuba	252	1.61	16
Tobacco	**856**	5.47	35
Farm Machinery	159	1.02	11
Amusements	51	0.33	21
Business & Office Equipment	107	0.68	11
Building	97	0.62	34
Paper & Publishing	89	0.57	28
Aviation	58	0.37	10
Rubber & Tires	88	0.56	21
Miscellaneous Utilities	90	0.58	31
Textiles	71	0.45	40
Miscellaneous Business	42	0.27	11
Land & Realty	25	0.16	8
Leather & Boots	162	1.04	20
Shipping Services	5	0.03	8
Garment Manufacturing	8	0.05	9
Shipping Operating & Building	9	0.06	9
Total	15,635	100.00	1,244

Source: *Wall Street Journal*, July 1932

The extent to which the change in the structure of the market is due to share-price performance rather than corporate activity can only be assessed from June 1926, when detailed sector performance data first became available. We cannot see the impact of sector price performance throughout the 1921-29 bull market, but we can view 1926-29, the most exuberant period of the "Roaring Twenties".

The 1920s bull market is often associated with the performance of the auto sector or Radio Corporation of America (RCA) stock, but the real stars were chemicals and electrical equipment. The electrification of American households and businesses accelerated during the decade, creating boom conditions for the electrical equipment manufacturers. The electrification business also boosted the performance of utility stocks, assisted by some dubious financial engineering in the sector. In the bust that followed, many of the utility holding companies failed and their CEOs – the likes of William Foshay, head of a Minneapolis based holding company, and Samuel Insull, head of Middle West Utilities - ended up on criminal charges.

Figure 46

KEY SECTOR PERFORMANCE - JUNE 1926 TO SEPTEMBER 1929	
Chemicals	+369%
Electric Equipment	+349%
Utilities	+326%
Financials	+275%
Business Equipment	+264%
Beer	+259%
Services	+223%
Steel	+180%
Autos	+174%
Telecoms	+157%
DJIA	+149%
Food	+102%
Retail	+95%
Transport	+85%
Construction	+83%
Tobacco	+64%
Oil	+48%
Textiles	+15%
Clothes	+42%
Coal	+39%
Wholesale	(65%)

Source: Kenneth R. French, 'Industry Portfolio Data'. Note: Total return with dividends reinvested.

The chemical industry benefited from the general economic boom, but by the 1920s investors were becoming increasingly excited about prospects for the new petrochemical industry. Cellophane had been commercially available since 1919, but when Du Pont added a waterproof coating to the product in 1927, its usefulness increased dramatically. As the 1920s progressed, synthetic methanol and synthetic nitrates went into commercial production. Investors could see development of petrochemicals as a path to huge growth in the production of synthetic raw materials. Other breakthroughs - neoprene, Perspex, polythene and nylon - were not to come until the early 1930s. However, the mere prospect of commercial success from petrochemical products helped boost the share prices of chemical companies in the second half of the 1920s.

The financials sector also performed well - this was driven by the mania for investment-trust shares. With many trusts rising to significant premiums to their asset values, and applying gearing to boost their returns, it is not surprising the sector produced good returns in a bull market.

The commodity sectors, which had led the last major bull market of 1917-19, lagged during the 1920s. This was a period when inflation in general was in abeyance and the prices for many commodities actually declined. Those who stuck with oil shares through the 1919-21 bear market were not to be rewarded - oil was one of the worst performing sectors in the 1920s. Only one sector of the stock market produced positive total real returns for investors in the 1929-1932 bear market - tobacco.

The scale of the declines shown in Figure 47 has to be considered against a background of a 33% decline in the wholesale price index over the same period. As well as this off-setting positive, most companies managed to maintain some form of dividend payment throughout the period. Cowles Foundation data, the broadest dividend data available for the market, shows a 48% decline in dividend payments from 1929 to 1932.

Figure 47

KEY SECTOR PERFORMANCE - SEPTEMBER 1929 TO JUNE 1932	
Tobacco	(38%)
Telecoms	(70%)
Clothes	(75%)
Coal	(74%)
Oil	(74%)
Food	(72%)
Utilities	(82%)
Chemical	(85%)
Beer	(86%)
Autos	(88%)
DJIA	(89%)
Transport	(90%)
Financials	(91%)
Electrical Equipment	(91%)
Steel	(92%)
Games	(93%)
Wholesale	(94%)

Source: Kenneth R. French, 'Industry Portfolio Data'. Note: Total return with dividends reinvested.

Seemingly defensive sectors of the market such as utility and food stocks offered little protection for investors. This was partly due to the over-valuation of all stocks by September 1929 but also due to the scale of the recession which produced volume declines in basics such as electricity and packaged foods. Packaged food was a relatively new growth concept in the nineteen twenties and thus there was ample room for demand declines. By 1932 85% of the bread consumed in America was baked at home. The tobacco sector was the only place to hide from 1929-1932 as volumes increased, raw material prices collapsed and selling prices held up.

The bond market in 1932

What does Father Moylan say? He tells what the bankers are doing. Loaning American money to Europe. If they had kept American money in America where it belongs, there wouldn't be any depression.

James T. Farrell, *Judgement Day*

On 1 June 1932, there were 1,587 bond issues aggregating $52,193 million of par value with a market value of $36,856 million listed on the NYSE. Based on market value, the NYSE-listed bond market was composed of the following key sectors:

Figure 48

COMPOSITION OF NYSE-LISTED BOND MARKET 1 JUNE 1932		
	%	Market value ($m)
US government	40.5	14,929
Foreign government	30.5	11,242
Railroads	13.4	4,953
Utilities	7.7	2,811
Industrial	4.9	1,812
Foreign companies	3.0	1,109
Total	100	36,856

Source: *Wall Street Journal*, 11 July 1932

Government securities made up the bulk of NYSE-listed bonds, though this was accounted for by just 11 issues. The average daily volume in the bond market in this period was around $10 million, of which some 40% was in US government securities. The total daily trading value of the other 1,576 issues was about $6 million. In May 1932, the month before the bond rally began, the total turnover in bonds on the NYSE was $169 million, the lowest May total since 1918. Bonds had not dropped as dramatically as stocks. As the total value of NYSE-listed bonds was $46,741 million on 1 September 1929, the value of the market had declined just 21% over the course of the equity bear market.

This relatively small decline in total market value and number of issues is, however, deceptive as the period saw steady prices for US government bonds and falling prices for other classifications. On 1 September 1929, there were 1,543 non-US government bond issues with an approximate market value of $33,809 million and by 1 June 1932 this had been reduced to $21,927 million of 1,574 issues. The steep decline in prices was a product of a general deterioration in corporate balance sheets wrought by deflation. While many corporate balance sheets were in dire straits, it was also true that many had been significantly strengthened through the long economic contraction. American Superpower, in 1932 a utility company and not a geo-political entity, was described as a "speculative issue" despite possessing a balance sheet which today seems highly conservative.

> While obviously a speculative issue, American Superpower common shares carry with them a certain appeal for the business man who is prepared to go without return on his commitment for what may prove to be an extended period. The company has no funded debt, and at the end of 1931 had in excess of $26,650,000 of United States government securities alone.[30]

Even companies making such balance sheet adjustments had seen the value of their bonds hurt by the economic deterioration. Figure 49, which shows the yields of key sectors in September 1929 and June 1932, provides some guidance as to the shift in the bond market over the period.

Figure 49

BOND YIELDS FOR KEY CLASSES OF BONDS SEPTEMBER 1929 AND JUNE 1932				
(%)	Government	Industrial	Railroad	Utility
September 1929	3.70	4.10	5.38	5.16
June 1932	3.76	6.80	9.14	7.21

Source: Federal Reserve, *Banking and Monetary Statistics*

The moderate decline in the market value of bonds outstanding was because government bond prices were largely unchanged over the period. The Treasury's three bond issues of $2.2 billion in 1931, its first in three years, also bolstered the total market value of bonds. One would have expected a government bond rally in deflationary times, which is what happened, at least initially. The bull market in government securities lasted from September 1929 to the second banking crisis in June 1931, when the yield reached 3.13%. With the added devaluation panic of late 1931, even the price of government bonds declined. However, the net situation was that the price of government bonds was largely unchanged from September 1929 to June 1932.

It was very different for other classes of bonds. Initially, while the recession remained of normal dimensions, bond prices rallied. From September 1929 to the peak of the rally in September 1930, industrial bond

---

[30] *Wall Street Journal*, 9 June 1932

107

yields fell 33 basis points. However in September 1930, everything changed - with the first banking crisis, industrial bond prices fell dramatically. Industrial bond prices were already below September 1929 levels by as early as December 1930.

This general pattern of a rally from September 1929 to September 1930 and then a dramatic sell-off was also true for railroad and utility bonds. The rally in company bond prices for 11 months after the October stock market crash is another factor suggesting the crash itself may not have played as large a role in the ensuing depression as is popularly believed.

Figure 50

US GOVERNMENT YIELDS MONTHLY - JANUARY 1929-JANUARY 1933

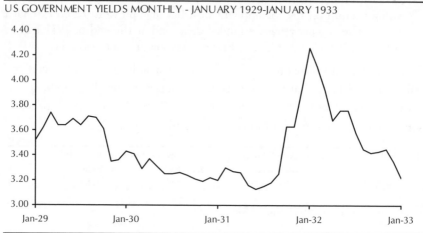

Source: Federal Reserve, *Banking and Monetary Statistics*

Figure 51

YIELD ON BAA CORPORATE BONDS - JANUARY 1929-JANUARY 1933

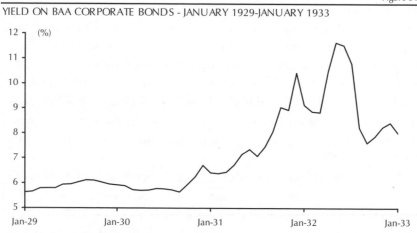

Source: Federal Reserve, *Banking and Monetary Statistics*

While bond prices may have been declining they were significantly outperforming equities and, even as the stock market bottomed, investment managers continued a high commitment to bonds. The *Wall Street Journal* of 11 July 1932 carried such regular news items as:

Anderson & Cromwell, managers of Fidelity Fund, Inc. report that on June 30 the portfolio was invested as follows: Bonds, 65%; stocks, 28.6%; cash, accruals etc., 6.4%.

Separate mention must be made of foreign government bonds. It may surprise most modern investors that the market value of these bonds outstripped that of domestic commercial concerns in June 1932. Although there were many more domestic corporate bonds listed on the NYSE, foreign governments tended to have much larger issues. During the 1920s, when Britain was still recovering from the war, the US became the key provider of global capital to the world. That rise in importance was signified by a dramatic increase in the number of foreign governments raising capital on the NYSE. At the end of January 1926, there were 116 foreign government issues listed on the NYSE, with a combined market value of $3,024 million. By the peak of the equity market in September 1929, there were 202 such issues with a combined market value of $16,012 million, comprising one-third of the total value of all bonds listed on the NYSE. Apart from the debt securities of major nations such as the UK, France and Canada, a US investor could add to his bond portfolio Bavaria, Bolivia, Bordeaux, Brisbane, Budapest, Costa Rica, Cuba, Haiti, Nuremberg, Oslo, Panama, Rotterdam, Warsaw, Vienna or Yokohama. By 1 June 1932, the market value of NYSE-listed foreign government bonds had declined to just $11,242 million, a 30% drop from the September 1929 level, with a small increase in the number of issues to 214. A selection of 1929 high and 1932 low prices provides some indication of the range of returns.

As Figure 52 shows, deflation wrought havoc with the price of most sovereign credits. Governments initially tried to live up to commitments to the gold standard and repay US-dollar debt. However, the internal deflation this demanded became politically unpalatable as unemployment rose and financial systems collapsed or neared collapse. By 1932, though the US remained on the gold standard, a long list of others had been forced to devalue - Bolivia, Bulgaria, Canada, Czechoslovakia, Denmark, Egypt, Estonia, Finland, Germany, Greece, Hungary, India, Japan, Mexico, New Zealand, Nicaragua, Norway, Portugal, Salvador, Sweden, United Kingdom, Venezuela, Yugoslavia.

Figure 52

FOREIGN GOVERNMENT BONDS LISTED ON NYSE - 3 SEPT 1929 PRICES, 1932 LOW

	3 September 1929	1932 Low
Australian external 5s	94 3/8	46 1/2
Australia 4 1/2s	85 1/2	41
Bolivia external 7s	84 1/2	2
Bordeaux 6s	100	98 1/4
Brazil 6 1/2s	88 1/8	14
Brisbane City 5s	90	32
Canada 4 1/2s	97 1/4	86
Canada 5s	101 1/8	87
Columbia 6s	77 7/8	13 1/2
Denmark external 6s	103 1/4	47 1/8
Finland ext 6 1/2s	85	40
French external 7's	109	109
German external 7's	105 1/4	41 1/4
Italy external 7s	95 3/8	82 1/2
Japan external 6 1/2s	100	52 1/2
Milan 6 1/2s	84 1/2	57 1/8
New South Wales	92	30 1/2
Norway 5s	94 1/8	63 1/4
Nuremberg City	83	15
Poland external 5s	94 3/8	43 1/2
Rome 6 1/2s	86 1/2	62
San Paulo 6s	83 1/8	7
Sweden external 5 1/2s	103 1/4	75
Tokyo external 5 1/2s	84 1/2	36
United Kingdom 5 1/2s	102	90
Yokohama	91	40

Source: *Wall Street Journal*

Not surprisingly, the ability of countries devaluing against gold and the dollar to repay US-dollar debt was significantly diminished. The best-performing sovereign credit during the period was the Republic of France which, having joined the gold standard with an undervalued currency in 1928, was able to maintain its commitment to gold until 1936. Of course, the end of the link to gold did not necessarily lead to a collapse in the price of sovereign credit. The UK and Canada had left the gold standard by 1932, but were pursuing sufficiently sound monetary policies that bond prices traded higher than those of Italy, which was not to abandon the gold standard until 1936.

At the bottom with the bear - Summer 1932

In my recent visit to the White House, I found this same hope prevailing in official circles, and I concluded that what we all must do is to get behind our president and push upward, to the next period of prosperity.

James T. Farrell, *Judgement Day*

The investment trenches were deep and muddy in the summer of 1932. But before we get into the tactics of the trenches, we need to take a strategic look at that battlefield investors call "the long term".

There are many ways 1932 stands out from other major bear-market bottoms of the 20th Century. The most important difference is the pace at which equities moved from overvalued to undervalued.

As we have already seen, stocks had become very cheap in 1921, primarily because equity prices had been moving sideways while the economy and corporate earnings had been growing. At its peak, before the 1919-21 bear market, the DJIA reached 119.6. While the US economy had boomed in the previous two decades the DJIA was not much higher than the 100.5 reached in November 1909 or the 102.7 level reached as early as January 1906. However, things were very different on the eve of the 1929-32 bear market - the Dow had reached 381.2 on 3 September 1929, an increase of almost 500% from the 1921 low. There was no slow return of value to equities, but a crash that was to turn overvalued equities into undervalued equities in less than three years.

We have already traced the growth of the US economy over a 20-year period after which the DJIA ended virtually unchanged in 1921. That comparison was useful in showing the huge strides made by the US economy at a time when equity prices were volatile but effectively going nowhere. Things were very different in 1929 following a prolonged bull market in equities, with the Dow peaking almost 220% above the previous bull market peak of November 1919. With such a dramatic rise in the price of equities, there can be no case for 1929-32 as being just the final down leg that exacerbated an undervaluation of the market. From very low levels the valuation of equities rose and rose over the course of the 1920s. Then dramatically, in the late 1920s and into the early 1930s, equities went from overvalued to undervalued. As we shall see, this dramatic valuation shift is in stark contrast to the slow burning, downward drift in valuations and then final slump that we see in all the other bear markets considered in this book. Because the 1929-32 bear market looms so large in the investment psyche, we still assume this is the model for all bear markets. However, this bear market is very much the exception in terms of the development of real value for investors in the stock market.

A key driver for the bull market in equities during the 1920s was that finally equity investors began to fully participate in the growth of the US economy. The numbers in Figure 53 show the pace of economic

111

development from the end of the bear market in 1921 to the end of the bull market in 1929.

Figure 53

ECONOMIC CHANGES IN THE US FROM 1920 TO END 1929

	1920	1929
Population (millions)	107	122
Number of immigrants per annum	430,001	279,678
Expectation of life at birth (years)	54.1	57.1
Number of physicians	114,977	152503
Average hourly earnings (manufacturing)	56c	57c
Total union membership	5,034,000	3,625,000
Wholesale price index	154.4	95.3
Nominal GDP ($bn)	87	104
Real GDP ($bn 2000 dollars)	607	865
School enrolment (000's)	23,277	27,810
Number of farms (000's)	6,518	6,512
Number of cattle on farms (000's)	66,640	58,877
Value of mineral products current dollars (m)	6,084	4,908
Index of physical volume of minerals produced	51	73
Crude oil production (000's barrels)	442,929	1,007,323
Value of new building permits (index)	88	187
Dwelling units started (000's)	247	509
Cigarettes produced (millions)	48,091	122,822
Total steel ingots and castings produced (000's long tons)	42,132	56,433
Railroad mileage	406,580	429,054
Motor vehicle registrations (000's)	9,239	26,704
Number of telephones (000's)	13,329	20,068
Net production of electricity by central stations (m Kwh hours)	56,559	116,747
Exports ($m)	8,664	5,441
Imports ($m)	5,784	4,755
Balance on goods and services ($m)	3,523	1,148
Real gross private domestic product per man hour (1929=100)	78	100
Total assets of banks ($m)	53,094	72,315
Total of deposits and currency ($m)	39,555	54,790
Volume of stock sales on NYSE (millions per annum)	227	1,215
Life insurance in force ($m)	40,540	102,086
Federal government expenditure ($m)	6,403	3,298
Public debt of federal government ($m)	24,299	16,931
Military personnel on active duty	343,302	255,031

Source: US Bureau of the Census

Headline GDP figures provide significant insight into the important deflationary trend in the 1920s. Measured in real terms, GDP increased

43% over the period, while nominal GDP growth was 20%. The bulk of this deflation occurred in the commodity price collapse of 1921, but the GDP deflator was marginally lower in 1929 than it was even at the end of 1921. As Figure 53 shows, economic growth, perhaps with the exception of the farming sector, was particularly high during the decade. However, none of the economic indicators covered in Figure 53 grew as fast as the stock market over the same period. This was in marked contrast to previous decades when, as we have already seen, an economic boom did not result in higher equity prices. So what explains this sudden transformation of the relationship between broad economic growth and the price of equities? Did corporate earnings growth outstrip growth in the economy and thus justify the almost 500% rise in the Dow Jones Industrial Average from August 1921 to September 1929? To what extent where the high returns for investors just a product of higher valuations for equities?

The best data available on earnings growth over the period is that compiled by the Cowles Foundation. In quantifying profit growth in the 1920s, picking a start date has a major impact on the outcome, due to the collapse in profits in 1921. Figure 54 provides the series of earnings from 1916-29 and indicates the volatility of earnings over the period.

Figure 54

EARNINGS OF S&P COMPOSITE STOCK PRICE INDEX (INDEX, 1929=100)	
1916	95
1917	80
1918	62
1919	58
1920	50
1921	18
1922	43
1923	61
1924	58
1925	78
1926	77
1927	69
1928	88
1929	100

Source: Robert J. Shiller, *Market Volatility*

The data shows the difficulty in assessing the level of profit growth of listed companies during the 1920s. It is clear the huge war-profit year of 1916 and the deflationary year of 1921 are not good starting points for launching any comparison with 1929. In order to cope with such problems throughout this book we refer to the cyclically adjusted earnings as providing the best guide to the underlying earnings power of listed

113

companies. The chosen cyclical adjustment is to compute a ten-year rolling average earnings figure as recommended by Professor Robert Shiller in his book *Irrational Exuberance*. However, even this approach to calculating normal earnings is complicated in this particular period due to the exceptionally high levels of profit earned from 1915-17. These wartime profits inflate even ten-year average figures for 1921 and indicate that cyclically adjusted earnings increased just 11% from 1921 to 1929. A simpler, but clearly more subjective, way of estimating profit growth is to look at the growth in earnings following the economy's recovery from recession in 1922 and 1923 to the peak of the market in 1929. Utilising this approach, and the numbers in Figure 54, it is a good rule of thumb to say that the profit of listed companies doubled during the great bull market of the 1920s. Importantly, the 1920-29 period, when reported earnings grew faster than economic growth, stands in marked contrast to 1871-1921, when the reverse was the case. In general terms, the economy expanded 43% over 1920-29, while earnings doubled. However, the stock market rose 220% above its previous highest level and almost five times above its August 1921 low. The 1920s augured a new era for equities. Reported earnings growth finally lived up to and exceeded economic growth, and against that background, perhaps not surprisingly, equity valuations rose. Finally some evidence arose that shareholders would directly participate in the economic emergence of America and this alone could begin to justify significantly higher valuations for equities.

This growing faith in investor participation in economic growth pushed equity valuations to extreme levels. As elsewhere in this book, we assess equity valuation with reference to the cyclically adjusted PE and the q ratio. Utilising the ten-year average rolling earnings figure to make the cyclical adjustment, the PE of the S&P Composite Index rose from 7.4x in August 1921 to peak at 31.6x in September 1929. The average cyclically adjusted PE had been just 15.3x from January 1881 to September 1929, and the previous peak level had been 26.5x in June 1901.

Clearly there was something in equity valuations in 1929 to suggest that a "new era" for future earnings growth had developed. The q ratio shows similar extremes of valuation by 1929. The data is only available for year-end and as the stock market had already declined significantly by 31 December 1929, the data does not register the September peak for the ratio. However, even utilising year-end data, the ratio was still 20% above the previous high recorded in 1905 and 80% above the 1900-29 average.

On the eve of the 1929-32 bear market, equities were very expensive, a marked contrast to the situation in 1919.

Figure 55

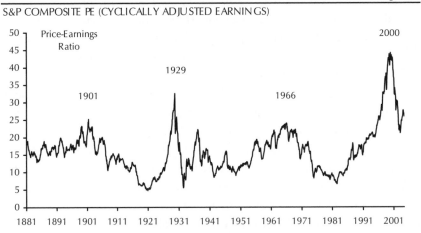

S&P COMPOSITE PE (CYCLICALLY ADJUSTED EARNINGS)

Source: www.econ.yale.edu/~shiller/data.htm

The idea behind **the q ratio** is basically very simple. It compares two different estimates of the value of US companies. The first is what Wall Street says the companies are worth and the second is their fundamental value. For the stock market as a whole, fundamental value is what it would cost today to replace all the assets of all quoted companies. Their value is what it would cost to create them, if we had to start from scratch and do it again. To calculate their fundamental value, we need to work out how much this cost would be. Their total value is thus the measure of what the companies are worth in terms of their assets, both physical and financial, minus their liabilities. This estimate is normally referred to as net worth. To find q, we compare the net worth of the corporate sector with the total value that the stock market puts on corporate shares. The ratio between the two is q.

- From Andrew Smithers & Stephen Wright, *Valuing Wall Street*

When the market peaked in November 1919, on the eve of the 1919-21 bear market, the cyclically adjusted PE was just 10.6x, 33% below the 1881-1919 average. As we shall see in Parts III and IV, the 1919-21 experience, of a slow decline in valuations ending with a dramatic slump, is more common than a rapid movement from overvalued to undervalued. **Popular memory sees 1929-32 as the typical bear market, when a rapid decline in price produces a move to undervaluation. To some extent this has** resulted in a rule of thumb that equities become cheap after a significant decline in price. The evidence from 1921 and, as we shall see, 1949 and 1982, is that this is not necessarily the case. The 1921 instance is more typical when the move from overvaluation to undervaluation took well over a decade. Bear markets, where three-year price declines make overvalued equities cheap, are the exception and not the rule.

The contraction in valuations from September 1929 to July 1932 was only part of the story. The 1929-32 bear market saw the DJIA fall 89%, and a collapse in earnings played an important role. The S&P Composite Index earnings declined 68% from September 1929 to July 1932. The contraction in valuation and decline in earnings together reduced the DJIA to 41.2 on 8 July 1932, just marginally above the 40.9 level on 26 May 1896 when the index was launched. In real terms, reported earnings of the S&P Composite Index in July 1932 were below those reported in October 1873 and in nominal terms were back to the level of December 1880.

This decline in earnings surpassed the scale of decline in economic activity. In nominal terms, GDP returned to around its 1917 level and in real terms to around its 1922 level, representing contractions of 43% and 26% respectively from 1929. The strategic picture of the 1929-32 bear market is of a market falling from near-historical peak valuations combined with a contraction in earnings that significantly surpassed the scale of the economic contraction. The most important component of the strategic picture for the investor on the front line in the summer of 1932 was whether the stock market was now trading below "fair value".

With earnings of listed companies reduced to 1880 levels by the summer of 1932, it is clearly not enough to assess the degree of "value" in the market in relation to those earnings. At issue was the correct level of normalised earnings, and assessing this was increasingly difficult by 1932. It was argued by some investors that the left-wing policies of a Roosevelt administration would result in a structural reduction in corporate profitability. As early as May 1932, even before his nomination as the Democrat candidate, Franklin D. Roosevelt was stating that, in the future, capital must be content with smaller returns relative to labour. Maybe past levels of profitability could now provide no guidance as to the future. Did the 68% decline in market earnings presage this new era of lower profitability?

This confusion as to the level of underlying earnings accounts for the dramatic differences in valuation parameters around the bear market bottom of July 1932.

Despite reported earnings being back to 1880 levels, the market capitalised even that level of earnings at only 10.2x in July 1932, a 26% discount to the 1871-1932 monthly PE average.

However, within 12 months the market was to value corporate earnings at 26.3x current earnings, a PE level only previously surpassed in one month (December 1894) and not to be seen again until March 1998. This still stands as the most dramatic recorded change in market PE in a 12-month period and is accounted for by the rise of the index and a 13% decline in earnings from the bottom of the market in July 1932.

The dramatic surge in the PE ratio in 1933 is often taken to indicate that equities were expensive - not so, they were very cheap. It is untrue that the PE indicated the market was expensive at 10.2 in July 1932, as the market was capitalising an earnings level first achieved in 1881. Only the most dyed-in-the-wool Republican could believe that the "New Deal" had reduced the earnings power of US corporations to such a permanently low level. The headline PE did become a very misleading indicator of value by 1933 as it neared its historical high, but the bull market underway in equities still had a very long way to run. On reported earnings, the PE suggested equities were around 26% undervalued in July 1932, relative to the long-term average PE. On any form of adjusted earnings, they were trading even further below fair value.

Calculated using 10-year rolling-average earnings, the market PE in July 1932 was almost 70% below its 1881-1932 average. The q ratio was also indicating equities were very cheap. At the bottom of the market in July 1932, the q ratio had probably fallen below 0.3x. As in August 1921, equities were now trading at more than a 70% discount to the replacement value of their assets.

The good news, then, for the entrenched investor in the summer of 1932, was that equities were very cheap unless one believed that Roosevelt was intent on destroying capitalism in America. The bad news was that, using the cyclically adjusted PE as a measure of value, equities had been below their long-term average valuation since the middle of 1931. Since then the DJIA had declined by almost 70%.

Stocks also crashed through all previously accepted limits imposed by considerations of book value. Helpfully, the *Wall Street Journal* provided a table comparing price-to-book and price-to-working capital ratios for 21 of the 30 Dow Jones Industrial Average stocks on 18 May 1932, with comparison to the low prices of 1921.

117

Figure 56

KEY DJIA MEMBERS – PRICE TO BOOK AND PRICE TO WORKING CAPITAL

	% low price to book value		% low price to working capital	
	1932	**1921**	**1932**	**1921**
Allied Chemical	56	61	114	425
American Can	61	12	----	----
American Smelting	15	22	----	----
Bethlehem Steel	9	16	----	----
Eastman Kodak	67	144	158	151
General Electric	100	73	252	150
General Motors	60	81	512	----
Goodyear	33	108	----	----
International Harvester	26	41	47	69
International Nickel	48	37	----	804
Liggett & Myers	123	242	138	922
Mack Tucks	19	85	34	708
Sears-Roebuck	39	75	80	140
Standard Oil of California	39	115	273	728
Standard Oil of New Jersey	41	71	508	238
Texas Corp.	256	77	263	203
Texas Gulf Sulphur	126	124	269	206
Union Carbide	68	82	275	241
United States Steel	13	28	----	----
Westinghouse Electric	25	51	58	122
Woolworth	154	184	507	583

Source: *Wall Street Journal*, 19 May 1932. Note: The 1932 and 1921 low prices for the 21 stocks are shown in percentages of book value, excluding intangibles, and of equities in working capital, after deducting full par value of all prior obligations.

On a simple average, the numbers in Figure 56 show the 21 industrial stocks reaching a price-to-book ratio of 0.66x compared to 0.82x at the 1921 low. Of course, 18 May was not the bottom for the market and the DJIA was to fall a further 22% before hitting bottom, by which time the price-to-book ratio of the industrials market was around 0.52x.

Investors who believed the 1921 low of 0.82x would mark the bottom for the price-to-book ratio in 1932 witnessed a further 27% decline in the price of equities.

This shift in investor perceptions of what constituted value may well have been a reaction to the doubtful value accorded stocks at the top of the market.

During the roaring days of the bull market, lack of full information about a company gave its securities a certain 'mystery' value. The long depression has done a great deal to eliminate 'mystery' value from consideration of the worth of a security.[31]

---

[31] *Wall Street Journal*, 15 June 1932

In the late summer of 1929 investors had placed a premium on "mystery", but by the summer of 1932 they would demand a 50% discount on hard assets.

Good news and the bear

'I know, all right. I tell you, I know times is going to get better, and I'm not just guessing.'

'Send a telegram to Hoover about him and let him in on the secret,' Studs said.

James T. Farrell, *Judgement Day*

By the summer of 1932, faith in the whole financial system had collapsed along with the stock market. There were probably few laughs when Charlie Chaplin, on returning from a world tour, remarked to the press: 'I am reputedly a comedian, but after seeing the financial conditions of the world I have decided I am as much an economist as financiers are comedians.'[32]

As if to sum up the general mood, a *Wall Street Journal* headline of 12 May 1932 stated 'Inspiration Shuts Down'. The story referred to the closure of a mine in Arizona by Inspiration Copper, rather than the general malaise in the country. There were still those awaiting the cyclical economic rebound, though it was taking a long time to materialise. Since 1854, the average duration of an economic decline from peak to trough had been just 20 months. By July 1932, the country was in its 35th month of economic decline. The 1921 bottom for the equity market coincided with the bottoming of the economy - the NBER reference date of July 1921 confirms this. However, things are not as clear cut for 1932. The NBER reference date for the bottom of the recession is March 1933. It would appear that the equity market bottomed nine months before the economy.

There was an economic recovery which began in the summer of 1932, but it was knocked off course by a third banking crisis, this time following the election of Roosevelt as president in November. The economic contraction associated with this third crisis reduced economic activity to even lower levels than those witnessed in the summer of 1932 - just. Indeed, a future chairman of the Federal Reserve, Arthur Burns, in a book co-authored with Wesley Mitchell, described these two periods, summer

---

[32] *Wall Street Journal*, 15 June 1932

1932 and March 1933, as representing a "double bottom" for the economy.[33]

Figure 57

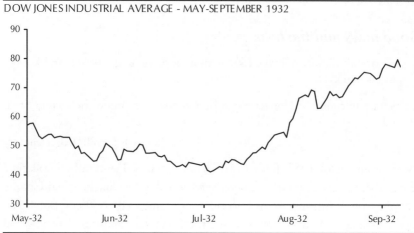

DOW JONES INDUSTRIAL AVERAGE - MAY-SEPTEMBER 1932

Source: Dow Jones & Co.

The stock market technically led the recovery in the economy, but it is almost as true to say that the market bottom coincided with this first bottom of the economy.

For those in the investment trenches in the summer of 1932, it is important to remember that the light seemingly peeping over the parapet proved to be a false dawn. The economic recovery had petered out by November 1932 and by March 1933 it was pretty much back where it had started in June 1932. The third banking crisis did not, however, return the DJIA to its July 1932 low. The index rose 94% from 8 July 1932 to 7 September 1932 and, by 27 February 1933, when it hit its low for that year, it was still 22% above the bear-market bottom of 8 July 1932. It is still debatable whether the equity market led, or coincided with, the recovery in the economy. It is clear, though, that confidence in the market never again subsided to the levels registered in July 1932.

In Part I, we heard a symphony of good news in 1921 from numerous sources as the stock market reached the bottom of the bear market, but investors seemed determined to focus on the negative. Things were different in 1932. By that July, the stock market had declined 89%, there had been two banking crises, wholesale prices had fallen 40%, and

[33]Arthur F. Burns and Wesley C. Mitchell, *Measuring Business Cycles*

industrial production had halved. The surprise collapse of banks and the ensuing consequences were beyond the experience of most investors. Even the great bear market of 1907 and the failure of the Knickerbocker Trust Company had not damaged investors on this scale. (On 21 October 1907, the National Bank of Commerce refused to honour cheques of Knickerbocker Trust, sparking runs on nearly every trust in New York.)[34] It is perhaps unsurprising that by July 1932, 34 months into the worst bear market and economic contraction in living memory, there was little left by way of optimism. Whereas in 1921 the newspapers were filled with largely good news, in 1932 good news was much thinner on the ground.

It should be stressed, however, that even at the darkest hour for American capitalism, not every piece of news was bad and not every commentator bearish.

Throughout this book we focus on the two-month period either side of the bear market bottom in an attempt to get a contemporaneous view of the market. Popular mythology has it that there is no good news around at the bottom of the market. If ever such an assertion was likely to be true, then one would expect it to be so as investors battled against the Great Depression. However, there was an ample supply of positive economic news in the pages of the *Wall Street Journal* in the summer of 1932:

9 May: An upturn in new passenger auto sales in excess of a normal seasonal gain in April. Reports at hand from seven states show an increase of 36% over March. The average gain from March to April in the preceding seven years was 30.5%.

10 May: The Norfolk plant of the Ford Motor Co. was in operation on a Saturday for the first time in four years.

16 May: April construction contract totals for the 37 states east of the Rocky Mountains showed an 8% gain over March in contrast to a loss of 9% between the corresponding two months of 1931. In public works the April gain over March was 93%.

16 May: Those people able to afford a new car, but who have not been buying, are now coming into the market.

16 May: Gradual industrial improvement noted in various parts of New Hampshire.

17 May: Building permits in 568 cities and towns of the United States during April showed a gain of 19.7% over the March figure, as compared with a normal seasonal expected decrease of 3.3%. The April total however was 30% below that for April 1931.

21 May: Increased employment reported in eight of the 16 major industrial groups.

---

[34] Robert Sobel, *Panic on Wall Street: A History of America's Financial Disasters*

121

22 May: The gradual stepping up of Ford output is having a marked effect in several quarters.

24 May: William Guggenheim, New York capitalist, in class reunion speech at University of Pennsylvania states: "A little light that brings with it a ray of hope is emerging from the industrial chaos and gloom. We are approaching the completion of the adjustments that were necessary."

24 May: Stutz Motor Car Co. has many new orders on hand and will begin operating on a 6-day weekly schedule effective immediately.

25 May: Inventories are at a low ebb and any demand of importance would find shelves bare of stocks.

30 May: H. A. Scandrett, president of St. Paul, said agricultural conditions in the road's territory were never better and that if they continued so there would be an early movement of grain traffic.

11 June: Chevrolet Sales Curve Rising.

13 June: Detroit - General Business Reflects Continued Pickup in Automobile Sales

15 June: Near exhaustion of consumer supplies points toward possible early trend upward of prices and recovery of business, according to P.A. O'Connell of Boston, president of National Retail Dry Goods Association, speaking at organization's annual convention in Pittsburgh.

17 June: The head of one of the leading wholesale hardware houses in Toledo declared that there had been a noticeable pick up recently in demand

from local dealers, who were building up inventories. He declared that similar upswings in demand from the same sources had preceded upturns in general business after previous periods of intense depression. He was inclined to regard the turn as most significant.

18 June: After an unprofitable first quarter, business of the Caterpillar Tractor Co. turned for the better in April with the result that net for the month of May aggregated $73,826 equivalent to 4 cents a share

20 June: Employment decreased 3.2%, in May and payroll totals 3.9%, as compared with April. Of the 16 groups of employment, decreases in both employment and earnings were shown in 10. The auto industry reported an increase of 1.5% in employment and a gain of 13.5% in payrolls.

21 June: Fisher's index of commodity prices slipped to another new low, but the wholesale price index of the National Fertilizer Association recorded the first gain in two months rising to 60 from 59.6. A greater number of commodity prices advanced than for any week during the last several months. Included on the list of commodities that showed advanced prices were cotton, burlap, lard, flour, sugar, corn, wheat, cattle, hogs, tin and gasoline.

25 June: Present indications are that both retail and wholesale distribution of seasonal merchandise is improving in the Chicago market area.

3 July: The upward tend which was begun a week ago in commodity prices continued during the past week, according to Professor Irving Fisher's weekly index for wholesale commodity prices in this country. For the week ended July 1, index rose 0.1 to 59.6, which compares with the record low of 59.3 established on June 17. This marks at least a temporary break in the prolonged drop in the index which continued from last March without interruption.

6 July: Danbury's hat industry, dormant since the short-lived 'Eugenie' hat boom, awoke suddenly today, with two of the largest factories swinging into capacity operation.

6 July: Belief that bottom of business depression has been reached is expressed by Charles Edison, son of Thomas A. Edison and head of Edison Industries, Inc., following his return from six weeks tour of United States.

7 July: Wholesale Price Index of the National Fertilizer Association advanced for a third consecutive week.

7 July: Asinof & Sons, Inc., Chicopee Mass., woollen clothing manufacturers, whose plant has been closed since May 1, announce work to be resumed on full schedule this week, giving employment to about 750 people.

8 July: New High For Sugar.

8 July: DJIA bottoms.

9 July: World commodity markets responded to the reparations agreement reached at Lausanne by a quickening of outside interest and by fairly sharp price mark-ups in several of them, led by hogs and sugar, both of which went into new high ground on the current movement.

11 July: Bank suspensions for the past week dropped to 24 from 41 the week previous, the American Banker reports.

14 July: Crop conditions in territory of Chicago & North Western Ry. show record promise and the season is practically far enough advanced that the only 'if' appears to be in prices, according to Henry W. Beyers, Vice-President in charge of traffic.

14 July: The advance in hide prices in the past ten days, up 35% from the lows reached a short while ago, should prove beneficial to U.S. Leather Co..

16 July: Hoover Cuts Own Pay 20% And Cabinet Members 15%.

21 July: Advance from 40 to 50 cents a barrel for cement in the Middle West is the first price increase of consequences since 1929. In May last year the final cut occurred, bringing prices to the lowest level in 15 years.

21 July: Although the radio business is going through its quietest period of the year, many dealers have been surprised at their volume of sales.

22 July: "Economic crises in the past century have all ended with a firming of commodity and bond prices. Both of these indications are visible today." Barnet, Fuerst & Co..

26 July: More than 15,000 idle New Englanders have been recalled to their jobs or given new jobs as result of a business spurt during the past few weeks, a survey reveals.

1 August: Travelling representatives of the automobile manufacturers, who have first hand knowledge of conditions in every section of the country, have found business generally firming up and the public in a more optimistic frame of mind.

1 August: Steel prices are holding better than at any time since the depression started.

1 August: Cocksure conclusions concerning the near future are not unlikely to prove embarrassing. But they are unnecessary at the present stage of affairs; what is more, they would be far less practical use than the definitely observable signs that ultimate recovery is on the way.

2 August: Surplus transportation, as represented by used car stocks, is being rapidly consumed. During June stocks of used cars in the United States were reduced by 10% and during the first 20 days of July by an additional 16%.

2 August: Willys-Overland stepped up its July production schedule 20% above that originally planned as result of demand for the new streamline series... compared with the first half of July last year, the gain this year was 23%.

3 August: Although business activity continued to recede during June, and in the early part of July, several recent constructive developments have contributed to an improvement in sentiment, the survey of current business, published by Department of Commerce, says.

3 August: Many favourable factors have appeared in trade and general business during the last few months, according to the monthly report of the Federal Reserve Bank of Dallas.

3 August: Shelves are bare, manufacturer, middlemen and retailers say any turn for the better in trade would turn a replacement business into an anxious demand which might in many industries be difficult to fill.

3 August: Bradstreet's commodity index of wholesale prices scored its second consecutive monthly advance on August 1st. It increased 1.0%. In all previous business cycles, Bradstreet's finds that the first improvement occurred in the very sensitive raw materials and then gradually, the betterment became more general, affecting semi-finished and then finished articles. This seems to be the present course of commodity prices.

6 August: Roy D. Chapin, new Secretary of Commerce, says there is no doubt "depression has run its course" and that "the job now is to unleash the buying power".

8 August: Dispatches from industrial centres, while furnishing testimony to the dullness of industry generally, detailed high hopes.

8 August: London Economist expresses belief that United States has passed crisis finding that credit expansion policy has been beneficial and that public psychology has become steadier.

9 August: Chicago - Operators of the leading State Street, neighbourhood and outlying dry goods stores here are unanimous in expressing conviction that their business is showing fundamental improvement.... Prices of leading lines are developing still further.

13 August: St. Louis - A pronounced spurt in orders for dry goods during the past few days, with unit volume exceeding that booked for any similar period so far this year and comparing favourably with sales a year ago.

15 August: The motor industry is feeling the first effects of the improved sentiment which pervades business.

Retail sales have been stimulated and buying interest has become more active. Interest is being revived in the higher priced cars, and increased sales are being reported.

17 August: There is a distinctly brighter outlook in American grocery industry, says Paul S. Willis, president of Associated Grocery Manufacturers, who finds public is turning to quality rather than low-cost goods.

19 August: F.A. Merrick, president of the Westinghouse Electric & Manufacturing Co., says "The natural forces of recuperation have begun to operate, and it is gratifying that evidences of their working are becoming increasingly apparent. The appreciation of prices of commodities and securities and the upturn in business of the smaller units must precede the full normal functioning of the business world as a whole."

19 August: "Steady improvement in business sentiment in all lines is being reflected strongly in a broader buying movement. The outlook is brighter than at any time in the last six months, and for some branches of activity better than at any time in the last two years." - Dun's Review.

19 August: While the advance in wholesale prices has continued for more than two months, retail prices have been lagging, but must of necessity soon begin a general rise if the wholesale price levels are maintained.

20 August: "Within the last two weeks unmistakable indications of a trend upward have made their appearance.... For 18 months we have purposely refrained from making predictions. Now we feel there is a tangible basis upon which to become definitely optimistic." A. Vanderzee, general sales manager of Dodge Brs. Corp.

22 August: The weekly steel trade reviews were more encouraging in tone. While operations for the most recent week are up only 1% there are definite signs of an increase in demand, particularly for light steel.

22 August: A renewal of confidence, increased activity, together with a decidedly improved sentiment, was evident in many lines of trade during the past week in Chicago.

22 August: Improvement in general business is indicated in reports of several Detroit manufacturing concerns.

22 August: US Employment Service states July saw the first really noticeable expansion in industrial activity that has occurred so far this year.

23 August: Recent commodity price increases caught many retail merchants 'short' and sent them scrambling to replenish inventories that had been cut to the limit.

29 August: One of the best recognized signs of better times is the fact that prosperity is hitting New England first, said W.L. Hinds, vice-president of the Crouse-Hinds Co., electrical manufacturers. "Because of the character of its industry, New England always leads the way out of a national business slump."

29 August: In some lines, particularly the rayon and textile industries, there has been a marked change for the better.

29 August: Responding to the improved tone of general business, truck sales have begun to pick up, particularly in lighter-weight lines. It is normal for the truck branch of the motor industry to feel the first effects of a recovery in general business. Due to hard usage replacement demand rises first.

30 August: Iowa's business morale has strengthened with the steady rise in hog prices. Hog prices made their 17th consecutive advance yesterday.

2 September: Inquiries received by Chicago Association of Commerce for products made in that district increased more than 35% in the past three weeks.

3 September: The most significant trend of consumer buying thus far in fall

lines is the rather clearly defined preference for better goods. This has brought with it a stepping-up of industrial operations, and many factories which had been idle for months again are turning their wheels in anticipation of a swelling tide of purchasing derived from the absolute necessity of replacing worn-out articles of every-day service and a venturing forth of idle funds in search of practical buying opportunities.

5 September: London *Economist*, edited by Sir Walter Layton, sees possibility of substantial economic recovery in United States "as result of existing natural forces backed by the stimulus of controlled inflation now being applied."

News reports alone do not provide the evidence that it was time to buy equities. But, reading back through them, any investor must reconsider whether all news must be bad before the market can hit bottom. Even in the darkest days of 1932 – when things were so bad President Hoover resisted pay cuts for soldiers in case he needed them to quell a revolution - there was still ample good news to be found.

As in 1921, the investor's ability to ignore good news, rather than the predominance of bad news, characterised the end of the bear market in 1932.

In both 1921 and 1932, the motor industry was in the vanguard of recovery and news of improvement from New England was particularly noticeable. In both periods, evidence of the pickup in demand, against a background of falling prices, became noticeable first in higher-quality, higher-priced goods. However, the most striking similarity in the two periods is that a positive chain of events began once evidence of price stability returned to the commodity markets. It is these price trends, evident from the headlines of the day, which provided the most accurate indicator that the bear market in equities was coming to an end.

Price stability and the bear

'Look, Bill, at that gorgeous black crepe. It's only twelve dollars. Clothes are dirt cheap now.'

James T. Farrell, *Judgement Day*

Signs of price stability, as in 1921, coincided with the bottom of the bear market in 1932. As in 1921, growing stability in selected commodity prices broadened to include more commodities and finally reached the wholesale price index.

We discussed in Part I the importance of price adjustments to the operation of the business cycle in a gold-standard regime. Stability in commodity prices seems to have played a role even when, in 1932 as in 1921, the US was one of the few nations still operating a gold standard. Whatever complications the free float of other currencies brought to assessing the outlook for the gold standard, the stability of commodity prices still seems to have been important in defining when the economic cycle was nearing bottom. At the first sign of an upturn in commodity and wholesale price indices in the long bear market from September 1929, the equity market stabilised and moved higher.

Figure 58

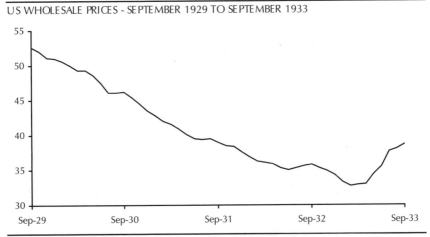

US WHOLESALE PRICES - SEPTEMBER 1929 TO SEPTEMBER 1933

Source: National Bureau of Economic Research

The key difference between July 1932 and August 1921 is that the improvement in wholesale prices that developed in 1932 was not sustained. Economic growth began to stall around November of 1932, and by March 1933 economic activity was probably just below the July 1932 level. A similar trend was evident for wholesale prices, the difference being that prices clearly fell below their July 1932 lows. The wholesale price index of the Bureau of Labor reached its 1932 low in June, but by February 1933, following a rally that ended in November, the index was 6.6% below the June 1932 level. However even at their 1933 lows equity prices remained 20% higher than the levels reached in July 1932. A sustainable advance in wholesale prices began in February 1933 and this coincided with the most dramatic period of appreciation in the equity bull market which was to last until 1937.

The lesson for the investor from 1921 and 1932 is that increasing stability in commodity and wholesale prices is an important indicator that the bottom of the stock market is close. In 1921, the sign that such stability was sustainable was the unwillingness of producers to sell their products forward, and that the country was operating with very low inventory levels. As the quotations above from the *WSJ* illustrate, similar considerations were noted in the summer of 1932. On 15 May 1932, the *Wall Street Journal* listed a much larger range of factors at play, under the headline 'Anti-Deflation Forces Spread', indicating commodity prices would stabilise. The factors were:

Federal Reserve purchases of government securities.

Excessively low return on capital in New York.

A probable cut in New York rediscount rate in near future.

Willingness of Bank of England to cooperate.

Successive reductions of Bank of England rate to 2½% from 6%.

Accumulation of £13,500,000 gold by British Treasury since March.

Piling up of idle capital in Paris, and in Switzerland and other "neutral" countries.

Suspension of the gold standard and currency depreciation in a score of countries.

Continued gold flow from India.

As in 1921, it was easier to watch for these signs of improvement rather than pick a price level in advance at which the adjustment process must be over. In 1921, many predicted deflation would have to carry prices back to pre-war levels. This did not occur, and prices and the equity market bottomed well before such an adjustment. Similarly in 1932, it was almost impossible to judge in advance at what level the price adjustment was complete. The wholesale price index sank below the 1921 cyclical low, below the 1913 pre-war level, and kept falling until it reached the 1907 level. Within this average measure of decline, some producers had to cope with even more serious adjustments. In early June 1932, Procter & Gamble cut the price of *Ivory* soap to its 1879 launch price. The price of sugar was back to its 1895 level, and copper, lead and zinc hit 50-year lows. Things were even worse in the cotton market, which bottomed around its 1848 level.[35] In this environment watching for key signs of price stabilisation was much easier than forecasting the "correct" price at which the wheels of commerce would begin again to turn.

Signs that such deflation was ending in summer 1932 proved a very bullish indicator for the equity market. As usual, some commentators were more prescient than others. John D. Rockefeller, who had the good fortune to be born on 8 July, sounded suitably upbeat in his announcement to the nation released the same day as the stock market bottomed. 'These are the days when many are discouraged,' he said.

> In the 93 years of my life, depressions have come and gone. Prosperity has always returned, and will again. And now on my birthday, I desire to reaffirm my belief in the fundamental principles upon which this country was founded - liberty, unselfish devotion to the common good, and belief in God.[36]

He urged Americans to 'recognize with humility our mistakes of extravagance, selfishness and indifference, let us, with faith in God, in ourselves and in humanity, go forward, courageously resolved to play our part worthily in building a better world'. Measured in today's terms, Rockefeller had amassed a fortune in excess of $200 billion, larger than Bill Gates and Warren Buffet combined. No doubt the American people were amused to hear that 'devotion to the common good' was one of the key principles that would bring them through hard times. Maybe they remembered the exhortations of the then 90-year-old Rockefeller in a statement issued on Wednesday 30 October 1929.

> Believing that fundamental conditions of the country are sound and that there is nothing in the business situation to warrant the destruction of

---

[35] *Wall Street Journal*, 10 June 1932
[36] *Wall Street Journal*, 8 July 1932

values that has taken place... my son and I have for some days been purchasing sound common stocks.[37]

Liquidity and the bear

If he kept it at home he might be robbed. If he socked it in a bank, the bank might go under. If he bought stock, the market might crash. Christ, what a goofy world it was becoming.

James T. Farrell, *Judgement Day*

Investors looking to find the end of equity bear markets often look for signs from the actions of the Federal Reserve and improvements in liquidity. In Part I, we saw just how difficult it was to forecast the gyrations in the new elastic currency. Assessing changes in liquidity is difficult enough, even with the predictability of the operation of the gold standard, but the liquidity forecasting business had been significantly complicated with the birth of the Federal Reserve System in 1914. In 1918-20 the elastic currency was expanded well beyond what almost anyone had predicted as the Federal Reserve Board sought to support the government's war financing activities. Unfortunately for Fed watchers the contraction of the elastic currency continued long after the stock market and the economy had bottomed in the summer of 1921.

Those awaiting stability in Fed credit outstanding to indicate better liquidity and a better stock market were still waiting in the middle of 1924, three years after the equity market had bottomed. The past inability of market commentators to forecast Fed activities and their impact on liquidity may account for the lack of positive comments on liquidity in the press in the summer of 1932. Of all the positive comments from the *WSJ* noted above on the outlook for the US economy only London's *Economist* mentioned improvement in liquidity as an important factor.[38] The general lack of enthusiasm for easier liquidity as a stock market indicator is particularly interesting when one considers the Fed began a material injection of liquidity into the financial system in April 1932 just prior to the equity market bottom.

The *WSJ* tried to explain to its readers how the Fed's new policy was

---

[37] Maury Klein, *Rainbow's End: The Crash of 1929*
[38] *Wall Street Journal*, 5 September 1932

supposed to work with the Federal Reserve buying government bonds and issuing checks for the purpose.

> The checks given for the bonds will be deposited in banks and thence pass back to the Reserve banks, either in payment for past rediscounts or for credit in the reserve accounts of the member banks, where the credit will serve as the reserve base for a possible expansion of member bank loans or investments in at least 10 times the volume.[39]

This all sounds straightforward and was presumably why Secretary of the Treasury Andrew Mellon believed the Federal Reserve System was the antidote to the business cycle. However how could one predict when the Fed would apply the antidote? Those invested in equities and relying on the provision of the antidote to cure the depression had lost most of their capital by early 1932. There had been a long-standing argument within the Fed as to the impact of putting money into circulation via purchase of government securities or bills. Famously, the Federal Reserve Bank of New York plunged into the market in late October 1929, buying $160 million of government securities despite only having explicit authorisation from the Federal Reserve Board for purchases up to $25 million. The Board strongly disapproved of the action and there was a general feeling that such actions would delay necessary liquidation and promote speculation. The New York Fed continued to lobby for a stretching of the elastic currency from November 1929 right through to the run on the dollar caused by the devaluation of sterling in September 1931. However the persuasive powers of the New York institution had been dented by the death in 1928 of its long-serving Governor Benjamin Strong. The Federal Reserve Board ignored the calls from New York for the administering of Andrew Mellon's antidote. So an investor seeking to find the liquidity turnaround in 1929-32 would have had to be privy to this debate and have realised that the Board would be victorious over the New York Fed.

The Federal Reserve System had been created to rescue the country from just the type of national financial emergency which was now developing. The institution's relative inaction, given its general activism since its creation in 1914, was a particularly difficult factor to understand and forecast in 1929-32. The Board continued to hold the upper hand over the New York Bank, and Federal Reserve credit outstanding showed no sign of increasing until late summer 1931. Then from August 1931 to October

---

[39] *Wall Street Journal*, 7 May 1932

1931, total bills and securities held by the Federal Reserve banks rose from $930 million to $2,062 million. However, this policy soon came to an enforced end on the devaluation of sterling. Even the Federal Reserve Bank of New York accepted that the expansive open market policy could not now continue as a drain on gold from the US developed. Not until January 1932 was the New York Bank again pushing the Board to launch a programme of open-market purchases. In April, the Board did again authorise a major purchase of securities, a move largely attributed to fear of Congress taking legislative action rather than any acceptance that the New York Fed's arguments were correct. The role of Congress in forcing the Fed's change of policy is further suggested by the fact that the expansion of Fed credit essentially ceased when Congress adjourned on 16 July.

Figure 59

PEAKS AND TROUGHS OF BILLS, SECURITIES DISCOUNTED BY FEDERAL RESERVE	
Peak October 1920	$3,358m
Trough July 1924	$827m
Peak December 1928	$1,766m
Trough July 1931	$906m
Peak October 1931	$2,062m
Trough March 1932	$1,635m
Highest level March 1932-March 1933	$2,407m

Source: Federal Reserve, *Banking and Monetary Statistics*

Figure 59 shows the inactivity of the Fed in providing liquidity to the system until July 1931. But the equity market did not respond to the injection of liquidity from August to October 1931, presumably as these open-market purchases coincided with a worsening of the international position and sterling's departure from the gold standard. When the Fed tried a similar policy in April 1932, investors were sceptical given the market's failure to react positively in the fall. Another reason was that the Fed's actions served to merely offset the impact of the gold outflow. The Fed's actions also coincided with a major series of bank failures in Chicago, which produced further withdrawals of cash from the banking system. From 8 June to 6 July, currency in circulation had increased by $32 million as the public withdrew further sums from the banking system. It seems the introduction of a 2¢ tax on cheques may also have played a role in persuading the public to hold ever more cash instead of deposits. The new policy of open-market purchases, even to the extent that it offset these negative factors, was not a success. The policy was accurately judged to be driven by short-term political expediency and commercial bankers were cautious in using the new funds.

It is now clearly apparent that banks are not willing to use the surplus funds being put at their disposal by the Federal Reserve until they have a clearer idea of taxes and the budget.[40]

Bankers rushed to defend their inaction. A report from the Guaranty Trust Company on 1 June explained that the banks would be happy to make more commercial loans and to extend lines of credit to deserving businesses and predicted that this would happen when domestic consumption picked up.

A resumption of normal purchasing by the public will be quickly followed by an expansion of bank loans. The latter must follow, but cannot precede, such action.

This reasoning may have been correct. The *WSJ* reported on 16 June even the pawnbrokers were flush with liquidity.

New York City pawnbrokers report sharp drop in business due to reluctance of people to incur indebtedness under current conditions and to depreciated value of pledged articles. Much of their money is lying idle.

By June 1932, the increase in the reserves of Fed's member banks was half the amount lost since the second banking crisis started. The improved financial condition of the commercial banks had no noticeable impact on their willingness to extend loans, and this was recognised very rapidly by the market as indicating 'very clearly a continuance of drastic deflation, despite the Federal Reserve's policy of controlled credit expansion'.[41]

This instant assessment of the credit policy proved correct. Some weeks showed an improvement and caused some excitement, but on a monthly basis the decline in loans continued until April 1933. The transmission mechanism had failed. However, something did happen at exactly this stage of the depression as commodity prices began to rise and the economy began to recover.

It is clearly difficult to link this response by commodity prices directly to the open-market purchases of the Federal Reserve, given that those actions did not succeed in producing credit creation. However, there may have been indirect effects and it is notable that the amount of currency held by the public peaked in July 1932, and the deposit-currency ratio improved marginally for the rest of the year. Willingness to maintain deposit levels showed improved faith in the banking system, perhaps because of the Fed's

---

[40] *Wall Street Journal*, 30 May 1932
[41] *Wall Street Journal*, 12 July 1932

action to create liquidity. The lessening of public fear may have helped to stabilise commodity prices and produce economic recovery in the summer of 1932. Whether it did, the lesson for investors was the high danger inherent in calling the bottom of the equity market based solely on the Fed's move to ease liquidity. One can speculate that the Fed's action played an indirect role in stabilising commodity prices and boosting economic activity but there is no evidence that it had the expected direct impact on the economy by boosting credit creation.

For an investor to bet that the Fed's new policy would work by indirectly producing a stabilisation in consumer sentiment and feeding through to an economic recovery would have been a risky one to make, given the absence of such a response to a similar policy pursued from August to October 1931. Entering the equity market when the Fed first adopted such a policy, in August 1931, would have meant exposure to a further 69% decline in the DJIA. Perhaps the brave investor, unperturbed, would have committed to the market in April 1932 when the second material open-market purchase drive was launched. But from April to July that investor would have lost one-third of the investment. Those who committed funds when the Fed's open-market operations indicated easier liquidity were badly burned from August 1931 to July 1932.

In Part I, we analysed the changes in broad money growth and credit growth in the search for indicators of a bear market bottom. The search yielded little in 1921 and, if anything, produced an even smaller harvest in 1932. It was 1935 before total loans of the US commercial banking system bottomed and credit growth resumed. A focus on broad money-supply growth also fails to point to any trigger point for buying equities in July 1932. If judged in either nominal or real terms, it would not be until the end of the first quarter of 1933 that an improvement in broad money could be said to have been underway.

Perhaps this was just not the time to expect monetary analysis to have all the answers. How could one analyse monetary statistics to assess the turnaround in a psychological malaise in which the very use of money itself was in question? The loss of faith is illustrated by the situation in South Carolina, where mill workers agreed to accept cloth in payment for an extra week's work a month. Merchants and farmers in the vicinity agreed 'in so far as possible' to accept the cloth in payment for goods.[42] And across the

---

[42] Wall Street Journal, 30 May 1932

civilized world, desire for gold had never been stronger.

> If we may judge by the 'premium' being paid - in francs be it noted! - of close upon 25% upon curb transactions in American double-eagles in Paris - and, where coin is not available, on slivers of gold cut from bullion.[43]

In such extreme situations, crunching monetary statistics in the search for evidence of financial stability is probably not the best use of one's time.

The bulls and the bear

> He thought of how his stock was now down to ten, and he had to make up his mind whether to hold it or sell. A drop from two thousand to eight hundred dollars, and Ike Dugan had said fluctuations. That bastard was going to have fluctuations the next time he met Studs Lonigan.

> James T. Farrell, *Judgement Day*

In 1932, as in 1921, there were many prognostications on the direction of the equity market. In 1932, as in 1921, those investors who advanced the theory that returning price stability would mark the turning point of the market were proven correct. As in 1921, trying to judge the bottom of the equity market using liquidity analysis was fraught with problems. In the investment trenches, though, there are often perhaps more tactical than strategic ways of assessing how the battle is proceeding and there are numerous comparisons between 1921 and 1932.

Figure 60

DOW JONES INDUSTRIAL AVERGAGE - 8 MAY TO 8 OCTOBER 1932

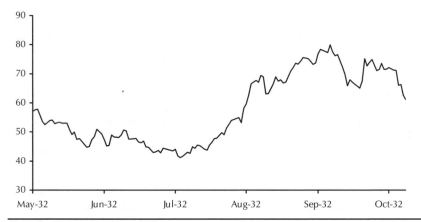

Source: Dow Jones & Co.

---

[43] *Wall Street Journal*, 7 June 1932

The following notes from the *Wall Street Journal* show the view from the investment trenches in the summer of 1932.

9 May: The absence of momentum of upswings had been due to unusually small shorting interest and lack of inducement for important buying.

9 May: Sharpest upward movement in months. Hoover's plea to balance the budget was the cause.

12 May: It is significant, in reviewing markets over the past month, that when volume of trading has been above the average, prices have been rising, whereas declines, for the most part, have been accomplished on a small volume of trading which has shown no disposition to increase as lower levels have been reached.

13 May: If the government's program, as finally outlined, contemplates a definite policy of embarking on inflation, a rise in stock prices undoubtedly would develop.

17 May: Action by the Senate Democratic leaders welcome - joining Republicans to urge speedy enactment of the tax bill touched off a late rally.

21 May: Overnight announcement of the formation of a committee of twelve bankers and industrialists to aid in putting to work the huge store of funds being poured into the market by the Federal Reserve Systems' credit expansion policy injected a new element of hope into the securities market yesterday. Just what the newly formed committee's program will be remained in doubt, buy any effect from its endeavours might well be first reflected in the bond market. While other developments may give a temporary fillip to the securities markets, it is hard to see how any rallies can make headway until Washington news is more constructive.

25 May: Weakest were the food company and the tobacco shares, which so far have held up the best in the long decline. In many quarters, weakness in these issues was attributed to the selling of stocks which had held up the best to protect accounts hard hit by weakness in other securities. New lows in the food group were numerous.

26 May: The sharp increase in volume yesterday indicated that the market might be approaching a climax.

27 May: AT&T into new low ground.

28 May: The apathy of an extremely dull pre-holiday stock market was shaken by a 60% reduction in the General Electric quarterly dividend.

28 May: Interest in stock market was practically non-existent in the morning.

2 June: Reports of a formation of a new stabilization corporation. The Federal Reserve's policy of controlled credit expansion has permitted the piling up of a huge amount of excess reserves by most important banking institutions. Some of these reserves, at least, will be put to work through purchases of debentures of the proposed corporation, according to indications. Stocks scored abrupt rallies early in yesterday's session, stimulated by the Senate's final passage of the tax bill. If the proposed economy measure is put through a balance budget should result. Since

March 8, the Dow-Jones averages of industrial, railroad and utility stocks have shrunk from around 50% to more than 60%. The very depth of the decline seems to indicate that the market is somewhere near a turn.

6 June: The recovery has been similar to a number of other swift reversals in the markets during the long deflation in security prices. Each of its predecessors has brought the hope that a definite turning point has been reached, only to have hopes dashed by the subsequent reaction.

11 June: In stocks the day saw a number of striking advances, but they were mostly at the expense of an overcrowded and nervous short interest, which was evidently impressed by what happened to the unfortunate group in Auburn. Starting out with an overnight gain of about 5 points, Auburn pushed steadily ahead, and at one time was up over 20 points. Other stocks with a large short interest showed abrupt upswings, particularly J.J. Case, Columbia Carbon and International Business Machine.

11 June: Not all the day's news was favourable but the market paid little attention to the bad.

13 June: On balance Europe appears to be buying American securities in the local market thus checking the steady wave of liquidation from overseas which was a contributing factor in the weak market New York experienced over the past several weeks.

15 June: Stock prices generally were higher, and at times the market gave clear indications of a disposition to turn definitely strong.

Strength of the dollar in comparison to foreign currencies gave impetus to the forward movement in stock prices which prevailed much of the session.

16 June: Considerable significance attached to manner in which the market acted during the day. Trading volume subsided during periods of reaction, and increased when stocks moved ahead. In addition, the fact that the leading stocks gave the best performance, and gave evidence of concerted buying, was considered noteworthy.

17 June: Street taking its cue from the bond market these days as the trading element realizes that without an advance in bonds, permanent improvement in stocks can hardly be anticipated.

21 June: Trading fell to approximately 400,000 shares for the full five-hour session, the lowest for any full days trading since June 2 1924. Monday's 400,000 shares contrast with 16,410,000 the record on October 29, 1929 when stocks broke badly. On that day the turnover in one issue - General Motors common - amounted to 971,300 shares (the record for an individual issue) or twice the total volume on Monday.

23 June: Though new lows were set in some of the leaders, the rest of the list was steady in the face of these declines.

24 June: Pressure from liquidation again was evident in individual issues, notably American Can, which struck a new low level during the session, and American Telephone. The latter hovered within a fraction of its previous low but recovered substantially in the afternoon and marked up a fair gain for the day.

25 June: The deflation in stock prices, and that is a mild word for it, has carried prices down to a level where better than 50% of the stocks traded in are selling for under $10 a share. In Thursday's trading, transactions took place in 422 issues. Of this number 226 sold at $10 a share or less... not a single common stock sold at $100 or better.

28 June: The breakthrough of the industrial average was distinctly disquieting. Alone, it is not a conclusive signal, but if it is confirmed by the rails, under the Dow theory it clearly indicates that the long deflation is not over. [Dow-Jones Industrials breaks May low].

29 June: The stock of General Foods was not disturbed by the reduction in dividend payments to 50 cents quarterly against 75 cents previously. New lows-US Steel, Coca-Cola, General Motors, National Biscuit, Sears-Roebuck, Union Pacific and AT&T.

30 June: During the day, the Democratic conclave in Chicago offered very little in the way of news to affect the securities markets... Dispatches from Lausanne served to confirm the impression, included in the overnight news, that the conference was near a complete breakdown, without having made any contribution to a solution of the pressing European economic problems.

2 July: Such stocks as represent equities in sound companies possessed of current financial strength and fundamentally good operating prospects, with a fair modicum of earning power even under present conditions, may be regarded as distinctly attractive for the long pull at present market prices. Following is a brief list of stocks of the type we have in mind: American Telephone & Telegraph, Consolidated Gas, United Gas Improvement, Pacific Gas & Electric, Chesapeake & Ohio, American Tobacco B, United States Tobacco, Procter & Gamble, American Home Products, Continental Can, E.I. du Pont de Nemours, William Wrigley Jr., American Chicle, Borden, Corn Products.

3 July: On June 27th the industrials closed at 42.93 more than a point below the previous bottom of 44.74 set on May 31st. To students of the Dow Theory, the break through in the industrials average was a warning, but not a clear signal, because confirmation from the rails was lacking and has been lacking since that time. The rail average set a low of 14.10 on June 1. On June 27 it fell to 13.76, only fractionally below the previous bottom, and so far has not gone a full point under the June 1 low....There have been very clear signs of resistance to selling pressure in the rails. Even in the face of the distressingly poor earnings statements for the month of May, the rails have held. The evidence of support in the railroad list and the ability of the average to hold only slightly under the resistance point are significant to the student of the averages.

8 July: [DJIA bottoms]

11 July: While Wall Street generally continues to pay more attention to fears of possible adverse news than to concrete actions which have tremendous potentialities for long-term improvement, there has been investment buying, both here and abroad.

11 July: Several leading stocks broke through their previous low levels late in the week, including American Telephone, Coca Cola, Eastman Kodak, Union Pacific, Public Service of N.J., International Shoe and International Business Machine.

11 July: Common stock of Coca Cola has been subject to considerable short selling... this selling, which has been by traders who believe that the return of beer of a higher alcoholic content than ½ of 1% is rapidly becoming a probability. Robert W. Woodruff, President of Coca Cola pointed out that in Montreal, where the sale of alcoholic beverages has been permitted for some time, sales of Coca Cola are more then double the per capita sales of the United States.

12 July: Shareholders of RCA numbered 103,851 on December 31, 1931. A year ago on June 30 the total was 93,000 and on the same date of 1928 there were 25,000 stock holders.

12 July: Notwithstanding the fact that at the close of the market on Tuesday, July 5, all of the Dow-Jones averages were within half a point or so of the lows for the year and for the depression, a long list of stocks and bonds listed on the New York Stock Exchange at that time showed advances of 50% or more from the low prices of the year. [List shows 67 stocks 50% or more above their 1932 lows the day the market bottomed on 8 July.]

14 July: The Anglo-French accord agreeing to a united front on political and financial matters affecting the welfare of Europe, was the chief matter of interest. Foreign buying of American stocks has been in somewhat larger volume in the past few days according to some sources...For a period of months, from early March until late June, foreign trading in the market, except for occasional short selling, was relatively negligible.

15 July: The action of stocks in the face of quite a number of unfavourable developments, was particularly encouraging. Unquestionably, the hope of nearby adjournment of Congress, which might provide a stimulus for a rally, remained the prime factor in the upswing. [Congress adjourned next day].

20 July: Interims coming to hand. The Street is resigning itself to the fact that most of them will not offer pleasant reading but on the other hand it is obvious that the securities of most of the companies reporting have long since discounted this fact.

22 July: At Thursday's closing price Aluminium Co. Stock was 80% above its low point this year of $22 a share and Gulf was 39% higher than its low of $22. The Dow-Jones industrial average has risen 13% from the 1932 low.

22 July: There was short covering in AT&T. Reports of such companies as AT&T, Auburn, du Pont, Nash, National Biscuit, Otis Elevator, Union Oil of California and United Fruit, showing that none of these companies earned its dividend requirements for the period are among those shares which have rallied in the last day or two some substantially.

25 July: IT&T holders number 100,745. On December 31 1929 there were 53,594. In the first annual report of the company as of December 31, 1921, the number of stockholders was given as 846.

25 July: Volume fell off materially on the declines and the market managed to consolidate its recent gains without yielding appreciable ground.

25 July: The importance of the recent advance in bonds is beginning to make itself felt in stocks. In many cases bonds are in marginal accounts for collateral purposes and any sharp rise in bonds gives such accounts greater buying power.

26 July: During periods of hesitancy when prices dipped off slightly activity was sharply curtailed. Volume picked up sharply as prices worked higher. The action of the market was in sharp contrast to the long period of decline from early March to early June, when volume dried up on any recoveries, and increased during periods of weakness.

26 July: Although sceptics have held that the current price advance is largely professional and therefore not to be taken too seriously, there has, nevertheless, been a substantial amount of buying by those who reason that their favourite stocks are cheap on current earnings even if there is no prospect of any immediate business improvement.

30 July: Trend line from September 1929 finally broken, providing in our opinion conclusive technical evidence that the major bear movement has definitely been succeeded not by a minor recovery but by a bull swing.

1 August: The reaction after the sharp upturn, looked for in many quarters has not materialized, and stocks have pushed steadily ahead, absorbing profit-taking and liquidation in fairly easy fashion.

Immediate cause for the break of the exchanges was found in the rush of

bears to cover their open short positions taken in forward dollar exchange during the flight from the dollar last spring. These positions for the most part were never closed in expectations of further unfavourable developments in this country...Previously convinced that the United States was headed for economic chaos, the sight of rising security prices brought conviction that the United States after all furnished the best opportunity for capital investment and appreciation.

5 August: In spite of evidence that many in the Street continued to fight the advance and that both short selling and profit-taking were in the market throughout the session, prices in most instances attained new highs in the most active market since October, 1931.

6 August: While prices eased during the afternoon, it was apparent that substantial resistance was being encountered on the decline, and there was no evidence of any major extension of the reaction.

8 August: The Street believes the short position in many stocks is still as large as it was a month ago a belief which the Exchange's figures on the short interest as of August tends to bear out.

9 August: All capitals of Europe have probably done more trading in our securities in the past week than in over a year and certainly more buying that at any time since the 1929 crash.

12 August: In the face of the largest month's percentage advance in the aggregate security values since the depression started, total known security loans declined $112,000,000 in July to the lowest level on record. Total known security loans have now declined

$8,518,000,000 since the peak of $13,205,000,000 was reached on September 30, 1929.

13 August: The stock market is ignoring the poor business figures that have been coming out and paying more attention to any indices which point to an upturn in the fall... For a long time the market reacted immediately to unfavourable news and did not discount prospects of cheerier developments.

16 August: The market practically ignored the reduction in the duPont common dividend to 50 cents quarterly from 75 cents.

So far evidence of any important change in business is lacking, but bond and raw material commodity prices have shown strength over a period of roughly two months.

16 August: Revival of British interest in Wall Street dates from the announcement of the war loan conversion offer and the adjournment of Congress. It is believed here that London led the way in Wall Street's upswing about a month ago. A London broker's circular published on July 26 set out two lists of 15 blue chip American and British industrial common shares which showed an average yield on the American shares of 10.4%.

17 August: A seat on the NYSE changed hands at $150,000 up 25% from the preceding sale and comparing with the low for the year of $68,000.

These were dark days indeed in the summer of 1932, but there were still plenty of bulls about. **One key change evident in the comments above, however, was that the market in general, and specific securities in particular, stopped posting negative price reactions when bad news was announced. During this period when the market seemed so stunned as not to respond to good or bad news a subtle shift began to develop.**

Although the general market was still declining, apparently ignoring the increasing good news, selected stocks had already begun to rise in response to specific good news. The day the market bottomed on 8 July, 67 issues were trading more than 50% above their earlier 1932 lows. In the dog days of early summer 1932, it was common for less than 450 issues to trade, so the movement of these stocks can certainly be considered material. None of these stocks were Dow constituents, and it is difficult to characterise them. However, one common trait is that they would benefit from higher commodity prices in general, and sugar prices in particular. Perhaps the ability of such a number of stocks to rally prior to the bottom of the market averages provides evidence that buying power was building.

One of the features singled out in the final days of the bear market by various commentators was the weakness in AT&T. This was the widest held stock in the market and major one-day declines were enough in themselves to make headlines. The ability of even this stock to hit such "air pockets" was perhaps a sign that small investors who had stuck with the market were now throwing in the towel. Did these major declines in AT&T signify that the last bull had turned bear? It is also noticeable that while a material number of selected stocks were rallying significantly through the last days of the bear market, there was a major collapse in the "safe" tobacco and foods sectors. The average weighted price of food stocks fell 23.2% in May and the tobacco sector declined by 21.3%. The average monthly price decline for these sectors during the 33 months of the bear market had been 3.4% and 1.3% respectively. However, the collapse in price of these "safe" sectors cannot, in isolation, be taken as a foolproof indicator that the market is reaching its bottom. In September 1930, the food sector saw a 27.9% monthly collapse and the tobacco sector a 21.3% decline. Investors who took this as a sign of final capitulation bought equities on 1 October and were to lose half their money by July 1932. If the precipitate decline in so-called safe sectors is indeed an indicator the bear market is ending, then it is a factor that must be considered in relation to other indicators.

A development noted as bullish in 1921 was that volumes tended to decline on a weak market and increase with a rising market. Once again, this trait was evident as early as June 1932 and in clear contrast to what had come before. The low volume on a falling market was thought to indicate there were fewer investors prepared to liquidate their positions. The rise in volume in a rising market was attributed to the arrival of the so-called "big constructive interests".

In 1921, this increase in volume was also partly attributed to shorts covering their positions in a rising market. Although this did occur in selected issues in the summer of 1932, this bear-market bottom was noticeable for the absence of any significant bear-market covering. While the shorts covered quickly in 1921, short positions continued to increase from the market bottom on 8 July to 27 July in 1932. Not until 3 August were short positions below their 8 July level. In that period, the DJIA rose 29%, so the shorts had to endure considerable pain before they entertained capitulation.

The failure of the shorts to cover in July was one positive sign as to why this particular rise in the stock market was likely to be sustained past July. The reluctance of bears to capitulate, or others to borrow and speculate, was a positive signal that the nascent recovery in stock prices could be sustained.

Figure 61

VOLUMES AND DOW JONES INDUSTRIAL AVERAGE AT BOTTOMS

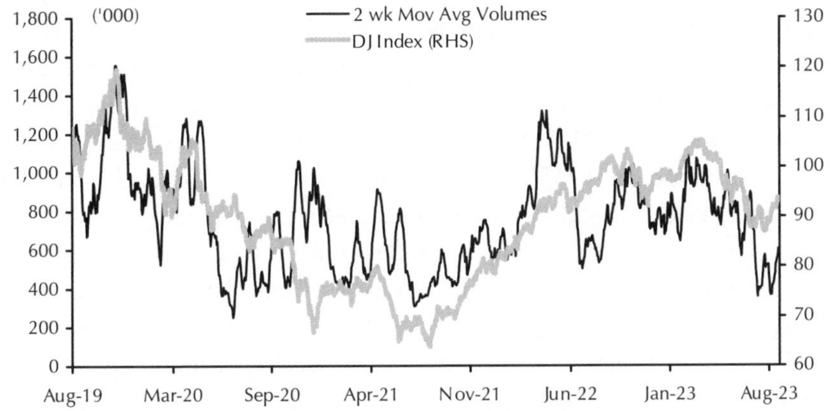

Source: Dow Jones & Co.

A stock market adage we investigated in Part I has it that bear markets end with a so-called "capitulation" event. Such an event is popularly described as a final sharp decline in the market associated with high volume as the last bulls sell out. In 1921 we see the final decline in the market happened on low volume. A similar situation was evident in 1932.

As Figure 61 shows, trading volume declined throughout the final few months of the stock market's decline. At the bottom of the market, two-week daily average volume was just less than 650,000 shares. By 23 July, two-week moving average volume was still less than 750,000 shares. There were then four consecutive days from 25 July, when daily volume exceeded one million shares, a level of activity not witnessed since early May 1932.

Once again the evidence shows the final market decline occurring on ever lower volume. It is only after the initial rise of the market that higher volumes develop. This pattern, also evident in 1921, is more indicative of a bear market bottom than the high-volume capitulation event of popular belief.

Investors who were awaiting an earnings recovery before returning to the stock market missed the bottom of the market in July 1932. The Cowles Foundation data for the S&P Composite Index shows earnings bottoming in December 1932. Given the delay in reporting earnings it would have been sometime in the second quarter of 1933 before it was evident to contemporary investors that earnings were improving.

Even in 1933 it was difficult to proclaim that earnings growth would be sustainable. Based on previous experience investors should have expected strong earnings growth as the economy recovered. However, in 1933 reported earnings were just 7% above their 1932 level. So at best investors awaiting an earnings improvement would have been holding fire until early summer 1933, but it is more likely that they would have kept their powder dry right through 1933. Indeed earnings growth in 1934 was an anaemic 11% and not until 1935 when earnings increased 55% could one see categorical evidence of the normal cyclical recovery in earnings.

As a group, listed companies never reported a loss at any period through the depression. However, there was a very different picture if one looks at US corporations in the aggregate.

The data in Figure 62 shows US corporations reporting losses in 1932, while S&P data for the listed sector reports profit for 1932, albeit 75% below the 1929 high. Data on the percentage of companies reporting profit provides some insight as to when the profit recovery began for corporations in general.

Figure 62

NET PROFIT OF ALL US CORPORATIONS ($M)	
3Q 1929	1,696
4Q 1929	1,406
1Q 1930	984
2Q 1930	727
3Q 1930	357
4Q 1930	132
1Q 1931	84
2Q 1931	(34)
3Q 1931	(185)
4Q 1931	(407)
1Q 1932	(361)
2Q 1932	(569)
3Q 1932	(677)
4Q 1932	(662)
1Q 1933	(604)
2Q 1933	(142)
3Q 1933	370

Source: Harold Borger, *Outlay and Income in the United States 1921-1938*

Awaiting signs of the earnings recovery would not have put investors in at, or near, the bottom of the stock market in July 1932. Even the most trusting investor could not have suggested a sustainable earnings recovery until the second quarter of 1933 and it is probable, given the anaemic recovery in the earnings of the listed sector, that not until 1935 could one bet on the sustainability of the earnings recovery. The DJIA bottomed on 8 July 1932 at 41.22. Investors buying in early summer 1933 would already be paying twice this price. However, the next leg of the bull market was not to find purchase until around March 1935. This second leg of the bull market saw it almost double again from March 1935 to February 1937. It is probable that investors focused solely on earnings growth would have participated in this second stage of the rally. They would still have made double their money while those lucky enough to invest in July 1932 had made four times their money.

In both 1921 and 1932, considerable effort was made to monitor the number of shareholders of listed companies. If the number of shareholders began to reach new highs this was taken as an important bullish signal. One would expect that in a bear market with waning public interest the number of shareholders would decrease. The reverse is the case. Of the 346 companies monitored by R.G. Dun & Co. in May 1932, the number of stockholders had increased 42% since May 1930. This trend, particularly for the stock market bellwethers, was so well known that market calls had been made for over two decades based on the diffusion of holdings in US Steel.

Figure 63

PERCENTAGE OF COMPANIES REPORTING PROFIT	
3Q 1929	94.3
4Q 1929	89.8
1Q 1930	84.1
2Q 1930	83.0
3Q 1930	71.6
4Q 1930	65.2
1Q 1931	67.2
2Q 1931	63.1
3Q 1931	53.3
4Q 1931	50.9
1Q 1932	45.7
2Q 1932	40.2
3Q 1932	39.5
4Q 1932	41.8
1Q 1933	38.6
2Q 1933	52.3
3Q 1933	70.0

Source G.H. Moore, *Business Cycle Indicators*

On a chart with a well-chosen base, it could be seen that when the price of US Steel fell below the number of its shareholders, the market was a buy. This chart had produced accurate buy signals in 1903, 1914, 1920 and 1923.

In the 1921-29 bull market, the number of holders of US Steel was unchanged. In 1929-32, the number of stockholders almost doubled. Presumably this represented investors rushing from more speculative issues back to the presumed safety of one of the country's largest corporations. The next buy signal on the US Steel chart, in terms of shareholder number relative to share price, was in early 1931, when the stock market still had a long way to decline. Not surprisingly this brought this particular method of analysis into some disrepute. However it is still irrefutable, based on the R.G. Dun data, that there were more shareholders in US corporations in 1932 than there had been in 1929. This fact, along with the fact that almost one-third of all NYSE-listed shares were traded in 1932, suggests that interest in the market was higher than is commonly believed. Those awaiting evidence of complete public distrust of the equity market were still waiting in 1932 when the market bottomed.

It is interesting that even the leading stock of the 1920s boom, RCA, saw a major increase in its number of shareholders in the 1929-32 bear market. The trend in both bear markets was for a movement of shares into the hands of the public at the expense of Wall Street and what would be described at the time as "big constructive interest". At the bottom, as in 1921, it was the return of professional buyers, stock brokers and rich capitalists that marked the bottom of the market. The move in stocks was then away from the public and back to the professionals as the bull market developed. In 1932, as in 1921, it was the concentration of stock back in the hands of bigger players that indicated the return of the bull market rather than any return of public enthusiasm.

One major error evident from investor comments at the time was the focus on the deteriorating fiscal position. The *Wall Street Journal* carries constant reference to changes in the fiscal outlook and the supposed positive or negative impact on the stock market. The pages of the *WSJ* suggest the culprit for the final plunge in stock prices was the prospect of an unbalanced budget. The DJIA halved in the four months from March to July 1932. By the standards of any bear market, that was a vicious and rapid final downturn. The scale of this final decline exceeded those endured in the October 1929 crash and in both banking crises. There was no doubt that government actions were undermining public confidence as the following extracts from the *WSJ* reveal:

> New Jersey Legislature 'walks out' on Theron McCampbell, militant legislator, who insists on reading a 1,500-word speech on the question 'Is

The New Jersey Legislature an Insane Asylum?', despite measures taken to prevent him, including hisses, cheers, songs, and turning out the lights. Recess declared as a last resort, but speech was read until finished.

Wall Street Journal, 25 May 1932

'Have we a government?' That is surely a 'mouthful'. Was there ever before such a shameless and cheap bunch of politicians in Washington? Shoot 'em again, only much severer. You are too easy.

Letter from Mr. Charles N. Thomson of Orient, Long Island,
Wall Street Journal, 17 May 1932

As it turned out, the constant call for a balanced budget before any improvement in the equity or bond markets could materialise was the most erroneous investment judgement made in 1932.

In 1931, the budget deficit amounted to just 0.60% of GDP, and there were numerous pro-spending lobbies in Congress who created a number of expansionary bills in early 1932 suggesting further fiscal deterioration. Contemporary reasoning was that this produced the final crash. As Congress came towards adjournment on 16 July 1932, the steady failure of these bills and the balanced-budget statements of President Hoover were seen as good news for the stock market. At the time, the improvement in the market was attributed to this step back from a supposed fiscal abyss.

A **fiscal deficit** results when government spending exceeds government revenue. The deficit in revenue is usually met by borrowing money through the issuance of bonds, although the sale of government assets is another option. Financial practitioners view fiscal deficits as a negative factor. However, at least since the abolition of the gold standard, there is little evidence a deteriorating fiscal position can produce or exacerbate a bear market in equities.

Also in July, the Democrats endorsed Roosevelt as their candidate for President. Roosevelt was also surprisingly vociferous in his demands for a balanced budget. If this was part of the reason for the recovery in the equity market, which began in July 1932, subsequent events were to show that it was misguided. Prior to the 1930s, the US had grown used to a federal surplus during periods of peace. In what was probably the largest economic contraction recorded in the US, in 1837, the fiscal deficit reached only 0.68% of GDP. In this context, the peace-time budget deficit of 0.60% in

147

1931 was enough to seriously frighten the investment community in 1932. However the deficit would escalate to 4.6% of GDP in 1932, 4.61% in 1933 and peak at 5.50% of GDP in 1934. It seems unlikely that anybody at the time would have foreseen one of the greatest bull markets in the history of US equities occurring while such an unparalleled fiscal deterioration was underway. Those who called for a balanced budget as an essential precursor for a recovery in equities could not have been more wrong. Government's desperation across the globe to balance their budgets may thus have been misplaced and the bird owners of Moravia may have suffered in vain.

> To raise money to meet municipal expenses, city of Hihenstadt in Moravia decided to impose tax on all pet song birds of $2.97 a year for each nightingale and lower for canaries and thrushes etc.[44]

This ability of equities to rise through a major fiscal deterioration from 1932 to 1937 suggests that the final downward lurch in the market from March to July 1932 was not caused by concerns over the fiscal situation. There was a major drain on US gold reserves at this time which clearly depressed the equity market but there were other potential catalysts for this drain. Some commentators in the WSJ attributed the decline in the equity market to the worsening political situation in Washington, which was causing the drain on gold reserve and the collapse of the market. It was not surprising that the Wall Street Journal, later described by President Truman as 'the Republican bible', should attribute a decline in confidence on the increasing probability of a Democratic President. There was however a more fundamental reason why gold would be leaving the US - the devaluation of almost all the country's major trading partners. Just how dramatically these currency changes could impact the trade position was becoming evident in early 1932, when the UK imported only 396 automobiles in the first four months of the year, compared with 5,188 for the whole of 1928. UK exports, in the same period, totalled 8,771 cars, an increase of roughly 50% over the like 1928 period.[45] The US trade surplus had already halved from 1930 to 1931.

The increasingly apparent trade deterioration, and the impact this might have on the country's commitment to the gold standard, played a role in producing capital flight from the US in this period. With the benefit of

---

[44] Wall Street Journal, 10 June 1932
[45] Wall Street Journal, 23 May 1932

hindsight, it is very likely the Federal Reserve's change in monetary policy in April 1932 was also a contributing factor to this gold outflow. In many circles, the move to boost liquidity, seemingly under political pressure, had to be a precursor to the abandonment of the gold standard. This persuaded foreign investors in particular that holding assets valued in US dollars was increasingly risky. From January 1932 to July, the monetary gold stock contracted 12% to $3.65 billion. The outflow of gold came to an end at almost the same time as the Federal Reserve ended its open market purchase programme and the adjournment of Congress. Contemporary opinion that a balanced budget was necessary to stabilise the equity market was wrong, and it was probably also wrong to blame events in Washington for the final terrible slump in the market. The combination of deterioration in the trade position and the launch of the Fed's liquidity injection were the key factors which persuaded many that the US was on the verge of leaving the gold standard. It was in this environment that the price of equities could halve in just four months.

The negative response to the Fed's actions must have been a bitter blow to those who believed it had the antidote to business recessions. Though many, including the New York Federal Reserve, had been arguing for liquidity injections into the system for some years, there is evidence the injection, when it finally came, and within the confines of the gold standard, may have resulted in capital flight, effectively neutralising the positive impact of the liquidity injections. Such actions earlier in the economic contraction, when the US trade surplus was larger and before other countries had devalued their currencies, may have produced positive rather than negative reactions. However by April 1932 confidence in the commitment to gold was already shaken and the Fed's action further undermined such confidence exacerbating the decline in the stock market.

The key question for investors is: What finally stopped this rout in July 1932? With the benefit of hindsight it appears that there was one event unique to 1932 that helped relieve the gold drain and bolster the stock market - the international agreement concluded at Lausanne on Germany's war reparations. From press reports of the time, it is evident that no breakthrough was expected on these negotiations.

Germany, as it had since the signing of the Treaty of Versailles, was arguing for smaller reparation payments. Others, in particular France, were arguing against any such reduction. This had been a long-running disagreement and the markets were inured to diplomatic compromise and obfuscation. Germany's reparations were agreed in 1921, but within the year it had defaulted on its payments and was granted a one-year moratorium. Before the moratorium expired, Belgium and France occupied the industrialised Ruhr and soon thereafter hyper-inflation swept Germany. The Dawes Plan of 1924 rescheduled Germany's debt and the country continued to meet reparation payments by borrowing funds in the US. From October 1921 to July 1930, Germany offered for sale in the US 135 dollar-denominated bonds - the par value of the outstanding obligations in August 1932 was just short of $1 billion. Despite the success of the debt issues, a further reduction in Germany's burden was needed in 1929, and this was achieved through the Young Plan. However, the burden of economic contraction in the Great Depression intensified Germany's economic problems, and President Hoover announced in the summer of 1931 a one-year moratorium on war-debt payments from the Allies and reparations from Germany. As this moratorium approached expiration, interested parties met in Lausanne and surprised everyone with a deal to abolish Germany's reparation obligations in return for bonds. This agreement amounted to a de facto reduction in Germany's financial burden of some 90%. France's longstanding antipathy towards a reduction of reparations had mysteriously vanished. (Not made public was the informal agreement that the US would cancel outstanding war debts owed by its European allies, an agreement the US Congress subsequently refused to honour.)

When the news of an apparent breakthrough on reparations was announced, the impact was particularly positive on commodity markets. Investors believed the international financial log jam had been broken and that consumption from Germany and the debtor nations was likely to rise. The *WSJ* on 24 June illustrated the positive consequences flowing from the agreement.

> France now ranks with Holland and Switzerland as one of the three countries with gold unit for unit circulation. World recovery depends, in part at least, on shifting this concentration of gold from these countries to the debtor and exporting countries. That will come about eventually, through economic processes, but it can be speeded up if political leaders can work out some solution of the present intergovernmental debt problems.[46]

The Lausanne agreement held out the prospect of just such a speeding up of the global economic recovery. In particular the agreement was a key

---

[46] *Wall Street Journal*, 24 June 1932

factor that helped stabilise commodity prices, which, in turn, was, as we have seen, an important factor in stabilising the stock market. Also at the time, the downward pressure on the Swiss franc following the agreement was thought to be a very important positive indicator for global financial markets. Capital had been attracted to Switzerland as it fully backed its currency in gold. The weakness in the Swiss currency following Lausanne was thought to signify that this "unemployed capital" was moving back into employment elsewhere in the world.

A further improvement in the international outlook occurred in Germany. There was increasing optimism about the outlook for German government bonds, widely held in the US, as the rise of the National Socialist party appeared to falter. In April 1932, Adolf Hitler was defeated by President Paul von Hindenburg in the presidential election. Despite some commentators believing Hitler would be good for business, the *Wall Street Journal* did not hesitate to refer to him as a "shoddy leader" throughout this period. Wall Street generally welcomed the fact that the Nazi party failed to increase its vote in the subsequent 31 July Reichstag elections, believing this would improve the chances of "order" in a country disrupted by civil strife. The *WSJ* gave a downbeat assessment of Hitler's future prospects.

> The opinion is growing, however, that the Hitler movement has reached its peak in Germany and that, the Nazi party will continue to be a troublesome element to those seeking orderly government, Herr Hitler will not be able to secure control of the government.[47]

Unfortunately for the world, Hitler's progress was not stopped by his failure to make progress through the democratic process.

As in 1921, the Dow Theory scored a notable success in 1932. There were moves to fractional new lows, but the Dow experts at the *WSJ* made it clear this could be a very bullish signal.

> Although the recent simultaneous entry of both the railroad and industrial averages into new low territory may be regarded as symptomatic of prospective continuance of the major downward movement, according to the theory, this interpretation is subject to confirmation by further market action. Normally, penetration of previous low, or high, points must be more than fractional to qualify as a definitive signal. A fractional penetration, though perhaps justifying some expectation of a further movement in the same direction, also has possibilities of interpretation as a double bottom or

---

[47] *Wall Street Journal*, 29 August 1932

double top, whose significance would be quite different from that of a breakthrough.[48]

A bullish double bottom was soon confirmed. Once again the *WSJ*'s analysis of the Dow Theory had suggested that the bottom of the bear market was imminent. William Peter Hamilton died in 1929, but the baton as leader of the Dow theorists was not passed to the next editor of the paper. Instead Robert Rhea, an independent commentator who studied the Dow Theory editorials of both Dow and Hamilton in the *Wall Street Journal*, became the new guru. Rhea called the bottom of the great bear market on 21 July 1932 - two-for-two for the Dow Theory.

Cynics might note that the Republican Advisory Committee of New York County had urged legislation to prevent casualty insurance companies from buying common stocks. The stock market bottomed within two weeks of the publication of this report. Panic may have been rife but it may be worth remembering that not everyone was concerned with the future for common stocks in the summer of 1932.

> Alex Stillman, 20-year-old son of James A Stillman, announced he plans to fly the Atlantic next year. He explained 'Dad had only about $65,000,000 left after the market crash so I may have to go to work.'[49]

Bonds and the bear

> 'I remember the panics of 1907, and 1893, and they were bad. But not as bad as now. I don't know how many millions of men there's on the streets.'

> 'How did the depression in those years end?'

> 'Well, they got to end. There's action, and then reaction, and then action again. When a thing goes up, it has to come down, and then when it comes down, it has to go up again.'

> James T. Farrell, *Judgement Day*

Something peculiar happened in this deflationary depression - the price of US government bonds declined. The daily average yield of long-term government paper in January 1932 was 4.26%, compared with 3.70% in September 1929. Over that same period, the wholesale price index had declined 31%. Given the decline in the general price level and the rising credit risk associated with other investments, most investors would have

---

[48] *Wall Street Journal*, 12 July 1932
[49] *Wall Street Journal*, 2 September 1932

expected government bonds to have risen through the economic contraction. Indeed this was the trend from September 1929 to June 1931, when the yield declined to 3.15% from 3.70%. However, June 1931 proved to be the high point for the government bond market and prices declined as the second banking crises took hold in the US and as the crisis was internationalised. Although prices drifted lower from June 1931 to August, the real slump in government bond prices came with the departure of sterling from the gold standard.

Sterling's departure from the gold standard prompted foreign central banks to liquidate US dollar assets and the gold stock declined. This external drain on liquidity occurred just as domestic depositors, shocked by a new surge in commercial bank failures, sought to hold an even greater proportion of their assets in US currency rather than deposits. To exacerbate the pressure on US commercial banks to liquidate assets, the Fed sprang to the defence of the gold standard exchange rate. On 16 October, the New York Fed raised its rediscount rate from 1.5% to 3.5%. This rise in interest rates put further pressure on bond prices.

Prior to September 1931, banks had been liquidating lower-quality corporate bonds, and yields on these instruments had already been rising from the third quarter of 1930.

By September 1931, both corporate bonds and US-government bonds were being dumped and the yields on both instruments now moved higher. A stabilisation of government bond prices was not evident until February 1932. While it is possible the fear of bigger fiscal deficits played a role in depressing the price of government bonds, this factor was probably minor, given that the market was rallying in February 1932, years before there was any prospect of a return to fiscal rectitude. It is noticeable however that the stabilisation in the government bond market did coincide with the establishment of the Reconstruction Finance Corporation in January 1932. The government-backed RFC had borrowing power of $1.5 billion (increased to $3.3 billion by the Emergency Relief and Construction Act of 21 July 1932) and was charged with lending money to banks and other institutions. This availability of new credit, which alleviated banks' needs to liquidate government bonds, seems to have been more important than any change in the fiscal situation in stabilising the government bond market. Another fillip for bond prices was the Federal Reserve's buying of government bonds, launched in April 1932, aimed at injecting liquidity into the system.

Figure 64

YIELD ON US GOVERNMENT LONG-TERM SECURITIES - SEPT 1929-SEPT 1932

Source: National Bureau of Economic Research

The collapse in government bond prices was rapid, and recovery was gradual. Government bond yields did not return to June 1931 levels until April 1934. The collapse has to be put into the context of a longer-term bull market in bonds, underway since August 1920. In this secular bull market yields declined from 5.67% in August 1920 to just 2.16% by June 1946. In this context, the June 1931 to January 1932 setback, when yields rose from 3.13% to 4.11%, may seem minor. However this collapse in the price of government bonds, during a period of historically high deflation, must have considerably disrupted investor perceptions of what represented "fair value" in financial assets. The impact on financial asset valuation in periods of declining prices and earnings but rising risk-free rates is particularly negative. Even in the worst deflationary times a collapse in the price of government bonds was thus proved possible. What other unexpected reactions might there be in financial markets?

Investors in the corporate bond market were also to be shocked by the scale of the bear. The performance of this market provides perhaps the best indication that investors expected a normal economic contraction to follow after the crash of October 1929. The yield on Baa-rated corporate bonds, the sector of the market with the lowest credit quality, actually declined from the September 1929 level through most of 1930. Not until the eruption of the first banking crisis in the third quarter of 1930 did the first decline in the price of Baa-rated corporate bonds begin. The average monthly yield on Baa corporate bonds in September 1929 was 6.12% and by September 1930 yields had declined to 5.65%. Although faith had been maintained in this asset for almost a year after the October 1929 crash, this faith was quickly demolished. By November 1930, Baa yields were already in excess of the September 1929 levels. The average yield exceeded 6.7% by December of 1930 and remained around that level until April 1931. It was then, with the second banking crises and the internationalisation of the crisis that the really dramatic bear market in corporate debt began. Between April and Dec 1931, the average Baa yield jumped from 6.72% to 10.42%.

Both the government bond market and the Baa corporate market stabilised in the first quarter of 1932. However, while this stabilisation marked the beginning of a new bull market for government bonds, there was another final crash coming for the corporate bond market. The Baa corporate bond market bottomed in June 1932 when the daily average yield for the market reached 11.52%. The trend in prices in the AAA corporate bond market was very similar to that in the Baa market, although the amplitude of change was more restrained.

While the bear market may have carried government bond prices back to 1924 levels, the bear market in corporate bonds was of a considerably larger magnitude. The historical data on bond yields by quality of issuer is limited, but the Baa yield of 11.52% was one-third higher than the highest yield previously recorded from when data became available in 1919. The yield of AAA corporate bonds averaged 5.41% in June 1932, the highest since December 1921. The Dow Jones Index of forty corporation bonds, which had been available since 1914, fell to a new low.

Figure 65

YIELDS ON BAA CORPORATE BONDS - SEPTEMBER 1929 TO SEPTEMBER 1932

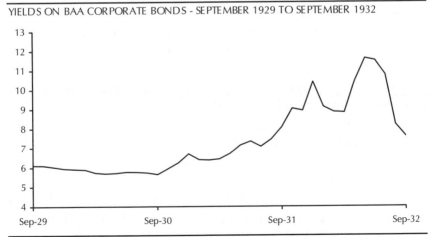

Source: National Bureau of Economic Research

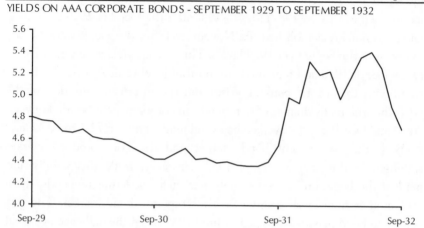

Figure 66

YIELDS ON AAA CORPORATE BONDS - SEPTEMBER 1929 TO SEPTEMBER 1932

Source: National Bureau of Economic Research

Whatever stabilised the government bond market in January and February of 1932, the chief suspect being the establishment of the RFC, it failed to have the same positive impact on the corporate bond market. It was not until June 1932 that the AAA and Baa corporate bond markets found their bottoms.

By the summer of 1932, the pages of the *Wall Street Journal* were full of indications that the end of the sell-off in corporate bonds was likely. As in 1921, the complete dearth of credit growth in the economy led the commercial banks to become ever larger buyers of bonds. While their original purchases may have been secure government bonds rallies in the prices of these instruments increased the attractiveness of corporate bonds. The prices of corporate bonds had fallen precipitously with the Dow Jones & Co Average of Second Grade Rail Bonds down 49% from the 1931 high. The commercial banks were joined in the corporate bond buying spree by the corporations themselves, tempted by the fact that some of their obligations could be cancelled at less than half of face value.

The most publicised new buyer for bonds was the American Securities Investment Corporation, formed by the largest commercial banks in the US. The idea was that this "pool" would buy bonds, thus spreading the risk among the nervous bankers. The market rose strongly on the announcement of the creation of the pool, and the little buying the pool actually implemented was at prices well above the 1932 lows. In terms of the general growing buying support for the bond market, the role of the

Resolution Finance Corporation (RFC) was very important. Of course, investors tend to discount the ability of government to fundamentally change markets, but there is no doubt the provision of financing by the RFC to distressed banks and railroads alleviated the selling pressure on the corporate bond market.

Once again, this period is marked by numerous commentators pointing out the investment wisdom of borrowing cheap, short-term money to buy the best quality corporate bonds. In 1932, unlike 1921, one key factor depressing bond prices was the worsening fiscal position. In 1932, there was a real threat Congress would endorse the so-called "Garner Plan" which 'called for the issuance of $1,000,000,000 bonds to raise funds for public construction'. The bond market constantly fretted about the impact such an increase in the supply of bonds would have on prices. The Garner Plan was not to make it into law, but over the next few years the fiscal deficit ballooned, without producing any major sell-off in the bond markets. Bond-investor fears about the negative impact from continued fiscal deterioration were misplaced. And whatever fears may have been expressed in the pages of the WSJ, the fact was that bond offerings were increasingly over-subscribed.

It is clear that the apparent agreement at Lausanne regarding the cancellation of German reparations had a big impact on the commodity markets, and its impact was also evident in the bond markets. The argument was that the removal of this burden on Germany, accompanied by some alleviation for the Allies on their debt repayments to the US, would reduce the logjam in international trade and demand. German bonds jumped ten points within days of the announcement of the deal at Lausanne. The agreement also coincides with renewed vigour in the upswing in the US bond markets. The rebound in bond prices was spectacular.

Figure 67

THE DOW JONES & COMPANY BOND AVERAGES		
	Close Saturday	Gain From Low
10 1st grade rails[1]	88.47	17.10
10 2nd grade rails	70.14	22.42
10 Public utilities[1]	91.49	8.99
10 Industrials	77.29	17.67
40 Bonds	81.85	16.07

[1] New highs for year. Source: *Wall Street Journal*, 22 August 1932

While the government bond market had seen its lows in January 1932, it was not until the first of June that corporate bonds bottomed, about five weeks before the equity market.

However, the fiscal deterioration was to reach levels not contemplated in June 1932, and yet the bull market in bonds, which commenced then, was to last until 1949. While bond investors may have thought the adjournment of Congress an important bull factor in 1932, the Congress would be back with bigger spending proposals and much bigger deficits, and still the bond bull market raged on. There were other reasons for the corporate bond market bottoming in early June, and once again the role of stabilising and rising commodity prices was to the fore and signs of such stabilisation were evident by late May.

The WSJ was reporting as early as 24 May that 'a few commodities' were showing 'a tendency to hold at present levels'. By the end of the month, commodity price rises were being reported in a broad range of commodities, and Fisher's index of wholesale prices posted three consecutive weeks of gain in the middle of July. By the end of August, there was general confidence that price rises were sustainable as 'the advance in wholesale prices has continued for more than two months'.[50]

The corporate bond market bottomed just as a number of commodity prices began to improve - two weeks prior to the broad indicators of wholesale prices revealing improvement. The deflationary process had wrought particular havoc with corporations' ability to repay fixed obligations, so there were good reasons why a rise in the general price level was seen as positive for investors. By the middle of the month, the news from Lausanne suggested a fundamental change in the global financial system, which would further underpin commodity prices.

There were several one-off events that also played a role in stabilising bond prices, the most notable of which were the creation of the "bond pool" and the launch of the RFC. The bottom of the corporate bond market coincided with rumours of the formation of the American Securities Investment Corp (ASI). As the government-bond buying programme of the Federal Reserve had failed to create credit growth, the ASI was formed to pool the funds of commercial bankers to buy a portfolio of bonds, utilising some of the liquidity created by the Fed, while spreading the risks of the purchasers. News that such an organisation had been created was enough to

---

[50] Wall Street Journal, 19 August 1932

cause a substantial bond rally. The turnaround was achieved without the corporation initially having to buy any bonds. At the right time when bonds were cheap, economic conditions improving and commodity prices rising, the support operation provided the necessary upward impetus for prices. If a private support operation played a role in stabilising financial markets in 1932 then a public support operation played an even bigger role. Although it is always difficult to desegregate cause-and-effect in financial markets, the formation of the RFC not only assisted bank liquidity and stabilised government bond prices, but it led to some improvement in credit quality in those sectors of commerce, notably railways, where credit availability improved. As well as these support operations there is also some suggestion that the conversion of Britain's £2 billion 5% war loan into a 3.5% perpetual loan also played an impact in stabilising bond prices in the US. On 2 July, about a month after the US corporate bond market had bottomed, the *Wall Street Journal* was reporting:

> The London Stock Exchange today witnessed frantic scenes of excitement and activity such as have not occurred since the boom days of 1928.... Instead of the minor conversion operations expected earlier this week, dealers were confronted with the largest single conversion operation ever staged.... Trading began at around 10.30a.m. when British funds soared with unprecedented advances. Gilt-edged securities usually move only in fractions of a point at a time, but at the opening this morning 4% consols rose 8 points to £110.... Even leading common shares among the industrials, mines and oils joined in the general advance.

It is noticeable from reading the *WSJ* for the summer of 1932 that "foreign buying" of all US securities was mentioned more by commentators following the British conversion. It is certainly possible the conversion sent funds overseas due to the reduction in interest rates, and the excitement in London over the conversion occurred just a few days prior to the bottom of the US equity market. There were thus these various important one-off considerations impacting the corporate bond market in the early summer of 1932. However, as in 1921, the key consideration for stabilising the bond market appears to have been the stabilisation of select-commodity and then general-wholesale prices.

Roosevelt and the bear

'But getting back to politics, boys, this spring is only going to be a preview of the presidential election in 1932. Then we'll have Democrats all the way from the White House to the street cleaners on every block. And there'll be better times, too,' Red said with smug pride.

James T. Farrell, *Judgement Day*

One cannot analyse the factors impacting the financial markets in the summer of 1932 without discussing the race for the White House. Was it merely coincidental that the stock market bottomed just a few days after the Democrats selected Roosevelt as their Presidential candidate? Both Republicans and Democrats held national conventions in June 1932 to choose candidates. The Republicans were bound to endorse their incumbent, Herbert Hoover. The contentious issue for them was how far they would go to change the law on Prohibition. With the public in open breach of the law, and the growth of organised crime around the alcohol business, it was clear that a more lenient stance could only help the party's election prospects. At the Democratic convention Franklin D. Roosevelt was the clear favourite to win the nomination. However, his campaign was badly managed and, although the Convention began on 27 June, the outcome was still uncertain on 1 July. The *WSJ* reported on 2 July of the excitement the deadlock was causing in the markets.

With the first three ballots producing a virtual deadlock, hopes were high that a compromise candidate, in whom business would have confidence, would be agreed upon, and prices for the list, as a whole strengthened perceptibly on later advices that Governor Roosevelt was losing strength.

According to the *WSJ*, Roosevelt as a likely President was depressing, rather than supporting, prices in the equity market. The market's excitement regarding a compromise candidate was short-lived as Roosevelt gave his nomination acceptance speech the next day. Thus from 2 July onwards, it was looking increasingly likely that Roosevelt would be the next President. The public's disgruntlement over the depression was very likely to produce a change in administration. John Nance Garner, Roosevelt's vice-presidential running mate, went on the record to say that the Democratic party would win the Presidential election if it could follow a 'sit still and keep quiet' policy. Of course, Republicans could hope that the public would not apportion blame for the Depression on the incumbent and the *WSJ* vainly argued the case.

14 July: This 1932 Presidential campaign is the most uncertain one since 1916. However, no neutral, and but few partisans, who have combed all possibilities, care to attempt a positive forecast at this time.... However, anyone who has talked with voters finds their wrath against the Democratic House of Representatives is probably greater than against Mr. Hoover, and the leader of the Democratic House is second man on the Roosevelt ticket.... The country is in a frame of mind to try new men and new measures. However, those sections which will determine the election do not appear to want this change to carry them toward radicalism or even advanced liberalism and that is the way the associates and the words of Governor Roosevelt seem to be heading him.

However, such optimism of opinion was refuted by the facts being reported in the same newspaper:

15 June: Survey of national political sentiment by Babson statistical organization says nation is now 60% Democratic and 40% Republican but that 'the tide has recently turned and is now clearly running toward President Hoover.'

23 August: President Hoover's chances for re-election have risen perceptibly in the past few weeks. However, at this time it cannot be said that Mr. Hoover has the advantage over Franklin D. Roosevelt, his Democratic opponent.

30 August: Down Town Republican Club of Los Angeles abandons plans for dinner and rally following poll of members showing 70% of them in favour of Governor Roosevelt for President.

1 September: Roosevelt Could Triumph.

No Presidential election is a certainty with more than four months to go. However, it was highly probable by the summer of 1932 that Roosevelt was to be the next President of the United States. It is a matter for the historical record that Roosevelt's nomination and the probability of a Roosevelt Presidency coincided with the bottoming of the US equity market. The rise in government bond prices, wholesale prices and the corporate bond market was underway prior to his nomination, but continued strongly thereafter. That the equity market had reacted positively to news on 1 July that Roosevelt would fail suggests the incipient recovery in financial markets was entirely coincidental with the increasing probability of a Roosevelt victory. In the summer of 1932, it was still unclear what Roosevelt meant for business. During his campaign, the Roosevelt camp was sending two very different messages. On the one hand

161

there was the radical message of structural change being delivered by both himself and his wife and reported in the *Wall Street Journal*:

> **23 May:** Governor Roosevelt, in commencement address at Oglethorpe University at Atlanta, Ga., asks for bold experimentation to achieve redistribution of the national income, stating that in the future capital must be content with a smaller return and reward for the worker must be proportionately greater if the modern system is to survive.

> **9 July:** Mrs. Franklin D. Roosevelt, wife of Presidential nominee, in speech at Chautauqua, N.Y., states that the overcentralization of big business is a factor in economic depression, which has demonstrated the interdependence of agriculture and urban industry and trade and of all nations in world commerce.

On the other hand Roosevelt also made a clear commitment to balancing the budget, criticising Hoover for spending too much and, on 19 October in Pittsburgh, promised to cut the cost of government by 25%. So Roosevelt was in favour of redistribution of the national income but somehow he expected to achieve this while slashing government spending. Having espoused a policy of 'bold experimentation' and 'redistribution of the national income' in May 1932, the policies offered during the campaign seemed much more conservative.

> The paradox of the 1932 campaign was that Roosevelt spoke out against spending, against unbalanced budgets and a bloated bureaucracy, while Hoover defended deficit spending and experimental measures - it was as if the speeches had gotten mixed up.[51]

Did the markets really expect great liberal and radical policies to follow the election of Roosevelt as President? In a report to clients on the eve of the Democratic Convention, The Guaranty Trust Co. stated that 'the Presidential Election still looms as a disturbing factor. Largely imaginary, for its actual economic influence will be of little importance.' Based on contemporary comments, it seems that Roosevelt's election if anything reduced confidence or, based on the Guaranty Trust report, had no material impact on the financial markets.

While it is always difficult to separate cause and effect in financial markets, the balance of evidence suggests the probable election of Roosevelt was not a key cause for the commencement of the equity bull market in July 1932. Indeed, the first setback for the bull market began with

---

[51] Ted Morgan, *FDR*

Roosevelt's election in November and lasted until his inauguration in March. There was great uncertainty in this period regarding Roosevelt's policies in general and his commitment to the gold standard in particular. As we shall see in Part III, the market finds Roosevelt adopting some very radical policies, but these did not prevent one of the greatest equity bull markets in US history.

There had never been a bear market like the bear market of 1929-32. The market declined 89%, far surpassing the worst previous market declines of 45% in the panics of 1857 and 1907. As in 1921, equity prices did not stop declining until they reached a 70% discount to replacement value. At the bottom of the equity market in July 1932, the same signals from the summer of 1921 were flashing green, with a few notable differences. On this occasion, the first reduction in the Fed discount rate came right at the beginning of the bear market rather than at its end. The other key difference is that the economic and price recovery of 1932 was not sustainable. However, the DJIA remained above its July 1932 lows and investors made spectacular returns over the next five years. Despite the incredible difference between the events leading to 1921 and 1932, our bear market bottom indicators signalled once again the death of the bear and the birth of the bull. By the next bear market bottom, the New Deal had transformed the structure of the US economy and the gold standard was gone. In that environment, could the same indicators succeed in marking the transition from bear to bull?

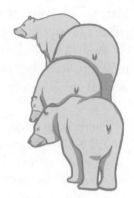

Part III
June 1949

He sat next to a stout man who lived in his hotel. Occasionally they would speak.

'How's the market?' asked the fat man, deciding not to read his paper.

'The market's doing fine, should go up.'

'Well, that sure is good news. I've a little bit that I'd like to put in it. I'd like to put it in something safe, though. You know of something safe? Something that's going to go way up, say?'

'Well, that's a hard question. It's very hard to tell just yet. Sugar's doing well,' said Robert Holton. He always said that same thing to these questions. No one cared what he said. They would repeat it to acquaintances, saying that a friend of theirs in Wall Street had advised them to buy sugar but they didn't feel it was such a good buy at this time.

'You was in the army weren't you?' asked the stout man suddenly.

Robert Holton nodded.

'Been out long?'

'Over a year.'

- Gore Vidal, *In a Yellow Wood*

When we isolate the four most profitable times to invest in stocks, June 1949 comes second on our list after July 1932, but well ahead of 1942, when the DJIA was at even lower levels. This is because, using a 40-year time horizon, an investor in 1949 benefited from the 1982-89 bull market. That is not to say the bear-market bottom of April 1942 should be ignored - it was one of those very rare times when the q ratio fell below 0.3x, making it a period worthy of inclusion in a wider study. The 1940s was a response to the Depression and the negative impact of that cataclysm on investor sentiment that had equities traded at deep discounts to their fair value for the entire decade. How, then, did one determine it was not until 1949 that the equity market would begin in earnest the longest bull market in the history of American equities? As we will see, there were numerous lessons to be had at the bottom of the 1921 and 1932 bear markets, indicating prices and valuations could only improve.

The road to June 1949

The world in 1949 was a very different place than it had been in 1932. Hitler, whose attempt to become President of Germany had failed in 1932, was dead and so were 55 million people killed in the world's bloodiest conflict. Over the period, the United States of America had increased its standing military force from a quarter of a million in 1932 to more than 12 million by 1945. Some 300,000 who left America to fight in the war did not return alive.

By 1949 more than 10 million Americans had left the military in search of civilian employment. In financial terms, the key changes were that the government now accounted for a much larger proportion of economic activity and that the investing public was once again a large holder of government bonds.

The equity market was a backwater for investment in the immediate postwar period. Daily equity turnover on the NYSE was often less than $500,000 and the public's speculative enthusiasm, such as it was, focused on the property market.

By the summer of 1949 there was another factor depressing interest in Wall Street - a record heat wave. On 13 June 1949, the day the DJIA reached its postwar low, a *New York Times* headline proclaimed '1,500,000

Cool off at City's Beaches; Temperature Hits 89.1, Only 0.7 Below Record'. Just three days later, in Detroit, New York's Jake La Motta was crowned middleweight boxing champion of the world; and in Manhattan, Gene Kelly and Frank Sinatra were filming *On The Town*.

Figure 68

DOW JONES INDUSTRIAL AVERAGE - JULY 1932-JULY 1949

Source: Dow Jones & Co.

The great bull market, which had begun in July 1932, did not end until March 1937. The DJIA rose from 41.22 to peak at 194.15. In terms of total capital return over the period 1932-49, it was all over by 1937. The DJIA did not surpass the 1937 high until December 1945 and, in total, from the 6 March 1937 high to the bottom of the 1949 bear market, it spent just 32 weeks above the 1937 high. Peaking at 212.5 in May 1946, less than 10% above its 1937 high, the market then entered a bear phase that was to end with the DJIA reaching bottom at 161.6 on 13 June 1949. A good gauge of investors' varying interest in the equity market over the period is provided by the average monthly market volume (see Figure 69).

The waning volume shows a dramatic decline in the willingness of investors to play the game. From the record trading day of 1929 to the low of 1942, volume on the NYSE declined 99%. The total value of trades in 1942 was 70% lower than in 1932, when the previous bear market had bottomed. In 1942 the dollar volume of trades in equities on the NYSE was below 1901 levels. While a portion of the decline in volume was due to the decline in market values, there was a further impact from a general decline in interest in the market. In 1929, the total number of shares traded accounted for 119% of all the shares listed on the NYSE. As late as 1937 this market turnover ratio was still as high as 30%. However, by 1942 annual trading accounted for just 9% of all shares listed and this had only risen to 13% by 1949. In the previous bear-market years of 1921 and 1932, the ratio was 59% and 32% respectively. The general disinterest, as measured by activity, was thus higher in 1949 than it had been even in the worst days of the Depression. The market capitalisation of NYSE-listed shares in 1949 exceeded that of the end of 1929, but almost no one wanted to play.

Figure 69

AVERAGE MONTHLY VALUE OF NYSE STOCK TRADES ($M) 1937-1949

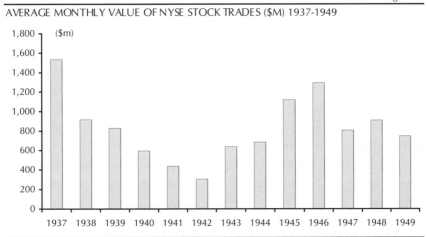

Source: NYSE

The crisis of confidence in equities was based on poor long-term returns and some disconcerting false dawns for the market and the economy. While investor enthusiasm had rebuilt in the 1932-37 bull market, the inability of the economy and the market thereafter to produce a normal, sustainable, cyclical recovery undermined faith in the long-term outlook for equities.

Not surprisingly, trading volume was severely curtailed during WWII. In the worst day's trading of 1942, only $206,680 in stock changed hands. There was renewed interest in equities from 15 August 1945, Victory over Japan Day, well into 1946 but, with the return of the bear market, volumes were on the slide once again.

Insiders' waning enthusiasm for the market, shown in the decline in the price of membership of the NYSE, was particularly pronounced.

Figure 70

NYSE MEMBERSHIP PRICES 1932-49		
Year	High	Low
1932	$185,000	$68,000
1933	$250,000	$90,000
1934	$190,000	$70,000
1935	$140,000	$65,000
1936	$174,000	$89,000
1937	$134,000	$61,000
1938	$85,000	$51,000
1939	$70,000	$51,000
1940	$60,000	$33,000
1941	$35,000	$19,000
1942	$30,000	$17,000
1943	$48,000	$27,000
1944	$75,000	$40,000
1945	$95,000	$49,000
1946	$97,000	$61,000
1947	$70,000	$50,000
1948	$68,000	$46,000
1949	$49,000	$35,000

Source: NYSE

While the DJIA bottomed in 1932, this was only the beginning of the bear market in NYSE seats. From the 1929 high to the 1932 low, the price of a seat had fallen some 90% - almost in line with the market. However, from 1932 to 1942, when the DJIA doubled, the price of a seat on the NYSE sagged a further 75%. Worth $495,000 in 1929, it had dropped to just $17,000 in 1942, recovered from 1942 to 1946, then slid again to bottom in 1949, when the long-term recovery in prices began. The long decline in the price of NYSE seats is further evidence of a growth in apathy towards equities, which continued long after the worst of the Depression was over.

The concern investors had about long-term capital returns from equities appeared justified by the record. By 1949, the DJIA was at the level it had first reached in February 1926. At its 13 June 1949 bottom, the Dow was still 57% below the all-time high set almost 20 years before in September 1929. Within this long period of 17 years from 1932 to the great bottom of 1949, there were two distinct bull and two distinct bear markets.

Why do we track the 1942-1946 bull market and 1946-1949 bear market, when the index in 1949 does not return below the 1942 level? Doesn't this mean the bull market began in 1942? On some measures this could well be the case, and April 1942 was one of those very rare occasions when the q ratio declined below 0.3x. However, we are choosing our bear market bottoms in relation to valuation parameters, primarily in relation to subsequent returns. Subsequent long-term returns from 1949 significantly exceeded those from 1942, and the q ratio was back below the 0.3x level in June 1949. For the long-term investor, 1949 was a better time to invest than 1942.

The course of the Dow - 1932-37

The period from July 1932 to March 1937 was one of the greatest equity bull markets in US history. The DJIA rose 370% during a period when the best available estimate of the GDP deflator shows an 11% rise in prices. As well as this spectacular capital gain, an investor who purchased at the bottom in July 1932 secured a dividend yield of 10%, based upon the dividends actually paid in 1932, and a growth in dividends to 1937 of 60%.

Underpinning the 1932-37 bull market was the increasing solvency of the financial system from 1933 onward. This stabilisation of a seemingly bankrupt financial system helped push equity valuations back up to more normal levels. The return from the brink of national insolvency was powerfully combined with an improvement in the economy and corporate earnings. In real terms, net national product grew at 12% per annum from the economic trough in 1933 to the peak in 1937. Such economic growth rates in the United States have not been recorded before or since, and earnings growth was even more dynamic. From the low in 1932 the earnings series for the S&P Composite Index show earnings increasing 176% to 1937, growth almost three times faster than nominal GDP.

Figure 71

DOW JONES INDUSTRIAL AVERAGE - JULY 1932 TO JULY 1937

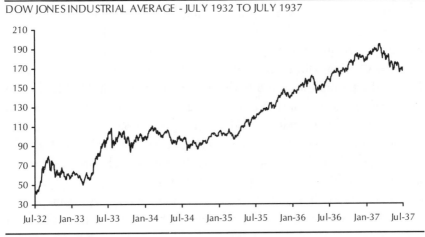

Source: Dow Jones & Co

Despite the dramatic rebound in economic growth, ample excess capacity throughout the system resulted in low inflation, and interest rates declined throughout this unparalleled economic expansion. Thus, there was a powerful positive mix for equity prices - surging earnings, surging dividends and falling interest rates.

The earnings and dividend recovery was dramatic, but not dramatic enough to lift either to new highs. Despite the 176% rise in earnings for 1932-37, the S&P data show market earnings in 1937 still below the levels reported in 1929, 1928, 1926 and 1925, as well as 1917 and 1916. The market's earnings at the 1937 peak were still 30% below and dividends 49% below the 1929 peak. At its peak in March 1937, the market was still 49% below its August 1929 all-time high.

So while this may have been the greatest five-year bull market in US history, only those who had purchased before March 1928 or after October 1930 could boast any capital gains. Those lucky enough to buy at the bottom in July 1932 had seen the DJIA rise 376% in just less than five years. It may not seem surprising that equity prices rose so dramatically from substantially undervalued levels in 1932 supported by this profits explosion and falling interest rates. However, it has to be remembered that these dynamics overpowered the numerous seemingly negative developments for American capitalism occurring at the same time.

The great bull market of 1932-37 occurred against the background of what many Wall Street commentators referred to as the introduction of "socialism" in America. To some these negative forces were already acting to depress prices in late 1932.

Although the DJIA bottomed in July 1932, the nascent economic recovery petered out in September of that year. At the time investors primarily attributed this to the increased uncertainty associated with the presidency of Franklin D. Roosevelt, which seemed certain by September 1932 and was confirmed on 8 November. At that stage in US history, the Inauguration was not until 4 March. There was a prolonged period with a "lame duck" administration and much speculation about Roosevelt's policies. In particular, there was a growing belief that FDR would remove the US dollar from the gold standard and the president elect refused to deny such rumours. The American public, for the first time in the Depression, now sold dollars to buy gold. A further tightening of liquidity began.

During this interregnum, the recovery in the economy, the stability in commodity prices and the recovery in bond prices all ended. The period also saw the third banking crisis, which ran from November 1932 to March 1933. Nevada declared a bank holiday in October 1932, Iowa in January, Louisiana and Michigan in February. By 3 March 1933, half the states of the Union had been forced to suspend operations.

Although this was the worst economic paralysis of the Depression, the DJIA's decline to 50 points was still almost 10 points above its July 1932 low. Whatever fears the market had about Roosevelt's policies, they failed to depress prices below the July 1932 low. According to the NBER, the economy reached its low point in March 1933, just marginally below the level of June 1932, and the stage was set for the bull market in equities to begin in earnest.

The great bull market in US equities coincided with the revolutionary "New Deal". By his inauguration in March 1933, few could have been in any doubt that FDR had major changes planned for financial institutions and financial markets in America. In his March 1933 Inaugural Address, Roosevelt declared that 'the money changers have fled their high seats in the temple of our civilization. We may now restore that temple to the ancient truths.' Within weeks, Roosevelt's first legislative action against Wall Street - the *Securities Act* of 1933 - passed through Congress, soon to be followed by the *Glass-Steagall Act* of 1933, the *Securities Exchange Act* of 1934, the *Banking Act* of 1935 and the *Public Utility Holding Company Act* of 1935. Against this background of encroaching legislation and regulation, the bull market in equities raged on.

The bull market in equities took place against a background of major experimentation with the monetary cornerstone of America - the gold standard. As early as his second day in office, Roosevelt decreed a "temporary" bar on the export of gold. There was some evidence that the move was indeed temporary as some banks were granted license to export gold in March and April. However, on 19 April it was announced to the world that Roosevelt would endorse the Thomas Amendment to the *Agricultural Adjustment Act*, which empowered the President to issue unbacked currency at his discretion. America had left the gold standard and Lewis Douglas, Director of the Budget, summed up the view of many in America when he remarked privately: 'This is the end of Western Civilization.'[52] Roosevelt then criminalised the hoarding of gold in private hands and abrogated government contracts promising payment in gold. Not

[52] John Brooks, *Once In Golconda - A True Drama of Wall Street 1920-1938*

until his mid-January 1934 State of the Union address did the President announce that America would be returning to the gold standard. The dollar was finally stabilised, following the passage of the appropriate enabling legislation, at the end of that month. In March 1933, the US Treasury had been redeeming every $20.67 for an ounce of gold, but by January 1933 it took $35 to buy the same amount of gold. Despite such legerdemain with the key monetary target that had anchored the financial system since 1879, and the dire warnings of most pundits, the bull market in equities continued.

Accompanying the new belief that legislation could make the financial markets safer and less volatile, the public sought scapegoats for the onset of the Depression. Almost as the stock market bottomed, President Hoover had asked Congress to investigate the stock exchange. The Senate Banking Committee hearings, which became known as the "Pecora" hearings for chief counsel to the committee Ferdinand Pecora, began in April 1932. The hearings produced lurid headlines for more than two years as they continued through to May 1934. Along the way, there was ample evidence of the misdeeds of Wall Street, and the public howled. Over the course of the 1930s, numerous Wall Street operators went before the criminal courts. Some convictions were not secured until the 1940s - many of those suspected of causing the stock market crash and the Depression went unpunished. Despite the publicity, the bull market in equities continued.

From 1932 to 1937, there was a vocal minority in America that believed the country was headed for socialism and that the "attack" on the financial markets was ideological in nature. There was ample evidence of such trends. In conjunction with the increased regulation of banking and financial markets, the government set up state agencies to provide services it believed the private sector could not provide.

The state's encroachment into the private sector progressed rapidly with the founding of Federal Home Loan banks in 1932, the Home Owner's Loan Corporation in 1933, the Tennessee Valley Authority in 1933 and the Federal Farm Mortgage Corporation in 1934, among others. The Reconstruction Finance Corporation, created by Hoover and massively expanded by Roosevelt, became the largest company in the world. A national minimum wage was introduced and the cost of labour rose further with the introduction of social security taxes and other government measures. Increasing government interference in the economy induced growing public deficits. Prior to the Roosevelt Administration, the greatest fiscal deficit reported by the US government, not associated with war financing, was 0.7% of GDP in the crash of 1837. The deficit was 4.7% of GDP in 1932 and rose through the recovery to peak at 5.5% of GDP in 1934.

Famously, Al Smith, a former Democratic candidate for presidency, in a speech in January 1936, damned the Democratic administration in comparing it with the administration in Moscow.

> There can be only one capital - Washington or Moscow. There can only be one atmosphere of government, the clear, fresh air of free America or the foul breath of Communistic Russia.[53]

Despite all the fears associated with gross public deficits, the New Deal and a move towards a socialist or even communist future, the bull market in equities raged on. Whatever theoretical or practical impairments Roosevelt's policies wrought upon the free market system in the US, the equity market thought them less important than the stabilisation of the financial system and a dramatic recovery in corporate earnings and dividends. If there was any structural impairment to the efficiency of the US economic system, the reaction of the equity market was that this was much less important than the powerful cyclical economic recovery.

The course of the Dow - 1937-42

In the vigorous economic recovery to 1937, real GDP rose marginally above the 1929 level, but rapid population growth meant per capita GDP had not recovered to its 1929 peak. Even at the peak of the recovery in 1937, the unemployment rate was 14.3% - half as much again as the previous high in 1900-30. With a normal economic recovery seemingly only in its infancy the economy then went into reverse gear. This interruption of the economic recovery at such an early stage shook investor faith in the surety of the business cycle.

It is unclear whether the abrupt end of the economic recovery in 1937 had a fiscal or a monetary cause. What is evident is that the decline did follow increases in reserve requirements by the Federal Reserve, which began in August 1936.

The Fed, utilising new powers granted by the *Banking Act*, also increased the margin on security purchases from 25% to 50%. With excess reserves in

---

[53] Address to the American Liberty League, 25 January 1936, Mayflower Hotel, Washington DC

the commercial banking system at such high levels, and lending moribund, it was considered that reserve-requirement increases would be the best way for the Federal Reserve System to regain control of the monetary reins. By 1937, there were reasons why the Fed might want to be in position to produce an effective tightening of monetary policy. Wholesale prices were rising strongly and the rising stock market caused concern about speculation.

Figure 72

DOW JONES INDUSTRIAL AVERAGE - MARCH 1937 TO MAY 1942

Source: Dow Jones & Co.

Given the slack in the financial system, it was not thought the Fed's moves would have a negative impact on economic activity. The Fed blamed the contraction that followed on a change in fiscal policy. Fiscal policy may indeed have been a factor; the federal deficit to GDP ratio declined from 4.2% in 1936 to 2.8% in 1937. Another factor may have been a sharp drop in corporate profitability in early 1937 associated with higher costs in general and rising labour costs in particular. On Wall Street, other culprits were sought for curtailing the cyclical recovery in the form of the stifling regulation of business flowing from Washington. Whether attributable to another Fed error of judgement or not, industrial production declined by a third from the 1937 peak to the 1938 low and S&P Composite Index earnings declined almost 50%.

Whatever the cause of the recession, the cyclical trough occurred in June 1938, just two months after the first reduction in reserve requirements by the Fed. This sharp economic contraction, before the economic recovery had any meaningful impact on employment, was far from normal and came as a particular shock for those who expected the economy to continue to expand until there was evidence of capacity restrictions and inflation. In the 12 months from 31 March 1937, the DJIA declined 49% and was back to mid-1933 levels. Stock market turnover suggests that this surprise economic recession within a depression played a bigger role than the Depression itself in producing the growing antipathy towards equities as an investment medium.

While the economy was recovering from June 1938, the bear market in equities did not abate. That equity prices failed to recover along with the rebound in corporate earnings suggests at the loss of faith in the ability of the economy to return to the pre-1929 normalcy. From the low in 1938, S&P Composite Index earnings doubled by December 1941, but the DJIA was unchanged. In an era of waning confidence in the economic future, equity prices could ignore even the strongest of earnings recoveries.

Perhaps more importantly, the increasing prospect of war in Europe was now playing an important role in determining the financial outlook. This is not to say that the equity market was necessarily depressed by the prospect of war. On the day the United Kingdom declared war on Germany, there was no panic selling on Wall Street - quite the reverse. In the first eight trading days of September 1939, as Germany swept into Poland, the DJIA rose 15%. Investors remembered US neutrality in WWI up to 1917, when flight capital flowed into the US and "war bride" stocks benefited so markedly from orders from Europe. How long would this beneficial combination of factors last this time? As German domination seemed increasingly inevitable, and materiel orders from a defeated Europe less likely, the market began to slip.

Hitler launched his *blitzkrieg* of Western Europe on 10 May 1940, and the tactic's success was clear to all within days. From 10 May to 25 May, as The Netherlands and Belgium surrendered and the British Forces were being evacuated from Dunkirk, the DJIA declined 23%. Flight capital fell away as Germany locked up European capital and US war orders appeared now only likely to come from the UK, though it was widely expected to pay in IOUs of dubious credit quality. By the end of May it was thus evident that the two positive factors which had produced the 1915-16 bull market were unlikely to recur.

The *blitzkrieg* changed everything and the pace of the bear market accelerated. As in WWI, the UK originally paid for materiel in cash, gold and securities. From the middle of 1940 to March 1941, there was thus an acceleration of capital inflows into the US associated with the war in Europe. With the US continuing to operate the gold standard, these capital flows produced acceleration in monetary growth.

The equity market had recovered somewhat during the summer-long Battle of Britain, supported by gold inflows from the UK, but by September 1940 it was becoming clear there would be more US involvement in the war as the US transferred ownership of 50 obsolescent destroyers to the United Kingdom. From this stage, the market's fears that cash payments would be diluted in favour of IOUs increased. The nature of the new form of US involvement became clearer in a radio address on 16 December 1940 when Roosevelt said the US would be "lending" materiel to Britain. The lend-lease programme began in March 1941.

In exchange for materiel, the US government now took credit or services from the Allies in lieu of cash or gold. The stock market did not respond favourably to the news. From September 1940 to 6 December 1941, the DJIA declined 14% as the US increased its lend-lease programme. The war was also producing direct inflationary pressures in the US, which was an added negative. From August 1939 to November 1941, wholesale prices rose 23% as raw material demand surged, with economies across the globe, including the US, gearing up for war. Although still neutral, the war had already enforced changes in legislation in the US which threatened to further undermine corporate profitability.

On 1 September 1941, the Federal Reserve took action against inflation, and imposed controls on consumer credit in "Regulation W", which stipulated minimum down-payments and maximum maturities for credit on certain listed articles. On 1 November 1941, the Fed increased the reserve requirement to the maximum available 25%. The DJIA was now back to 1938 levels but there was worse to come.

The attack on Pearl Harbor on 7 December ended speculation about US involvement in the war. As in 1917, the increased prospect of direct military involvement depressed the price of equities. However the immediate market impact of the attack on Pearl Harbor was not as dramatic as the impact following Britain's declaration of war on Germany, or the success of Hitler's *blitzkrieg*. The market continued the trend of the gradual decline evident from September 1940 and took almost five months to fall a further 20% to bottom on 28 April 1942.

However, this was not to be the best time in the 1940s to buy equities -

investors had to endure a further bull and bear market. Still, an investor using the q ratio as a guide to extreme undervaluation would have noticed that, in April 1942, equities were trading at more than a 70% discount to their replacement value. This was a level of undervaluation only previously recorded in 1921 and 1932. From 1942 began the second bull market of 1932-49, and the DJIA rose 128% to May 1946.

The course of the Dow - 1942-46

The bottom of the bear market in equities in April 1942 coincided with a major change to the US financial architecture and defeat of the country's military forces in the Philippines.

Figure 73

DOW JONES INDUSTRIAL AVERAGE - APRIL 1942 TO MAY 1946

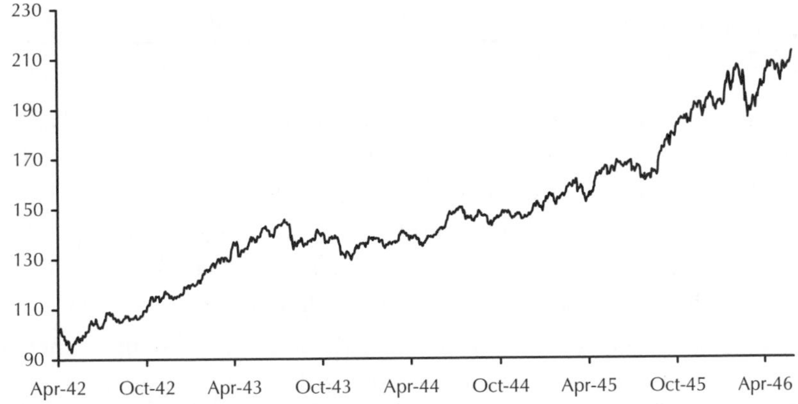

Source: Dow Jones & Co.

As in 1917, the Fed abandoned all other financial goals to further the ability of the government to finance the war effort. In April 1942, the Fed stated that it would fix the rate on Treasury bills at three-eighths of one per cent by intervening in the market. It was understood this rate would be fixed for the duration of the war. In fact, some form of intervention policy was to remain in force until March 1951. Although only the commitment to intervene in the Treasury bill market was explicit, in practice the actions of the Federal Reserve created a capped federal debt yield curve. The rationale behind these actions was that it would encourage investors, who would not be speculating on higher future interest rates, to buy War Bonds and thus reduce the cost of financing the war. The de facto maximum permitted yield on the longest-term government bonds was 2.5%. The capped rates effectively enshrined the positively sloping yield curve, which the market was dictating prior to April 1942, for the duration of the war and beyond. Not surprisingly the investing public and the commercial banks flocked to the long end of the market, where the risk of capital loss had been eliminated for the duration of the war, and ownership of the T-bill market passed increasingly to the Federal Reserve. During this period, the Fed, in the words of its chairman Marriner Eccles, 'merely executed Treasury decisions'.[54]

Figure 74

DE FACTO YIELD SUPPORT FOR GOVERNMENT SECURITIES DURING WWII	
Treasury bills	0.375%
One year certificates of indebtedness	0.875%
Short bonds	2.0%
Longer bonds	2.25%
Twenty-five to thirty year bonds	2.50%

Source: Sidney Homer and Richard Sylla, *A History of Interest Rates*

As in WWI, unlimited monetary fuel was made available by the Fed as needed to finance government bond sales and support bond prices. By buying bonds directly for its own account, the Fed boosted commercial bank reserves. The commercial banks, unlike in WWI, utilised the expanded reserves to buy government securities directly rather than to make commercial loans to others to do the buying. Between 1941 and 1945, the Treasury made seven war-bond issues, and this huge increase in financing was achieved without surging yields, due primarily to the allocation of these issues to compliant commercial banks. With the Fed intervening in the Treasury market, the rise in interest rates normally associated with large fiscal deficits and strong economic growth did not ensue. The low yields in the treasury market acted to dampen other yields. From April 1942, the monthly average prime corporate bond yield fell from 2.63% and it averaged 2.55% in 1942-46.

With inflation already rising steeply from 1939 to 1941, and bond yields now effectively fixed at low levels, it is not surprising that investors saw equities, yielding in excess of 11% in 1942, as offering better opportunities. While bonds offered fixed future payments investors in equities could normally expect growth in dividend payments.

---

[54] Marriner Eccles, *Beckoning Frontiers - Public and Personal Recollections*

The headline figures of low yields on fixed-interest securities and rising inflation persuaded many investors that equities would be a better long-term investment. However, even the headline figures underestimated just how powerful the dynamics for equities had become by 1942. Although the average annual rate of inflation from November 1941 to August 1945 was just 4%, this headline rate was achieved only via price controls and, for certain goods, rationing. Inflation would undoubtedly have been higher without price controls (introduced in January 1942). For those purchasing goods on the "black market", inflation was considerably higher than the reported level. Fixed-interest securities were even less attractive than reported figures suggested and thus the relative attractiveness of equities was even greater.

While the outlook for equities may have been improved by the government's rigging of the debt market, wartime finance produced other off-setting negatives. The US had financed its participation in WWI primarily by issuing debt securities. However, entering WWII federal debt levels were, as a result of the Great Depression, much higher than they had been in 1917. This time the government opted to place the burden of war financing more squarely on the taxpayer. Tax receipts as a percentage of GNP rose from 7% in 1941 to 21% in 1945. The highest rate of income tax reached 90%, on incomes of $1 million or more, well in excess of the 66.3% reached in WWI. This environment of strongly-rising tax rates was a head wind against which equities had to make progress.

Another problem for equities was the muted corporate profit growth from 1942 to 1946. While US business might have been expected to report bumper profits during WWII, this was not to be the case. The US government took numerous administrative actions to control prices during the wartime emergency and this put it in de facto control of corporate profit margins. The allocation of resources and capital passed from the markets to bureaucrats. Between the War Production Board, the War Labor Board and the Office of Price Administration, corporate profit margins were far less subject to the laws of supply and demand and could be squeezed to further the war effort. Also, the US administration, desperate for tax revenue and mindful of profiteering during WWI, dramatically ratcheted up corporate tax rates. From 1940 to 1942, the top rate of corporation tax rose from 19% to 40%, and an excess profits tax, introduced at a top rate of 50% in 1940, reached a flat rate of 95% by 1943. As a result, reported S&P Composite Index earnings and dividends were basically unchanged in 1946 from their

179

1942 level.

The 1942-46 equity bull market had been driven entirely by an expansion in equity valuations against a background of low real yields on fixed-interest securities.

While part of this rise in valuations may have reflected US progress in the war, the evidence suggests this impact was limited. The nadir for US involvement in the war can best be dated as 9 April 1942, when US forces in The Philippines surrendered at Bataan, and 6 May, with the surrender at Corregidor. The DJIA bottomed on 28 April. By early June there was already positive war news, when the Battle of Midway evened up the naval balance of power in the Pacific. In August, the US was on the offensive, landing troops at Guadalcanal. In November 1942, with the Allied victory against German and Italian forces at El Alamein, the war news began to improve significantly. In the same month, the Soviet counter-offensive at Stalingrad encircled Hitler's Sixth Army.

The first leg of the 1942-46 bull market was underway during this period and lasted until July 1943. However, despite the increasingly positive war news, the DJIA did not see a steady rise as the prospect of victory improved. The DJIA traded sideways from July 1943 to the end of December 1944 as the Allies liberated Sicily, Rome, Romania, Paris, Brussels, Antwerp, Athens, Wake Island, Saipan, Guam and Leyte. By December 1944, Allied troops had entered Germany from the west and the Soviets were fighting in East Prussia, but the DJIA was unchanged from the previous year, when the Russians had been almost a thousand miles from Berlin and the other Allies were massing at Dover.

Despite these moves towards victory, it was not until early 1945 that the bull resumed its run. Even then, the market rose only gradually, tempered by a minor economic contraction from February 1945. The economic downturn constrained equity prices and rises in margin requirements - from 40% to 50% in February 1945, and to 75% in July - also hampered progress. Not until VJ Day did an accelerated rise in stock prices begin, even though the economic contraction continued until October.

With the authorities aware of the possibility of undue speculation, in January 1946 margin requirements on shares increased from 75% to 100%. On 2 January 1946, Harry D Comer of Paine, Webber, Jackson & Curtis summed up the reasons to be bullish about the outlook for US equities.

Strongly fortified by elimination of excess profits taxes, net earnings of industrial companies as a group promise to be some 30% higher than in

1945... Dividends in total should increase fully proportionately with earnings. During the war, distributions to shareholders were only moderate; the resulting improvement in balance sheets will permit more liberal dividend policies in 1946.[55]

Buoyed by such optimism over earnings and dividends, the bull market continued until May 1946, finally surpassing the 1937 high and reaching levels only previously exceeded from July 1928 to September 1930. At this new peak the DJIA was still 44% below its all-time high of September 1929.

The course of the Dow - 1946-49

Bulls of the US market in 1946 saw the upside for equities from an economic boom based on pent-up consumer demand and a return of corporate tax rates to normal levels. The economy was bouncing back strongly from the 1945 recession. However, bears remembered how postwar euphoria in the 12 months after the 1918 Armistice had produced soaring inflation and that this had been followed by the sharpest annual bout of deflation in US history, accompanied by a vicious bear market in equities. Bears with even longer memories remembered the other necessary deflationary adjustment that followed the end of the country's previous major conflagration, the Civil War. As we have seen, the bull market that began in the darkest days of 1942 continued for one year past VJ Day. By the end of summer 1946, however, the bears were back in control.

Figure 75

DOW JONES INDUSTRIAL AVERAGE - MAY 1946-JULY 1949

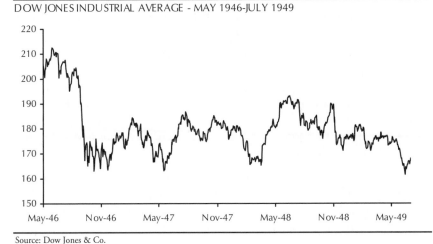

Source: Dow Jones & Co.

---

[55] *Wall Street Journal*, 2 January 1946

The index slide of late August and early September 1946, with the Dow declining 17%, was the sharpest decline in stock prices since the *blitzkrieg* of May 1940. The causes for the sharp break were spelt out in the *Wall Street Journal* on 30 August 1946.

> Robert S. Byfield of Lewisohn & Co. lists the following factors contributing to the decline in quotations '(1) The legislative struggle over O.P.A., (2) the acute indigestion in the market for new securities, (3) the evidence that interest rates had passed their low point and were beginning to firm slightly.'

During August and September, investors worried that President Truman would succeed in extending the wartime price controls administered by the Office of Price Administration (OPA), which were due to lapse in June 1946. This would put the squeeze back on corporate profit margins. Ultimately, Truman failed in his bid to extend price controls which, following a brief "emergency" extension, finally ended in November 1946.

Numerous other factors played their part in depressing the market. Continued demand for higher wages was a key concern. Many thought that inflation would only be conquered by a rerun of the destructive deflationary episode of 1920-21. In his State of the Union Address of 5 January 1949, even Truman was prepared to admit that bad times were probably just around the corner. 'We cannot afford to float along ceaselessly on a postwar boom until it collapses,' Truman told the nation. The feared postwar adjustment seemed increasingly likely. In *Money of the Mind*, James Grant relates the impact the 1920-21 deflation had on the economic outlook of one prominent business man in 1949, Sewell Avery, of Montgomery Ward.

> When an economist at Montgomery Ward handed him a diagram of commodity prices reaching back to the beginning of the nineteenth century, the chairman studied it raptly. Prices rose and fell recurrently. They rose in wartime inflations and fell in subsequent postwar deflations. The pattern had repeated itself as recently as 1919-1920... To Avery, a postwar depression was therefore a foregone conclusion. 'Who am I to argue with history?' he asked, and kept on asking.[56]

Avery's bet on deflation went wrong and his decision to stock up on government bonds rather than invest in the future of his business was disastrous. However, in 1949 most commentators believed some form of a re-run of 1919-20 was on the cards and the higher the rate of postwar

---

[56] James Grant, *Money of the Mind: Borrowing and Lending in America From the Civil War to Michael Milken*

inflation the greater would be the price correction. Of the various factors mentioned by contemporary commentators, it is clear, with the benefit of hindsight, that rising inflation and interest rates were the most important causes of the 1946-49 bear market. The fear was not of the inflation but of a deflationary reaction which was seen as inevitable by most investors.

Evidence of building inflationary pressures grew and grew from 1946 to 1949. In 1946 it looked possible that the US could witness a similar explosion in prices to that which had erupted in 1919. In the first half of 1946, wage settlements were rising sharply in response to a wave of strikes. Worker-days lost to strikes in January and February exceeded all those days lost in 1943 and 1944 combined. Not surprisingly, a sudden surge in inflation occurred later in 1946 when price controls were lifted. The wholesale price index rose 32% in 1946, primarily in the second half of the year. It was believed by some that the structural changes in the economy would institutionalise inflation. The composition of the economy had changed and the government sector now accounted for 15% of GDP, compared with 3% at the end of the 1920s. Investors had to ask whether this would be a one-off upward adjustment in prices or whether structural changes would now make inflation endemic.

As well as an increase in the power of government, there had been a rise in the power of labour. Would this structural alteration in the economy also produce more ingrained inflation? Union militancy reflected the fact that, by 1949, non-agricultural union membership had reached 33% of the workforce, up markedly from 13% in 1932. With particular piquancy, unions even demanded FDR's birthday be a holiday in new employment contracts.

For some, taking a view opposite from Sewell Avery, it seemed these structural changes could result in inflation becoming institutionalised in the postwar period. While the majority expected a postwar deflation and equity prices declined in anticipation, the minority saw a new era for inflation. The rise in inflation was, far from being a pre-cursor to a major price correction, an indication of the shape of things to come. The commitment to "maximum employment", enshrined in the *Employment Act* of 1946, suggested the postwar inflation outlook would be very different from that in 1919. Also, by 1946, it was evident there would be no attempt to reconstruct the gold standard, considered an institutional bulwark against inflation. The new international monetary arrangement thrashed out at Bretton Woods in July 1944 was, at its core, aimed at making deflationary periods less likely. If this was the case, investors could expect over the course of the business cycle inflation to be higher than it had been under the gold standard. Despite these institutional changes investors still expected the postwar period would suffer a period of deflation similar to that which followed WWI. With interest rates rising and the seemingly inevitable crash just around the corner, the duration of the decline in the DJIA reached record proportions by early 1949.

The 1946-49 bear market in equities was accompanied by a muted bear market in bonds. Bond prices declined, although the decline in government bond prices was halted by the continued actions of the Fed to support prices at pre-determined levels. Rising inflationary fears began to hurt debt markets as early as April 1946, finally ending the great bull market for bonds that began in 1920. With the war over the floor put on government bond prices could not be expected to continue. Official interest rates were not altered, but market-determined rates, trading well below caps enforced by the Federal Reserve, started to rise in April 1946. The yield on AAA-rated corporate bonds reached what remains their all-time low of 2.46% in April 1946, before rising steadily to 2.86% by December 1947.

Figure 76

YIELD ON AAA-RATED CORPORATE BONDS – JANUARY 1942 TO DECECEMBER 1949

Source: National Bureau of Economic Research

There was a pause in the rise of market-determined interest rates from the end of 1946 to the middle of 1947, as government bonds had risen towards capped levels. However, over the course of 1947, the support of shorter-term government securities was discontinued and the support price for longer-term government securities was lowered. In July 1947, the posted buying rate for Treasury bills, of three-eighths of one per cent, was lifted and the T-bill yield rose gradually to reach 1.25% by the end of 1948. Apart from the negative impact of rising market-determined interest rates, investors also worried over the government response to rising inflation. Official concern was so great that Truman sought powers in the fall of 1947 to reintroduce price, wage and credit controls. Congress denied his request.

While market interest rates had been rising since April 1946, the first increase in official rates only materialised in January 1948. The discount rate was raised 25 basis points in that month and a similar rise in August 1948 brought the rate to 1½%. Rises in reserve requirements were implemented in February, June and September, and in August, Congress restored, for a 12-month period, the Fed's ability to implement credit controls. All of these actions finally began to dampen demand and economic activity peaked in November 1948.

In the two years following the sharp decline of August and September 1946, the DJIA range-traded between 163 and 190. The final leg of the bear market then began in November 1948 with the commencement of the recession and the surprise election of Truman as President in his own right. The DJIA fell from 190 in November 1948 to its low of 162 on 13 June 1949.

In the 1946-1949 bear market, S&P Composite Index earnings increased almost two hundred percent. The optimism concerning earnings for 1946 was misplaced but earnings exploded after 1946. In 1947, reported earnings finally exceeded the 1916 level and this was to prove to be a level finally reached on a permanent basis.

Dividend growth, however, lagged earnings growth significantly, as the retooling of America for the consumer society called for heavy corporate investment. Dividends increased just 31% in the two-year period. The extent to which investors were concerned about possible deflation is evident from the fact that this scale of earnings and dividend growth occurred against the background of a bear market in equities.

While economic factors, in the form of the great debate on inflation or deflation, were the key driver of the 1946-49 bear market, the deterioration in US/Soviet relations during the period also played an important role.

The deterioration in the US relationship with the USSR had been increasingly weighing on the market. As early as March 1946, Winston Churchill famously told a Missouri audience that 'an iron curtain' had descended across Europe.

> In a great number of countries, far from the Russian frontiers and throughout the world, Communist fifth columns are established and work in complete unity and absolute obedience to the directions they receive from the Communist centre. Except in the British Commonwealth and in the United States where Communism is in its infancy, the Communist parties or fifth columns constitute a growing challenge and peril to Christian civilization.[57]

By March 1947, the Truman Doctrine offered financial support to 'free peoples who are resisting attempted subjugation by armed minorities or by outside pressures'.[58] Soon thereafter, the US began supplying monies to the Greek government to fund the resistance against the Soviet-backed communist guerrillas in the north of the country. The birth of the Marshall Plan soon thereafter produced further tension between the US and the Soviets as Moscow saw the plan as an attempt to expand US influence in Europe. In May 1948, the Soviets upped the ante and blocked the western powers ground access to Berlin, prompting the Allies to implement an air lift of supplies to the city. Tension continued to mount. The formation of the North Atlantic Treaty Organisation (NATO) in April 1949, was deemed by the Soviet Union to be an "openly aggressive" alliance and in breach of the charter of the United Nations. In the infancy of the new bull market developing by the summer of 1949, the *Wall Street Journal* on 12 July quoted broker Sam Smith, of Bache & Co, as crediting Soviet failure to take action over NATO's formation as an important bull factor.

> For over three years fears of what is now occurring in the business world have dampened market sentiment, preventing normal price-earnings relationships. When this weight is lifted, a welcome change in psychology should evolve with a tonic effect on our markets. There should be room for plenty of cheer in the realisation that: There isn't going to be a war...

By July 1949, the much expected deflationary episode was finally underway but the prospect of war with the Soviet Union seemed to be abating. Despite the occasional hot episode such as soon erupted in Korea, a "peaceful war" ensued, based on an arms race, which had decidedly better implications for equity investors than the third global conflagration that seemed to be getting closer between 1946 and 1949. With the Soviet Union detonating its first atomic bomb on 29 August 1949, the prospects of

---

[57] Address at Westminster College, Fulton, Missouri, 5 March 1946
[58] President Truman's address to Congress, 12 March 1947

some form of stand-off rather than outright warfare increased. For investors this global environment of de facto US neutrality combined with a rearmament boom had some of the very positive characteristics of the boom 1915-16 market. This slide into a "cold" rather than "hot" war played an important role in stabilising the equity market in the summer of 1949. The stage was now set for a bull market which would last for almost 20 years.

Structure of the market in 1949

On one side of the room were the doors of offices; the other side was covered with tremendous pictures of factories and ships and railroads. The pictures were Mr Golden's idea. He wanted to explain to customers the real meaning of the stocks they were buying. Mr Golden always wanted people to feel that the stock market was a creative, a productive thing.

Gore Vidal, In A Yellow Wood

The stock market in 1949

By the end of May 1949, the total market value of all NYSE-listed stocks was $64 billion. While market capitalisation was still a third lower than it had been in September 1929 it was four times larger than it had been at the bottom of the 1932 bear market. As in 1932, NYSE listings accounted for almost 90% of the total market capitalisation of US-listed stocks. At the end of 1949 there were 1,457 listed equity securities on the NYSE being only a marginal increase from the 1,293 issues listed at the end of 1929. With 1,043 companies listed on the exchange, the average market capitalisation of a company was $58 million. The size of the market needs to be put into the context of an investment management industry decimated by depression and war. In June 1949 there were just 150 investment management companies registered with the SEC and their total funds under management were $2.7 billion. Even had this industry completely eschewed bond investment it would have owned less than 5% of the US equity market.

At the bottom of the market, in early July 1949, an average of just over 900 of some 1,500 equity issues listed were traded on a daily basis. This compares to the peak of activity at the top of the market in 1946, when about 1,000 of 1,300 issues were trading. In 1946, monthly stock volume on the NYSE reached $1,946 million in January and had already declined to $1,432 million when the market peaked in May of that year. By the time the Dow reached its low in July 1949, monthly volume was just $526 million. The market was trading half-days on Saturday, so the average daily volume in July was just $23.4 million. While the DJIA had declined 24% from its May 1946 high, average trading volumes were down 70%. The peak volume for the market was still $16.4 million on 19 October 1929. The lowest daily volume in 1949 was $541,360, almost 97% below levels of 20 years earlier.

Over the 17 years since 1932, the composition of the market had changed considerably.

Figure 77

NYSE TEN BIGGEST CAP SECTORS VERSUS TOTAL MARKET CAP, 1949 RANKINGS		
(%)	1932	1949
Utilities	15.5	6.7 (5th)
Oil	10.9	16.0 (1st)
Communications	10.8	6.2 (7th)
Railroads	8.7	5.1[1] (9th)
Foods	8.0	6.2 (8th)
Chemicals	7.8	9.0 (2nd)
Tobacco	5.5	2.3 (14th)
Retail	5.4	7.9 (3rd)
Autos	4.3	7.5 (4th)
Steel	3.7	6.4 (6th)
Electric Equipment	2.4 (13th)	3.5 (10th)
Top Ten Total	**80.6**	**74.5**

Source: Kenneth R. French, *Industry Portfolio Data*. Note: [1] All transport, including railways.

Figure 77 shows how the ten largest industrial sectors listed on the NYSE changed over the course of the Depression and the war. While the importance of the utilities sector had waned somewhat, oil was even more important in 1949 than it had been in 1932. In 1949, oil and chemicals together accounted for a quarter of market capitalisation. The rise in the importance of petrochemicals was of particular importance for the chemical companies. The war-born plastic called polyethylene was finding 'new uses daily' and production had quadrupled in a year to the annual output rate of 50 million pounds.[59]

With the German chemical industry largely destroyed, the outlook for US companies was particularly bright. The drugs business had also exploded, with exports of penicillin alone adding up to more than the total drug exports of the country before the war. Other areas of the market which

---

[59] *Wall Street Journal*, 6 July 1949

had become significantly more important since 1932 were retail and autos. By 1949 the auto sector, prevented from producing cars during WWII, was retooling in an attempt to satisfy long waiting lists. In contrast, utilities, tobacco and communications were much less important than in 1932. Figure 78 shows the role of sector performance in the changing structure of the market.

Figure 78

BEST, WORST NYSE INDUSTRIAL SECTORS - JUNE 1932-JUNE 1949 (TOTAL RETURNS)	
Best	(%)
Beer	3,993
Games	2,606
Wholesale	2,396
Autos	2,201
Services	2,199
Worst	
Utilities	280
Tobacco	398
Coal	489
Household	523
Communications	527

Source: Kenneth R. French, *Industry Portfolio Data*. Note: Calculated on basis of dividends re-invested.

A simple description of the sector performance over the period can be taken from Matthew's Gospel - 'The last shall be first and the first last.' Sectors outperforming in the 1929-32 bear market - utilities, tobacco and telecommunications - underperformed in 1932-49.

The brewers performed particularly well due to the repeal of prohibition. The repeal of prohibition was increasingly likely in June 1932 as the prospects of a Democratic President grew. Still, the repeal in December 1933 had a major positive impact on the beer sector. With ample advance warning, investors were still richly rewarded by investing in the sector. The sector performance illustrates the importance of new equity issuance in the 1932-49 period in changing the structure of the market. Over the period the number of shares outstanding had increased by 59% while the number of companies with listed securities had increased just 27%. In particular the rise in importance of the chemical industry was as much due to its ability to attract new capital as to its share price performance.

The bear market of 1946-49 was long in duration, but mild in magnitude. Equities became very cheap in 1949, not because of the scale of the bear market, but because of the boom in earnings over the period. In this mild bear market, from May 1946 to June 1949, the utility sector once again showed its defensive qualities.

Figure 79

RETURN OF TEN LARGEST INDUSTRY SECTORS (JUNE 1949) - MAY 1946 TO JUNE 1949	
Oil	+5.8%
Chemicals	-8.06%
Utilities	-9.7%
Retail	-15.5%
Food	-16.2%
Communications	-17.7%
Steel	-17.9%
Autos	-21.5%
Electrical Equipment	-27.5%
Transport	-33.4%

Source: Kenneth R. French, 'Industry Portfolio Data'

The oil sector performed particularly well through the bear market as it had the fewest problems shifting from wartime production. Amazingly, oil demand was higher in 1946 than it had been in 1945 and, unlike other industries, few changes in the product were necessary to cater for the civilian, rather than military, market. The oil industry benefited in the period from both rising demand for its products and rising prices. The auto sector faced a more difficult transition as, with the collapse in demand from the military, it needed substantial retooling to shift back to civilian production. The transport sector was composed largely of railroads and continued to be burdened with government regulation. The difficulty in securing freight rate rises in the postwar, high inflation, period further undermined the industry's profits.

The bond market in 1949

> He stopped at his desk. It was a dull olive colour. His different books of statistics were piled neatly on one corner; notebooks and papers were scattered over the top and it looked as if he were busy.
>
> Gore Vidal, *In A Yellow Wood*

By 1949, the market value of NYSE-listed bonds had reached $128 billion compared to just $32 billion in 1932. Over the same period, the government bond price index rose 16% and the corporate high-grade bond index rose 43%. In July 1949 the *WSJ* explained how the NYSE bond market had changed.

> There were more than 1,600 issues of bonds listed on the Board in 1932. By the end of 1940 there were still nearly 1,400. Today there are only 912, and

75 of these are represented by United States Treasury and World Bank issues - which are traded entirely by dealer specialists in the over-the-counter market.

The number of NYSE-listed bonds was reduced to a level not seen since 1905. The difference in trend between the size of the market and the number of issues was driven by the increased importance of a few large issues by the federal government. The corporate bond market had been shrinking for many years. In every year from 1932 to 1945, with the exceptions of 1936 and 1938, the monetary value of corporate bond retirements exceeded new issues. In total over that period there were net corporate bond retirements of $42.8 billion and by 1949 the total value of corporate bonds outstanding was probably less than $30 billion.

Figure 80

MARKET VALUE OF NYSE BONDS & EQUITIES			
($bn)	Bonds	Equities	Equities as percentage of total
1928	47.4	67.5	58.75
1929	46.9	64.7	57.97
1930	47.4	49.0	50.83
1931	37.9	26.7	41.33
1932	32.0	22.8	41.61
1933	34.9	33.1	48.68
1934	40.7	33.9	45.44
1935	39.4	46.9	54.35
1936	45.1	59.9	57.05
1937	42.8	38.9	47.61
1938	47.1	47.5	50.21
1939	49.9	46.5	48.24
1940	50.8	41.9	45.20
1941	55.0	35.8	39.43
1942	70.6	38.8	35.47
1943	90.3	47.6	34.52
1944	112.6	55.5	33.02
1945	143.1	73.7	33.99
1946	140.8	68.6	32.76
1947	136.2	68.3	33.40
1948	131.3	67.1	33.82
1949	128.5	76.3	37.26

Source: New York Stock Exchange

NYSE statistics show the bond bull market, which had been underway since 1920, happened against a background of declining volumes. The peak year for NYSE bond trading was 1922, when trading volume exceeded an average of $15 million per day. As equities dominated investor interest during the 1920s, bond volumes declined to $11.4 million per day by 1929. While volumes in the equity market reached bottom in 1942, the lowest trading interest in the bond market was not registered until 1949, when daily average volume reached just $3 million a day. In total, less than $1 billion in bonds was traded on the NYSE in 1949, less than 1% of the $128 billion market value of outstanding issues.

As early as 1924, annual trading volume in the NYSE bond market had been almost 14% of the total market value of those bonds listed. In terms of volumes traded on the NYSE, bonds remained more important than equities throughout the period. Only in 1929 did even the highest trading day for equities see the monetary value of equities traded exceed the average daily volume for bonds. By 1949, bond volumes on the NYSE averaged $3 million per day, while equity trading volume ranged from $2 million to $500,000.

It has to be stressed, however, that this is an analysis of the bond market utilising only NYSE data - the only complete data available, in terms of trading volumes of bonds. However, over this period there was an important change taking place in the US bond market. As Figure 81 shows, the NYSE remained the most important venue in the US for the listing of corporate bonds.

Figure 81

LISTING STATUS OF US CORPORATE BONDS - PAR AS % OF TOTAL PAR VALUE			
(%)	NYSE	Other exchanges	OTC
1900	60	11	29
1908	51	5	44
1916	56	5	39
1924	62	5	33
1932	57	20	23
1940	66	12	22
1944	66	10	24

Source: W.Braddock Hickman, *Statistical Measures of Corporate Bond Financing Since 1900*

While the NYSE remained important for the corporate bond market its importance to the government bond market had been on the wane for many years. C.F. Childs explains how the dynamics of the government bond market, even by the time of WWI, were increasingly operating outside of the NYSE.

> ... virtually all purchases and sales of government securities were customarily made through dealers specializing in those bonds. The nominal quotations issued by the Stock Exchange had always been recognized as reflecting merely a general official price record for appraisal reference rather than the actual going market for large amounts. For every $1,000 Government bond sale recorded on the Exchange there were $1,000,000 par value unrecorded transactions made by a very few banking houses which were known as

192

Government bond dealers.[60]

The government bond market had only become a significant financial asset for individual investors following the explosion of government debt during WWI. Liberty Bonds were primarily traded on the NYSE and, in 1919, 76% of all bond trading on the NYSE was in government bonds. However, this was a high-point for individual ownership and, as the bonds moved to institutional ownership, large off-market transactions once again came to dominate the market.

Despite the explosion in the amount of federal debt outstanding, less and less trading in these securities occurred on the NYSE. It had decreased to non-material sums by 1940. Even with the rise of the individual holder of bonds during WWII finance drives, the NYSE was not to attain a position of importance in the government bond market.

Thus NYSE data provides an increasingly inaccurate picture of the US government bond market as time progresses. A better indication can be garnered from studying the growth in total outstanding government debt over the period. Even before the US had entered WWII, total gross debt of the federal government was $48.9 billion in 1941 and it then peaked at $269.4 billion in 1946. The public debt was now almost ten times higher than it had been following the end of WWI. By March 1946, individuals alone held $167.6 billion of government debt. In 1932 the nominal value of issued government bonds was $14.2 billion, with notes and bills bringing the total to $19.5 billion. By 1949, the face value of government bonds was $168.6 billion, with $56.3 billion of this comprised of savings bonds. The balance of the total public debt was made up by $82.2 billion in notes, bills and special issues. The federal debt market alone was thus almost three times larger than the equity market in 1949.

In describing the US bond market in 1949, it is worth mentioning the foreign issues market. While the 1920s are remembered as a period of US public speculation in equities, there was also a similar euphoria for the bonds of foreign issuers. The US had been enfranchised as the key creditor nation to the world because of WWI. Although foreign sovereign credits had been seeping onto the market for some time, the 1920s saw a new issuance boom fed by enthusiastic public participation.

On 30 June 1914, prior to the outbreak of war in Europe, only two foreign bonds, Argentina and Japan, traded on the NYSE. Britain, the

---

[60] C.F. Childs, *Concerning US Government Securities*

world's previous creditor nation, had had its first terrible introduction to the world of foreign bonds in the early 1820s. There had been several surges in new issues and bull and bear markets at decent intervals thereafter. In the US, this was a new market and it met with an enthusiasm that had all the hallmarks of British foreign debt manias of the 19th Century.

By September 1929, there were 202 foreign bond issues trading regularly on the NYSE and they accounted for one third of the bond trading volume on the Exchange. Not surprisingly, a global depression and world war had whittled down the number of foreign bonds still trading in 1949. When the DJIA bottomed on 13 June 1949, only 46 foreign bond issues were listed on the NYSE. There remained only 20 sovereign issuers with bonds trading on the Exchange and many of these issues traded below half their par value: Chile, Colombia, Costa Rica, Greece, Italy, Mexico, Peru, Serbia and Yugoslavia. Just over half of all the foreign bonds still trading were paying interest in full. At the end of 1948, there was $1,030 million of European dollar bonds paying no interest, 64% of this accounted for by Germany.

Following the attack on Pearl Harbor, the Securities and Exchange Commission had banned dealers from quoting prices or dealing in the $1,250 million in face value of dollar bonds issued by the Axis powers. This had ended trade in the debt of seven nations - Germany, Italy, Austria, Romania, Hungary, Bulgaria and Japan. Even by 1949, the market in these securities, with the exception of Italy, had not been reopened.

One reason provided for the continued suspension was a fear that German government securities, repurchased by the government prior to December 1941, had been accumulated in Berlin but not cancelled. It was now feared those bonds were in the hands of the Soviets. It is a fair generalisation to say that the first rush of enthusiasm by US investors for foreign government bonds had been just as disastrous as the British involvement in the 1820s. Benjamin Graham, writing after the war, was able to dismiss the entire asset class with some disdain, arguing that foreign bonds had 'a bad investment history since 1914', made worse by two world wars and a world depression.

> Yet every few years, market conditions are sufficiently favourable to permit the sale of some new foreign issues at a price about par. This phenomenon tells us a good deal about the working of the average investor's mind - and not only in the field of bonds.[61]

---

[61] Benjamin Graham, *The Intelligent Investor*

At the bottom with the bear - Summer 1949

'We should have a big rush soon. I'm doing a report now. Well, not really a report; I've been getting some statistics on aircraft stock ready for the front office. It's been some job.'

Gore Vidal, *In A Yellow Wood*

In both 1921 and 1932 there were large slumps in equity prices. The bear market that ended in summer 1949 was very different. From the peak in May 1946, at a 16-year high, the market declined just 24% to reach its low in June 1949. However, despite the lack of drama, this bear market was, in one key respect, similar to that of 1921. In 1929-32, equities crashed from high valuations to low. This sudden lurch from over-valuation was exceptional. As we have seen in 1921, equities had spent a long time seeking lower valuations before reaching them in a final material price decline.

In 1949, the final price decline was more muted, but the prolonged downdrift in valuations echoed the pre-1921 experience.

Figure 82

S&P COMPOSITE INDEX CYCLICALLY ADJUSTED PE - 1933-49

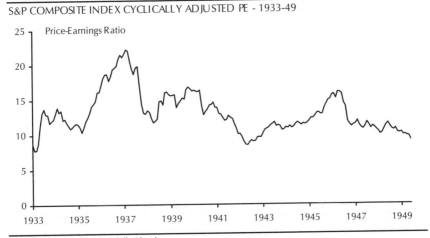

Source: www.econ.yale.edu/~shiller/data.htm

A key driver for the prolonged decline in equity valuations, as it had been prior to 1921, was the failure of corporate profits to fully benefit from the growth of the economy. The path for the US economy from 1929-46 had been a lot more rocky than it had been prior to 1921. Despite the Great Depression in the intervening period, the US economy had expanded while the DJIA was back to levels first seen in 1926.

Figure 83

ECONOMIC GROWTH 1926 AND 1949

	1926	1949
Population (millions)	117	149
Number of immigrants per annum	304,488	188,317
Expectation of life at birth (years)	57	68
Number of physicians	149,521	201,277
Average hourly earnings (manufacturing)	55¢	$1.43
Total union membership (000's)	3,502	13,213
Wholesale price index	100	155
Nominal GDP ($bn)	97	267
Real GDP ($bn 2000 dollars)	794	1,634
School enrolment (000's)	27,180	28,491
Number of farms (000's)	6,462	5,722
Number of cattle on farms (000's)	60,576	76,830
Value of mineral products current dollars (m)	5311	10,580
Index of physical volume of minerals produced	66	92.1
Crude oil production (000's barrels)	770,874	1,841,940
Value of new private an public construction $m (1947-49 Price)	23,752	23,527
Dwelling units started (000's)	849	1,025
Cigarettes produced (millions)	92,523	385,046
Total steel ingots and castings produced (000's long tons)	48,293	69,623
Railroad mileage	421,341	397,232
Motor vehicle registrations (000's)	22,250	44,690
Number of telephones (000's)	17,746	40,079
Net production of electricity by central stations (m Kwh hours)	94,222	345,066
Exports ($m)	5,017	12,160
Imports ($m)	4,755	7,467
Balance on goods and services ($m)	826	6,359
Real gross private domestic product per man hour (1929=100)	94	162.7
Total assets of banks ($m)	65,079	170,810
Total of deposits ($m)	54,416	156,488
Volume of stock sales on NYSE (millions per annum)	451	271
Life insurance in force ($m)	77,642	213,672
Federal government expenditure ($m)	3,097	39,506
Paid civilian employees of federal government (000's)	548	2,102
Public debt of federal government ($m)	19,643	252,770
Military personnel on active duty	247,396	1,615,360

Source: US Bureau of the Census

While the equity market had gone nowhere since 1926, the economy had expanded materially. Real GDP was below its 1926 level as late as 1935 and the entire growth in the economy in the period happened from 1935 to 1949. Continued population growth prevented a doubling in real GDP per capita, but it still increased 62% in the 1926 to 1949 period. One possible reason for the discrepancy between the expansion of the economy and corporate profit growth was the rise in importance of both government and labour. Figure 83 shows how the government sector had become an increasingly large portion of the US economy. Over the 1926-49 period, government expenditure as a percentage of GDP had risen from 3% to 15%. While the first half of the period was calamitous for labour, there was a marked improvement in the second half. The consumer price index rose 73% from 1935 to 1949 but the average hourly earnings of manufacturing workers increased 155%.

Despite the growing role of the government and the unionisation of labour, the reported profits of listed companies did grow marginally faster than nominal GDP in 1932-49. However it is very dangerous to measure corporate profitability solely by the increase in profits over one specific period. The ability for corporate profits to grow in line with nominal GDP from 1932-49 is not particularly impressive when one considers how depressed profits were in 1932. The S&P Composite Index earnings series for listed companies began in 1871 and by 1872 profits were already higher than they were to be in 1932 in both nominal and real terms.

Given the very depressed nature of earnings in 1932, the 10-year average reported earning figure, compared with the 1949 equivalent, provides a better general estimate of "normalised" earnings. This comparison shows "normalised" earnings in 1949 to be 33% higher than "normalised" earnings in 1932. Given the growth in nominal GDP over that period, corporate profitability had clearly been disappointing.

The total growth in listed company profit from 1932 to 1949 contains two very different periods. Almost two-thirds of all growth in reported profit in the 13-year period occurred between 1945 and 1949. The repeal of the excess profits tax in 1945 played an important role in this sudden surge. As we have seen this profits surge coincided with the final decline in equity prices.

This suggests that investors doubted the sustainability of the postwar profits explosion and were treating the very low levels of profitability in 1945 as more indicative of the earnings power of US corporations. Thus even the sub-par profits growth from 1932 to 1949 was treated as perhaps an over-generous representation of the future earnings power of listed companies. This lack of faith in the continuation of even this low level of profitability was evidenced by a decline in valuations.

For many investors it must have been difficult to believe that equity valuations could decline from their very low 1932 levels. When the DJIA reached its lowest level in June 1932 the market was trading on a modest PE of just 9.4x current earnings, compared with the 1871 to 1932 average of 13.7x. As the earnings contraction had not run its course by June 1932, the PE was much higher on a prospective earnings basis. Reported earnings hit their lows for the Depression in December 1932, and based on that level of earnings the market was trading on 11.6x PE in June 1932.

Even at this very depressed level of earnings, a level already surpassed from April 1872 to June 1876, the market was valuing equities at a very steep discount. An investor in June 1932, even foreseeing the further contraction in earnings might have expected that the valuation, over the long term, was likely to rise towards the 13.7x 1871-1932 average level. However by June 1949 the S&P Composite Index PE had fallen even further to 5.8x earnings. Earnings did have a little bit further to contract in 1949 but even taking this into account the market was trading on just 6.4x in June 1949.

Investors buying at the bottom in 1932, expecting that at least valuations of equities would rise, saw those valuations decline a further 40% by the bottom of the 1949 bear market. Earnings growth was poor over the period, but the ability of equities to reach ever lower valuations was the key driver of poor returns - particularly post 1937.

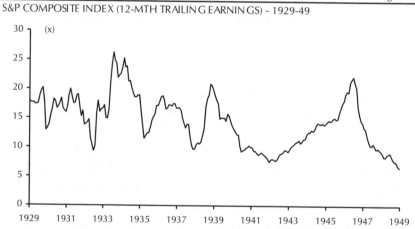

Figure 84

S&P COMPOSITE INDEX (12-MTH TRAILING EARNINGS) - 1929-49

Source: www.econ.yale.edu/~shiller/data.htm

The year-end *q* ratio for the US market declined from 0.43x at year-end 1932 to just 0.36x at year-end 1949. By 1949, equities had become exceedingly cheap and the scene was set for the longest bull market of the 20th Century.

Good news and the bear

'Although I have the greatest personal esteem for the opinions of yourself and associates, uh, in re to the stock market, I must, in this instance, disagree with you, for I am of the opinion that this is a rising market and will continue to be so. All statistics at hand... no, available, point to just that. Hoping to hear from you again, and so on.'

Gore Vidal, *In A Yellow Wood*

The summer of June 1949 was more like 1921 than 1932. Investors had not recently suffered a calamitous collapse in prices. By mid-1949, investors had been through a prolonged period of sideways trading despite better economic conditions and, since 1945, dramatic improvements in corporate earnings. Tempering the better economic and earnings picture was the fear of a postwar depression and deflation, as had occurred in 1921, or a continued heavy government involvement in the economy which would stifle corporate profitability in the long term. Despite this general uncertainty, the recovery of equity prices preceded the recovery in the economy.

The DJIA bottomed in June 1949, while the NBER reference date for the end of the recession is October 1949.

Yet, even for investors who could foresee the economic improvement there were good reasons to be cautious. In the long period since 1932, there had been two previous occasions, June 1938 and October 1945, when recessions had ended and economic expansion had recommenced. On neither occasion did the economic turnaround produce a sustainable rise in equity prices. To be prepared to invest in equities in June 1949 an investor had to believe that this time it was different.

One of the great market truisms is that the end of a bear market will be signalled by the absence of good news and optimism. As we have seen this was not the case at the bottom of the market in 1921 and 1932. Similarly in 1949 there was ample good news and optimism at the bottom of the market.

The economy may not have bottomed until October 1949 but there had been plenty of good economic news in the pages of the *Wall Street Journal* that summer.

21 April: ... first quarter reports have been better than generally expected.

22 April: International Harvester Co. thus far in its current fiscal year, which started last November 1, has produced at least 30% more farm equipment then in the like period a year ago.

22 April: 'A number of economic observers have reached the conclusion, or are veering to the view, that the readjustments which are progressing in our economic situation will ultimately set the stage for a vigorous business revival.' Sam Smith of Bache & Co.

22 April: W.W. Axe president of Axe-Houghton Fund Inc., writes stockholders in part: 'There are a number of factors which are likely to limit the duration of a business decline. One of the most important is the credit supply, which is large and probably will be increased by the Federal Reserve Bank operations. Government expenditures probably will be increased if there is further contraction in business. There is also a great deal of construction work which must be done, notably in the utility field. A decline in process and improvement in labour efficiency would probably bring in new demand. Finally, the downward trend in general business activity should modify legislation likely to be passed by Congress. The situation is very unlike that obtaining at the start of a really severe business decline in the past, such as 1907 and 1920. But a short, perhaps sharp business contraction in 1949 is a real possibility.'

25 April: Evans Wollen Jr. president of the American Bankers Association- As strong spots in the business picture Mr. Woollen enumerated these: An important pent-up demand for goods:

the large amount of money in the hands of the public: the European aid program, which while it involves serious problems over the long term is certainly a stimulant to business currently and the expected military aid to this country's associates in the Atlantic Pact.

28 April: The budgets of first quarter reports, led by such companies as U.S. Steel, Du Pont and General Motors, include many improvements but investors are not concerned with history and are trading on what may take place in coming months.

28 April: Sales of gasoline by Standard Oil Co. of Ohio in the first quarter were about 8% ahead year on year.

2 May: Earnings of the 197 firms topped $732 million more than 21% greater than 1948. [WSJ survey of 1Q 1949 in 20 major listed industries]

12 May: Secretary of the Treasury Snyder said postwar 'adjustments' are now 'practically completed' in many lines of business.

14 May: Announcement after the close of the cent-a-pound increase in the price of scrap copper heartened the constructively minded in Wall Street.

21 May: It is reported that U.S. Pipe & Foundry has noted an improvement in new orders in the second quarter. Municipalities and public utility firms, its major customers, are expected to maintain its operations at a high rate for some time.

23 May: The bulk of indication is the recession will be a light one.

3 June: Private residential construction in May fell 15% below the like month last year. For the first five months of 1949, residential building was down 15% from last year....For the first five months of this year, all construction ran 3% above the like period last year....Public construction hit a more positive note.... For the first five months this year public construction was 40% over last year.

8 June: Followers of the aircraft shares say Boeing's 1949 sales should be double last year's and earnings considerably above those of 1948.

9 June: Dropping for the 20th consecutive time, business loans fell another $152 million during the week ended June 1, the Federal Reserve Board reported. Real estate loans, running an opposite trend, advanced to a new record high of $4,092 million at leading city banks June 1. Real estate loans were $324 higher than a year ago.

16 June: About a year - that's how long many businessmen think the downtrend will last.... President Spang of Gillette, for instance, suggests the downswing will be over in four to six months.

16 June: President George B. Beitzel of chemical-producing Pennsylvania Salt says, 'In the last few days we've noticed more activity in certain lines. Most of us in the company feel by fall we will be active again.'... A big paint company notes a recent sales pickup. Its explanation is that dealers stopped buying to cut inventories and then found consumer demand was still pretty strong. Would be buyers complain store stocks are skimpy in wanted items.

16 June: 'Rolling recession' is a term used more and more to describe the situation. A White House economic adviser gets credit as the phrase coiner.

By rolling he means industrials have been hit in series rather than all at once. Some such as cotton, textiles, airlines, frozen foods, radio sets, distillers, luxury goods ran into trouble a year or more ago. There has been some comebacks in this list. Still other industries haven't really felt the downswing. Autos an important example. Drug makers another. Electric power sales continue to top those of a year ago. Telephone company has a big backlog of orders. Truckers profitably busy partly at the expense of competing railroads. The government's economic pulse-takers suggest that on the average it appears to take about a year for each industry to complete the slide from its lofty postwar business peak to a levelling off place.

16 June: If a business recession seemed to be gaining momentum early this year, a good many U.S. consumers weren't too worried about it.... According to figures collected for the Federal Reserve Board, they had more money to spend than ever before, felt pretty optimistic about their future prospects and intended to buy automobiles, houses and other durable goods.... The results said one 'looked queer compared with what other things we know about the economic picture.'... They note a slump on appliance sales continuing through April then a pickup less than seasonal but enough to indicate that lower prices were stimulating sales. Federal Reserve banks report that dealers who go after customers most aggressively with price cuts and advertising get results.

22 June: Walter Maynard of Shearson, Hammill & Co.: 'Evidence seems to point to an upturn in both business activity and the stock market in July. Under the circumstances, investors would do well to adopt a somewhat more aggressive attitude.'

29 June: Ralph Rothem of Harris Upham & Co. 'It is just possible that business activity may be able to recover some in coming weeks because of the need for increased production of certain non-durable goods where inventories have been reduced.'

30 June: The rayon business, which has dipped steeply of late, is showing signs of perking up.... A spokesman for North American Rayon and American Bemberg Co. both under the same management says: 'This is a definite turn from the bottom. We consider it significant and expect better business for the rest of the year.'

1 July: Considering the intervening price reductions, physical volume at retail is so far holding up remarkably well in the aggregate. The rise in unemployment has not yet made much of an impression n the general exercise of purchasing power. The difference between industrial production and distribution to consumers is obviously accounted for by reduction of inventories. Baring such contingencies as prolonged work stoppages and great loss of wage income, consumption must in due course over-take production and call for greater activity at the mills and factories. The automobile and building construction industries remain conspicuously active.

1 July: There have been scattered instances of business improvement, notably in the rayon field. There has also been a slight break in the clouds blanketing the international economic outlook. Those who had been warning of an imminent devaluation of the pound sterling for a week or two past now believe that no such climax to Britain's economic crisis is likely for a month or two, or until after the meeting of commonwealth finance ministers in London.

2 July: Unemployment jumped to a seven year high of 3,778,000. But there was no increase in the number of adult jobless the department said. The 489,000 increase over May figures came in the 25-and-under age group.... The increase in non-farm employment reversed a five-month decline and was attributed to expansion of construction and outdoor work.

6 July: 'It is becoming quite popular now to predict that our current recession will tend to bottom out in the fall and that a gradual pick-up in over-all business activity will occur in the spring of next year.' Daniel F. Rice & Co. of Chicago

8 July: Lucien Hooper of W.E. Hutton & Co. - 'Field reports, gathered from a wide cross section of industry, indicate that the usual conditions which precede a major depression are lacking.'

8 July: Sales of electricity to the nation's larger industrial plants in May declined below the like month a year ago.... It was the first year-to-year decline in any month since August 1946.... Sales to residential customers in May totalled 4,470 million kilowatt hours, or 14.2% above the like month a year ago, and sales to commercial consumers amounted to 3,625 million kilowatt hours, or 7.2% above the May, 1948, total.

11 July: The brass industry, whose production has slumped 50% in the past six months noted a substantial pick-up in sales late last week.

12 July: Sam Smith Bache & Co. - 'For over three years fears of what is now occurring in the business world have dampened market sentiment, preventing normal price-earnings relationships. When this weight is lifted, a welcome change in psychology should evolve with tonic effect on our markets. There should be room for plenty of cheer in the realization that: There isn't going to be a war; there won't be a tax increase; we have no vicious labor bill; we re rapidly heading for business normalcy; costly inventories are shrinking; excess inefficient plant space is being idled or scrapped; public needs are still huge and purchasing power enormous; vast additional markets will be tapped with the return to realistic prices; money is cheap and credit plentiful; and stocks are low and yields are high.'

14 July: Textile makers are encouraged by 'feelers' from cotton and rayon cloth buyers. New England mills say this preliminary nibbling by cutters and garment makers for fall goods is the first evidence of real buying interest in these fabrics in over a year.

18 July: Outdoor advertising firms, which sense the general advertising trend first, report 1950 is shaping up as another big year.

21 July: Trade at retail stores has been relatively stable since the beginning of the year, the Commerce Department said. In the first six months the total variations on the adjusted index from the first six months of 1948 has been only 1% it added.

22 July: The appliance industry has reached the bottom in its readjustment in the opinion of James J. Nance president of Hotpoint... 'Price reductions for electrical appliances, which took place around the end of the

first quarter of this year, were rapid and thorough. They have brought appliance prices well within... levels of the nations economy.'

23 July: Corporation Dividends Paid in May Were 14% Above like 1948 Month- For the three months ended May 31, cash dividend payments totalled $1,373,300,000, up 10% from the $1,251, 900,00 paid out in the same period of 1948.

25 July: New England, Hit Hard By Business Dip, Sees Hints of Recovery. New England with a high proportion of consumer goods industries is usually the first section of the country to feel a business change for the better or for the worse.

1 August: Business continued to decline in July but at a slower rate than in May and June, the National Association of Purchasing Agents said... At the same time order booking revealed its greatest strength since the start of the decline last October with 30% of the purchasing executives reporting increases compared with 28% showing decreases. Survey shows these commodities increased in price in July-Copper, lead, zinc, alcohol, new burlap, ceramics, corn, limerock, cottonseed oil, tung oil, rosin and starch.

4 August: Steel mills report a definite pickup in demand.

5 August: Indeed this newspaper, which has had the unfortunate chore of reporting 'bad' news for several months, has carried enough such cheering items lately to bring forth comment from President Truman at yesterday's press conference. For once he is pleased with us.

6 August: After the close the Federal Reserve Board announced cuts to be made over the next few weeks in reserve requirements of member banks.

The reductions will increase by $1,800 million the amount of bank funds available for investment in government securities or loans to business.

10 August: Bache & Co said. 'The beginning of a new spirit can be sensed in Wall Street. This could easily be the foundation for the next major expansion in American business activity.'

10 August: Hemphill, Noyes & Co. 'Nevertheless, we believe that a severe business depression will be avoided that war is improbable and that any adverse effects here from sterling or other currency devaluations will be temporary.'

Of course, there was plenty of bad news as well. But the above excerpts again show that those who await the universal bad news that mythically signals the end of a bear market will miss the boat. **As in 1921 and 1932, the market's failure to respond to good news was more indicative of the end of the bear market than any proliferation of bad news. There were numerous other similarities, in 1949, with the signs of nascent economic recovery in 1921 and in 1932. On all three occasions, it was remarked that the economic recovery, to spread through the country, began in New England. Another factor common to all three bear market bottoms is that the auto industry expanded while the general economy continued to contract.**

With auto production halted in February 1942, only 749 new cars, taken from inventory, were sold in 1943 and 1944. Motor vehicle registrations in 1945 were still below 1939 levels. This lack of production produced a very abnormal auto market which distorted pricing for many years after the war. The pent-up demand for car ownership had sent second-hand car prices to large premiums and created a queue for new cars after the war. From the *Wall Street Journal* of 5 April 1949 comes this item:

> **Used Car Doldrums** - Lower prices and slower sales mean sliming profits for used car men who have watched their fabulous market crack slowly but surely in the past two years. During the war and early postwar they could sell any car that ran for almost any price. In the winter of 1946-47 sales of fantastically-priced luxury models began to skid. Business boomed through 1947 but consumer resistance grew gradually and more new cars came off assembly lines complete. In the 1947-48 winter prices slipped 10% to 20%, in September 1948, they were off an estimated 25% from 1947 peaks. Business this past winter dipped to postwar lows... A 1937 Chevrolet that cost $900 new would probably have been marked off about $250 the first

year, $200 more the next year and $150 more the next, bringing it down to one-third its original price in three years. After the war, a 1946 Chevy listed at $1,200 new was likely to sell in a used car lot for $1,500 early in 47, $1,300 early this year and maybe $1,100 today - three years later. A three-year-old Cadillac that listed at $2,500 new in 1946 would have sold for just about that early this year. Today it would bring $800 less.

One expert estimated, in the same *WSJ* story, that there were 40,000 dealers in the US compared with 19,000 pre-war. The declining premium on second-hand cars and the decline in the number of second-hand car dealers signalled that the market was returning to normality.

In the first full year of peace, in 1946, US factory sales of autos totalled 2.1 million and this was to reach 5.1 million in 1949. While price declines on new cars did not begin until 1949, they did not progress far before resurgence in demand occurred. The 5.1 million sales figure seemed high relative to the 3.8 million units sold in 1941, the last year of peace for the US. Not surprisingly, investors worried that sales could not be maintained at such high levels once the wartime pent-up demand had been satisfied. Such concern was unjustified as postwar sales continued to grow strongly. Some foresaw continuation of the postwar boom. William F. Hufstader, General Motors' vice president in charge of distribution, was quoted in the *WSJ* on 4 June 1949 as saying:

> The average age of cars in use during 1948 was 8.73 years, compared with 5.33 years in 1941; nearly 13 million cars on the highways in the United States last year were 10 years old or older compared with about 5 million before the war; disposable income is at a record high, population has increased and a larger proportion of people are in income brackets generally regarded as the new car market.

Car dealers had their own unique ways of clinching a sale, according to the *WSJ* of 11 August 1949:

> Got a horse? A New York City Ford dealer will accept one (or a mule or a goat) as a $300 allowance on a new truck.

In 1921, 1932 and 1949 rising demand for autos presaged a more general improvement in demand. This resilience may be based on the fact that auto ownership was still rising from what would subsequently be proved very low levels. For such products with low diffusion rates, it may be that the sign of the unleashing of pent-up demand provides an important indicator of general economic improvement. While autos seemed one of the very first products on the buying lists of the reinvigorated consumer the spending urge soon spread to other products. There may of course be other products at the top of consumers' shopping lists when their confidence returns. On 4 May 1949, the *WSJ* pointed out another industry already undergoing something of a boom.

> **Business Booms Again At Las Vegas** - In the bar of the Flamingo, Ben Goffstein, one of the managers, says, 'I get reports from other parts of the country that liquor sales are off as much as 40%, but the last few weeks our bar gross has been 10% better than a year ago.'... Gambling in Nevada is no sure-fire economic weathervane. But as one guide to luxury spending, it has been accurate in the past. For example, a slump in Reno gambling in the winter of 1947-48 preceded by several months the national let down in demand for luxuries. Las Vegas hopes soon to pass the 30,000 population level of Reno to become the biggest metropolis in Nevada.

This interview took place just three years after Bugsy Siegel had opened the Flamingo. If ever there was an industry and a town in a structural growth phase it was Las Vegas in 1949. The city that hoped to have a population in excess of 30,000 can now boast almost two million people living within its metropolitan area and 36 million visitors a year.

Price stability and the bear

In the summer of 1949, the *Wall Street Journal* chronicled numerous economic improvements. As in 1921 and 1932, there was rising demand for products at lower prices. This echoes an important change underway at the bottom of both the 1921 and 1932 bear markets. Perhaps autos and gambling saw strong demand first, being products benefiting from structural growth. But rising demand was soon evident in more mundane products and commodities. An important indicator of the 1921, 1932 and 1949 bear market bottoms was the first evidence of increased demand for commodities appearing at lower prices. In 1949 as in 1921 and 1932 this provided a clear indication that deflation was ending. As it had been deflation that was crushing corporate earnings, it is not surprising that the equity market responded so positively to the first evidence of price stability. The rise in demand and prices happened at different times for different goods and commodities.

In 1949, as in 1921 and 1932, a return of general price stability coincided with the end of the bear market in equities. As in 1921 and 1932, spreading demand for and price stability of selected commodities augured well for general price stabilisation.

In 1949, as in 1921 and 1932, low levels of inventory in the system suggested that any price rises might be sustainable.

It seems the tendency to overstock can impact even those industries with more predictable demand characteristics, as the *Wall Street Journal* reported on 19 May.

Lower Death Rate Hits Casket Manufacturers The biggest factor in declining production is that many funeral directors, like purchasers in other lines, bought heavily last year - and are now overstocked.

Inventory liquidation had played a role in depressing prices so, now that inventories were at rock bottom, perhaps deflation would abate. For the economy as a whole, inventory liquidation had erupted in late 1948. According to the Department of Labor's wholesale price index, the postwar peak for prices came that same month. This was exactly three years after the end of the war. The continuation of wartime inflation had lasted almost twice as long as it had done following the end of WWI. By the time the DJIA bottomed in June 1949, the wholesale price index had already fallen 7.5% from the August 1948 peak, and as Figure 85 shows, there was only a further marginal decline to come.

Figure 85

US WHOLESALE PRICE INDEX 1939 TO 1951

Source: National Bureau of Economic Research

The consumer price index performed very similarly to the wholesale price index. So, while the equity market bottom did not coincide with the bottom for general price levels, it did occur as the period of sharp decline in prices ended. As in 1921 and 1932, growing indications of stability in commodity prices proved a good indicator of the change in trend of general prices and the end of the equity bear market.

There was ample evidence of this change in the pages of the *Wall Street Journal* in the summer of 1949. As early as April a rise in the price of rents and food was evident within the retail price index. The market price of wheat and oil improved in June. A key confirming feature of the rise in prices was the fact that inventories were low and that there was evidence of rising demand at lower prices. As the *WSJ* put it on 8 July, 'the public is willing to spend if it considers the price is "right"'. By July, price rises in lead, rayon, poultry, zinc and copper were remarked upon as further evidence that general deflationary trends were abating. The wholesale price index marked a marginal rise in prices in July and the accelerating pace of deflation, frightening the markets, was nowhere to be seen.

The big call for investors in 1949 was the degree of deflation that would necessarily follow the war. When would it end? The crucial answer to that question came from the performance of general prices, and not the economy in general, or the equity market itself. In particular, signs of increased demand for commodities at lower prices leading to prices stabilising in the summer of 1949 suggested the scale of deflation would have to be much smaller than occurred in 1920-22. As in 1921, and in 1932, close scrutiny of price trends in general and commodity prices in particular was a key element in determining when equity prices were approaching their nadir.

The total decline of 7.9% in the wholesale price index from August 1948 to June 1950 was in marked contrast to the 45% decline in prices following the post-WWI peak for prices. It is clear from the pages of the *WSJ* that a much greater degree of deflation had been expected. The bear market in equities during 1946-49, when corporate earnings doubled, also suggests that investors expected a much greater degree of deflation. For the investor who saw commodity price stabilisation as the first sign of general price stabilisation there were very cheap shares to be bought in the summer of 1949.

Of course, the key question is whether it was any easier to forecast this change in prices than it was to forecast the bull market in equities. In particular, was it possible to foresee that deflation would be of such minor magnitude compared to 1921 and 1932? While there may have been many reasons for the constrained 1948-50 price decline, key institutional changes between 1921 and 1949 did strongly suggest price declines in the post-WWII economic cycle would be more muted. It is clear from a former vice-president at the Teachers' Insurance and Annuity Association that the prospect of a new era for inflation was being actively discussed.

> Eminent authorities believe that our economic system is now 'replete with
> built-in inflationary bias,' especially in periods of war or international
> tension accompanied by heavy expenditures for defense. They point to the
> tax structure, escalator wage clauses, parity prices, budget deficits,
> government borrowing from commercial banks, low rates of interest, cost-
> plus contracts, subsidies and the like. Some point to Keynesian economics,
> emphasis on full employment, the public welfare state, disinclination to
> return to the gold standard.[62]

So there were those who foresaw that the postwar deflation would be
muted. These investors presumably were increasing their exposure to cheap
equities throughout the 1946-49 bear market. It did indeed turn out to be
different this time. For those with such foresight, there were good profits to
be made in buying equities in the summer of 1949, confident a postwar gross
deflationary adjustment was not on the cards. However, as already suggested
above, investors did not necessarily need to have such an expert grasp of the
changing institutional architecture dictating a "built-in inflationary bias".
As in 1921 and 1932, there was no need to pre-judge the level at which
prices would stabilise. One could wait and assess evidence in the summer of
1949 that prices were stabilising.

The analysis so far has focused on how signs of pricing stability for
commodities have been an important tactical consideration in timing entry
into the equity market. Of course, there is an increasingly evident strategic
message from the importance of changes in the general price level. It is
evident that the periods of extreme undervaluation for equities have all
followed a shock to the general price level. In 1921 and 1949 investors were
pondering just how much of the gross wartime inflation would have to be
reversed. The answer was very different on both occasions but the massive
uncertainty regarding future prices and corporate profits depressed equity
prices. In 1932 there had been no inflationary surge associated with the
previous bull market. This perhaps resulted in further uncertainty as
deflation erupted and investors had to guess at what level prices would
stabilise.

In this book, we are studying those periods when equity prices were very
cheap and provided excellent subsequent returns. Can it be merely a
coincidence that in 1921-49 we find equities reaching their cheapest levels

---

[62] William C Greenough, A *New Approach to Retirement Income*

following material disturbances to the general price level? This has important ramifications for investors. It suggests the safest time to buy equities is following a major price disturbance. If no such price adjustment is associated with a decline in the stock market then this may not be one of these great buying opportunities.

This is not to say that one can't buy into declining equity prices in the absence of a major disruption of the general price level. However it is to say that the absence of such a price disruption may mean that equities have not reached such a low level as to permit one to pursue a long-term buy and hold strategy. Low valuations, when combined with a return to normalcy in the general price level, are likely to provide the best prospect of above-normal returns for investors.

The **general price level** refers to the prices of all goods and services in the economy. The term is used in this book to avoid confusion with the regular references to more specific price changes. A disturbance usefully covers either a rise or a fall in prices. But what is a material disturbance? It is a term of convenience, but it is used here to reflect that the magnitude of the disturbance to the general price level was significant enough to have had a major impact on the market.

Liquidity and the bear

> A nurse with a baby carriage was hurrying streetward. It was late, probably much too late for her to be out with the baby. As she passed him he caught a glimpse of the child and saw that it was staring vacantly ahead, concentrating upon growth.

> Gore Vidal, In A Yellow Wood

For each of the four key episodes covered by this book we look at how useful liquidity analysis has been to those seeking to find the bottom of the bear market. In 1921 and 1932 we looked at what role increases in Federal Reserve credit outstanding and other changes in monetary policy had on the stock market. In Part I and Part II, we saw how the creation of the Federal Reserve, to work in conjunction with the gold standard, had significantly complicated the business of forecasting liquidity trends. By 1949, the Fed had been operating for almost 35 years, and this should have resulted in an increased ability to forecast its actions. However, as we have seen, inconsistency and error in its policy settings over those 35 years meant that Fed actions were probably as difficult to predict in 1949 as they had been when it opened for business in November 1914.

The bad news in 1949 was that the monetary mechanism had changed and this made Fed watching even more difficult. The Fed's wartime responsibility to support government securities at pre-determined levels meant it was a provider of unlimited amounts of high-powered money. Little had changed by 1949 and although support prices for Treasury bills and certificates were discontinued in 1947, the Fed remained committed to supporting government security prices of longer maturities. The support price for government bonds was lowered on Christmas Eve 1947, but the new price remained in place throughout 1948. In practice this policy meant that the "elastic currency" would have to keep expanding as long as the Fed needed to buy such securities to support their price. Thus when market forces were forcing government bond prices below their support level the Fed's key monetary tool was placed on de facto auto-pilot. In this situation the expansion of the "elastic currency" was an administrative certainty and not an indication of the Fed's preferred monetary stance.

The commitment to support government bond prices produced other distortions in the normal operations of the monetary system. Raising reserve requirements was not as effective as it would have been in periods of normalcy. There was a rise that began on 27 February 1948, aimed at slowing economic activity and inflation, and this forced banks to sell government securities. However the Fed was then forced to intervene in the market to support the prices of these securities, thus raising Fed credit outstanding. The Fed thus found themselves in the ridiculous position of having to expand the "elastic currency" in response to their own measure aimed at curtailing economic activity. While market forces sought to push government bond prices below their support levels such distortions to the monetary system were inevitable. Investors could have no conditioned response to changes implemented by the Fed. If it had been difficult to work out what the Fed was up to in 1921 and 1932 it was much more difficult now.

With the key monetary tool on auto-pilot investors had to look at other actions of the Federal Reserve to assess its future monetary intentions. Since the 1935 banking legislation the Fed had the power to determine margin requirements for security purchases. The margin requirements had been reduced from 100% to 75% in February 1947. The subsequent decisions not to make any further reductions, despite a prolonged bear market in equities, suggested that the Fed was not unhappy with the price adjustment. In August 1948 another administrative power was added as the Fed regained powers to regulate consumer credit, which Congress had removed in November 1947. As early as September 1948 these new powers were being used to restrict consumer credit. The use of the administrative measures also indicated the Fed favoured a tighter policy.

The reaction of the economy to the administrative measures was swift. The peak for prices had already been reached in August 1948 and economic activity peaked in November of that year. With the economy slowing and prices falling in the first quarter of 1949, those trying to time a movement into the falling equity market would have been seeking guidance on future liquidity trends. When would the Fed signal a change in policy and how, given the confusing joint targeting of the time, would such a change in stance be visible?

Fortuitously, a change in market conditions occurred in 1949, which restored some freedom of action to the Fed and allowed it to show its hand. The Fed's legal obligation was to intervene to buy government bond prices at the support level, but clearly this obligation ended if market forces pushed prices above the support level. This is exactly what happened in the last quarter of 1948 and in that environment the Fed's actions could now be seen as providing a true sign of its intentions. Should the Fed permit the market-led rally to continue this indicated that they favoured lower interest rates and an easier policy? However, if the Fed now intervened to sell government securities and restrain the rally this would result in a contraction of the elastic currency and a clear indication that it favoured a tighter monetary policy. The Fed responded to the market rally by selling government bonds and in January 1949 alone effected a five percent contraction in the elastic currency. As soon as an opportunity had arisen the Fed had moved swiftly to implement an important contraction in their credit outstanding. Now investors prepared themselves to cope with the postwar deflation which had been so long expected.

There were those who expected a re-run of the post WWI contraction, and as a guide would have looked to the behaviour of Federal Reserve credit outstanding in that period. These investors expected dramatic deflation as Fed credit outstanding had declined 50% by the time the equity market bottomed in 1921. The decline did not end until July 1922, when the Fed had orchestrated a total decline in its credit outstanding of 69%. Would this be the scale of contraction in the elastic currency the Board of Governors deemed necessary after WWII?

The Fed had permitted another major contraction in its credit outstanding from 1928-31, even though there had been no previous inflationary excesses which needed erasing. From November 1928 to May 1931, a 50% decline in Fed credit outstanding was permitted before the Fed began to stretch the elastic currency. With the Fed contracting credit outstanding by five percent in their first month back in control it was easy to see why investors expected a re-run of the 1919-21 and 1928-31 experience.

Such a major contraction was particularly likely as there had been a very large increase in Federal Reserve credit outstanding during WWII. From Pearl Harbor to VJ Day, Fed credit outstanding increased from $2.3 billion, still 32% below its 1920 peak, to $22.9 billion, almost six times its pre-war high. The amount peaked at $24.7 billion in December 1946. Would there now be a 50-60% decline as the Fed's previous actions suggested? By the time the Fed finished squeezing the wartime inflation out of the system after WWI, its credit outstanding was just 60% larger than it had been when war was declared. If this was the standard operating procedure then investors could now expect an 85% decline in the elastic currency. It was the prospect of this magnitude of monetary contraction which produced a bear market in equities from 1946 to 1949, while corporate earnings doubled.

The rapid tightening evident in January 1949 continued. In just eight months from December 1948 there was a 25% contraction in Federal Reserve credit outstanding. This is just what the bears had expected and they awaited the completion of the expected 50-85% contraction which history suggested was likely. It never occurred. The contraction was over by October 1949 and the elastic currency had been stretched back to its December 1948 level by September 1951. The Fed decided to stop the contraction of Fed credit outstanding after what could only be described as a mild liquidity squeeze by historic standards. There was no element of *force majeure* about this decision as government bond prices continued to trade well above their support level. This decision was made by the free will of the Board of Governors but who could have guessed that they would permit the elastic currency to remain so stretched relative to its pre-war level. A focus on Fed credit outstanding would not have been suggesting cause for optimism until the final quarter of 1949 while the stock market had bottomed in June of that year.

An investor focusing on the Fed balance sheet would have been unlikely to guess the DJIA would bottom in June 1949. The contraction in Fed credit outstanding was in full swing and a historical analysis suggested that the contraction was, at best, only half completed. As in 1921 and 1932 it cannot be said that detailed analysis of the Fed balance sheet produced any clear indication that the bottom of the bear market had been reached.

While not providing a good buying signal in 1949 this approach was still much more successful than it had been at the bottom of the 1921 and 1932 bear markets. While those analysing the Fed balance sheet in 1949 may have been about five months late for the party this was much better than the signal provided to commit funds in July 1931 and in the summer of 1924.

In 1921 and 1932, credit expansion significantly lagged the improvement in the equity market and the economy. In 1949, things were very different and commercial bank loans bottomed in July 1949, just after the bottom of the equity market. From there, credit grew steadily, if slowly, through the rest of the year. Those prepared to act on the July data might have been buying equities by August, but it is more likely that any action would have been postponed for a few months until a new trend was evident. In 1949, waiting for a credit expansion before buying equities was a sounder policy than at the bottom of the other bear markets. However, it was still a lagging, rather than a leading, indicator of any improvement in equity prices. Waiting for an improvement in broad-money growth proved as misleading in 1949 as in 1921 and 1932. The earliest indication of any improvement in broad-money growth was in the second quarter of 1950, long after the equity market had bottomed. Even this improvement was short-lived, and the major trend of decelerating growth in broad money did not come to a halt until 1953. Inflation-adjusted M2 growth shows noticeable improvement from August to September of 1949. This measure of monetary alteration thus appears to have had some value in both 1921 and 1949, although its turnaround was well after the bottom of the market in July 1932.

Though the balance sheet of the Fed did not give a good indication of when to buy equities, changes in its policy stance did provide timely signals. The first easing of credit controls imposed in September 1948 came as early as March 1949, providing clear evidence the Fed believed that, if anything, the pace of the economic contraction was too rapid.

From March 1949, it was evident the Fed probably believed it had squeezed the economy hard enough. A series of reductions in reserve requirements began on 1 May. On 29 June, the *WSJ* reported Federal Reserve officials confirming they would stop intervening to prevent a rise in the price of government bonds. Although this did not result in a rise in Fed credit outstanding until October, it was another policy statement that made it clear the Fed preferred an easier monetary policy. These signs of policy changes were a much better indicator that the liquidity squeeze was more likely to end than any detailed analysis of the Fed balance sheet.

Investors buying equities on the first sign of easier monetary policy, in March 1949, were to see the DJIA decline a further 10% before bottoming on 13 June. As the commercial bankers were responding to both policy announcements and the availability of Federal Reserve credit, their balance sheets proved a better indicator of altering liquidity conditions. Commercial bank loans outstanding bottomed in June 1949 and had already expanded 3.2% by November of that year. This resumption of credit growth was occurring, while Fed credit outstanding continued to contract. Readers of the *Wall Street Journal* were aware of the turnaround in commercial bank behaviour by the end of July 1949, when business loans by New York City banks broke out of a record 27-week decline. The end of the contraction in commercial bank loan books was underway about three months before the Fed began to increase its own credit outstanding.

The good news for investors in 1949 was that they had very little time to wait before the stock market responded to the first signs of easing, the reduction in consumer credit controls in March, from the Federal Reserve. The subsequent 10% decline in prices was in hindsight not an extreme price to pay to invest at the bottom of what was to be one of the greatest bull markets in US history. In 1921, investing on the first sign of a policy change, a reduction in discount rate, would have had investors committing funds to equities in May of that year and seeing a decline in the DJIA of 20% before the index bottomed on 22 August. On both occasions following changes in the Fed balance sheet, as opposed to change in policy signals, would have brought investors to the market after the first significant rises in equity prices.

The major problem for those seeking to invest at the bottom of bear markets was that pursuing a similar policy in the 1929-32 bear market would have been disastrous. Reductions in Fed discount rates were already underway by November 1929 when the bear market had a very long way to go. Searching for the ease in liquidity is best done by watching the Fed's policy stance, rather than changes in its balance sheet.

Even then, one would have to discount the 1929-32 period as a one-off event in order to say that buying equities on the first sign of a change in Fed policy is a fruitful tactic.

The bulls and the bear

> Mr Heywood spoke of the market, of stocks and shares, of the state of the Union. He spoke convincingly because his manner was convincing and, also, because his ideas and facts had been given him by many clever men.
>
> Gore Vidal, *In A Yellow Wood*

As we have seen, contrary to popular mythology, there is plenty of good economic news around at the bottom of bear markets. The need to see the dominance of bad news proved misleading in 1921 and 1932. A similar market canard has it that one should be a buyer of equities when everybody else is pessimistic. If one determines pessimism by reference to the press and the broking community, then it was as absent in 1949 as it had been in 1921 and even 1932. There were plenty of bulls ringing the bell for equities at the bottom of the market.

13 April: Broad Street Investing Corp. notes that in its history the average annual income return on its diversified investment fund was above 5% only in 1932, 1911 and 1942, 'which hindsight proved to have been highly auspicious buying occasions'. Current yield 5 ¼%.

18 April: 'We think it noteworthy that while the bulk of recent news has not been cheerful, the market has failed to break down.' Sam Smith of Bache & Co.

19 April: Harry D Comer of Paine, Webber, Jackson & Curtis 'Review' listed 20 common stocks yielding 8% to 12%, about which he said 'Besides bearing extra-liberal dividends, each of these selected stocks earned at least 50% more than the dividend payments in 1948. Also each stock holds a record of uninterrupted dividends for 20 years or more, some of them over 50 years.'

19 April: W. Maynard of Shearson, Hammill & Co.: 'Viewed purely from the point of view of the market, there is some fairly persuasive evidence that adversity of a good deal more serious nature than many companies are likely to encounter has already been thoroughly taken into consideration by both buyers and sellers.'

25 April: L.O. Hooper of W.E. Hutton & Co said 'There are a number of things to remember about this market. The progress of the bear market since the summer of 1946, nearly three years ago, has been highly irregular and some stocks are much more liquidated than others; price earnings ratios should rise as earnings decline and the percentage of profit paid out increases, we should begin to look for new price factors rather than think that the same old influences are going to govern sentiment indefinitely, and, more than half of the time in recent years stock prices have moved inversely to the business index and profits.'

25 April: Said Arthur Weisenberger & Co. stock prices have never been lower in relation to dividends, except at the critical points of WWI and II and in the depths of our worst depressions, in 1932 and 1873.

25 April: Norman Funk of E.F. Hutton & Co.: For the present the stock market may have to remain on the defensive but the soundness of its underlying position is indicated by its general stability in the face of adverse trade reports over a period of months and by the very large short interest revealed by the recently revealed figures.

28 April: George G. Bass of Harris, Upham & Co.: 'The inability of the market to make headway at this time is scarcely surprising, but it is, of course, evident that the day-to-day play of favourable earnings and other news is exerting practically no market influence.'

2 May: Traders adopted a wait-and-see policy toward developments abroad last week and investors apparently were more concerned with increasing signs of deflation at home.

2 May: Failure of the ample budget of good news early in the week to result in anything but the feeblest rally raised bears expectations of an early test of February lows.

2 May: Several of Wall Street's largest houses have reported they currently are lending 'more stock than at any time since 1929' and 'more than at any time in our history'. Such statements lend credence to widespread belief in the Street that the short interest again has expanded in the last two weeks. If so, the cushion against any forthcoming decline may be comfortably deep, according to the dwindling herd of bulls.

2 May: Coffin, Betz & Co., Philadelphia: 'Once again, as at the bottom in late November there are a lot of little bears hoping to make a profit. They rarely do.'

9 May: Although there was no follow through, volume contracted during subsequent fractional sell-offs and the over-all technical picture was said to be favourable.

10 May: Hugh W Long & Co. 'For almost a decade there has been little or no relationship between the level of business activity and the level of security prices. Thus it cannot be assumed that the current business readjustment will surely be accompanied by a commensurate adjustment in securities prices...'

10 May: A.J. Messing of Hertzfeld & Stern 'It is out of such divergences as we are witnessing now that important reversals occur and I am now ready to express the definite opinion that the lows of the year have been made.'

12 May: Kenneth Ward: 'When so many high-grade stocks are selling on a price basis all out of proportion to even a substantial decline in earnings, then it is usually close to buying time.'

12 May: H. Hentz & Co.: 'The investor today has, in our opinion, the opportunity to avail himself of unusually attractive values.'

13 May: L.O. Hooper- ' Technical factors, in our opinion, lean in favour of a worthwhile seasonal rise sometime early this summer.'

13 May: The stock market deadlock continues. It even survived the lifting of the Berlin blockade which the bulls claimed stood in the way of an advance. Further the list of stocks lending at a premium is larger than in many months.

14 May: Announcement after the close of the cent-a-pound increase in the price of scrap copper heartened the constructively minded in Wall Street.

14 May: Edmund W. Tabell of Walston, Hoffman & Goodwin said 'My technical work indicates that the market is very rapidly reaching a sold-out condition. Some further pressure may be required but it would appear that we are near the start of an important upside move.'

14 May: For the past six month, in spite of all the bad news about business, the DJIA has been in a 7% trading range.

19 May: Release of short interest figures after the close made even bigger news than Wall Street had forecast. The increase of 130,058 shares in the month ended May 13 made the bear position of 1,628,551 the largest in more than 16 years, or since the report of February 27, 1933.... Technicians found it even more significant that the short position as of the most recent report represented 213 days trading based on average daily turnover in the past month....First second and third largest short positions were in Pepsi Cola, Hudson Motors and General Motors.

20 May: With a fairly firm under structure stocks continue in the trading rut. This ability to take the light selling

has inspired many broker commentators, chartists and other students of market movements to say the upside has more substance than the down in the face of a lot of deflationary news.

24 May: The market moved a long stride nearer the critical 171.10 resistance level in the industrial average yesterday. The fact that the reaction was accompanied by reduced volume was not lost on technicians, who have forecast that a further easing of prices on even smaller volume than the 750,000 daily average of recent weeks would be a bullish factor second only in importance to an advance on increased turnover.

25 May: Vance, Sanders & Co. of Boston; 'With the exception of the depression years of 1932-33 common stocks are selling at about as low a level in relation to dividend payments as they have for 50 years.'

1 June: The consensus was that 1949s test of the 163-165 triple bottom, defined by the lows of 1946, 1947 and 1946, is at hand.

3 June: On the other hand, and no less a factor in the consensus of market opinion, are the continued high yields for stocks of companies in strong balance sheet positions. Doubt is expressed that anything short of violent surprise in the day-to-day developments would persuade holders of large blocks of such securities to pitch them overboard at this juncture.

4 June: Stocks completed one of the sorriest weeks in recent market history by sinking further into the rut just above the historically important resistance area measured by the industrial average at 163-165. Volume indications, if not bullish, at least gave no immediate cause for alarm. Turnover yesterday was only 700,000 shares.

6 June: L.O. Hooper of W.E. Hutton & Co. has compiled a list of 225 stocks which sell at less than working capital.

10 June: 'For our part,' said L.O. Hooper, of W.E. Hutton & Co., 'We would prefer to buy than sell, for trading purposes if a bear market is recommended by the industrials selling through 160 and 40 respectively. Remember that this intermediate move is of above average age already, the stock market never was as high as business and business profits, the short interest is large, we are approaching a 'saturation point' in pessimism regarding business, institutions are showing a greater buying interest, and a mid-summer rally is traditional, even in bear markets.'

11 June: Another fact partially obscured by gloom was the failure of the railroads to reach new lows for the year, although industrials closed at a new two-year bottom. Finally, turnover of 800,000 shares compared with 1,380,000 and 1,240,000 on the preceding post-Memorial Day breaks....On a closing average basis, industrials are 1.49 above a low dating form 1945, railroads 1.54 above their 1947 bottom. There was agreement on one point between bulls and bears as the weeks trading closed. Next week should be interesting.

13 June: DJIA bottoms at 161.6

14 June: All closing average resistance points were swept aside and stocks reached new postwar lows in the fourth major decline in the past 10 sessions. Industrials dropped 3.01 to their lowest

level since August 7, 1945. Railroads slipped 1.67 through all bottoms set since October 3, 1944. Volume once again failed to reach 'climactic proportions' but rose 540,000 shares above Friday's total to just under the turnover generated on the break a week ago.

14 June: Management of National Securities Series, one of the largest trusts to report for the fiscal year ended April 30 believes this to be 'a good time for long-term investment in carefully selected income-producing securities. The year 1949 will in our opinion be good for income to investors.'

15 June: One thin barrier to lower prices again remained inviolate, however. That was the intra-day lows of the industrials and the railroads, set October 30 1946 and May 19 1947 respectively.

15 June: May 29th marked the third anniversary of the present bear market. Already it has lasted longer than any other, exceeding even that from September 1929 to July 1932.

16 June: Said Kenneth Ward 'In the past few years Dow Theory spots have been closer on the upside for selling purposes and on the down for buying opportunities. This is a selective buying time not selling time in this writer's analysis.'

17 June: The turnover in the final hour however when prices were at the lows of the day was little more than half that generated in a rising market after 2pm on Wednesday.

17 June: L.O. Hooper of W.E. Hutton- 'The bear market has some of the features of being in its final stages.

Volume of trading it is important to observe falls on each succeeding attack on prices.'

21 June: The small reduction in the short interest announced after the close came as somewhat of a surprise to Street sources who had been expecting a further crowding of the bear side.

25 June: Some analysts say that a higher premium is being paid for the safety inherent in 'defensive' stocks today than at any time since 1942 and suggest that swing in emphasis to more speculative groups is on the cards.

29 June: Over a period of years the 30 stocks in the average have sold at about 15 times earnings noted the Keystone Co. of Boston. In bull markets they sell as high as 25 times earnings. In recent bear markets they have sold at about 10 times earnings. Today they are selling a 6-7 times the latest reported 12-month earning.

1 July: A/M. Kidder & Co. 'We refuse to be stampeded into the bearish camp by the occurrence of events that were anticipated weeks and months ago'

5 July: The interest depressing aspect of the decision of the Federal Reserve System to let government bond prices rise was discouraging to bank share dealers who were looking to a responsive market in anticipation of favourable second quarter earnings.

6 July: Sam Smith of Bache & Co. said: 'Precedents readily can be found where a reversal in the trend of security prices was instituted by strength in Treasuries. In time, such demand over-flowed into other grades of bonds and stocks, ultimately embracing practically all categories. The constant search for

better yields and the confidence imbued by the rise in government bonds gradually exerted their effect. It may be premature to assume at this time that this pattern will evolve in the current instance, but one should bear such possibilities in mind.'

7 July: More stock was traded in the final hour yesterday than in any full session since June 15. The 810,000 shares which changed hands after 2 pm were the most for any 60-minute period since May 17, 1948 and swelled turnover for the day as a whole to its highest point since March 30, when the abortive spring rise ended. Thus, volume yesterday exceeded anything generated on the downside during repeated intervening selling drives, a point whose importance technicians emphasized after the close.

8 July: The anticipated reaction following five consecutive days of rising prices failed to get far and was accompanied by a contraction in volume.

8 July: A modest technical rally became a budding 'summer rise' on Wednesday when volume on the fifth consecutive day of advance exceeded anything generated during the repetitive selling drives of the second quarter.

14 July: The market took another puzzling step up yesterday. In the face of disquieting labor news, unrelieved tension abroad and an impaired technical position, all three averages reached recovery highs as volume once more surpassed the million-share level. It was also considered significant that in a much broader market with 1016 different stocks appearing on the tape, compared with 941 Tuesday.

14 July: Stocks followed a recently familiar pattern yesterday by doing their best in the final hour. In an attempt to explain this persistence of late session improvement in prices brokers said that such demand probably stemmed from timid shorts who were wary of constructive overnight news developments.

16 July: In the face of a seemingly certain strike in the steel industry and unsatisfactory labor relations in several others the market advanced rather persistently for several days this week.

19 July: W.E. Buford & Co. of Charlotesville Va. Has issued a memorandum on 'Ploughed Back Earnings' which says in part: 'Results of a study of some 3,000 stocks disclose that about one-fourth currently are selling for less than the ploughed back earnings of the past six years.'

20 July: Said the manager of one of America's large private fortunes 'I'm not inclined to follow this rally, but the large number of investors readying programs to be initiated 'after the next market break' makes me nervous about my own position. In matters like these I don't like too much company.

20 July: Carl M. Loeb Roades & Co.: 'It seems to bear out the comments current among confident investors for the past year or two. They argued that a market which was never guilty of exaggerations of optimism and which began predicting a business decline two years before the fact would not suffer the usual slump when depression actually struck.'

21 July: By the most recent count there were 1,644,313 shares short, all representing stock which must be purchased at some future date. This almost exactly matched the figure of 1,643, 047 in January, 1933. The ratio of the latest figure to daily average trading in the month ended July 15 is 2.40 to 1. This is the highest point at which this compilation has stood since May, 1938. Technicians said it might be significant that on both those prior occasions the bears were wrong.

25 July: Herbert G. King: 'Traders should not overlook that the market is resting on a potential keg of dynamite. Stocks have been going into very strong hands for some time and the latent power of the extremely large short interest is tremendous. One thing appears certain: Very few of the amateur shorts will succeed in making money out of their short positions.'

5 August: 'It will be noted that during the boom year 1929 when common stocks were highly inflated in value, the yield on bonds was actually in excess of common stocks by about 1¾%. In the depression year, 1932, the yield on stocks was almost the same as bonds and in 1937 the gap amounted to only a little over 1 ½% in favour of stocks. During 1942 when stocks were reflecting the extremely adverse war outlook, the yield gap increased to over 3% in favour of stocks. Stocks are now selling to yield 4%, more than bonds which is at a greater variance of spread than we have experienced during any one of the past 20 years.' Ralph Rotnem of Harris, Upham & Co.

9 August: G.H. Walker & Co, in its Securities Outlook, said of the stock market: 'As matters now stand it is likely that another buying opportunity at lower levels would be welcomed by a great number of potential stock purchasers.'

14 August: L.O. Hooper of W.E. Hutton-'One of the confusing things about this market at the moment is that so many people still 'do not believe in it.'... This investor scepticism makes for technical health rather than technical weakness. As a matter of fact those chartists who believe that the current advance is of historical and technical proportions, assert that the turn down will not begin until we have had some climactic advances with large volume.

So, at the bottom in 1949, as in 1932 and 1921, there was plenty of optimism concerning the outlook for the equity market.

As we are looking at the four extreme cases from the 20th Century, it should not be a surprise that value investors were banging the drum for equities in 1949. But they had been enthusiastic too early in the decline, as equities reached ever-lower valuations. Value had been evident in the market from around January 1947 when the S&P Composite PE ratio declined below its 1871-1947 average. This was almost 18 months before the market was to bottom, though on this occasion the DJIA declined just a further 10%.

The arrival of value was delivered by a mild decline in the market, but with an explosion in earnings. By June 1949 the S&P Composite Index PE was almost 60% below the 1871-1947 average PE. For those seeking to find the bottom of the bear market, the clarion call of value investors is not sufficient.

Although the decline below fair value in 1949 was associated with only a 10% price decline, we have seen in 1932 how much larger declines in prices were racked up even after equities had already become cheap. Of course, value investors are never fixated by the current earnings outlook and the current PE. Those who looked at the underlying value of the assets of the corporate sector would have seen that equities had been undervalued for a very long time.

As early as 1939, the *q* ratio of the market was below its geometric mean, indicating that the market was trading below fair value from 1939 to 1949. In seeking the bottom of the bear market it is important to determine that equities are below fair value but it is also important to look at other factors if one is to avoid investing too early and watching cheap equities become very cheap.

Many commentators noted in May and June 1949 that the failure of the market to react negatively to bad news was a key sign that future declines may be limited.

Figure 86

Q RATIO

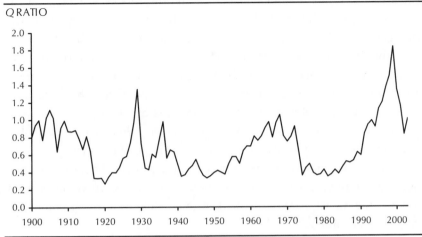

Source: Smithers & Co

Such resilience was evident in the last period of the bear market and in the early stages of recovery. The general apathy towards good and bad news perhaps signals that bears are not covering their shorts, but at the same time are unable to drive the market even lower. If this is the case, then the supply/demand outlook for the market is improving markedly when the market shows general apathy to news announcements. This position is of particular importance when seen in conjunction with the large short position, which had been growing for a very long time.

One particular feature of the end of the 1946-49 bear market is that, particularly on the rebound, volumes often reached their highs in the final hour of trading. This might suggest that bears, awaiting a setback for the market, considered it prudent to decrease their exposure when another day passed without such a setback developing. There was a string of strong late sessions in the 1949 rebound which suggested that those waiting to buy equities at lower prices were throwing in the towel.

The combination of a large short position in conjunction with a market that does not decline on bad news was a positive indicator of a rebound in 1921, 1932 and 1949.

A potential underlying reason for the potency of the combination is that it signifies that everybody who can go short has already done so. The increasing number of "little bears" on the short side seems particularly important. This appears to be the reverse of the so-called "mania" periods, when numerous small and inexperienced investors rush to participate in

223

bull markets. When a similar mania for shorting stocks is evident by an increase in the number of "little bears", this is an indication that the willingness and ability to short stocks is reaching some kind of limit.

In the first stages of the market rebound, which occurs on low volume, the short interest appears not to be shaken in its determination. There is usually a lag of a few weeks before any sign of "capitulation" by these bears is evident. Whether this capitulation is triggered by rising prices combined with higher volumes, or itself causes the higher volumes, is unclear. For equity investors, the conclusion is clear that a failure of the short interest to cover on a bounce increases the prospects of the recovery being sustainable. More importantly, should shorts keep failing to cover when volumes begin to rise at the higher level of the market, this should be a trigger point for a sharp rise in equities.

History shows that technical analysts are right to view declining prices accompanied by declining volumes and rising prices accompanied by rising volumes as important elements in the overall picture associated with market bottoms. Whatever role shorts play in increased trading volume, it is clear volumes increase after the initial surge in prices. It is this rise, evident in 1921, 1932 and 1949, that confirms prices can be sustained at the new higher level. Figure 87 shows rising volumes following the initial rise in the market and, once again, the absence of the capitulation event.

Figure 87

DOW JONES INDUSTRIAL AVERAGE, TWO-WEEK MOVING AVERAGE VOLUMES

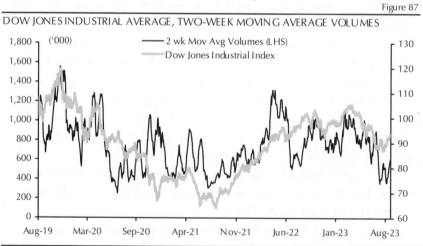

Source: Dow Jones & Co. and NYSE

As in the other bear markets there is a final accelerated decline in the market just at the end of the bear market. However, this final decline is not associated with any surge in volume. **As we have seen, a bear market is marked by a final decline on no volume, rather than high volume.**

As in 1921 and 1932, the replacement of bears by big constructive interests was a key indicator that the bear market was ending. Despite such general comments, less attention was paid in 1949 to the general diffusion in stock holdings. This was considered a key indicator of the bear's demise in 1921 and 1932, as the greater diffusion of holdings to historically high levels was seen as a good indication that a concentration in the hands of big constructive interests was imminent. However, the ability of the US Steel price to rebound when diffusion rates on its shareholder register reached high levels, which had been a very good indicator of a change in the market up until the 1930s, had since produced some erroneous signals. The fall in accuracy of this particular indicator probably accounts for the lack of comment in 1949 regarding the diffusion of stock holdings.

However, the appearance of constructive interests, the big holders that over time reduce the diffusion of holdings, is still mentioned as an important sign the end of the bear market is near.

Once again the bottom of the bear market is more generally associated with limited retail buying. The pages of the *Wall Street Journal* reveal a picture of widespread ownership of US equities, but with limited activity by the numerous small shareholders. On 20 April 1949, the largest-ever stockholder vote in US history took place as 19 million shares of AT&T's total of 23 million shares were voted. The counting process may well have been epic as 94% of AT&T shareholders held 100 shares or less in the company. At General Motors, 59% of shareholders held fewer than 26 shares each. At the General Electric meeting in April 1949, the company disclosed that 45% of shareholders were women. This diffusion of share holdings among small holders was the normal situation in bear markets and the bulls awaited evidence that the big constructive interests were appearing to consolidate holdings. While the brokers awaited the return of the rich man, the push for business from the "little man" continued:

> 'He's about concluded,' said one Wall Streeter, 'that he must either sell to the little man or look for another job.' Taxes have turned the "rich man" into a lean customer.... Some stock and bond merchants think one of their biggest problems is education. The wartime and postwar inflation has put money into the hands of many folk unaccustomed to buying securities.[63]

---

[63] *Wall Street Journal*, 7 June 1949

Education classes were already in full swing as Merrill Lynch, Pierce, Fenner & Beane were to launch a drive for retail investors, which was to pay handsome dividends in the future. In May 1949 the company launched a 'For Women Only' investment class because, in the words of a Merrill's spokesman, 'A man never thinks of boring his wife telling her about such things.' (WSJ, 20 May). Interest among some women was obviously very high and the Federation of Women Shareholders in American Business Inc. was already actively pressing for female representation on the boards of major US businesses. When such a proposal was put to bring 'the women's viewpoint' to the National Dairy Products board of directors, the WSJ reported: 'A stockholder - a bachelor - said he was sure married directors were already getting the women's viewpoint 365 days a year.'

Inviting attendance at coeducational investment lectures, Merrill Lynch placed ads in the Detroit Labor News, an American Federation of Labor paper. One worker who showed up said he had heard so much about brokers being a "bunch of crooks" that he thought he had better check it out himself. He later opened an account. There are usually a lot of small holders around in a bear market but they are in the safest of stocks and they are holding and not trading.

In the summer of 1949 the WSJ was awash with comments from technical analysts stressing the importance of the 160-165 support level for the DJIA. This did indeed prove to be an important support level and the DJIA bottomed at 161.6 on 13 June and a strong rebound then began.

The Dow Theory, as it did in 1921 and 1932, scored another notable success in 1949. Reporting on the market of 14 June, the day after it hit bottom, the WSJ pointed out that the intra-day lows of the industrials and the railroads had not been breached. In the WSJ on 16 June, Kenneth Ward cited the Dow Theory in recommending selective buying. The Dow Theory now had a life outside the Wall Street Journal. A key proponent, E. George Schaefer, famously wrote a very bullish newsletter for his clients dated 18 June 1949:

> Up to this writing, the market has not penetrated the intra-day lows of its 20-year trading range. Until a decisive breakout of this area occurs, the averages could advance and test the upper limits of the area, or continue to fluctuate within that range for an extended period of time. The industrial average established an intra-day low of 160.49 in October, 1946, and the rail average recorded its extreme intra-day low of 40.43 in May, 1947. These lows were closely approached by both averages during the past week, but were not violated. On Tuesday, the extreme intra-day lows of the current

bear market were recorded at 160.62 and 40.88. A slight decrease in volume was noted at the lows, while odd-lot short sale orders skyrocketed to 121 on the very low day. The fact that the market refused to give a decisive downside penetration of its long 20-year trading area implies that a rally from those lows will develop after a sufficient test of those lows has been made.[64]

In 1921, 1932 and 1949, the Dow Theory was used to correctly forecast the bottom of the DJIA to within just a few days.

Bonds and the bear

Robert Holton looked at him. Mr Murphy could not tell what he was thinking for his face was relaxed and calm. 'Well,' said Holton, 'I don't know. I don't want to be out of my depth. I'd like to make more money. I like the idea of buying and selling stocks. I like that idea very much. In fact, that's one of the reasons I came here.'

'Of course, there's a lot of work to knowing about stocks and bonds. You realize all the work that's involved.'

'Yes.'

Gore Vidal, *In A Yellow Wood*

The unnatural condition of the bond market in the postwar era has already been discussed at some length. The Federal Reserve's de facto commitment to buy government securities at set yields along the curve distorted market yields. This floor on the prices of federal securities obviously played a role in influencing the price of commercial fixed-interest securities, which are influenced by the price of government securities but still trade in a free market.

By 1946, US government long bonds traded below the de facto yield support of 2.25% and reached a yield low of 2.03% in the second week of April 1946. Prices declined thereafter and the Fed's balance sheet indicates that not until November 1947 was any material intervention necessary to prevent prices breaching the support level. A large support operation was then necessary throughout 1948 and the value of government bonds held by the Federal Reserve System increased by 129% over the year. With signs of a declining general price level increasingly evident, a rally began in November of 1948 that was not to end until yields reached 2.18% in

---

[64] E. Geogre Schaefer, *The Dow Theory Trade*, 18 June 1949

November 1949.

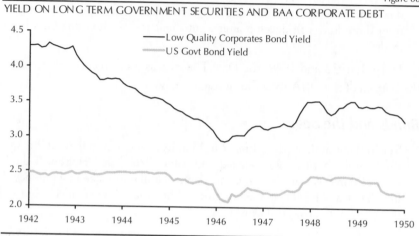

Figure 88

YIELD ON LONG TERM GOVERNMENT SECURITIES AND BAA CORPORATE DEBT

Source: Dow Jones & Co. and NYSE

The yield on Moody's AAA-rated corporate bonds, like the yield on government bonds, reached a low in April 1946. From that low yield of 2.46% it then rose to 2.90% in the first week of January 1948 and from that level a gradual rally began, ending with yields at 2.57% on the last trading day of December 1949. A similar pattern is evident in the yield changes on Moody's Baa-rated paper. The average yield, which reached a low of 2.94% in April 1946, rose to 3.56% in the first week of January 1948, before a major rally began. However, the rally in Baa paper was to be prolonged over a much longer period than that of AAA-rated paper and was not to end until yields reached 3.16% in February 1951. The price of AAA and Baa corporate bonds had bottomed in January 1948, ten months before the rally in government bonds and sixteen months before the bottom of the equity market. This was a different sequence from 1921 and 1932 when the prices of government bonds, corporate bonds and then equities stabilised in that order.

Although corporate bonds did rally prior to government bonds, it was muted until the rally in government bonds began in November 1948. From January to November, the yield on Baa-rated corporate bonds declined from 3.56% to 3.54%.

Although there was a different relationship in 1949 than in 1921 and 1932, the rally in corporate bonds, prior to the rally in government bonds, had been minor.

This difference in order between the corporate bond market and the government bond market in 1949 may have been caused by the distortions in the latter bond market. Yields in the corporate bond market would also be distorted in such an environment due to the impact of bond investors switching between the two markets. The Fed was forced to support the government bond price from November 1947 to November 1948. In this situation it may have been that the rally in corporate debt, evident from January 1948, was effectively a result of investors switching away from the pegged rate in the government market to higher rates in the corporate market. Thus the fact that the corporate bond market rallied ten months before the government bond market could be an anomaly associated with Fed's support of the latter market.

While recognising the different sequence for the commencement of bull markets in financial assets in 1949, the abnormality of the postwar situation must be remembered. It seems more likely the 1921 and 1932 sequence of stabilisation of government bonds followed by corporate bonds followed by equities is more likely to be the normal sequence of events.

As had happened in 1921 and 1932 US equity prices stopped falling when they reached a 70% discount to the replacement value of their assets. All the same signals were positive as in 1921, with the exception that, with Fed interest rate policy constrained in 1949, it was a reduction in credit controls that indicated the bear market was in its final phase. In all three instances, the US was operating a fixed-exchange-rate policy of varying degrees of stricture. Perhaps one could expect these indicators to work in such an environment where other factors adjusted in predictable ways to keep the external value of the currency steady. The acid test for validity is whether they worked in the last great bear market bottom - 1982. The US dollar was in a free float, there was no constraint on the "elasticity" of the currency and deflation was a distant memory. Would the same indicators from 1921, 1932 and 1949 provide the same positive indicators of the birth of the bull?

Part IV
August 1982

The old textile plants given over to discount clothing outlets... acres of dead railroad track and car shops and stockpiled wheels and empty boxcars stick in the heart of the city like a great rusting dagger.

John Updike, *Rabbit is Rich*

It was a long road from 1949 to 1982. During this period, investors had to cope with something they had never seen before - systemic inflation. There had been bursts of inflation before, mainly associated with war, but the basic pattern was for inflation during economic expansion, followed by deflation in economic contraction. By the 1960s, it was becoming evident that inflation would not necessarily be extinguished even by an economic contraction. Many argued that this "new era" would be positive for equities, as management would be able to protect and even bolster profit margins. So did this "new era" alter the characteristics of equities? Did it change the nature and ultimate denouement of bear markets? By August 1982, the S&P Composite Index was, in real terms, back where it had first been in August 1906. The scene was now set for the transformation of America and a bull market in equities that ran for almost 18 years.

The road to August 1982

In the sweltering summer of 1949, with Wall Street languishing in the doldrums, New Yorkers cooled off in open-air cinemas watching the big summer release, *The Girl From Jones Beach*. They watched as the lead character, Bob Randolph, a magazine illustrator, created the "perfect girl" only to later meet her living personification on Jones Beach. Randolph seized the situation and, posing as a lowly Czech immigrant to ingratiate himself with the girl, tried to profit from the promotional opportunities. Despite fully utilising the talents of Virginia Mayo, the movie flopped. However, the actor who played Randolph fared much better and, by 1982, Ronald Reagan was president of the United States. The country had changed somewhat since Reagan's beach outing on Long Island in 1949. One thing remained the same, however. Wall Street was in the doldrums.

The road from the summer of 1949 to the summer of 1982 is the longest between two periods of extreme undervaluation covered in this book. This in itself may suggest that extremes of valuation are becoming less prevalent, but one must be very careful about such a statement. It is in the nature of selecting just four bear market bottoms for analysis that other, similar, episodes are excluded. If five bear market bottoms were studied, then 1974 would be included in the analysis and the distribution of periods of undervaluation would appear very different. For many modern investors, December 1974 is the very embodiment of a great bear market bottom. Hence, we need to take a brief diversion to explain why December 1974 ranks only as the fifth of the great bear market bottoms of the 20th Century. As Figure 89 shows, by 1974, equities were almost as cheap as they had been in 1921, 1932 and 1949.

Figure 89

THE Q RATIO AT THE FIVE BEAR MARKET BOTTOMS		
	Q ratio Year End	Q Ratio Estimate at Market Bottom
1921	.35	.28
1932	.43	.30
1949	.36	.29
1974	.36	.35
1982	.38	.27

Source: Smithers & Co.

Looking at year-end data, equities appear particularly cheap in 1974 as the DJIA bottomed in December of that year. But in all the other years covered in Figure 89, there had already been major rallies by year-end. If one adjusts the q ratio for the rebound in the DJIA from the summers of 1921, 1932 and 1949, it is evident equities were cheaper in these periods than in 1974. A similar picture emerges if one values the market with reference to the ten-year rolling earnings figure to calculate the cyclically adjusted PE. The cyclically adjusted PE in December 1974 of 11.2x is well above the 7.4x reached in August 1921 and 4.7x in July 1932. The cyclically adjusted PE in 1974 is marginally lower than the 11.7x in June 1949, but still higher than the 9.9x racked up in August 1982. When one looks at the q ratio and cyclically adjusted PE, then 1974 ranks fifth in the pantheon of great bear-market bottoms.

Of course, as well as determining the biggest bear market bottoms by reference to valuation criteria, this study also selects periods for analysis by reference to subsequent returns to investors. In particular, we focus on those periods when investors could confidently pursue a buy and hold strategy and achieve above-normal returns. As Figure 90 shows, the December 1974 market bottom created a great trading opportunity, but it is less clear that it produced a great buy and hold opportunity.

Figure 90

DOW JONES INDUSTRIAL AVERAGE - JANUARY 1965 TO DECEMBER 1984

Source: Dow Jones & Co.

There is a clear contrast between the gyrations of the market after December 1974 and the broad advance in prices, which set in after 1921, 1932, 1949 and 1982.

A further important factor that relegates 1974 to fifth position in the history of great buying opportunities on Wall Street is inflation. Investors achieved excellent subsequent real returns after 1921, 1932, 1949 and 1982. However, the real price index of the S&P Composite Index in 1982, as calculated by Yale Professor Robert Schiller, was 13% below the December 1974 level[65]. In 1921, 1932 and 1949, subsequent inflation was quiescent and did not materially reduce the real returns of investors. From 1982, inflation was high and falling, and although a drag on real returns, did not prevent positive real returns accruing to investors. As Figure 91 shows, real capital gains to investors were muted in the five- and ten-year periods from December 1974.

Figure 91

CHANGES IN THE S&P COMPOSITE REAL PRICE INDEX FROM MARKET BOTTOMS			
	5 Years	10 Years	15 Years
1921	+106%	+152%	+211%
1932	+209%	+46%	+92%
1949	+84%	+237%	+343%
1974	+9%	+21%	+114%
1982	+143%	+163%	+414%

Source: www.econ.yale.edu/~shiller/data.htm

Taking a punt in 1974, investors achieved excellent returns over 15 years, but this was due to returns achieved after the bear market bottom of 1982. While it is true that December 1974 was a great time to buy equities, it was not a repeat of August 1921, July 1932, June 1949 or August 1982. On both a valuation basis and on the basis of subsequent returns, 1974 does not find itself in this study of the four great bottoms for American equities.

Of the best four periods to buy equities in the 20th Century, two fell in the first half, with the third mid-century and the fourth in the final quarter. As we have seen, a study of five periods of undervaluation would create symmetry of distribution, with two periods of undervaluation in the final quarter of the century. Given the structural changes in the economy one might have expected proclivity to undervaluation to have diminished.

Throughout the century, the elasticity of the US currency increased. There was the move from the gold standard to one of gold exchange standard, implementation of Bretton Woods, and then a free-floating exchange rate. The increasing ability of the Federal Reserve to provide a monetary response in periods of distress might suggest that the return of equities to fire-sale prices would become less prevalent. It is interesting that

---

[65] Robert Shiller, *Market Volatility*

such a phenomenon is not evident in the data. The oscillation of the q ratio around the geometric mean does not appear to be any more volatile in the first half of the century than it was in the second. Despite the institutional advances since 1900, it appears equities are just as likely to be reduced to gross undervaluation today as they were a century ago. How easy was it, then, to spot the last gross undervaluation of equities in 1982 and what can we learn from that period in the history of Wall Street? To understand the dynamics of the market in 1982, it is first necessary to understand the prelude and the course of the Dow from 1949 to 1982.

In the 33-year period from 1949 to 1982, it is possible to pick out a series of bull and bear markets on Wall Street. By one definition regularly employed, any decline in the index of more than 10% is a bear market and, using this measure, 16 bear markets can be identified amid the events leading to the summer of 1982. However, to understand how equities came to be so undervalued by 1982, the period is best seen as marked by one bull market and one bear market.

The course of the Dow - 1949-68

If we use the DJIA as a guide, the bull market began in June 1949 and ended in February 1966. However, the broader S&P Composite Index shows the bull market did not end until December 1968, when the DJIA was still one percentage point shy of its 1966 high. The peak for the broader index, which coincided with particularly high trading volumes, is generally recognised as representing the end of the bull market.

Figure 92

DOW JONES INDUSTRIAL AVERAGE - JUNE 1949 TO JANUARY 1969

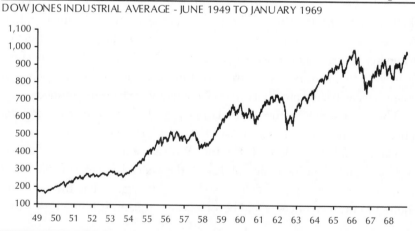

Source: Dow Jones & Co.

While the DJIA may not have made any progress from 1966, monthly average trading volumes on the NYSE jumped 48% from 1966 to 1968. The two-year period also saw a conglomerate-led takeover boom and the growth of new aggressive approaches to investment management. As we shall see, there is little doubt the great postwar bull market ended in 1968, and not 1966. Within this great bull market there were numerous index corrections in excess of 10% which, by some definitions, also constitute bear markets. Figure 93 shows all the DJIA corrections in excess of 10% for 1949-68.

Figure 93

BEAR MARKETS IN 1949-1966 - PERCENTAGE DECLINES IN THE DOW JONES INDEX	
June to July 1950	13%
January to September 1953	13%
July to October 1957	19%
January to October 1960	15%
December 1961 to June 1962	27%
May 1965 to June 1965	11%
February 1966 to October 1966	25%
September 1967 to March 1968	13%

Source: Dow Jones & Co.

The biggest of these bear markets, named after the President of the time, was the so-called "Kennedy break" of 1962. In this sorry episode for the market, the newly elected John F. Kennedy was branded anti-business for preventing the steel companies from raising their prices. The subsequent downturn in the market, caused by the supposed threat to corporate profit margins from Kennedy's actions, stands out for its scale and rapidity of decline. The scale of this panic is particularly severe when one considers that, during the Cuban Missile Crisis of 22 October to 28 October, the market posted a small advance. The next sharpest decline was in 1966, a result of a crisis in confidence when, as Adam Smith explains in *The Money Game*, Wall Street stopped believing in anything:

> They don't believe Johnson, they don't believe anything in Washington, they believe taxes are going to go up but not enough, they don't believe we'll ever get out of Vietnam, and... nobody will believe any earnings.[66]

These were indeed vicious corrections. Brief bouts of bearishness notwithstanding, 1949-68 was broadly bullish, with a 662% rise in the S&P Composite Index representing a 413% rise in real terms.

As Figure 92 shows, it took some years for the market to get up to full

---

[66] Adam Smith, *The Money Game*

steam. There was a strong rebound from June to December 1949, but the market recovery then slowed with the index having risen just 29% by September 1953. The dominant theme of the postwar period on Wall Street became the rise of the defence industry. While the administration initially sought to constrain public spending and hence defence spending, the Soviet Union's launch of Sputnik in October 1957 resulted in a change of plan. The US began to build its first permanent armaments business separate from wartime exigencies, and this promised great profits for investors in selected stocks. The rise of the industry was rapid, so much so that outgoing President Dwight D Eisenhower's final public address in January 1961 warned of 'unwarranted influence' by this 'military-industrial complex'. Investors in this 'military-industrial complex' had been reaping financial rewards throughout the second half of the 1950s.

The high growth levels of some of these companies were rewarded with high valuations by Wall Street and, with listed equities trading at discounts to replacement value throughout the 1950s, there was growing takeover activity. With the benefit of such highly-rated shares defence/electronics businesses such as Litton Industries were able to launch aggressive acquisition strategies as early as 1958. An acceleration of takeover activity was important fuel for the bull market into the 1960s.

It was a surprise to many investors that the 1949-68 bull market came against a background of regular fiscal deficits. In 1949-68, the federal government reported a surplus in only four of the 19 years. In the buoyant decade of 1958-68, only one fiscal surplus was reported. Growing fiscal deficits had often spooked equity investors, and this was a period of fiscal deterioration. Whatever negatives assumed to flow from fiscal profligacy were more than offset by the positive factors driving prices higher.

Throughout this bull market, interest in the equity market was to remain low by historical standards, as Figure 94 shows. The low point was 1942, when just 9% of the average number of s listed hares traded. As the market began to rise, interest and volumes did increase. However, as Figure 94 shows, annual turnover rates in 1949-68 of just 17% never approached the remarkable levels witnessed in the first half of the century. Peak turnover in 1949-68 came at the apex of that cycle, when annual turnover reached 24%, a level surpassed in every year from 1900 to 1937, a period encompassing at least two major bear markets. This low level of market activity in the 1949-68 bull market contrasts with much higher levels of activity in the century's other great bull markets. At the time, the reason given for the restrained trading activity, relative to the first half of the century, was the growing institutionalisation of the market. This may well have been the case, but, if so, it stands in marked contrast to the much higher turnover rates the same institutions were creating by the end of the century.

Figure 94

TURNOVER OF NYSE - SHARES TRADED AS A PERCENTAGE OF TOTAL LISTED

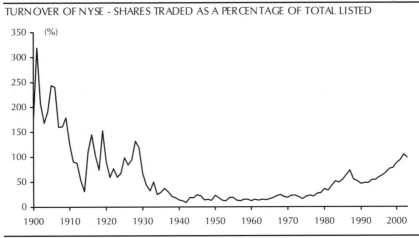

Source: NYSE

While general interest in stocks was low throughout the bull market, the price of NYSE memberships indicates a sea change in total interest in the market in the second half of the 1950s.

Figure 95

PRICES PAID FOR NYSE MEMBERSHIPS - 1949-68

	High	Low
1949	$49,000	$35,000
1950	$54,000	$46,000
1951	$68,000	$52,000
1952	$55,000	$39,000
1953	$60,000	$38,000
1954	$88,000	$45,000
1960	$162,000	$135,000
1961	$225,000	$147,000
1962	$210,000	$150,000
1963	$217,000	$160,000
1964	$230,000	$190,000
1965	$250,000	$190,000
1966	$270,000	$197,000
1967	$450,000	$220,000
1968	$515,000	$385,000

Source: NYSE

As late as 1954, the price of a seat on the NYSE was below levels achieved at the bottom of the bear market in 1949. A marked rise in the price of memberships was evident from the late 1950s, but it was not until 1968 that the price of NYSE membership finally surpassed the $450,000 paid in 1929, even though the DJIA had exceeded its 1929 high as early as November 1954. The lagged rise in the price of NYSE membership is due to the low trading volumes associated with the postwar market. It was not until 1963 that the annual number of shares traded on the NYSE exceeded the 1929 high. Even then, the price of NYSE membership was two-thirds lower than its 1929 high. This lag in membership prices is partly explained by increasing competition as it was also in this period that the increasingly powerful institutions were able to trade off-market in large blocks of NYSE-listed stock. By 1968, when the 1929 high prices for NYSE membership was finally surpassed, annual volume was 160% higher than 1929. The slow rise of NYSE prices in the postwar period indicated the nature of the new, institutionalised Wall Street with longer holding periods and lower volumes.

As the 1949-68 bull market played out, there was an institutionalisation of the market, with the mutual fund becoming an increasingly important vehicle for private investors, and pension funds and life companies increasing exposure to equities from very low levels. During the 1950s, the number of mutual-fund shareholder accounts increased from one million to five million. By the end of the 1960s, there were 10.7 million. The number of individual shareholders doubled during the 1960s, but their power diminished, down from just over 50% of trading in 1961 to one-third by 1969.

A key driver for the bull market was the endorsement of the equity as a suitable investment for pension funds. In 1949, total pension assets of US citizens amounted to $14.3 billion, compared with a gross national product of $258.1 billion. These pension monies were invested primarily in government bonds or insurance company general accounts. This industry was transformed in the postwar era and its transformation played an important role in fuelling the bull market in equities. The rapid growth in pension funds was spurred by a decision of the National Labor Relations Board in 1948 forcing Inland Steel to include negotiations on pensions as part of the collective bargaining process. Not only did strong growth in assets ensue from this decision, but employers were prepared to consider more risky asset allocations with a view to enhancing returns and restraining the size of future corporate contributions to these funds. In pursuit of higher returns, pension fund portfolios' weightings in equities increased.

Figure 96

KEY SAVINGS VEHICLES IN THE USA AND THEIR COMMITMENT TO EQUITIES

	1952		1968	
	Total Financial Assets ($bn)	Corporate Equities as % of total	Total Financial Assets ($bn)	Corporate Equities as % of total
Life Insurance Companies	67.78	3.3	183.07	7.1
Other Insurance Companies	13.2	22.2	45.31	32.2
Private Pension Funds	9.26	15.6	111.39	55.2
State & Local Govt Retirement Funds	5.87	0.7	48.05	12.1
Mutual Funds	3.61	83.9	51.23	90.0
Closed-End & Exchange Traded Funds	2.27	79.7	8.92	71.1

Source: Federal Reserve, *Flow of Funds Accounts of the United States.*

Figure 96 shows the general growth from 1952 to 1968 in funds managed by key US savings institutions. Over the 16-year period, the total size of funds under management increased more than 300%. Private pension fund assets increased 11-fold and mutual funds 13-fold. With the exception of the small, closed-end fund sector, there were material increases in the holding of corporate equities within all types of portfolios. The process was slow and, in the case of life insurance companies, increases in equity weightings were only possible following changes in restrictive state legislation. While total funds increased by just over 300% in 1952-68, the total holding of equities increased almost 12-fold. In 1952, when flow-of-funds statistics were first published by the Fed, holdings by these institutions of corporate equities represented just 9.5% of NYSE equity market capitalisation. By 1968, this figure had risen to 21.3%. As late as 1960, institutions accounted for just one-third of the dollar value of trading on the NYSE; by 1968 this had risen to 60%. Following the "Great Crash" of 1929, equities had been shunned by conservative investors. The story of the 1949-68 bull market is in part about the rehabilitation of the equity as a long-term-savings medium.

There were many reasons why investment institutions increased their commitment to equities, but the root cause was a change in inflationary expectations. As we have seen in 1946-49, investment practitioners debated the extent to which the general price level would have to deflate in the postwar period. Particularly prescient were those who believed a new global financial framework would make inflation more prevalent. Such "new era" thinking was ridiculed by some but these investors correctly identified the key change in the postwar investment arena.

As the 1950s and 1960s progressed, investors began to accept that structural changes reduced the prospects of material deflationary episodes in the future, which meant fewer periods when bonds would be so clearly preferable to equities. While the management of companies could adjust and hopefully profit in the new environment the real value of fixed payments to bond holders would be undermined by inflation. The shift by institutional investors out of bonds and into equities was at least partially driven by the evidence that the inflationary outlook had changed to favour higher returns from equities relative to bonds.

As long as there had been equities, the dividend yield on these instruments exceeded bond yields. Only dangerous "new era" thinkers believed this fundamental long-running relationship could be upset. The existence of the so-called "yield gap" in favour of equities was one of the few constants investors could rely on. On this occasion, the relationship that existed from the founding of the NYSE in 1792 ceased to be a constant and the new era thinkers proved to be correct. The flow of funds in favour of equities pushed the yield on the S&P Composite below long-term government bond yields in July 1957, a state that became entrenched by September 1958, and the "reverse yield gap" grew into the 1960s. By the equity market peak in December 1968, the yield on the S&P Composite was 2.88% and the long-term government bond yield was 5.65%.

This fundamental change in valuation between bonds and equities goes much of the way to explaining how a bull market in equities from 1949 to 1968 coincided with a bear market in bonds. The sell-off in government bonds began in January 1950, just six months after the end of the bear market in equities, when the yield on US long-term government bonds began rising from 2.19%. In the equity bull market which followed bond yields doubled and the dividend yield on equities declined almost 60%. Even the new era thinkers of 1949 would have had difficulty believing such a massive realignment in yields was possible. For once it had been right to say that it was different this time. The difference was a new postwar financial and social infrastructure that made inflation much more prevalent. For almost 20 years, equity investors reaped the rewards for the financial markets' adaptation to the newly created permanence of inflation.

It was this change in the valuations of equities, and not corporate profit growth, which resulted in the long postwar bull market. As we have seen,

S&P Composite Index earnings bottomed in 1946 and increased throughout the 1946-49 bear market. The much-forecast profit downturn for 1949 turned out to be brief and minor, and was ignored by a rebounding market. From the prevailing low level of December 1949, reported earnings increased 150% to December 1968. This compares with a 240% increase in nominal GDP over the same period. The 150% rise in reported earnings in nominal terms compares with a rise of 662% in the S&P Composite. As Figure 97 shows, those who profited from holding equities over the 1949 to 1968 period owe their excess returns to rising valuations and not rising profits.

Figure 97

RISE IN EQUITY VALUATIONS 1949 TO 1968			
	q ratio - 12 Month Year End	PE-trailing earnings	Cyclically adjusted PE
1949	0.49x	5.8x	11.7x
1968	1.06x	18.5x	25.1x

Source: Smithers & Co; www.econ.yale.edu/~shiller/data.htm

Equities moved from undervaluation to overvaluation and, as in any bull market, there were plenty of experts around to justify the overvaluations. By the mid-1960s, there was a new, younger generation who understood why equities had to trade on higher valuations than they had before. For the first time in the institutionalised markets, a performance-oriented and youthful sector of Wall Street emerged, fully versed in the new economics. John Brooks writes in *The Go-Go Years* that there was a belief only someone under 40 could understand and foresee the growth of fast-moving and unconventional companies.

> Wall Street, which lives on dreams and fashions, was, for all of its pretensions to rational practicality, precisely the milieu within which the new gospel of youth could proliferate.[67]

By 1966, however, the belief in the value of the "new economy" had to be increasingly reconciled with the evidence of trouble in the real economy. The crux of the growing concern for investors was the seeming inability of the Federal Reserve to get control of inflation against the background of the fiscal spending associated with Johnson's "Great Society" programme. This government programme, produced by Lyndon B. Johnson in January 1965, was only rivalled by Roosevelt's New Deal in its largesse. As the

---

[67] John Brooks, *The Go-Go Years - The Drama and Crashing Finale of Wall Street's Bullish'60s*

inflationary implications of the Great Society and the increasing military involvement in Vietnam became clear, the bond market was spooked. As Figure 98 shows, the yield on government long-term securities rose to ever-higher levels.

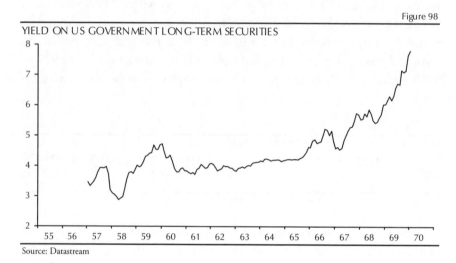

Figure 98

YIELD ON US GOVERNMENT LONG-TERM SECURITIES

Source: Datastream

By the mid-1960s, the bond market was suggesting something had changed. That change was the shift from the sound monetary policy pursued by the Federal Reserve since 1951 to increasing reliance on an activist fiscal policy as the key tool of economic management. The re-engagement with Keynesian management tools, launched by President Kennedy, resulted in a major boost to economic growth under President Johnson. The Fed seemed to acquiesce in this shift in policy. Philip Coldwell, then-chairman of the Dallas Fed, is quoted in William Greider's *Secrets of the Temple* as saying Johnson believed the economy was flexible and could accommodate higher defence spending for the war in Vietnam. Coldwell said the message was 'the Fed shouldn't be stiff-necked' about monetising the increase in debt.

> A number of us on the Federal Open Market Committee argued very strongly that we should have greater restraint. But others were saying, 'Well, we are in a war and we have to support the war effort.' We never did it.[68]

The Fed's monetary inaction was evident. The discount rate, at 4.0% in October 1967, was the same as in September 1959. Over the same period,

---

[68] William Greider, *Secrets of the Temple*.

inflation had risen from 1.23% to 3.56%. Monetary tools were held in abeyance and the politicians were supposed to reduce inflation. However, the necessary fiscal restraint proved politically impossible due to spending on the war in Vietnam and increased social safety nets. The lack of a fiscal solution to inflation would eventually put even greater pressure on the Fed, in the words of its then-chairman William McChesney Martin, to 'lean against the wind' of inflation. Not until November 1967 were monetary measures finally mobilised. The 50bp rise in the Fed funds rate in that month was the first move in an attack on inflation which was to see the rate exceed 9.0% within two years - a new high.

Wall Street was slow to react, and the equity market's ability to ignore rising interest rates in 1968 may have been spurred by President Johnson's announcement that he would not run for re-election, improving the prospect for a Republican administration. There were also the Paris peace talks between the US and North Vietnam to buoy the equity market, and the Republican presidential candidate, Richard M. Nixon, was promising to deliver 'peace with honour'. The prospect of fiscal relief from this quarter was to prove illusory and the continued steady march to higher interest rates finally brought the 1949-68 bull market to an end. The market peaked soon after Nixon's November 1968 election victory and America entered a prolonged period of malaise and a 14-year bear market.

The course of the Dow - 1968-82

Figure 99

DOW JONES INDUSTRIAL AVERAGE - DECEMBER 1968 TO SEPTEMBER 1982

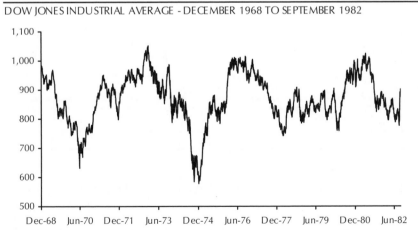

Source: Dow Jones & Co.

The key events that shaped the period from 1968 to 1982 were the demise of the Bretton Woods agreement and the acceleration in inflation. Speculation on the sustainability of the international monetary agreement had been growing for years. As early as 1960, Yale Professor Robert Triffin had warned, in his book *Gold and the Dollar Crisis*, that the US would be forced to run regular current account deficits to provide the rest of the world with the necessary liquidity to grow.[69] He pointed out that the long-term result of these deficits would be to undermine faith in the dollar as the world reserve currency and thus the stability of the Bretton Woods system itself. Eleven years later, Triffin's prediction came to pass when, on 15 August 1971, President Nixon declared the US was suspending the redemption of dollars for gold. The US dollar devalued in December 1971, from $35 to $38 an ounce of gold, and early in 1973 it was devalued to $42. By March 1973, any possibility of resurrecting Bretton Woods was dead and the dollar entered free float. With the gold link gone, a key factor for economic discipline to contain inflation was removed. The equity and bond markets had been worried by inflation in the late 1960s and the end of the Bretton Woods agreement exacerbated these concerns.

Inflation, and the fight against it, drove the 1968-82 bear market.

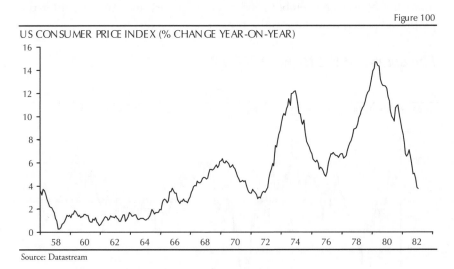

Figure 100

US CONSUMER PRICE INDEX (% CHANGE YEAR-ON-YEAR)

Source: Datastream

In 1969, investors were coping with a vicious decline in equity prices as the Fed pushed short-term interest rates above 9%. The Fed had finally

---

[69] Robert Triffin, *Gold and the Dollar Crisis: The Future of Convertibility*

upped the ante against inflation just as it announced a new chairman - Arthur Burns. President Nixon had tried to kick the incumbent chairman, William McChesney Martin, upstairs to the Treasury Department immediately on his election in 1968. Martin, Governor since 1951, had refused to leave and it was not until his term expired on 30 January 1970 that Burns finally became Chairman. On swearing in Burns as the Fed chairman, Nixon remarked:

> I respect his independence. However, I hope that independently he will conclude that my views are the ones that should be followed.[70]

The views of Nixon and Burns were indeed regularly to coincide and the Fed's reputation as a guardian of price stability was to suffer. With the benefit of hindsight, it is clear the Fed ceased to be tough on inflation and the result was a roller-coaster ride through the 1970s for interest rates (see Figure 102) and the stock market. Within the first year of Burns' tenure, short-term rates were back below 4.0% and below the average level maintained in the 1960s. However, by the middle of 1971, rates were on the rise again, accompanied by the first price controls since 1949. There was some evidence the medicine was working and annual inflation was back below 3% by the middle of 1972. In 1973, Nixon dismantled price controls and inflation was quickening, and the equity market declining, when along came the "oil shock" as the Organisation of Petroleum Exporting Countries (OPEC) more than tripled the price of oil - from $3.12 a barrel in October 1973 to $11.63 in December. Annual inflation, running at 2.9% in August 1972, surged to 12.5% by December 1974.

There were actually **two oil shocks** in the 1970s. The first began in October 1973, when Arab members of the OPEC announced they would no longer ship oil to countries supporting Israel in its war with Egypt. The oil price had tripled by Christmas 1973. The second oil crisis was caused by a decline in oil exports from Iran following the revolution of January 1979. By year-end, the oil price had risen 150%. Within 12 months of both oil shocks, G7 GDP contracted. From December 2002 to June 2005, the oil price has risen 160%.

This would have been bad enough for investors, but the huge surprise

---

[70] Quoted in William Greider, *Secrets of the Temple*

was that the sharp recession, from November 1973 to March 1975, failed to bring inflation under control. In April 1973, the term "stagflation", a combination of low growth and inflation, made its first appearance in the pages of the *Wall Street Journal*. Such a cocktail could only be bad news for equity investors.

The Fed's response remained mild, and the Federal Funds rate was only 75bp higher in January 1977, when inflation was 6.1%, than in January 1960 when inflation was just 1.1%. By early 1977, the annual rate of inflation was rising again and this continued until it reached a new high of almost 15% in March 1980. A further impetus to this inflation was political crisis in Iran, which resulted in an anti-US Islamic theocracy, and another leap in the price of oil. The bottom line was that, despite the dramatic bull and bear markets of the 1970s, the DJIA spent all but a few days of the decade trading below its 1968 highs.

Stagflation is used to describe the unusual combination of economic stagnation and inflation, and was supposedly coined on 17 November 1965 by Conservative Party MP Ian Macleod in the House of Commons. He needed a new word because this was a new phenomenon. Within five years, Macleod was appointed Chancellor of the Exchequer. Whether he had a remedy for the condition he defined will never be known. He died after only a month in office.

In this new inflationary environment, equities failed to deliver positive real returns. In the 1950s, consumer-price inflation averaged 2.2%, and was 2.3% in the 1960s. Through those two decades, investors secured above-normal real returns from equities. The bear market in equities really got going in 1969 as inflation moved above 3%. The 1970s saw inflation averaging 7.1% and a threshold of inflation seemed to have been passed, beyond which equities could not provide positive real returns. This is not to say that there weren't false dawns and hopes that inflation had finally been licked. In real terms, the S&P Composite Index declined 63% from December 1968 to July 1982. This long decline was punctuated by dramatic swings in the market. The 33% decline in the DJIA, from the December 1968 high to the lows of 1970, was the first phase of the secular bear market. It was not to be the most dramatic. Following a major rally to a new high in January 1973, the Dow dropped 45%. When it bottomed in

December 1974, the market was down 37% in nominal terms and 57% in real terms from 1968.

For many investors, returns had been even worse. By 1972 many investor portfolios were composed of so-called "one-decision" growth stocks labelled the "Nifty Fifty". It was believed that the "Nifty Fifty" would produce future earnings and dividend growth to render irrelevant the price paid for them. It was the rise of these 50 stocks that took the DJIA to new highs in early 1973, while broader-based indices such as the Value Line Index failed to surpass previous highs. Investors buying in 1972 paid a historic price earnings multiple of 42x for the "Nifty Fifty", which then suffered an average price decline of 62% in the 1973-74 bear market. By December 1974, the market in nominal terms was back to levels of 1958. This was bad enough but, in real-terms, returns had been even worse.

By December 1974 the S&P Composite Index, expressed in real terms, was back to levels first seen in November 1928. The Index bottomed in nominal terms in December 1974, but in real terms there was still worse to come. The DJIA fell in real terms below even its December 1974 level in April 1980, again in September to October 1981, and in January to September 1982. At its low in real terms in July 1982, the S&P Composite Index was 13% below its December 1974 low. In real terms, the Index was now back to levels first surpassed in June 1905. Investors had been entirely reliant on dividends to provide positive real returns.

The **Nifty Fifty** was a group of 50 stocks. In December 1972, the average PE ratio for the group was 42x earnings. Although all 50 of these stocks were part of the S&P Composite Index, the PE of the broader index was just 18x at that time. It was thought the future earnings growth of these stocks could justify such extreme valuations. In the short term, this proved incorrect as the average price of a Nifty Fifty declined 62% in the 1973-1974 bear market. However, for those investors who hung on, the Fifty did deliver some of this promise. Professor Jeremy Siegel points out in his *Stocks for the Long Run* that the annual return on the Nifty Fifty from December 1972 to November 2001 was 11.62%, just below the 12.14% of the S&P Composite Index over the same period.

Although equity prices rebounded strongly from the December 1974 low, 1974-82 was a period of further volatility, false dawns and poor returns. A general sense of despair hung over the financial markets in the second half of the 1970s. Even a renowned financial commentator such as Sydney Homer, the father of modern bond market research at Salomon Brothers, joined the chorus in November 1976.

> The complete blind confidence of the 1950s in the dollar, and hence in our status in the world, can never return.[71]

Homer likened the "unprecedented rise" in bond yields to the crash of 1929-32 and warned: 'It will be remembered for generations ahead, and this memory will tend to hold up yields and limit economic growth.' This lack of faith in America, even from the most acute of analysts, acted to produce rising bond yields and declining equity prices through the late 1970s and early 1980s.

The losses that accrued to equity investors in 1968-82 were due to both poor earnings growth and a reduction in valuations. In nominal terms, reported earnings per share increased just 143% in the period, compared with an increase in nominal GDP of 246%. The increase in reported earnings represented a 12% decline in real earnings over the period. This would have come as something of a surprise to investors in the 1950s and 1960s who, foreseeing the new high-inflation environment, bought equities to benefit from rising profits. Investors had assumed that management could adapt to a higher inflationary environment with increased operating margins to ensure the necessary higher returns, though Warren Buffett, among others, was keen to point out the fallacies of that argument.

> Recent statistical evidence... does not inspire confidence in the proposition that margins will widen in a period of inflation. In the decade ending in 1965, a period of relatively low inflation, the universe of manufacturing companies... had an average annual pre-tax margin on sales of 8.6%. In the decade ending in 1975, the average margin was 8%. Margins were down... despite a very considerable increase in the inflation rate.[72]

In 1949-68, inflation played an important role in pushing the valuation of equities higher and creating the "reverse yield gap". Inflation of the 1970s perpetuated the relative performance of equities against bonds, but it did not produce positive real returns for equities. Equity valuations continued to rise in the 1960s, even though the average yield on government long bonds was 4.67%. By 1968, equities were at the top end of their valuation range trading on a PE of 18.5x historic earnings and at a *q*

---

[71] Quoted in Marc Faber, *The Great Money Illusion* (Longman, 1988)
[72] Warren Buffett, "How Inflation Swindles the Equity Investor", *Fortune*, May 1977

ratio of 1.06, only previously surpassed in 1929 and 1905. With equity valuations at such high levels already, it is unsurprising that the rise in long-term government bond yields to more than 15%, while the return on equity was largely unchanged, acted to depress valuations from 1968 to 1982.

The widening of the "reverse yield gap" was driven by the collapse of government bond prices and thus, despite the shift in the bond-equity relationship, the valuation of equities declined. By July 1982, the historic PE of the S&P Composite Index had fallen to 7.8x, against 18.5x in December 1968. Cyclically adjusting earnings using the 10-year rolling average earnings level show equities declining from 25.1x in December 1968 to 9.9x in August 1982. From December 1968 to December 1982 the q ratio for the market declined from 1.68x to 0.38x. The market looked cheap, but it had done so for some time as the historic PE had been below ten times since March 1977. By 1982 the market q ratio had been below its geometric mean for almost nine years.

Despite the chaos in the economy and the equity market in the 1970s, market activity never declined to the low levels seen in the 1940s and 1950s. The low point for the NYSE was 1974, when turnover was 16%, still above the average turnover rate for 1949-68. Interest picked up steadily in 1974-82 to reach a turnover rate of 42% in 1982. This was almost double the level reached at the top of the bull market in 1968 and the highest level recorded since 1933. Interest in the equity market was rising long before the bottom of the bear market in August 1982.

While market activity reached its nadir in 1974, the price of NYSE memberships did not bottom until 1977. From 1968 to 1977 the price of a seat declined 93% in nominal terms during a period when the general price level almost doubled. In 1977-82, prices rose almost ten-fold, reflecting the surge in volumes on the NYSE. Rising turnover rates and higher NYSE membership prices show rising interest in equities in the second half of the 1970s, well before the market bottomed in 1982. The rising turnover rates indicate much shorter holding periods for investors. The average holding period of just over six years in 1974 had been reduced to less than two years by 1982. This was an occasion when rising interest in the market did not augur the birth of a new bull market, but rather an adaptation by investors to a new era of increased volatility. Throughout the period, institutionalisation of the market continued.

Figure 101

KEY US SAVINGS INSTITUTIONS – 1968-82

	1968		1982	
	Total Financial Assets ($bn)	Corporate Equities as % of total	Total Financial Assets ($bn)	Corporate Equities as % of total
Life Insurance Companies	183.07	7.1	527.02	7.70
Other Insurance Companies	45.31	32.2	196.46	14.90
Private Pension Funds	111.39	55.2	577.23	41.99
State & Local Govt Retirement Funds	48.05	12.1	233.61	18.90
Mutual Funds	51.23	90.0	58.97	58.52
Closed-End & Exchange Traded Funds	8.92	71.1	6.83	52.42
Total	**447.97**		**1,600.12**	

Source: Federal Reserve, *Flow of Funds Accounts of the United States.*

The growth in total funds of US savings institutions increased by slightly more than GDP over the course of the bear market. While equity weightings for the key institutions declined, the total funds committed to equities increased almost 300%, even as the DJIA declined by more than 20%. Institutions continued to increase holdings of equities, although increasingly slowly throughout the 1970s, and the turnover rate on the NYSE increased substantially, but still the bear market persisted.

The situation was reaching a climax by 1978, when President Jimmy Carter appointed G. William Miller, a CEO and corporate lawyer, as chairman of the Federal Reserve. Extreme policies followed, with the US borrowing from the IMF, as well as borrowing foreign currency in international markets to supplement support of the dollar. For the markets, there were clear signs of desperate short-term support measures, but no long-term solutions to America's economic problems. By August 1979, the price of gold exceeded $300 an ounce, compared with the $35 an ounce maintained under the Bretton Woods agreement. Miller's term as chairman of the Fed was brief and he moved on to become Secretary of the Treasury. Few could have foreseen that Miller's departure would augur a new era for America.

The path out of the malaise came with the appointment of Paul Volcker as Fed chairman on 6 August 1979. Within a month, he pushed through a rise in interest rates on a four-to-three vote in the FOMC. Volcker then called another, secret, meeting of the FOMC on 6 October, which pushed interest rates higher. Importantly, it was accompanied by a new Fed policy of targeting the growth of the M-1 monetary aggregate and thus permitting interest rates to adjust to whatever level this policy necessitated. To accommodate the potential change in interest rates, the Fed announced with immediate effect the permissible range for the Fed funds rate would be

11.5-15.5%. With the Fed targeting the monetary aggregates, there was huge uncertainty as to the future level of interest rates that would result.

Before there was a Greenspan there was a Volcker. **Paul Volcker** was Chairman of the Federal Reserve System from August 1979 to August 1987 and is credited with bringing runaway inflation under control. When Volcker took office, inflation was almost 12%. When he left, it was just 4%. Initially, the war on inflation was fought through targeting the growth of the monetary aggregates, such as M-1, rather than targeting interest rates. Implementation of the policy was fraught with difficulty and resulted in volatile, and often very high, interest rates. In 1995, Volcker asked Alan Greenspan: 'Whatever became of M-1?' His successor replied: 'It was once the name of a pretty good rifle.'[73]

Figure 102

FED FUNDS EFFECTIVE RATE 1970-1983

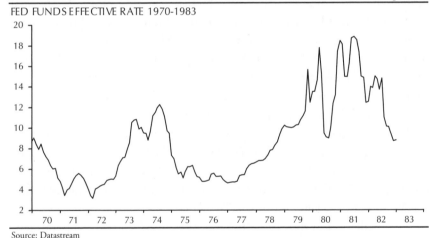

Source: Datastream

In the short term, it was evident the Fed's M-1 growth target would necessitate tighter liquidity and thus higher interest rates. From just over 9%, US government long-bond yields were approaching 13% within 12 months of Volcker's appointment. The markets remained sceptical about the impact on inflation, and the price of gold doubled in his first year. Indeed, inflation continued to rise and President Carter used his powers to impose credit controls. In a television address on 14 March 1980, he recommended the American public to stop spending. To everybody's

---

[73] Quoted from Martin Mayer, *The Bankers - The Next Generation*

surprise, this is exactly what happened, and in the second quarter of 1980 GDP declined at the fastest rate ever recorded. The collapse in consumer spending and M-1 was so rapid the Fed was soon easing monetary policy, with the Fed funds rate dropping from 20% to 8% in three months. It is clear the economy's reactions also came as a surprise to the Fed chairman:

> It is all recorded in the books as a recession, but in retrospect it was an odd, almost accidental occurrence. There was a sharp decline in production, but it only lasted about four months.... As the fright about an economic emergency dissipated and the credit controls were removed, spending (and the money supply) picked up rapidly.... The net result might not have been much of a recession, but there wasn't much progress against inflation either. It continued running at double-digit levels, and with the money supply rising strongly again we were in the uncomfortable position of tightening money and raising the discount rate only a few weeks before the election.[74]

The Fed's reaction against the continued strong growth in money supply pushed the Fed funds rate to a new high by the end of 1980. The Fed continued to steer by the monetary star and, as a result, a decline in short-term interest rates began in early 1981. In May and June 1981, annual inflation fell below 10% from its March 1980 peak of almost 15%, but bond investors continued to push yields higher. While the Fed may have been gaining some credibility, there was real concern the supply-side tax reforms being pursued by the new Reagan administration would undermine the Fed's progress against inflation. These concerns seemed to be backed up by accelerating growth of M-1. The Fed felt it could not take any risks and by May 1981 the fight to slow money supply growth was pushing interest rates higher yet again. The Fed funds rate, which had fallen from 20% in January to 13% in March, again exceeded 20% by July.

The oscillation in short-term interest rates since Volcker's appointment was unparalleled and greatly added to the uncertainty of financial forecasts. Not until September 1981, two years after his appointment, was there any sign the bond market believed the Fed chairman was succeeding in his battle with inflation. In that month, a rally in government bonds began which was to last more than 20 years.

Meanwhile, the equity market continued to slump. With inflation falling, real interest rates were still the highest investors had had to live with since the Depression. Fiscal deterioration continued. In Washington,

---

[74] In Paul Volcker and Toyoo Gyohten, *Changing Fortunes: The World's Money and the Threat to American Leadership*

the Reagan Administration and Congress were at odds over tax and spending cuts. Donald Regan, Secretary of the Treasury, recalled a meeting with Volcker in March 1982 that illustrates the dynamics keeping real interest rates high.

> Volcker had assured me that he would try to be accommodating to the Administration - he would ease money to bring interest rates down if he could see some movement by us on the deficits.[75]

While this stand-off continued, a major recession was underway. The prospect of higher short-term interest rates as a response to strong money supply growth in the first half of 1982 did not augur well for imminent recovery. This prospect, combined with interest-rate volatility, which many had forecast as the result of monetary aggregate targeting, unsettled equity investors. While the dollar benefited from high interest rates, and the government bond market rallied as inflation and short rates declined, the equity market continued to fall.

The rally in the government bond market was not the only improvement in financial markets to be ignored by equity investors. Through the 1970s, investors had the triple negative of a weak dollar, a weak bond market and a weak equity market. The first financial market to improve had been foreign exchange. Volcker's policy of targeting monetary aggregates produced higher real rates of interest, which finally created confidence in the greenback. Funds flowed to the dollar and the currency bottomed in mid-1980, rising strongly through 1981. However with the economy in sharp recession, the DJIA continued to decline. The equity market bottomed eleven months after the government bond market and almost two years after the dollar.

The bottom for the equity market coincided with an international financial crisis. It was clear in early 1982 that Mexico was in trouble and its largest company had gone bankrupt. The Fed believed there was a real risk of sovereign default and it began to offer Mexico, which had borrowed heavily from US banks, de facto bridging loans as early as 30 April 1982. In May, Drysdale Government Securities went bust. Then in early July a small Oklahoma institution, Penn Square Bank, failed. The bank itself was small, but it had had originated more than $1 billion in loans sold on to Continental Illinois and other large commercial banks. Bank examiners realised similar problems were likely to exist in the loans sold on to other

---

[75] Donald T Regan, *From Wall Street to Washington*

banks. Panic was avoided, but it was clear that the financial stability of the US banking system was under question. By August it was public knowledge that Mexico was bust. A rescue package was put together but major US commercial banks faced calamity as the public became aware of the scale of write-downs on their Mexican debt. Walter Wriston, head of Citibank, described the atmosphere at the annual meeting of the International Monetary Fund in Toronto in August 1982:

> We had 150-odd finance ministers, 50-odd central bankers, 1,000 journalists, 1,000 commercial bankers, a large supply of whiskey... [which] produced an enormous head of steam driving the engine called 'the end of the world is coming'. It was the Titanic. We were just rearranging the deck chairs.[76]

The FOMC convened on 30 June, fully aware that Mexico would soon default on its debt. Despite M-1 growth remaining strong, the prospects of a financial crisis resulted in a change in direction.

> Actually, by the summer of 1982 the financial fabric of the United States itself was showing clear signs of strain. Against the background of the spreading problems of the savings and loan industry and some well-publicized failures of marginal government dealers, the bankruptcy of the high-flying but obscure Penn Square National Bank in Oklahoma exposed that billions of dollars of oil loans that it had originated were virtually worthless. Some very large and well-known banks were involved; the proud Continental Illinois Bank, largest in the Midwest, was shaken to its foundations. All that contributed to the timing of our decision to ease policy in July 1982.[77]

This was a *de facto*, if not *de jure*, abandonment of money-supply-growth targeting. The Fed funds rate, above 14% in early July, was below 9% by early September. It was clear the Fed was no longer steering by the compass of the monetary aggregates alone. Importantly the bond market was not spooked by the change in policy, and the decline in long-term rates accelerated. It was with the public announcement of the Mexican crisis and the Fed's change in policy that the equity market finally hit bottom in August 1982.

---

[76] Phillip L Zweig, *Citibank and the Rise and Fall of American Financial Supremacy*
[77] Paul Volcker, in Volcker and Gyohten, *Changing Fortunes*

Structure of the market in 1982

The stock market in 1982

> Charlie emits a sardonic, single-syllabled laugh, and explains, 'The little man is acting like the oil companies now. I'll get mine, and screw you.'
>
> 'I don't blame the oil companies,' Harry says tranquilly. 'It's too big for them too. Mother Earth is drying up, is all.'
>
> John Updike, *Rabbit is Rich*

By 1982, the stock market was no longer a financial sideshow in America. At the end of May 1949, the total value of all NYSE-listed stocks was just $64 billion, or 23% of GDP. In the bull market to December 1968, NYSE market capitalisation increased to $693 billion, or 76% of GDP. Despite the bear market, which began in 1968, market capitalisation continued to rise and by the end of 1981 reached $1,143 billion or 36% of GDP. Growth in market capitalisation outstripped even the 11-fold increase in nominal GDP for 1949-81. The public's ownership of equities, primarily through financial intermediaries, also soared - from 4% of the adult population in 1952 to 28% in 1985. Activity in the stock market had been rising since 1974, and in 1982 the highest percentage of listed shares traded since 1933. The value of shares traded on the NYSE in 1982 was 350% higher than at the peak of the bull market in 1968. By 1982 public participation and interest in the market was at high levels. Activity was also very high, with the average holding period just exceeding two years, compared to the five-year average period evident from 1949 to 1981.

Through this period, the NYSE continued to provide a good representation of the overall market. While today's reader sees the rise of NASDAQ as increasingly important in relation to NYSE activity this was not the key threat to the NYSE in 1982. In a longer-term time horizon the rising importance of NASDAQ has to be set against the continued decline in the importance of the American Stock Exchange (ASE). At its peak in 1968, the ASE accounted for almost 18% of all the volume conducted on registered stock exchanges in the US. By 1982, this had declined to less than 4% and the NYSE's share of trading volume on the registered exchanges had risen from 74% to 85% over the same period. In 1982, references to the NYSE can still be equated with references to "the market" in more general terms.

255

The growth in the number of listed companies lagged far behind the growth in NYSE market capitalisation. The number of companies with NYSE-listed stocks increased from 1,043 in 1949 to 1,273 by the end of the bull market in 1968. By the end of 1982, there were 1,526 companies with shares listed on the NYSE. With only a 46% increase in the number of listed companies since 1949 the story of the growth in the market was of a rise in average market capitalisation. The average market capitalisation of a listed company by the middle of 1982 was around $639 million, up from $543 million at the end of 1968 and $58 million in the middle of 1949. By June 2005, there were 1,780 companies listed on the NYSE, with an average market capitalisation of $5 billion.

While much changed in terms of the industrial sectors comprising the market, there was something that seemed always to stay the same - the importance of oil. Though industry sector breakdowns only became available in 1926, oil was probably only second in importance to the railroad sector in 1921. At the bear-market bottoms of 1932, 1949 and 1982, oil had the largest market capitalisation of any sector. Even at the top of the big bull market of 1929, oil remained the third largest industrial sector of the market. The importance of this sector for investors is generally understated in the story of Wall Street, where the focus is so often on the new thing. Figure 103 shows the shift in importance of the key industry sectors from 1949 to 1982, the continued importance of the oil sector and the rise of new industries.

Figure 103

TEN LARGEST NYSE SECTORS (MARKET CAP RANKED BY SIZE)		
	1949	1982
Oil	16.0%	12.6% (1st)
Chemicals	9.0%	3.5% (9th)
Retail	7.9%	5.5% (6th)
Autos	7.5%	3.4% (10th)
Utilities	6.7%	7.1% (4th)
Steel	6.4%	1.4% (20th)
Communications	6.2%	4.7% (7th)
Foods	6.2%	3.3% (11th)
Transport	5.1%	1.7% (18th)
Electric Equipment	3.5%	1.1% (22nd)
Finance	2.1% (16th)	11.7% (2nd)
Business Equipment	2.3% (13th)	11.3% (3rd)
Health	1.6% (17th)	5.7% (5th)
Household	1,5% (19th)	4.6% (8th)

Source: Kenneth R. French, 'Industry Portfolio Data'

Railroads, the most important sector of the US stock market from the

middle of the 19th Century until the end of the 1920s, had largely
disappeared from investor radar screens by 1982. Similarly, with heavy
industry such as steel, autos and chemicals declining in importance to
investors, service-orientated businesses such as finance, business equipment
and health gained in importance. The most important change in the period
was the rise and rise of the financial sector. In 1949 the finance sector was
lowly weighted and composed largely of investment trusts and some
consumer-finance companies. It was only in the postwar period that already
well-established banking companies took full NYSE listings and finance,
the sixteenth largest sector in 1949, became the second most important
sector by 1982.

Despite the myriad changes in the US economy over the period, there
has been a surprising permanence amongst the largest sectors of the stock
market. In the three periods for which hard data is available - 1932, 1949
and 1982 - six sectors always appeared in the 10 largest by market
capitalisation: oil, utilities, retail, communications, chemicals and autos.
The importance of the 10 largest sectors has varied little over the years,
accounting for 76.6% of market capitalisation in 1932, 74.5% in 1949 and
73.4% in 1982. Prior to this, the market's industry concentration was likely
to have been even higher due to the dominance of the railroad sector. The
key change in the stock market between 1949 and 1982 was the shift from
heavy industry to services. Figure 104 shows how service-orientated
industries provided particularly good returns from 1949 to 1982 and thus
became increasingly large portions of market capitalisation.

Figure 104

TOTAL RETURNS FOR INDUSTRIAL SECTORS ON NYSE - JUNE 1949 TO JULY 1982	
Best	
Business Equipment	80.2x
Health	62.7x
Meals	55.1x
Electric Equipment	53.2x
Services	46.3x
Worst	
Coal	6.1x
Chemicals	16.9x
Communications	17.7x
Steel	17.9x
Textiles	19.1x

Source: Kenneth R. French, 'Industry Portfolio Data'

While share-price outperformance played an important role in the rise
of the business equipment and health sectors, this was not the case for the

finance sector. The finance sector index shows a 29.5x total return over the period, below the 32.5x average sector total return. The rising importance of the finance sector was driven by new listings. The communications sector was the seventh largest sector by market capitalisation in both 1949 and 1982. That the sector index produced very sub-par performance over the period indicates this continued importance was due to large capital raisings rather than exceptional returns for investors. The reverse impact is obvious for the electrical equipment sector, where the importance of the sector declined markedly despite it producing the fourth-best return of any of the 30 sectors. The performance of the 10 largest sectors in 1949, from 1949 to 1982, indicates how the oil sector maintained its importance to investors partly by providing excess returns.

Figure 105

INCREASE IN TOTAL RETURN INDEX - MAY 1949 TO JULY 1982	
Electric Equipment	53.2x
Oil	52.9x
Autos	34.6x
Foods	25.6x
Retail	20.0x
Utilities	21.2x
Transport	21.0x
Steel	17.9x
Communications	17.7x
Chemicals	16.9x

Source: Kenneth R. French, 'Industry Portfolio Data'

By 1982, the composition of the market had been transformed. The finance, health and business equipment sectors accounted for less than 7% of market capitalisation in 1949 - they now represented almost 30% of the market. In terms of the most important stocks, 1949-82 marked the rise and rise of IBM. In the first *Fortune 500* list of companies, compiled in 1955 and including only US industrial concerns, IBM ranked 61st by sales. By 1982, its profits were the second-largest of any American corporation.

The 1968-82 bear market was very different from the other major bear markets analysed in this book. While the 1921, 1932 and 1949 bear markets occurred against a background of deflation, 1968-82 was dominated by high, and rising, inflation. When one accounts for reinvested dividends, an investment in the S&P Composite Index increased in value by 82% over the period. The consumer price index increased 174% over the same period. While just one of the largest-30 industrial sectors produced negative nominal returns, when one includes the impact of reinvested dividends only five sectors produced any positive real return to investors.

Figure 106

SECTORS GENERATING REAL TOTAL RETURNS - DECEMBER 1968 TO AUGUST 1982	
Tobacco	+420%
Telecoms	+194%
Oil	+185%
Health	+180%
Coal	+180%

Source: Kenneth R. French, 'Industry Portfolio Data'. Note: Total return % includes dividends reinvested

Tobacco, which proved itself the best performing sector in the deflationary bear market from 1929-32, turned out to be the best performing sector in the inflationary bear market of 1968-82. Management's ability to adjust prices to maintain margins in the sector in differing inflationary climates seems almost unique. The oil sector was the fifth-best-performing sector in the deflationary bear market of 1929-32 and the fifth-best-performing sector in the inflationary bear market of 1968-82.

The average unweighted return from the key 30 industrial sectors over the period was 107%. Apart from the sectors listed above, which produced real returns for investors, only four other sectors produced a higher return than the average of 107% - food, electrical equipment, utilities and mines. Once again, the simple strategy of over-weighting utility and tobacco stocks in a bear market produced very favourable relative returns. Interestingly the oil and health sectors, which out performed from 1946 to 1968, also outperformed in the 1968-82 bear market.

The bond market in 1982

> You think fourteen per cent is catastrophic, in Israel they live with a hundred eleven per cent, a color television set costs eighteen hundred dollars. In Argentina it's a hundred fifty per cent per year... the US consumer still gets the best deal to be had in any industrialized nation.
>
> John Updike, *Rabbit is Rich*

By 1982, the NYSE no longer represented an accurate reflection of the structure of the bond market. The trade in government fixed-interest securities had been swinging away from the NYSE for almost 100 years, and even the NYSE's corporate bond market was dwindling in importance. As early as 1958, the market value of all corporate and foreign bonds listed on the NYSE was just 33% of the total value of those instruments outstanding. By the end of 1981, NYSE listings accounted for just 28% of that total market. A more accurate picture of the change in the bond market over the

259

period is provided by the flow of fund statistics published by the Federal
Reserve since 1952.

Figure 107

MARKET VALUE OF KEY COMPONENTS OF US FIXED INTEREST MARKET ($BN)		
	End 1952	**2Q 1982**
Treasury securities	220.8	858.0
Agency securities	2.8	351.4
Municipal securities	29.7	474.2
Corporate & foreign bonds	49.6	562.8
	302.9	2,246.4

Source: Federal Reserve, *Flow of Funds Accounts of the United States*

Figure 107 covers fixed-interest securities of all maturities. It shows US
fixed-interest markets in 1952 being 1.8x larger than the equity market.
The ratio was basically unchanged up to 1982. Surprisingly, the fixed-
interest market managed to grow marginally faster than GDP over the
period, despite the significant decline in bond prices. The scale and relative
importance of this bear market in bonds is put in context by Sidney Homer
and Richard Sylla in *A History of Interest Rates*:

> If a constant maturity thirty-year 2½% bond had been available throughout
> this second bear market of the century, its price would have declined from
> 101 in 1946 to 17 in 1981, or 83%.[78]

Despite the severity of this bear market, buyers were found for ever-
larger issues of government bonds. The boom in bond issuance was not
confined to the government and quasi-government bodies. From 1952 to
1982, the private sector's share of the bond market increased from 16% to
25%. Despite the collapse in prices, there was an active and growing market
in both government and private debt throughout the bond bear market.

The two big changes over the period for bond investors were the
exponential growth of the quasi-government fixed-interest security and the
rise of yields. The few agency securities available in 1952 had been issued by
those agencies created as part of the New Deal. While these securities
amounted to less than one percent of all fixed securities in 1952, they had
become almost 16 percent of the market by 1982. Investors had to
understand this new asset class and also the dynamics behind the new
record level of yields in the early 1980s.

Figure 108 shows how bond investors in 1982 were steering through

---

[78] Sidney Homer and Richard Sylla, *A History of Interest Rates*

uncharted territory. By February, the yield on Moody's Baa-rated corporate bonds had exceeded 17%. This contrasted markedly with the deflationary corporate bond bear markets in 1921 and 1932, when yields peaked at 8.6% and 11.6% respectively. At the bottom of the last equity bear market in 1949, equity investors were assessing the impact of Baa yields just below 3.5%. By 1982, with yields in excess of 17%, bond investors were in a much more nervous condition and anything seemed possible.

Figure 108

YIELD ON LONG-TERM GOVT SECURITIES & MOODY'S BAA CORPORATE BONDS

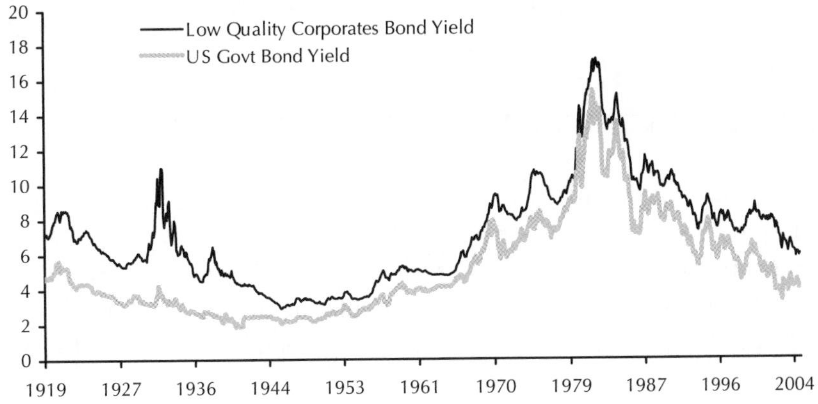

Source: Federal Reserve.

At the bottom with the bear - Summer 1982

Oil going up takes everything up with it... It's just like the Weimar thing, people' savings are being washed right down the tube, everybody agrees there's a recession coming to curl your hair.

John Updike, *Rabbit is Rich*

A prolonged bear market reduced equities to good value in the summer of 1982. By August, the DJIA had returned to a level first seen in April 1964. In real terms, the capital index was back to April 1928, and just 22% above the heights of 1916. **Equities were cheap. Using year-end data, the q ratio was just 0.38x, and adjusting for the low level of the market in the middle of 1982 it was probably nearer 0.27x. The cyclically adjusted PE of 9.9x, calculated using the ten-year rolling-earnings figures, was well below the 1881-1982 average of 15.8x.** These valuations are in marked contrast to the q ratio of 1.06x and the cyclically adjusted PE of 25.1x reached at the peak of the bull market in 1968.

It took almost 14 years for equities to move from an overvalued to an undervalued position. This might seem a long time, but in the context of this study it could almost be described as normal. Figure 109 shows the duration of the swing from high valuations to low as measured by the q ratio and the cyclically adjusted PE.

Figure 109

DURATION IN YEARS OF SWING FROM OVERVALUATION TO UNDERVALUATION		
	q ratio	Cyclically adjusted PE
To 1921 Bottom	16	20
To 1932 Bottom	3	3
To 1949 Bottom	13	13
To 1982 Bottom	14	17

Source: www.econ.yale.edu/~shiller/data.htm, Smithers & Co.

As discussed in Part II, the bear market of 1929-32 was very different from the other great bear markets of the 20th Century. How one measures the duration of the swing from overvaluation to undervaluation depends on whether this incident is included in calculating average duration. If one includes this episode, the average duration is around nine years, but if it is excluded as atypical, the period is around 14 years. (These durations are based on the change in the q ratio. They are even longer if one focuses on the cyclically adjusted PE.) It is evident that we should not model our ideas on the course of a normal bear market on the events of 1929-32. While it is possible equities could go from extreme overvaluation to extreme undervaluation in just three years, it is unlikely under "normal" circumstances. The modern investor should remember that to achieve this rapid value realignment in just three years the DJIA had to decline by 89%.

History suggests that, barring such a major rapid collapse in prices, it takes about 14 years for equities to make the journey from overvaluation to undervaluation.

Good news and the bear

'Won't the bubble burst?'

'Precious metals aren't a bubble. Precious metals are the ultimate security.'

John Updike, Rabbit is Rich

By 1982, the bear market in equities had been underway for almost 14 years, and yet it ended with a bang, not a whimper. In the 15 months from April

1981, the DJIA fell another 30% to bottom in August 1982. While the price of equities declined, commodity prices were contained and reduced, the dollar rallied and, from September 1981, the government bond market finally firmed. This combination of price changes provided encouragement that the Fed's battle with inflation was being won. However, equity investors were focused on the price of the victory, and in particular the havoc being wreaked on the economy.

Something changed in August 1982, and a very strong rebound in equity prices began. Was this rebound driven by a change in the outlook for the economy? **Based on the NBER reference date, the rebound in the equity market preceded the rebound in the economy, which bottomed in November 1982. However, GDP bottomed in the first quarter of 1982 and, based on this data, the rebound in the equity market lagged improvement in the economy.**

This near-coincidence of the bottoms for the economy and the equity market is also evident at the other great bear market bottoms. In 1921, the economy bottomed in July, according to the NBER reference date, and the equity market in August. In the 1930s, things were not so clear-cut, but the equity market bottom in July 1932 coincided with the first of what was later described as the double bottom for the economy. In 1949, the market did lead the economy as it bottomed in June, while the NBER reference date for the end of the economic contraction is November. Calculating an average lead for the market from these four incidents is likely to mislead. **What is clear is that the popular myth that the stock market leads the economy by six-to-nine months is not correct.** While it may have some validity if one examines all economic rebounds, it does not hold true for the four great bear-market bottoms of the past century. At these extreme times it seems the bottoms for the economy and the equity market were much closer together and the economy might have led the stock market.

This ties well with our observation from the *Wall Street Journal* that there is often ample good and improving economic news at the bottom of a market. This all suggests the risk to investors at these extreme times may not be as great as often assumed. An investor need not buy equities based on his forecast that the economy will start to improve in six-to-nine months. At the great bear market bottoms there is likely to be growing evidence the economy is already on the mend.

14 June: In inflation-adjusted dollars, business inventories were cut at an annual rate of $17.5 billion in the first quarter, the sharpest reduction for any quarter since World War II.

14 June: In discussing the rise in business inventories, Robert Dedrick, assistant commerce secretary for economic affairs, took a somewhat upbeat tone. 'While inventory liquidation may not be over it clearly has diminished in intensity,' he said. 'The abatement of the inventory cutback suggest that a major drag' on the economy is easing.'

14 June: The improvement in consumer expectations, which generally foreshadow actual economic events by three to four months, lends credibility to the prevailing professional view that business will begin recovering from the present recession in the months immediately ahead.'

14 June: Sales of new cars in May rose 5.9% from a year earlier.

14 June: Even the employment situation is providing some reason for hope. The unemployment rate in May rose to 9.5% of the labor force, up from 9.4% in April and the highest rate since World War II. But employment rose by 777,000 jobs last month to a seasonally adjusted 100.1 million. That's not far from the 101 million reached in May 1981.

14 June: 'The growth in real disposable income has been unusually strong in this recession,' says Elisabeth Allison of the consulting firm of Data Resources Inc., 'largely because of a decline in inflation the automatic stabilizers of unemployment compensation and Social Security' and high interest income- the bright side of the high interest rates.

14 June: As for fiscal policy, the 10% tax cut July 1 is generally expect to give an upward push to consumer outlays.

15 June: Despite conflicting signals, 'the second quarter still expected to mark the end of the recession,' said Donald H. Straszheim of Wharton Econometric Forecasting Associates, Philadelphia.

16 June: Are auto sales on the road back? Many industry officials believe that a recovery, if not already underway, is imminent.... Including imports, the latest 10-day sales pace worked out to a seasonally adjusted annual rate of about 8.3 million units- topping May's 8.2 million rate and substantially above April's 7.2 million.... The first pleasant surprise for car makers was last month's 15.8% increase in sales from May 1981, largely because of a rebound at GM.... The average age of cars on the road today is estimated at 7.5 years, up from 5.7 years in 1972.... In fact with inventories at their lowest levels since 1964, some analysts think that any sizable surge in demand could leave the companies short of cars.

16 June: Paul Volcker, Federal Reserve Board Chairman, said that recent strengthening of consumer spending and slowing of inventory reduction are signs 'that tend to accompany a levelling out of a recession and the beginning of a recovery.'... He declined to predict when rates will fall, but said 'I don't see any place for those interest rates to go but down.' [Before Joint Economic Committee of Congress.]

17 June: Possibly signalling a long-awaited recovery, housing starts climbed a surprising 22% in May and rose above the one million-unit annual level for the first time in 10 months.

17 June: Weekly take-home pay of median-income family will climb $6 in the second phase of Reagan's individual tax rate cut beginning July 1.

21 June: Last month's moderate rise in personal income, coupled with robust increase in consumer spending, provided fresh evidence that a consumer-led recovery from the recession is beginning to take hold.

22 June: The U.S. economy appears to be expanding in the current quarter at a 0.6% annual rate after inflation, the first growth since the 1981 third quarter, preliminary government figures show. David Stockman, White House budget office director, told reporters that 'We are past the trough of the recession.'... Meantime, White House spokesman Larry Speakes said the preliminary GNP figure indicates that 'the recession has bottomed out.'... Treasury Secretary Donald Regan told a gathering of accountants that 'we can begin to see the vistas of recovery' as a result of the preliminary current-quarter GNP figure.

23 June: 'Recent economic data continue to support the case for moderate economic recovery.' Said Erich Heineman, vice president of Morgan Stanley & Co.

23 June: The first signs of recovery are clearly stirring in the land. Auto sales and housing starts have picked up a bit, as have retail sales. Consumer demand can be expected to perk up further next month on the start of higher Social Security benefits and lower personal tax withholdings (the first significant yield from last year's tax bill).

Business corporations, with anaemic balance sheets to begin with, are wondering how the recovery can be financed without a relaxation by the Fed and, quite possibly, a new outbreak of inflation. These doubts, plus the rise in business loan demand already occurring, give us some clue to why interest rates got stuck on their downward path.

1 July: The tax cut will enrich consumers by $32 billion at an annual rate. And the 7.4% cost-of-living increase in Social security payments is to pump an additional $11 billion into the economy at an annual rate.

1 July: The Commerce Department's composite index of leading indicators rose 0.3% in May, the third consecutive monthly increase.... Before the March rise, the index had fallen or remained unchanged for 10 months.

1 July: Alan Greenspan, President of a New York forecasting firm and a close adviser to President Reagan, contends that 'in a matter of weeks.' The nation will see the signs of recovery.

6 July: Believers in a strong economic upturn are getting support from an uncommon source: Robert Wilson the prominent New York investor who heads a money-management firm bearing his name. Over the years, Mr. Wilson has been best known for borrowing shares of what he regards as overpriced stocks, and then selling them short. But currently, Mr. Wilson isn't short all that many stocks. He's intrigued by the notion of an economic recovery amid high interest rates 'just because everyone says it can't happen.'

12 July: Starting roughly now, the consensus sees a sustained economic recovery, albeit weaker than normal. It's a forecast buttressed by many key barometers to business ahead, from building permits to the money supply.

12 July: Invariably, the market has begun to rise at or just before a recessionary trough in the business cycle, and then kept on climbing briskly well into an ensuing recovery period. The market may have predicted some recessions that didn't come... but it hasn't signalled any recoveries that didn't arrive.... If a new recovery has indeed begun, it will be he first one in which at the outset the stock market has fallen rather than climbed briskly.

14 July: U.S. retail sales fell 1.5% in June but many economists predicted consumers soon would step up their buying, spurring a modest recovery from the recession.   Sales in 2Q were 3.1% higher than in the preceding period.

29 July: President Reagan asserted that an economic recovery is beginning, but he conceded that 'it's going to be slow.'

2 August: 2Q price deflator 5% half the 1981 level of 9.4%.

5 August: An economist at the U.S. Chamber of Commerce noted in a recent report: 'The improved quality of corporate profits has contributed to a strong performance in corporate cash flow - measured as the sum of earnings plus depreciation charges. On a seasonally adjusted annual basis, corporate cash flow during the first quarter was higher than that for (all) 1981.'

6 August: Perhaps the nearest thing to a consensus forecast can be found in Blue Chip Economic Indicators, a monthly survey of more than 40 prominent forecasters by Robert J. Eggert of Sedona, Ariz. On the average the Blue Chip group predicts growth of 3.3% in inflation-adjusted gross national product in the year ahead. All those polled anticipated at least some growth, but the estimates range from as low as 1.3% to more than 6%. The latest average of 3.3% for instance, is down from 3.6% in the June survey.

12 August: Sales at the nation's retail stores rose 1% in July, providing further evidence that the U.S. economy will emerge slowly from the recession.

18 August: Mr. Regan [Secretary of the Treasury], the former chairman of Merrill Lynch & Co., welcomed Mr. Kaufman's projection of falling interest rates but disputed the analyst's reasoning- that rates will fall because the economy will remain weak. 'He's got the right answers for the wrong reasons,' Mr. Regan said. 'What he's missing are emerging signs of a healthy economy.'

23 August: The 3.2% increase in factory orders for durable goods in July, the first rise since March, may presage improved industrial production in coming months.

22 September: The U.S. economy appears to be growing at a 1.5% annual rate after inflation in the current quarter.... The revised report shows that in the second quarter the economy expanded at a seasonally adjusted 2.1% annual rate.

27 September: So it might come as a surprise that business start-ups are at a near-record high. A reduction of the capital gains tax last year to a maximum of 20% vs. the maximum 49% in 1978 has encouraged more investment in small companies.

1 October: Alan Greenspan, a New York economist who advises President Reagan, expects the 'real' gross national product, of total value of all goods and services adjusted for inflation, to grow at an anaemic 2.3% annual rate in the fourth quarter and about the same pace in the 1983 first half.

5 October: The confidence of business leaders in the U.S. economy has improved for the third consecutive quarter, the Conference Board disclosed.

The government's preliminary economic figures suggested the economic recovery was already underway in the second quarter of 1982. Real GDP in the second quarter did indeed post a quarter-on-quarter growth rate commensurate with an annual rate of expansion of 2.2%. The consensus expectation of 3.3% economic growth in the following 12 months was accurate, as the economy grew by 3.2%. The bottom of the 1982 bear market occurred against a background of an improving economy and a high degree of optimism regarding the economic future.

Once again, as in 1921, 1932 and 1949, the bottom of a bear market is not marked by the absence of good news, but rather by an increasing supply of good news ignored by the market. Analysis of all four bear markets suggests the auto sector provides an important lead indicator for investors. In 1982, a recovery in the auto sector was evident well before the economy in general and the stock market bottomed. The monthly low-point for new car registrations was January 1982, when registrations declined 20% year-on-year.

By June 1982, new car registrations were down only 4% from the previous year and this improvement was widely discussed among investors. The pattern in our four periods is that there is a pent-up demand for this important consumer durable which is triggered by declining prices. In 1921, 1932 and 1949 a decline in the price of autos themselves was evident. In 1982 the situation is not as clear as the price of autos did not decline. On 1 September 1982, the *Wall Street Journal* was reporting that GM was raising the price of its 1983 models by 1.9%. However, while the price of a new auto continued to rise, the cost of buying one was falling quickly. The US prime lending rate, which had been above 20% for most of 1981, had already fallen below 16% by the beginning of 1982. This decline in financing rates, combined with muted price rises, meant cars were cheaper to buy in 1982 than they had been in 1981. Once again, this de facto price decline triggered an improvement in demand and, as in 1921, 1932 and

1949, augured improved demand in the economy in general and an economic recovery. Investors who see equities reduced to low valuations by an economic recession would do well to watch the auto sector as a leading indicator that the recession and the bear market are coming to an end.

A feature of the major bear market bottoms we have noted is that the economic recovery, which triggers the commencement of the new bull market, is generally presaged by news of recovery in New England, and on 19 July 1982 the *Wall Street Journal* was reporting:

> ... some of the perennially depressed states of the Northeast have been coming through with flying colors.... New England used to be the prime example of a stagnant region. In the last few years, it's been on the verge of a boom [derived] from the shift to micro-computers, telecommunications and high technology in general as the engines of the nation's growth. New England by and large made this transition a decade before the rest of the country.

The quote above indicates the degree of transformation of the New England economy over the period. Despite this transformation, the fact remains reports of improvements in the economy of New England have preceded, by just a few weeks, the four great bottoms for equities.

Price stability and the bear

We have seen in the preceding Parts how emerging price stability has been the most important factor signalling the end of the bear market in equities. The end of deflation marked the end of the decline in equity prices for all the three previous great bottoms. The inflationary environment was very different in the 1980s, with inflation falling from very high levels in the recession. Indeed, if we measure deflation as a decline in the CPI index then deflation in this period was not evident until November 1982. In the final quarter of 1982, the CPI declined by 0.6% compared to its level in the third quarter. This very minor and brief deflation is in great contrast to the events of 1921, 1932 and 1949. In 1921 and 1932, the gold standard played a major role in enforcing deflation and in 1949 the postwar adjustment of the economy was a key structural factor. One could see why deflation could occur in those periods and why its abatement would be so positive for equity prices. However things were very different in 1982. The last formal external constraint on the Fed's monetary policy was long gone. Also the financial markets, sickened by almost two decades of rising inflation, were in a mood to panic if it appeared the Fed had lost another battle against inflation.

What is most surprising about 1982, then, is that the great bottom for equities was once again marked by the end of deflation. In 1982, the market was not buoyed by the end of the decline in the general price index, as the CPI did not decline until the new bull market was already underway. In 1982, the key turning point for equities was, as it had been in 1921, 1932 and 1949, stabilisation of commodity prices.

As we discussed in the previous Parts, the prices of key commodities stabilised and led a more general stabilisation in commodity prices and then the general price level. Equity prices reacted positively in 1921, 1932 and 1949 to these first signs of stabilising commodity prices indicating general price stability would follow. Interestingly, despite an entirely different inflationary background, a similar pattern is evident in 1982. While any deflation measured by the CPI in this period was limited, it was much more marked if one's guide to deflation was commodity prices. The Commodity Research Bureau (CRB) index of commodity prices declined more than 30% from its November 1980 high to its October 1982 low. Figure 110 shows, from 1982, how general commodity prices bottomed in October, while the metals component of the index bottomed in June.

Figure 110

COMMODITY RESEARCH BUREAU INDEX, INDEX OF SPOT METALS (JAN-DEC 1982)

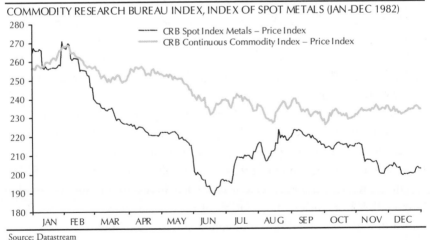

Source: Datastream

While the October low for general commodities came two months after the bottom for equity prices, the bottom for the metals component was two months before the bottom for equities. This coincidence is particularly surprising in 1982, when one might have expected investors would have been spooked by rising commodity prices. By 1982, investors could expect the Volcker Fed to come down very hard on any signs of inflation, and a rebound in commodity prices might be seen to augur even higher real interest rates. With so much pinned on the Fed finally defeating inflation, wouldn't a rebound in commodity prices have warned investors that the Fed had once again failed to conquer inflation? The remarkable thing is that despite this background to the rebound in commodity prices, the end of commodity deflation once again marked the end of the bear market in equities.

In all four of the great bear market bottoms analysed in this book, the end of the decline in commodity prices marks the end of the great bear market in equities.

Figure 110 provides data for general commodity prices and metal prices. The reason for the inclusion of the metal prices series is that a rebound in metal prices in general, and the copper price in particular, appears to precede more general price stabilisation. By May 1982, the price of copper had already declined 16% from its peak in August 1981. From May to June, the price slumped a further 17%, then quickly rebounded, and by the time the equity market bottomed in August the price of copper had returned to its May level. The rebound in copper from the June lows was the first sign that commodity prices may have bottomed. The CRB spot-metals index reached its low in June 1982 and, unlike the general commodity index, remained well above that level for the rest of the year. At the other great bear market bottoms, the copper price bottomed in August 1921, June 1949 and July 1932 (though the price would again hit a new low during the banking crisis of early 1933).

On every occasion, the rebound in copper prices preceded or coincided with the rebound in the equity market. This rule held even in 1982, when, to some investors, higher copper and commodity prices may have presaged the rebound of inflation and tighter monetary policy. So, if stabilisation of commodity prices is a good indicator of the end of the bear market in equities, stabilisation of the copper price may be the best indicator a general stabilisation in commodities is imminent.

The strong rebound in commodity prices pushed the CRB index 24% higher in the ten months after October 1982. The bull market in equities continued throughout that period. The fact that the stabilisation of commodity prices is beneficial for equity prices in these very differing inflationary/deflationary environments may indicate commodity prices carry more important information. It may be that in periods when equities are undervalued and prices still falling that stabilising commodity prices provide evidence of imminent economic improvement. Even in 1982, when the Fed could be relied upon to jump on any signs of inflation, stabilising commodity prices at least indicated there was some evidence of improving final demand. With the bond market already buying into the prospect that the Fed had won the war on inflation, perhaps the stabilisation of commodities was more important as a signal of an imminent improvement in the economy, rather than a concern about future inflationary pressure. This combination of falling interest rates and an indication of an improving economy could account for the more than 50% rise in the DJIA in less than a year from August 1982. Whatever the reason for the positive relationship, equity investors should be looking for a stabilisation in commodity prices in general and copper prices in particular to confirm a bear market in equities has ended.

There is a difficulty in predicting the future course of one set of prices, equities, by predicting the future course of another set of prices, commodities. Forecasting one may be no easier than the other thus invalidating this form of analysis. In this regard it is important to stress the confirming role of low inventory positions in the process of bottoming commodity prices. **In the *Wall Street Journal* in 1921, 1932 and 1949, the low level of inventory throughout the system is featured as a key reason for bullishness regarding the future. A similar situation was evident in 1982, with inventory reduction in the first quarter the most rapid recorded in real terms since the end of WWII.** For commodities, any price reversal may be fleeting, but this is clearly less likely when inventory levels are very low. While investors do need to believe in the sustainability of the price rise in commodities, it is not necessary to buy equities when commodity prices are declining and hope they will improve. History suggests equity investors can wait to see a rising copper price before taking the decision as to the sustainability of the price rise. In a recessionary period, when equities have been reduced to cheap valuations, an equity investor looks for rising commodity prices combined with low inventory positions. If there is also evidence of rising final demand for autos, and not just predictions of higher future demand, then history suggests one is very close to the bottom of the equity market.

One of the key problems in comparing equity bear-market bottoms over a lengthy period is that institutional frameworks change. Is it valid to use one event as a guide to the future if there had been a radical change in the

271

institutional framework in the intervening period? In particular, can such comparisons be valid in a period when the monetary system itself has changed dramatically?

Between 1921 and 1982, the US monetary system underwent radical change with the final abandonment of any form of fixed exchange rate. One would expect adjustments in internal pricing to play a more important role in periods when the exchange rate is fixed. In this environment, internal price adjustments, given the restriction on exchange-rate adjustments, play a crucial role in driving the business cycle. Similarly, one would expect internal price alterations to be less important in the business cycle as the US moved towards the freely flexible currency. Whatever the truth of this for the economy, price changes still imparted important information for the equity investor in 1982, despite the change in the monetary framework. Despite the removal of the external anchor for monetary policy, the lessons from 1921, 1932 and 1949 remain valid in this one area where they are most likely to have been undermined by structural change.

Liquidity and the bear

> Ask yourself sometime who benefits from inflation. The people in debt benefit, society's losers. The government benefits because it collects more in taxes without raising the rates. Who doesn't benefit? The man with money in his pocket, the man who paid his bills.

> John Updike, *Rabbit is Rich*

We have seen throughout this book that so-called "Fed watching" is more of an art than a science. By focusing throughout on changes in the Fed's balance sheet the aim has been to provide some objective guide as to the ability of Fed watchers to pick the bottom of the equity market. We have discovered there is more to Fed watching than simply analysing balance sheet alterations. Very similar lessons are to be learnt from events in 1982.

By the summer of 1982, investors had very clear guidelines from the Fed as to what to expect in terms of its balance sheet adjustments. The Fed had set a course for the growth for the non-borrowed reserves of the banking system, which it believed was consistent with its target for the growth of the monetary aggregates. If the monetary aggregates were growing too fast, this would force the banks to borrow reserves, thus placing upward pressure on the Fed funds rate. Such a rise in interest rates was then supposed to dampen demand and reduce the growth of the monetary aggregates.

Alterations in the growth of non-borrowed reserves provided investors the best indication of how the Fed was responding to the latest money supply data. Figure 111 shows the growth in non-borrowed reserves from the adoption of the monetary growth targeting policy in 1979.

Figure 111

NON-BORROWED RESERVES OF US DEPOSITORY INSTITUTIONS ($M)

Source: Datastream. Note: Seasonally adjusted.

There is some indication from Figure 111 that the growth of non-borrowed reserves did accelerate in 1982, indicating the Fed was pursuing an easier monetary policy. The Fed's first tightening of liquidity in 1980 produced a sharply negative economic reaction and, as the chart shows, Fed policy was rapidly reversed. Following the reversal of the early 1980 squeeze, non-borrowed reserve growth had been muted. The seasonally-adjusted figures show non-borrowed reserves had increased by just 1.8% in the 21 months from July 1980 to April 1982. There was then a change in May 1982, with seasonally-adjusted, non-borrowed reserves growing 2.4% month-on-month. This was to mark a new growth track for non-borrowed reserves, which expanded 10.6% in the next eight months. While the change in growth is evident from the complete set of data, it is not always so easy to spot these trend changes at the time, and it was not until August that one could see a new trend emerging from the fog of statistics.

While the evidence of a higher growth rate in non-borrowed reserves was increasingly evident from May, an investor still had to decide whether this was simply a response to on-target monetary aggregate growth or a new monetary policy. Interpreting the accelerated growth in non-borrowed reserves in relation to money-supply growth was not easy given the

273

volatility of the money supply data. The pages of the *WSJ* in the summer of 1982 show how the growth in non-borrowed reserves could be considered meagre in the light of one month's money supply data but excessive in the light of the next month's data.

By the middle of June the M-1 annual growth rate was 6.7% well in excess of the Fed's target of 3.5%. It was thus reasonable for investors to expect that the Fed would act to slow the growth in non-borrowed reserves with a view to reducing the growth in M-1. However, there was a complicating issue. A recent banking innovation had seen the creation of "NOW" accounts - interest-bearing cheque accounts. This innovation encouraged depositors to have more funds in their current accounts than was previously the case. This alteration could be expected to promote higher growth in M-1 than would otherwise have occurred, although it did not necessarily mean that depositors were getting ready to shop rather than save. So the market was confused and this confusion wasn't helped by the fact that, according to a Bank of International Settlements (BIS) report published on 16 June, the Fed had exceeded its money supply targets for the past three years. If missing the targets was the norm, then forecasting future Fed action, in reaction to M-1 data, was particularly difficult.

The volatility of the data added to the problem. The suggestion of strong M-1 growth changed in the first week of July, the *WSJ* reporting: 'Those figures showed the basic money supply, known as M-1, plunged $3.7 billion in the week ended June 30, bringing the weekly number well within the Fed's target range.' So, while some may have regarded this as a signal that a relaxation of monetary policy would follow, the key message was that weekly money-supply data could be highly volatile. Further confusion was evident by September, when M-1 growth accelerated at an annual rate of 16%. Any investor who saw that as auguring a tightening of liquidity by the Federal Reserve was to be completely wrong-footed.

What did the acceleration in non-borrowed reserves mean when the Fed had regularly failed to meet its money supply growth targets and when the growth of NOW accounts distorted the data? In June it looked like the growth in non-borrowed reserves was being permitted despite high money supply growth. By July, it seemed the Fed was adding liquidity in response to the "steep decline" in money supply. The difficulty in interpretation is evident from the opinions of the experts quoted by the *Wall Street Journal*.

If commentators were generally wrong-footed by their focus on the monetary data, the concern about the fiscal deterioration also led to forecasting errors. The *WSJ* reported on 14 June that Federal Reserve Board Chairman Paul Volcker had told Congress action on the budget was a 'pre-requisite for easier' credit conditions. So it was not surprising that the inability of the politicians to make ground on this issue convinced many that easier money was not around the corner. Presumably this fiscal impasse was one of the reasons why the BIS confidently predicted at its AGM that world interest rates would rise in the second half of the year. Even the most astute economic forecasters believed the outlook for lower interest rates was very unlikely:

> **6 July:** 'I had expected a compromise would be struck on the budget during the first half, and I was wrong,' said Alan Greenspan, president of a New York consulting firm and an economic adviser to President Reagan. Mr. Greenspan had predicted a prime rate of 11¾% by June 30, a three-month Treasury bill rate of 8.8% and a 30-year Treasury bond yield of 12.9%. By contrast three-month bills closed June 30 at 12.6%, while the Treasury bond closed at 13⅞%. 'I can't be optimistic about the long-term outlook in view of what is happening on the budget,' Mr. Greenspan said. 'It is going to require a rededication of effort by Congress to budgetary restraint.'

While the future chairman of the Federal Reserve was aligned with the consensus that interest rates could not decline, Volcker was prepared to propose a different outlook:

> **21 July:** The Treasury borrowing that will be necessary to finance record federal budget deficits doesn't present 'an insuperable obstacle to lower interest rates during this period,' the Fed chief told the Senate Banking Committee. While government pressure on the capital markets will keep rates from falling quickly, Mr. Volcker said he is 'hopeful' that 'we could get through this period with declining interest rates.'

When the seemingly impossible combination of lower long-term interest rates and continued fiscal impasse did develop, commentators were adamant a reversal was imminent. As the bond market rallied, disbelief mounted, with the *WSJ* reporting 'the bulk of the Fed's easing is probably behind us' (2 August), 'many economists warn that mortgage rates aren't likely to decline significantly this year' (3 August), 'but most economists don't think that the drop has much further to go' (19 August), 'most analysts, however, believe that any kind of recovery, even the weak one in prospect, would set a floor under rates over the next year' (13 September). If there was one reason such fears about the fiscal impasse proved misplaced, it was because a financial crisis was developing that would create a demand for the safety of government bonds surpassing the increase in supply.

Evidence that the Fed was permitting accelerated growth in non-borrowed reserves as early as May 1982 was not that easy to interpret as an indicator of future monetary policy. Most commentators had been conditioned to view all the Fed's actions in the light of the money supply data. The key change in the summer of 1982 was that the Fed in effect abandoned that policy. No announcement of this policy change was made, but for those schooled in interpreting the words of chairman Volcker, it was clear in late July something had changed. On 21 July the *Wall Street Journal* reported Volcker saying at the midyear review of monetary policy to the Senate Banking Committee:

> 'Moreover - and I would emphasize this - growth somewhat above the targeted ranges would be tolerated for a time in circumstances in which it appeared that precautionary liquidity motivations, during a period of economic turbulence, were leading to a stronger-than-anticipated demand for money.'

Couched in the most restrained language was the admission that money supply growth targeting would be abandoned if there was a period of 'economic turbulence'. Under questioning, Volcker admitted the recent bankruptcies of Drysdale Government Securities and Penn Square Bank did not constitute such 'economic turbulence'. What Volcker knew and the public didn't was that the bankruptcy of Mexico was imminent, and a government bond dealer, Lombard Wall, was in trouble. The 'economic turbulence' that would justify the new policy was already evident and the Fed had, in effect, already abandoned its money supply growth targets. The catalyst for the change in policy was the potential impact on the US banking system of further debt defaults by sovereign credits. It was evident in July that bank balance sheets were in worse condition than they were prepared to admit and the Mexican situation could only exacerbate the situation. The *Wall Street Journal* editorialised on 30 July:

> Unlike the thrift institutions, which are losing billions of dollars a year, most banks are continuing to earn enough to defray heavy loan losses.... Curiously, little of the surge in problem loans showed up in bank earnings reports through the first quarter. In fact a 24-bank index compiled by Keefe, Bruyette & Woods a bank-consulting firm in New York, indicated that troubled loans were still only half as bad, as a percentage of assets, as they had been five years earlier.... Increases in nonperforming loans Continental Illinois's were up 54% to $1.3 billion and Chase's 47% to $1.05 billion.... Perhaps the shakiest house of cards is being built up overseas.... About two thirds of Citibank's loans and 50% of Manufacturer's Hanover are

overseas.... One securities analyst, however, says, 'Not one dime is classified as bad debt even though there is no way Poland can pay it back.'... In the past the big banks have defended their loans to such countries by saying that nations don't go bankrupt.

By 15 September, a clearer picture of the scale of the disarray in the international banking system was evident, prompting the *WSJ* to comment:

Poland, Mexico, Argentina, East Germany, Brazil, Nigeria, Chile, Zaire, Yugoslavia, Bolivia, Nigeria, Venezuela, Peru, Tanzania, Sudan, Indonesia, Romania, and a dozen others. The list is an international banker's nightmare. The first two countries - Poland and Mexico - already have run out of cash and are near default.... The other countries are among the imponderables in bankers' portfolios.

Many bankers and government officials fear that if Argentina and Brazil default on their loans, a 'domino effect' would impel other countries to do likewise, thus pushing many large banks over the brink and setting off a world-wide financial panic that ultimately could lead to a global depression as happened in the 1930s. All told the debt burden of developing countries had soared from $100 billon in 1973 to about $540 billion at the end of last year. It is expected to reach $640 billion this year. Some $327 billion of this is owed to commercial banks in the West.... Walter Seipp, the chairman of Commerzbank, one of West Germany's largest foreign lenders, recalls that until the Polish and Mexican troubles, it was an accepted principle among bankers that 'it was inconceivable that a sovereign country would allow itself to go into default.' Any large bank that stayed out of international lending in the 1970s 'would not have stayed a large bank,' he adds.

Given the increasingly perilous condition of commercial bank balance sheets, the momentous decision to ignore money supply growth targets and provide further liquidity had been taken by the Federal Open Markets Committee on 1 July. Volcker's comments on 21 July were the first subtle indication that a new policy had been adopted.

While the Fed was explicitly tolerating money supply growth above its targets, there was a hidden agenda to prevent any undue rise in the Fed funds rate. This discussion on "capping" interest rates at the FOMC meeting was the background against which the "toleration" of higher money supply growth was agreed. This was a subtle shift as the Fed was targeting both money-supply growth and interest rates. It was this change in policy which was to permit the continued acceleration in non-borrowed reserves and easier monetary policy despite the fact money supply targets were exceeded. For those able to interpret the Chairman's runic comments, this was the best signal easier money was on the way.

Had one known that money-supply targets had been abandoned, all the liquidity signals from the Fed were now flashing "go" for the buyer of equities. In the six months from 19 July, the discount rate was reduced 350bp. The change of emphasis from money-supply growth targets was finally formalised in October 1982, when the Fed issued a statement that the Fed funds rate would also be targeted. Importantly, at no stage was the government bond market spooked by the prospect of easier money. From August to December, the long-term government bond yield fell from around 14% to 10.5%. The rally in equities occurred against a background of declining short- and long-term interest rates. All of this followed from the arrival of the "economic turbulence" evident to all in early August with the announcement of the economic collapse of Mexico. Liquidity analysts struggled to interpret Fed policy in the light of the old targets and could not foresee the degree of monetary easing that occurred in the second half of 1982. Those who profited were those who understood, from Volcker's guarded comments, that monetary targets had been abandoned and, as a result, a much easier monetary policy would follow.

In general, analysing the Fed's balance sheet for indications of liquidity change seems a dangerous way of trying to find the bottom of the equity bear market. It proved to be wrong in 1921 and 1932, and there were extreme difficulties of interpretation of the data in 1949. It was a much more accurate indicator of the end of the equity bear market in 1982. However, on this occasion the trigger for the easing of liquidity was growing evidence of financial distress in July 1982.

In 1982, the Fed had a free rein to respond to such distress without limitations imposed by the gold exchange standard or Bretton Woods. It was not necessary to engage in sophisticated liquidity analysis in July 1982 to realise the statement of the Fed chairman augured for easier liquidity at least for the duration of the "economic turbulence".

The equity market bottomed just as the scale of the lesser-developed-country debt crisis became known, and the worse the news on sovereign defaults, the greater the rise in the price of equities and the price of US government bonds. If one can draw lessons from just one bear market episode, it is that the price of equities will respond positively in a situation where the Fed is riding to the rescue of an imperilled financial system. In 1982, it didn't seem to matter how bad the news was, so long as investors were certain of a positive Fed response and so long as the bond market was not spooked.

The Fed had come to the support of the financial system in one previous great bear market bottom. By summer 1931, the Fed was making concerted efforts to ease liquidity and support the financial system, but this policy was abandoned as the devaluation of sterling put pressure on the dollar. In 1982, such external constraints had long ceased to be a factor, and any Fed response was more likely to be greeted with the enthusiasm evident that year, rather than the capital exodus that emerged in 1931. Whether the record-high foreign ownership levels of US government bonds today would act as an informal constraint on monetary policy is, of course, the subject of much debate.

Throughout this book we have assessed the usefulness of changes in broad money in finding the bottom of bear markets. In 1921, 1932 and 1949 it did not prove an accurate signal, and the same was true in 1982. Whereas a rebound in monetary growth had lagged bear-market bottoms in 1982, it significantly led the improvement in the equity market. From around April 1981 a rebound in broad-money growth, in nominal and real terms, became increasingly apparent. However, that rebound coincided with a vicious bear market that saw the DJIA decline almost 24% in the next 16 months. By 1982, broad-money growth, in nominal and real terms, had reached a plateau following the 1981 acceleration. There was nothing in the data in 1982 or 1983 amounting to acceleration in broad-money growth. A focus on credit growth would have provided very similar signals. In both nominal and real terms, a rebound in credit growth began in the final quarter of 1980 - long before the stock market bottomed. Those finding buy signals for equities from credit growth would have been badly stung in the 1980-82 bear market.

We have focused primarily on changes on the Fed balance sheet as indicating a period of easing liquidity. This indicator provides the acid test of when the Fed is seeking to expand what used to be known as the "elastic currency". One can also look at the key Fed-controlled interest rate, the discount rate, as providing some indication of its future stance. In all but one of the four periods under examination, the discount-rate trend proved successful. The Fed's first cut in the discount rate, in May 1921, was followed by the end of the equity bear market in August 1921, and an intervening loss to investors of 20%. In 1949, the change in credit controls in March was the first signal the Fed believed it had probably squeezed inflation hard enough. The equity market bottomed in July and, in March-July, investors had lost about 10 % of their money.

279

It was October 1981 when the Fed implemented the first reduction in the discount rate. Although the equity market was not to bottom until August 1982, once again the capital loss in the ensuing period was less than 10%. Taking the first reduction in Fed interest rates as an indicator of future, easier liquidity has been quite successful, with minimal capital losses compared with the scale of the capital gains that have followed rapidly thereafter.

The main problem is that an investor following this policy would have been plunging into the market on the first reduction in the Fed discount rate on 1 November 1929 and would have incurred dreadful losses.

It might be possible to set aside the 1929 example and simply say reductions of Fed interest rates in Fed-induced recessions are a good time to buy cheap equities. Recessions were clearly the result of Fed policy in 1921, 1949 and 1982. The first sign the Fed thought the economy had had enough anti-inflationary pressure was a good time to buy. On all three occasions, the Fed had raised rates to combat inflation and reduced rates when it believed the war was coming to an end. This was not the case in 1929. Inflation had been in abeyance in the 1920s and the malaise that swept the US from late 1929 was almost certainly not the result of a Fed-induced recession, but rather the inevitable consequences of a global financial system that had been unbalanced by German reparations, Allied debt repayments and the inept reconstruction of the gold standard. If the 1929-32 bear market is the exception, rather than the rule, then investing in equities following the first discount rate cut is a sound policy. Perhaps the rule-of-thumb should be that an investor should await a further decline of 10% in the stock market before contemplating investment. History suggests the downside would then be minimal and the upside very significant.

A further caveat is necessary regarding this policy of investing in equities following the first reduction in the discount rate. As we have seen the initial implementation of the Fed's monetary targeting regime produced a dramatic reversal of policy in the middle of 1980. Investors taking the plunge into equities following a reduction in the discount rate in May 1980 saw a rise in the discount rate before it declined again and had to wait until August 1982 before the equity market bottomed. On this occasion, the capital loss was again less than 10% before the market bottomed in August 1982, but it was almost double this in real terms. This zig-zag of official rates was a direct consequence of money-supply growth targeting. This reversal in the discount rate, necessitated by that particular monetary policy, might prove to be an event confined to periods when such targeting is underway. **With November 1929 and May 1980 in mind, investors should tread warily, but be prepared to buy cheap equities when a reduction in the discount rate signals the beginning of the end for a Fed war on inflation.**

The bulls and the bears

> He loves Nature, though he can name almost nothing in it. Are these pines, or spruces, or firs? He loves money, though he doesn't understand how it flows to him, or how it leaks away.

John Updike, *Rabbit is Rich*

It is a myth that bulls are extinct at the bottom of a bear market. The bulls were certainly not extinct in 1982. The *Wall Street Journal* carries numerous comments by pundits who saw not just the end of a bear market, but the start of a major bull market.

14 June: Daniel S. Ahern Wellington Management/TDP&L says signs of improved consumer atmosphere include an upturn in auto sales last month, and gains in general retail sales in April and May, the best in several months. He notes the 'sizable' stimulus that will be provided by the 10% income-tax rate cut next month and by the inflation adjustment on Social Security payments.

15 June: Eric T. Miller of Donaldson, Lufkin & Jenrette said, 'We continue to think that most stocks have seen their lows and that... the market has absorbed poor economic news quite well.'

18 June: The ultimate 'gold bug' has turned from the metal. After 20 years of advocating bullion investments, James Dines has sent telegrams to subscribers of his advisory service telling them to sell their gold holdings.... With these words, some market followers say, came the end of the 'gold bug' era.

23 June: 'Bear markets end in either a selling climax (a sharp drop accompanied by a volume surge) or flat

period when prices do little or nothing, and we appear to be in such a dead period,' contended Alan C. Poole, vice president of Laidlaw Adams & Peck Inc.

28 June: 'We're more bullish on equities than we have been in a long time because we think we're walking along a market bottom,' asserts James R. McCall, senior vice President of Keystone Custodian Fund Inc., Boston.

2 July: The $1.6 billion Dreyfus Fund has been trimming its utility-stock holdings that did so well for it in 1981. And a growing part of its cash reserves are going back into the stock market. 'I can see a 50% gain in these stocks a lot more easily then in most,' says Howard Stein, president of the fund.

14 July: The eminent brokerage firms of Merrill Lynch, Pierce, Fenner & Smith; Goldman Sachs; Bear Stearns and E.F. Hutton each can produce rather lengthy lists of stocks deemed worthy of purchase. They have something else in common, however.

Their top strategists all think investors would be better off in bonds.

28 July: 'The historical implications of the drops in interest rates we've seen since last year combined with the assumption that corporate profits won't decline further would indicate the stock market has reached a bottom.' John S. Brush of Columbine Capital Services, Colorado Springs, Colo. He added: 'It seems crystal clear that inflation is going to be cooling for the next few years.'

27 July: 'It was a normal correction as the market pulled back and digested the recent declines in interest rates,' asserted vice president Ralph Acampora of Kidder Peabody, encouraged that 'volume tended to dry up' when prices were falling. And he added that 'any time a pickup in the market has occurred recently there's been a ground-swell in the consumer stocks.'

30 July: Leon G. Cooperman, investment policy committee chairman at Goldman Sachs & Co., asserted that 'entry into a classical bull market must be validated by a further and sustained decline in interest rates.' He added: 'Lower interest rates are the essential market tonic and necessary for one to gain confidence that an economic recovery of substance can proceed and price-earnings (multiples) expansion can develop.'

2 August: 'I'm usually suspicious of the consensus view, but I have to agree with the current consensus that stocks can't go anywhere until interest rates come down,' Robert Kirby, chairman Capital Guardian Trust Co., Los Angeles. Mr. Kirby says he doubts that the market has ever sold lower relative to book value over the past 50 years to 60 years

than it did each time the industrial average fell below 800 this year.

6 August: 'The spirit of the bear is still with us- fear of financial collapses, both banking and corporate, high interest rates, rekindled inflation, political disarray, poor second-quarter earnings and Middle East hostilities are all keeping grizzly's image in the fore.' Said Alan R. Shaw senior vice president at Smith Barney, Harris Upham & Co.

12 August: DJIA bottoms

13 August: Lacy H. hunt the chief economist of Philadelphia's Fidelity bank says: 'The confidence problem now has more to do with fiscal policy than monetary policy. Unless the political process can deal with the entitlements programs, including Social Security, we'll have bigger and bigger deficits in 1984, 1985 and beyond.'

13 August: That the stock market recently has 'demonstrated no ability to mount a sustained rally on good news probably indicates that a selling climax will be required to end the bear market.' Said Richard E. Minshall, president of Capital Advisors Inc. of Tulsa.

18 August: 'Interest rates are going to plummet, the real cost of money above the inflation rate won't last, and this is going to stimulate one of the great booms in the history of this country,' Seth Glickenhaus, chief of money-management firm of Glickenhaus & Co. 'The Dow is going so much higher, it is foolhardy to predict, but I can see it surpassing 1200 eventually.'

18 August: An early-morning signal yesterday from Goldman Sachs which, like Solomon Brothers, deal primarily with institutions was also given part of the credit for the advance of the stock prices. Goldman told its clients to increase their equity holdings to 55% of portfolios from 35% and to reduce holdings in bonds and cash reserves.

18 August: Yesterday's heavy trading was widely linked to the surprise pronouncements of a single analyst. Salomon Brothers credit analyst Henry Kaufman, reversing his long standing pessimism on financial markets, told the firm's clients he expects substantial drops in interest rates within the next 12 months. Mr. Kaufman said the rate on long-term Treasury bonds could fall to as low as 9% from the current level of about 12.5%, and he predicted a decline of as much as three percentage points in short-term rates.

18 August: 'This isn't going to stop here,' predicted Jonathan F. Gutman, a broker with Ferris & Co. of Washington. 'We were due for a bounce, but 38 points isn't a bounce. Some are saying this is the start of the 1980's boom.'

18 August: Alfred E Goldman A.G. Edwards & Sons. 'On of the classic ingredients of a real bottom (in the market) is when you've had a capitulation (heavy selling) by the institutions, a high level of disgust and lack of confidence…But they've been complacent, confident. It's unusual to get a bull market with so little pain.'

19 August: Heavy institutional buying pushed trading volume on the NYSE to a one-day record while the small investor mainly remained on the sidelines. Other brokers said the small investor seems sceptical that the bear market and recession are over.

23 August: Technical analysts at Merrill Lynch believe last week's price surge was a false start. Richard McCabe, market analyst, said that institutions didn't reach a state of desperate selling prior to the rally, as they have prior to other long-lasting bull moves.

24 August: Last Tuesday, when the NYSE saw almost 93 million shares change hands, there were 95,000 trades, compared with 130,000 on a comparable day in 1981, when small investors played a larger role.

25 August: Blue chips tumbled sharply yesterday, but the broader market continued to move ahead in large volume of nearly 122 million shares, the second highest on record…. 'The pullbacks were shallow, barely allowing time to get aboard, while the broad market, remained on the plus side, which is action typical of a bull market,' asserted Hildegard Lagorski second vice president of Bache Halsey Stuart Shields Inc.

2 September: 'With institutional cash reserves still large despite the frenzied activity of recent weeks, and with good value still present in equities,' he said, 'It is likely that further retrenchment in stock prices may be short-lived.' Jacques S. Theriot Harris, Upham & Co.

3 September: 'Until there are more definitive signs that cash (reserves) has been expended, it is unlikely that a sustained setback will occur,' asserted Donald Kimsey, vice president and senior market analyst at Dean Witter Inc. 'In the past, once psychology shifted from bearish to bullish, the market has not shown a penchant for allowing players easy entry.'

10 September: James H. Farrell Jr. of Cashman Farrell & Associates, Philadelphia, asserted that according to

283

'conventional wisdom' every major market upswing is followed by a substantial pullback. However he believes that people waiting for such a major pullback soon 'will be disappointed because it will be mild.' The reasons, he said, are that 'there's still lots of cash waiting to get into the market and pension fund managers would be embarrassed to show large cash reserves in their reports at the end of the current quarter.' Also, there's lots of nervous money world-wide seeking a safe haven in the U.S. stock market,' he contended.

17 September: Lee H. Idleman, investment policy committee member at Dean Witter Reynolds Inc., asserted that 'if the stock market action of the past few weeks is, as we believe, the start of the new bull cycle, then even the fireworks of August are only a small part of what is to come.' He added that initial phases typically show gains of 30% and 'more likely 50%'.

21 September: 'The market was digesting some of its recent gains,' asserted Peter J. DaPuzzo, executive vice president at Shearson/American Express, Inc. 'The fact that volume tended to dry up as the market was retreating was positive. Individual

investors were nibbling at some of the secondary issues.'

23 September: Michael T. Murray, vice president at Loomis Sayles Inc., Chicago, asserted that changes give the appearance of a highly volatile market, the overall momentum established in recent weeks suggests that the market has much farther to go on the upside. He added that 'the critical fact in this process is disinflation, which ultimately rewards the equity investors.'

23 September: Noting the 25% jump in the Big Board short interest in the month to Sept. 15, Newton D Zinder of E.F. Hutton & Co. asserted that 'very large increases in the monthly short interest often occur in the early stages of major bull phases.' He cited big short-interest percentage gains in Feb 1975, June 1970 and June 1962.

29 September: 'We believe we are in the early stages of a bull market' and the bulk of it 'still lies ahead,' asserted Leon G. Cooperman, invest policy committee chairman at Goldman, Sachs & Co. He said the average postwar bull market 'has lasted 30 months and yielded an average trough-to-peak advance of 66%'.

There were plenty of bulls around at the bottom of the market in 1982 and there were some who foresaw the forthcoming turnaround, quite correctly, as the beginning of the great bull market of the 1980s.

The 1982 bear market bottom is again marked by the absence of a final slump in stock prices on high volumes. The great final slump in prices on rising volume was as absent in 1982 as it was in 1921, 1932 and 1949. The belief in the necessity of such an episode discouraged some investors in 1982. Indeed one commentator, Alfred E Goldman, of A.G. Edwards & Sons, stated that the absence of such high volume selling in the market's final decline indicated that the bear market was not over.[79] Ten days after the rally began, Richard McCabe of Merrill Lynch doubted the sustainability of the market rise in the absence of the capitulation event. This is not to say this event does not sometimes occur, but it did not occur at any of our four great bottoms, when equities were at their cheapest. There were numerous turning points in the trading market from 1968 to 1982 and perhaps, in this trading environment, the final high-volume sell-off was more of a feature.

Figure 112

NO CAPITULATION: THE DJIA AND NYSE VOLUMES (TWO WEEK MOVING AVERAGE)

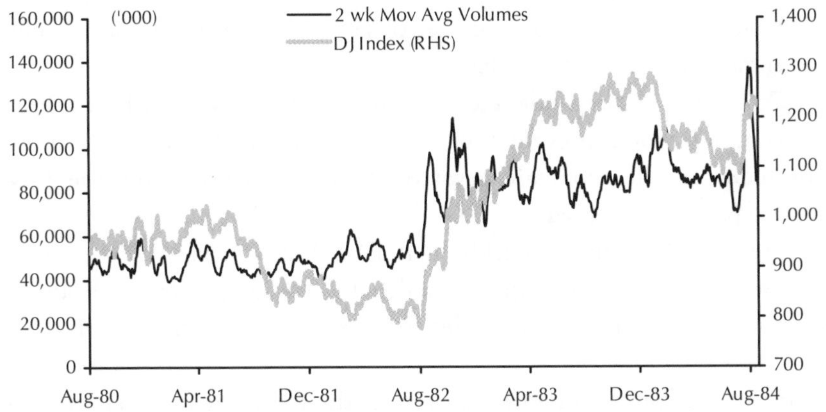

Source: Dow Jones & Co., NYSE

If one had to characterise the end of a bear market when equities are cheap, then it would be just like 1982, with a market trading sideways or drifting downwards and then slumping lower on low volume. In the period of sideways movement, the market has a much more subdued reaction to both good and bad news than one might have expected. It might recover on limited volume or, as in 1982, large volume, but at the new, higher level volumes will start to increase. It is the higher volume at higher levels that confirms the bear market is over.

Some features common to 1921, 1932 and 1949 did not recur in 1982. One key difference is that volumes had been picking up in the market for many years prior to the 1982 bottom. At other turning points for the equity market general interest, as measured by turnover rates, had not seen such rises in previous years. There seems to be little that one can learn in

---

[79] *Wall Street Journal*, 18 August 1982

relation to market bottoms from absolute levels of the turnover ratio. The annual turnover rate in 1982 was 42%, compared with 13% in 1949, 32% in 1932 and 59% in 1921. Another key difference in 1982 is that the initial rebound in equity prices occurred on very high volumes, whereas in other episodes the rebound came on low volumes.

Numerous technical indicators have proved useful in spotting the end of the 1968-82 bear market. Common to all the great bear market bottoms has been the proclivity of the market to decline on low volume and rise on high volume. This was taken correctly to indicate liquidation pressures were abating.

A clear consensus in the summer of 1982 was that equity prices could not climb unless interest rates fell.

There was a preponderance of opinion that the continued fiscal deterioration would prevent such declines in interest rates. Once again, this focus on the economic negatives that would flow from the fiscal malaise proved misplaced.

Interest rates declined quickly in 1982 and continued to do so through the 1980s, despite ever-growing fiscal deficits. The trigger for the decline in interest rates was not to come directly from the domestic economy, but from overseas.

It was the signs of financial distress in the global financial system that proved the catalyst for the reduction in short-term interest rates despite the worsening fiscal deficit. The extent of the decline in such rates was surprising, but the real surprise was the collapse in long-term interest rates. It was not surprising that equity prices rallied dramatically in this environment, but who could possibly have foreseen the collapse in long-term rates that would warrant such a rise in valuations? In 1982, the answer to that question was Henry Kaufman. Kaufman's change of forecast for long-term interest rates occurred on the day the major rally on Wall Street began. The significant rally on large volume that followed was, at the time, largely attributed to his comments.

Kaufman, dubbed "Dr Doom", had a solid reputation as an interest-rate forecaster due to his calculations on supply and demand for credit. In his autobiography, he describes why, on his 17 August return from a European vacation, he stopped being a bear and published a bullish forecast:

> So after catching up on some urgent business at Salomon, I called together my associates to review the data on the current interest rate situation. After doing so, I concluded that a significant interest rate decline lay ahead. What

had changed? To begin with, the economy was stalling, which was likely to moderate inflation. Second, financial blockages and intense international competition were straitjacketing the economy. Businesses were coming under intense pressure to refurbish their balance sheets. At the same time, financial institutions no longer were enjoying conditions favourable to aggressive lending and investing. Another factor that was restricting lending - domestically and internationally - was the huge burden of international debt.[80]

Although the interest-rate forecast was predicated on bearish economic conditions, Kaufman's change of opinion spurred the biggest one-day rally in the DJIA ever recorded. His forecasts proved correct, and the big surprise for the consensus was that such major declines in long-term interest rates were possible despite continuing fiscal malaise. In June 1982, the Senate budget resolution called for a deficit of $103.9 billion for fiscal 1983 (the actual reported deficit in 1983 turned out to be $208 billion). The rally in interest rates continued, despite this marked fiscal deterioration. The fiscal deficit in 1982 reached 3.9% of GDP, the highest since the end of WWII. The deterioration continued, with the deficit peaking at 5.9% of GDP in 1985, surpassing the peace-time peaks racked up by Roosevelt in the 1930s. That interest rates declined, and the economy recovered against this background, was the biggest surprise for investors in the summer of 1982. Some of the brightest commentators had difficulty foreseeing such an outcome:

> Alan Greenspan, president of a New York forecasting firm and a close adviser to President Reagan, contends that 'in a matter of weeks' the nation will see the signs of recovery.... He said interest rates will remain high until financial markets are convinced that Congress is committed to lowering federal deficit spending in future years.[81]

A similar fear of fiscal deterioration had stalked the markets in the summer of 1932. The gross fiscal deterioration that ensued did not prevent the strongest economic growth in US history and a bull market in equities. There is clear evidence from both periods that a continued fiscal deterioration will not necessarily prevent a rally in bonds and equities, and an economic recovery.

The Dow Theory, as interpreted by Hamilton, Rhea and Schaefer, had provided excellent timing signals for those seeking the bottom of the equity

---

[80] Henry Kaufman, *On Money and Markets: A Wall Street Memoir*
[81] *Wall Street Journal*, 1 July 1982

market in 1921, 1932 and 1949. Unfortunately, the Dow Theory is not entirely mechanistic, and different Dow theorists often arrive at different answers regarding the direction of the market. By 1982 there were numerous Dow Theorists, not all necessarily saying the same things. **On at least some interpretations of the Dow Theory, a "buy" signal for equities was seen in October 1982. By this stage, the DJIA had risen almost 30%, just a small portion of the total return to emerge over the course of the 1982-2000 bull market. Although the evidence is less clear-cut for 1982, the Dow Theory again appears to have assisted the investors' ability to determine the bottom of this great bear-market bottom..**

At previous equity bottoms, a key sign of the sustainability of any rally was the initial refusal of shorts to cover. In 1982, not only did shorts not cover in the explosive high-volume rally of August, but they actually increased positions. A peak of 103.6 million shares sold short was reached on 14 May, declining to just 96.4 million by the middle of August. However, when the market rallied in August, a sharp increase in shorting occurred and short positions reached a new record of 120.5 million on 15 September. The refusal of the shorts to capitulate on the initial rally proved the rally in the stock market had characteristics of a price movement likely to be more permanent in duration.

The pages of the *Wall Street Journal* in the summer of 1982 indicate equity investors were focused on the outlook for interest rates. There was less comment on the outlook for corporate earnings in 1982 than at any of the other bear market bottoms. This may have been driven by the Fed's new operational target which, in 1982, seemed certain to keep interest rates very high and prevent any earnings recovery. In this environment, it seemed very likely corporate earnings could not recover until interest rates declined. This focus on interest rates and not earnings was justified. The equity market bottomed in August 1982 when the real rally in the bond market began and short- and long-term interest rates declined.

Those investors who waited for evidence of an improvement in corporate earnings would have kept their powder dry until the second quarter of 1983. At each of the four great market bottoms, the nadir for earnings has come some months after the bottom for equities. The range of lag in earnings had been four-to-seven months, the average lag almost six months.

Bonds and the bear

The little stone house, once a gardener's cottage, in Penn Park cost $78,000. Janice wanted to put down $25,000, but Harry pointed out to her that in inflationary times debt is a good thing to have, that mortgage interest is tax-deductible, and that six month $10,000-minimum money market certificates are paying close to 12% these days.

John Updike, *Rabbit is Rich*

Figure 113

US GOVT BOND YIELD (LONG-TERM), YIELD ON MOODY'S BAA

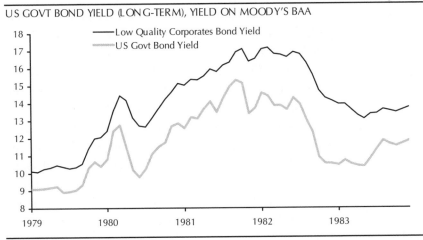

Source: Federal Reserve

The bear market in bonds, in its fifth decade, ended in October 1981. The yield on long-term US Treasuries had risen from 2.03% in April 1946 to 15.1% in the first week of October 1981. The government bond market had been unimpressed by declines in inflation. The annual rate peaked in March 1980 at 14.6%, and by September had declined to 11.0%. The bond market had also been unimpressed by the decline in commodity prices. The CRB futures index peaked in November 1980 and declined 20% by September 1981. There was ample evidence inflation was coming under control, but the key factors unsettling the bond market were the very high level of short-term interest rates and the fiscal implications of a supply-side orientated White House and a Democrat-controlled Congress.

Since October 1979, the Fed had targeted money-supply growth, which allowed short-term interest rates to adjust to whatever level necessary to achieve the monetary targets. Nobody knew the level of short-term interest rates that would result. The Fed funds rate was hitting 20% in the early

289

summer of 1981 as a result of this policy. By September, the rate was nearer 15%, but the volatility of the rate under the monetary-targeting regime made it difficult to forecast that this was the beginning of any sustained decline in interest rates. The change in investor perceptions began in the final quarter of 1981. **From early October 1981 to the end of July 1982, the yield on the US long-term government bond declined some 200 basis points to 13.1%.**

One key driver of the decline in long-term interest rates was a continued rapid decline in inflation. The annual rate of inflation declined by almost four percent in that period, and by July 1982 it had more than halved from its March 1980 peak. The continued decline of inflation and the evident determination of the Fed to stay the course on this occasion finally began to encourage bond investors. While nominal yields on government bonds declined, real rates of interest rose steadily. The real yield on government bonds, calculated using the September 1981 and July 1982 levels of consumer price inflation, had risen from 4.4% in September 1981 to 7.4% in July 1982. The first stage of the great bond bull market had begun, but the soaring real rates indicated bond investors still remained sceptical about the long-term outlook. The pages of the *Wall Street Journal* in the summer of 1982 provide an insight into the concerns that kept interest rates so high, and also an insight into the events of 17 August 1982, when a change in market sentiment occurred.

Among those issues which the *WSJ* reported as keeping real yields high were 'the current epidemic of corporate bankruptcy filings', 'the U.S. Treasury's huge borrowing needs' and 'the recent default of Drysdale Government Securities Inc'. The attitude was summed up by William H. Gross, a pension fund manager at Pacific Investment Management Co., when he told the *WSJ* on 15 June: 'The system has been undergoing an extensive period of pressure, and that can lead to accidents. It's better to be safe at times like this.' Indeed, it was the intensification of this fear which sent investors stampeding into bonds on 17 August. Henry Kaufman's bullish call on bonds had a positive impact, but probably because it was predicated on further deterioration in the economic outlook. In such an environment, with the stability of the financial system already under question, the desire 'to be safe at times like this' pushed government bond prices higher. Indeed it was not just US investors who suddenly fund an appetite for government bonds. 'Investors around the world are pouring more of their funds into gold and the US bond market because of growing nervousness about the plight of Mexico and rumors of potential problems in Argentina' (*WSJ*, 3 September). The positive change in the psychology of the government bond market followed on from the first real signs of risk to US financial stability.

It was only with the advent of clear signs of financial distress that the bond market began to accept short-term interest rates were unlikely to surge again and the real rally in the government bond market began. In this environment, the prospect, and then reality, of ever-larger fiscal deficits did not prevent substantial declines in short-term and long-term interest rates. **While the government bond market technically bottomed in September 1981, it was not until July 1982, when the Fed's fixation with money supply growth targeting ended, that the major rally in government bond prices began.** The coincidence was ironic. The FOMC constantly fretted about the negative impact on the bond markets if they were seen to be reneging on their monetary growth targets. Bond investors ignored the shift by the Fed and were instead driven into the security of government bonds by the increasing evidence of a likely financial collapse. This fear factor swamped concerns about the Fed's anti-inflation commitment and fears about fiscal profligacy.

In 1982, as in 1921 and 1932, the corporate bond market lagged the improvement in the government bond market, but led the improvement in equity prices. In 1949, government bonds rallied before the corporate bond market, but this was an aberration caused by the Fed's policy of capping the government bond yield. Both markets in 1949 recovered before the equity market. In 1982, the long-term US treasury market bottomed in the first week of October 1981, whereas the yield on the Moody's Baa corporate bond index did not peak until the middle of February 1982.

From the peak yield in mid-February 1982 of 17.3%, the Moody's Baa corporate bond index saw little improvement and by the middle of July the yield had declined to just 16.8%. The yield premium for Baa corporate bonds continued to rise from February 1982, and continued rising after the major bull market in corporate and government bonds that developed in July 1982. The peak for the Baa yield premium over government bonds was not reached until November 1982. The rise in the Baa yield premium, despite the rally in the corporate bond market, is not surprising when one considers that investors were piling into government bonds partly due to the prospect of a financial crisis. Thus, 1982 followed the sequence evident at the bottom of the other great bear-market bottoms of a rally in government bond prices, followed by a rally in Baa-rated corporate bonds and finally followed by the equity market. Investors waiting to buy equities after the apparent peak of the Baa-yield premium were committing funds to equities well after the bottom.

Growing evidence of stability in selected commodity prices has proven to be a lead indicator for an improvement in equity prices. The same is also true for corporate bonds. The same basic relationship seems to exist even in 1982, even though the entire monetary framework has changed and the Fed was fighting inflation rather than deflation. The marginal improvement in corporate bond prices from February to July occured against a background of falling commodity prices. However, the Baa corporate bond premium, which peaked in November 1982, declined markedly thereafter as commodity prices improved. This improvement could be coincidental, but once again this sequence of events mirrors 1921 and 1932.

Suffice to say, the indicators that signalled the bottom of the bear market in 1921, 1932 and 1949 worked again in 1982. This is particularly encouraging for investors seeking patterns - the new monetary regime in 1982 suggested bear-market bottoms would be very different this time around. This book is aimed at making sure investors are looking at the right indicators. However, the investor must still determine whether the positive changes in those indicators are sustainable. It is appropriate, then, to conclude our examination of bear-market bottoms with some questions about where the US stock market is in 2005 and where it is headed.

Conclusions

Exit, pursued by a bear.

William Shakespeare, *The Winter's Tale*

Perhaps surprisingly, the same indicators that helped identify the end of the bear market in 1921, 1932 and 1949 worked again in 1982. The similarities between all four bear-market bottoms are particularly intriguing when one considers the huge changes to the institutional framework over the period. Investors should focus on these indicators. We can refer to these as "Einstein's questions". All that's missing are answers that are better than most everyone else. The following is an attempt to answer those questions, which serves to map out the future for the US equity market over the next decade.

Strategic

As this book is concerned with the four periods when equities produced the best subsequent returns, it is axiomatic to say equities are cheapest at the bottom of the market. One indicator of value available to investors at the time was the q ratio. It fell below 0.3x at all four bear market bottoms. The cyclically adjusted PE provides the next best contemporary indicator of value, but its range has been rather wide at the bottom - from 4.7x in 1932 to 11.7x in 1949. Even calculating cyclically adjusted PE using inflation-adjusted earnings, the range is still a wide 5.2x to 9.1x.

Equities become cheap slowly. On average, it took nine years for equities to move from peak q ratios to their lows. If one excludes the 1929-32 bear market, the average period for the adjustment in valuations was 14 years. The US equity market reached its highest-ever valuations in March 2000, and all extremes of valuation have been followed by this slow move to undervaluation.

With the exception of 1929-32, our bear markets occurred against a background of economic expansion. On average, real GDP expanded 52% over the course of our three long bear markets. Nominal GDP expanded by an average of 285%.

Reported corporate earnings growth, at least in real terms, is muted during our bears, but it too has a wide range. Inflation-adjusted earnings growth ranged from -67% to +28%. For nominal earnings in the four bear markets, the range is -67% to +119%.

A material disturbance to the general price level will be the catalyst to reduce equities to cheap levels. On three occasions - 1921, 1949 and 1982 - the disturbance was a period of high inflation followed by deflation, although in 1982 deflation was confined to commodity prices. There was no initial inflation in 1932, but there was still a material disturbance to the general price level in the form of severe deflation. In such periods of price disturbance, there is great uncertainty as to both the level of future corporate earnings and the price of the key alternate low-risk asset - government bonds. This in turn leads to a decline in equity valuations.

We have seen that all four of our bear-market bottoms occurred during economic recession. We have also seen that a return of price stability, following a period of deflation, signals the bottom of the bear market in equities. In particular, stabilising commodity prices augur more general price stability ahead and signal the rebound in equity prices. Of all the commodities, the change in the trend of the price of copper has been a particularly accurate signal of better equity prices. In assessing whether price stability is sustainable, investors should look for low inventory levels, rising demand for products at lower prices, and whether producers have been selling below cost.

We have seen that a sell-off in government bonds accompanies at least part of the bear market in equities. Things were slightly different in 1929-32, when bonds rallied from September 1929 to June 1931. Only then did a sell-off begin, lasting until January 1932. But even in the two bear markets associated with high levels of deflation - 1921 and 1932 - there was some sell-off in government bonds.

Tactical

Investors should look out for the key strategic factors when attempting to assess whether the move from overvalued to undervalued equities is nearing completion. When the strategic factors suggest this process may be coming to an end, there are a host of tactical considerations to be considered in attempting to find the bottom of the market. As we have seen, a recovery in government bond prices precedes a recovery of equities. In 1932, equity prices bottomed seven months after the government bond market. In 1921, 1949 and 1982, the lags were 14, nine and 11 months respectively. The price decline in the DJIA following the bottom of the bond market was 23% in 1921, 46% in 1932, 14% in 1949 and 6% in 1982.

The birth of a new bull market for corporate bonds will precede the end of the bear market in equities. The recovery in corporate bond prices led equities by two months in 1921, one month in 1932 and five months in 1982. In 1949 the lead was much larger - 15 or 17 months - depending on how one defines it, but this was probably due to the distortions to the bond markets in the post-war era.

In our three long bear markets, reductions in interest rates by the Federal Reserve preceded the bottom for equity prices. The lag before equity prices bottomed was three months for 1921 and 1949, and 11 months for 1982. On all three occasions, the decline in the DJIA over the period of the lag was less than 20%. It was a different story in 1929-32. The Fed cut rates in November 1929, while the bear market was still in its infancy.

A number of further tactical conclusions can be summed up briefly:

Economic and stock market recoveries roughly coincide. Recovery in the auto sector precedes recovery in the equity market.

Bear market bottoms are characterised by an increasing supply of good economic news being ignored by the market. While numerous bulls bang the drum for equities even at the bottom of the market, they will be ignored.

Many commentators will suggest the worsening fiscal position will prevent economic recovery or a bull market in equities. They will be wrong.

Decline in reported corporate earnings will continue well past the bottom of the market.

The bottom is preceded by a period in which the market declines on low volumes and rises on high volumes. The end of a bear market is characterised by a final slump of prices on low trading volumes. Confirmation that the bear trend is over will be rising volumes at the new higher levels after the first rebound in equity prices.

There will be a large number of individual investors shorting stocks at the bottom of the market. Short positions will reach high levels at the bottom of the equity market and will increase in the first few weeks of the new bull market.

Dow Theory works to signal a buy for equities.

These are the identifying features of the bear and its bottom. Just as the possession of fur does not, of itself, permit the identification of an animal as a bear, the possession of any one of the features above should not be considered as constituting positive identification of its financial equivalent. Our list is the financial equivalent of Einstein's questions. In trying to identify the bear-market bottom you will have to find the answers to most, if not all, of the questions.

Then and now

As far as I am aware, we cannot as yet point a copy of a field guide at a wild creature and ask it for positive identification. However, for this particular field guide, which aims to be as practical as possible, failure to venture a positive identification would be somewhat remiss. Utilising the strategic features from the checklist above, one would have to assert that the US bear market that began in 2000 is in its early days.

At the end of 1999, the q ratio for US equities reached an all-time high. A similar new all-time high was reached for the cyclically adjusted PE. The

q ratio was 2.9x, its geometric mean, and the cyclically adjusted PE was 170% above its 1881-to-June 2005 average. There is no history of anything but a fall to deeply-discounted valuations following from such peak levels. As we have seen from these high levels there has been, with the exception of 1929-32, a slow shift back to low valuations. One should expect the adjustment to take from nine to 14 years. Our current market peaked five years ago.

From the June 2005 level, the cyclically adjusted PE would have to decline 40% to reach its long-term average. Assuming it declined to the low levels seen at the bottom of the great bear market bottoms, one would expect a decline in the range of 60% to 84%. Just how large a decline this will be in prices will depend upon how earnings perform over the period.

At the end of June 2005, the q ratio was 44% above fair value. If it is to approach the level recorded at the bottom of all the four great bear market bottoms of the 20th Century, it will have to decline 67% from there. Once again the degree to which this alteration occurs due to price declines will depend upon the growth in the replacement value of assets over the period.

There has yet been no disturbance to the general price level to create the uncertainty to push equities to cheap levels. But it is normal for the decline in valuations to have been underway for many years before the general price disturbance comes along to prompt the final price adjustment. If, as Milton Friedman asserts, inflation 'is everywhere and at all times a monetary phenomenon', the next general price disturbance is likely to be inflationary, given the current institutional framework.

The decline in the price of government bonds has so far been muted. This is also true for the decline in the price of corporate bonds. History suggests a larger adjustment in these prices is necessary.

There has been no reduction in interest rates by the Fed - quite the reverse.

There is no recession.

So, if this bear is going to look like the other bears, quite a few things still have to happen. Equities will have to fall to below fair value and the likely catalyst for this will be a bout of deflation or, more likely, inflation. There will have to be a bear market in bonds and a recession. Before the bear market is over, the DJIA is likely to decline by at least 60% - perhaps something more than 80% (given the current level of earnings and replacement value of assets).

This bear market will likely come to an end sometime after 2009, though probably nearer to 2014. Sometime around then you could perhaps reread this book and see if it can help you recognise the bear market bottom. In the meantime, if you have to go down to the woods, keep your wits about you.

Bibliography

In my research for this book, I have mined an extensive personal library and consulted colleagues and friends on useful source material that would lead to a better understanding of the nature of bear markets. This bibliography, by no means exhaustive, covers material directly related to that search. Publisher, edition and date of publication relate to the particular copy I had to hand, and web addresses refer to the home pages from where to find relevant data.

Bruce Barton, *The Man Nobody Knows* (Bobbs-Merrill, 1962)

Nathan Balke and Robert Gordon, *The Estimation of Pre-war GNP: Methodology and New Evidence* (NBER Working Papers 2674)

Paul F. Boller, Jr., *Presidential Campaigns* (Oxford University Press, 1984)

Linda Holman Bentley and Jennifer J. Kiesl, *Investment Statistics Locator* (Oryx Press, 1995)

Peter L. Bernstein, *Capital Ideas: The Improbable Origins of Modern Wall Street* (The Free Press, 1992)

Warren Buffett, "How Inflation Swindles the Equity Investor" (*Fortune*, May 1977)

Harold Borger, *Outlay and Income in the United States 1921-1938* (National Bureau of Economic Research, 1942)

John Brooks, *Once in Golconda: A True Drama of Wall Street 1920-1938* (Harper & Row, 1969)

John Brooks, *The Go-Go Years: The Drama and Crashing Finale of Wall Street's Bullish 60s* (John Wiley & Sons, 1999)

Hugh Bullock, *The Story of Investment Companies* (Columbia University Press, 1959)

H. Burton and D.C. Corner, *Investment and Unit Trusts in Britain and America* (Elek Books, 1968)

Ron Chernow, *The House of Morgan: An American Banking Dynasty and the Rise of Modern Finance* (Touchstone, 1991)

CF Childs, *Concerning US Government Securities: A Condensed Review of the Nation's Currency, Public Debt, and the Market for Representative United States Government Loans, 1635-1945, Also a Chronology of Government Bond Dealers* (R.R. Donnelley & Sons, 1947)

Harold van B. Cleveland and Thomas F. Huertas, *Citibank 1812-1970* (Harvard University Press, 1985)

David Colbert, *Eyewitness to Wall Street: 400 Years of Dreamers, Schemers, Busts and Booms* (Broadway Books, 2001)

Elroy Dimson, Paul Marsh, Mike Staunton, *Triumph of the Optimists: 101 Years of Global Investment Returns* (Princeton University Press, 2002)

Michael J. Clowes, *The Money Flood: How Pension Funds Revolutionized Investing* (John Wiley & Sons, 2000)

Charles D. Ellis with James R. Vertin (editors), *Classics - An Investor's Anthology* (Business One Irwin, 1989)

Charles D. Ellis with James R. Vertin (editors), *Classics II - Another Investor's Anthology* (Business One Irwin, 1991)

Barry Eichengreen, *Golden Fetters: The Gold Standard and the Great Depression 1919-1939* (Oxford University Press 1992)

Marc Faber, *The Great Money Illusion* (Longman, 1988)

Marc Faber, *Tomorrow's Gold* (CLSA Books, 2002)

John Kenneth Galbraith, *The Great Crash 1929* (A Mariner Book, Houghton Mifflin, 1997)

James T. Farrell, *Judgement Day* (Penguin Books, 2001)

F Scott Fitzgerald, *The Great Gatsby* (Penguin Classics, 2000)

Milton Friedman and Anna Jacobson Schwartz, *A Monetary History of the United States, 1867-1960* (Princeton University Press, 1993)

Martin S. Fridson, *It Was a Very Good Year: Extraordinary Moments in Stock Market History* (John Wiley & Sons, 1998)

Charles R. Geisst, *Wall Street: A History: From its Beginnings to the Fall of Enron* (Oxford University Press, 2004)

Benjamin Graham, *The Intelligent Investor* (Harper & Row 4th Revised Ed., 1973)

James Grant, Bernard M. Baruch, *The Adventures of a Wall Street Legend* (John Wiley & Sons, 1997)

James Grant, *Money of the Mind: Borrowing and lending in America from the Civil War to Michael Milken* (Noonday Press, 1994)

William C Greenough, *A New Approach to Retirement Income* (CFA, New York, 1951)

William Greider, *Secrets of the Temple, How the Federal Reserve Runs the Country* (Touchstone, 1987)

Alex Groner and the Editors of American Heritage and Business Week, *The American Heritage History of American Business and Industry* (American Heritage Publishing, 1972)

William Peter Hamilton, *The Stock Market Barometer: A Study of Its Forecast Value Based on Charles H. Dow's Theory of the Price Movement. (With an Analysis of the Market and Its History Since 1897)* (Fraser, 1993)

W. Braddock Hickman, *Statistical Measures of Corporate Bond Financing Since 1900* (Princeton University Press, 1960)

W.Braddock Hickman, *The Volume of Corporate Bond Financing since 1900* (Princeton University Press, 1953)

Sidney Homer and Richard Sylla, *A History of Interest Rates* (Rutgers University Press, 1996)

Matthew Josephson, *The Robber Barons* (Harvest, Harcourt Inc., 1995)

Henry Kaufman, *On Money and Markets: A Wall Street Memoir* (McGraw-Hill 2000)

Brian Kettell, *Fed-Watching* (Financial Times/Prentice Hall, 1999)

Maury Klein, *Rainbow's End: The Crash of 1929* (Oxford University Press, 2001)

William Leach, *Land of Desire: Merchants, Power, and the Rise of a New American Culture* (Vintage Books, 1993)

Martin Mayer, *The Bankers: The Next Generation* (Truman Talley Books/Dutton, 1997)

Martin Mayer, *The Fed: The Inside Story of How the World's Most Powerful Financial Institution Drives the Markets* (Free Press, 2001)

G.H. Moore, *Business Cycle Indicators* (National Bureau of Economic Research, 1961)

Ted Morgan, *FDR* (Grafton Books 1987)

Alasdair Nairn, *Engines That Move Markets:Technology Investing from Railroads to the Internet and Beyond* (John Wiley & Sons, 2002)

Wilbur Plummer, *Social and Economic Consequences of Buying on the Instalment Plan 1927* (American Academy of Political Science, 1927)

Donald T. Regan, *For The Record: From Wall Street to Washington* (Hutchison, 1988)

Jeremy J. Siegel, *Stocks For The Long Run: The Definitive Guide to Financial Market Returns and Long-Term Investment Strategies* (McGraw-Hill, 3rd Ed., 2002)

Mark Singer, *Funny Money* (Alfred A. Knopf, 1985)

Robert Shaplen, Kreuger, *Genius and Swindler* (Alfred A Knopf, 1960)

Robert J. Shiller, *Irrational Exuberance* (Princeton University Press, 2000)

Robert J. Shiller, *Market Volatility* (MIT Press, 2001)

Robert J. Shiller and Stanley B. Resor, www.econ.yale.edu/~shiller/data.htm

Andrew Smithers and Stephen Wright, *Valuing Wall Street: Protecting Wealth in Turbulent Markets* (McGraw-Hill, 2000)

Robert Sobel, *Panic on Wall Street: A History of America's Financial Disaster's* (Macmillan, 1968)

Robert Sobel, *The Great Bull Market - Wall Street in the 1920s* (W. W. Norton, 1968)

Adam Smith, *The Money Game* (Random House, 1967)

Richard Smitten, *Jesse Livermore: World's Greatest Stock Trader* (John Wiley & Sons, 2001)

John Steele-Gordon, *The Great Game: A History of Wall Street* (Orion Business Books, 1999)

Gordon Thomas and Max Morgan-Witts, *The Day The Bubble Burst: A Social History of the Wall Street Crash* (Doubleday, 1979)

John Updike, *Rabbit is Rich* (Penguin Books, 1991)

Dana L. Thomas, *The Plungers and the Peacocks* (G.P. Putnam, 1967)

Gore Vidal, *In a Yellow Wood* (William Heinemann, 1979)

Paul Volker and Toyoo Gyhten, *Changing Fortunes: The World's Money and the Threat to American Leadership* (Time Books, 1992)

James P. Warburg, *The Long Road Home: The Autobiography Of A Maverick*

(Doubleday, 1964)

Lloyd Wendt, *The Wall Street Journal: The Story of the Dow Jones & the nation's business newspaper* (Rand McNally, 1982)

Barrie A Wigmore, *Crash and Its Aftermath: A History of Securities Markets in the United States, 1929-1933* (Greenwood Press, 1985)

Barrie Wigmore, *Securities Markets in the 1980s Volume 1: The New Regime 1979-1984* (Oxford University Press, 1997)

Daniel Yergin, *The Prize: The Epic Quest For Oil, Money, And Power* (Touchstone, 1992)

Phillip L Zweig, *Citibank and the Rise and Fall of American Financial Supremacy* (Crown Publishers, 1995)

Board of Governors of the Federal Reserve System, *Banking and Monetary Statistics 1914-1941* (1943)

Board of Governors of the Federal Reserve System, *Flow of Funds Accounts of the United States*

U.S. Bureau of the Census, *Historical Statistics of the United States, Colonial Times to 1957* (Washington, DC, 1960)

The Economist

Fortune

Journal of Finance

The New York Evening Post

The New York Times

The Wall Street Journal

Read more from Russell Napier in CLSA's *Solid Ground* series

Going for broke revisited - February 2005

In last year's 'Going for broke' report, we felt a major decline in the $ was imminent. With foreign ownership of US liquid assets up dramatically in the past 12 months, we felt the need to update the situation to 3Q04.

Going for broke - February 2004

US Inc's P&L, aka the current account, is in an appalling state, and the balance sheet, as represented by net international investment, looks like that of a banana republic. Russell Napier asks if the international role of the $ is under threat.

Plaza, Dubai and you - January 2004
The Dubai agreement in September 2003 increases the probability of a weak US dollar and the outperformance of Asian equities. Apart from Japan and China, Asian countries will resist revaluation pressures.

US fiscal deterioration - September 2003
Fiscal deterioration and federal debt is haunting the US. What does this mean for equity investors? We analyse fiscal deterioration since 1800 and find growing fiscal deficit in itself is not bearish for equities. In fact, it can be the time to buy.

Inflation through deflation - January 2003
It is easy to accuse emerging China of threatening the world with structural deflation and say that emerging USA did the same in the late 1800s. We conclude that China s key deflationary threat is to global labour and perhaps land prices.

Great Hong Kong bottoms - November 2002
Fundamental valuation techniques are dangerous in a deflationary era, but history suggests that relative activity in key HK-dollar assets may hold the key to finding the bottom of the Hong Kong equity market.

US equities - It ain't over... - September 2002
Out rings the cry: capitulation! – and we see an illogical dumping of equities and panic signalling the end of a bear market. Does the dramatic slump since June 2002 represent such a despairing defeat? Not yet. First we need to see a rush to liquidity.

The new golden age - May 2002
The annual gross cross-border capital flow from the developed world is larger than all but the world's two largest economies. In 1980, there was $372bn in cross-border flows from the developed world. By 2000, the annual total was $3,111bn.

US credit system - February 2002
Plus ca change...Consensus believes that the US credit system has been immeasurably strengthened since the last recession and banking crisis of 1990-1992. It is time to end the illusion that in this US recession things are different.

The weak underbelly of the $ - US bank options,the $ and Asia – May 2000
If the $ pays the price for the irrational exuberance of the past, Asian equity markets will face the negative impact from lower US economic growth but will be major beneficiaries from lower US interest rates and a lower $.

Intrinsic value - Alive & kicking in Asia - April 2000
It is time to look again at the intrinsic value of Asian equities now that a greater degree of certainty regarding domestic risk-free rates has been established. The most undervalued equity markets in Asia are Singapore, Taiwan and China.

The $ crisis and continued outperformance of Asian equities - September 1999
The US dollar will likely weaken as the US current account grows and corporate ROE contracts. This will drive outperformance of Asian equity markets, as Asian governments ease monetary policy. Eastern Europe and LatAm will underperform.

Table of figures